W9-CDW-876

BIBLO & TANNEN PUBLICATIONS

Abbott, F. F.:   Roman Political Institutions
Abbott, F. F.:   Society & Politics in Ancient Rome
Budge, E. A. W.:   The Mummy
Cave, R. C.:   Medieval Economic History
Childe, V. G.:   The Bronze Age
Clark, E. D.:   Roman Private Law — 4 vols.
Cook, A. B.:   Zeus. Vol. 1
Cook, A. B.:   Zeus. Vol. II — 2 vols.
Davis, W. S.:   A Day in Old Athens
Davis, W. S.:   A Day in Old Rome
Dodge, T. A.:   Caesar — 2 vols.
Evans, A.:   Palace of Minos at Knossos — 4 vols. in 7
Ferguson, W. S.:   Greek Imperialism
Hamburger, M.:   Morals and Law
Hasebroek, J.:   Trade & Politics in Ancient Greece
Henderson, E. F.:   Select Historical Documents of the Middle Ages
Judson, H. P.:   Caesar's Army
Minns, E.:   Scythians and Greeks — 2 vols.
Pausanias   Description of Greece — Trans. J. G. Frazer 6 vols.
Pendlebury, J. D. S.:   The Archaeology of Crete
Petersson, T.:   Cicero. A Biography
Power, E.:   English Medieval Nunneries
Powicke, F. M.:   Ways of Medieval Life & Thought
Previte-Orton, C. W.:   Medieval History
Reymond, A.:   Hist. of Sciences in Greco-Roman Antiquity
Rostovtzeff, M. I.:   Out of the Past of Greece and Rome
Sayce, R. U.:   Primitive Arts and Crafts
Scott, J. A.:   Unity of Homer
Seymour, T. D.:   Life in the Homeric Age
Smyth, H. W.:   Greek Melic Poets
Thomson, J. O.:   History of Ancient Geography
Tozer, H. F.:   A History of Ancient Geography
Wace, A. J. B.:   Mycenae

BOHN'S ANTIQUARIAN LIBRARY.

SELECT HISTORICAL DOCUMENTS OF THE MIDDLE AGES.

SELECT

HISTORICAL DOCUMENTS

OF THE

MIDDLE AGES

TRANSLATED AND EDITED

BY

ERNEST F. HENDERSON

BIBLO and TANNEN
NEW YORK
1965

Reprinted with the permission of G. Bell and Sons Limited

Biblo & Tannen Booksellers and Publishers, Inc.
63 Fourth Avenue   New York, N. Y. 10003

Library of Congress Catalog Card Number: 65-15247

Printed in U.S.A. by
NOBLE OFFSET PRINTERS, INC.
NEW YORK 3, N. Y.

GENERAL PREFACE.

IN putting before the public a work like the present I am aware that I run the risk of being relentlessly criticised. "Was there ever seen a more motley collection of historical sources? Is there any one train of thought followed out, any system at all of selection? The documents chosen cover the modest period of nine hundred years of the world's history, and vary in length from one page to one hundred and twenty! Law, religion, politics, and general civilization are *among* the topics chosen for illustration." Such objections as these are not unfounded, but in spite of them my book may and ought to be of use for the class of readers for whom it is intended: namely, for students of history—not specialists as yet—who have an interest in the monuments of the past and who seize the first convenient opportunity of acquainting themselves with them. To search them out and to translate them for oneself is a labour for which few have time or inclination, even if they have sufficient knowledge of Latin and of history. It has taken me almost two years to collect and translate the pieces here given—the reader will be able within a few days or weeks to familiarize himself with them and to determine which, if any, will reward, in his case, a study of the original text. Such documents as I have chosen are the very framework of history. How little are they known, even by those who have perused volumes of references to and comments upon them! Clauses from them have,

during centuries, been woven again and again into histories
of Europe, but how few people have ever read them in their
own rugged simplicity! And yet a great document is a
far greater monument of a crisis in history than is any description of a battle or characterization of a man. It is the
corner stone, the last development after many battles, the
crystallization of all that has ebbed and flowed during
long constitutional struggles. A constitution, for instance,
can not lie; a treaty can not give a garbled view of a transaction—it is the letter of the law. And how much do such
documents tell us! Is not the Magna Carta at once a
summary of all the wrongs of all the men of England, and
a record of the remedies applied? Can the inner life lived
for centuries in monasteries possibly be understood without
reading the Rule of Benedict? Can the bitterness and
venom of the war of the investitures, or of the other
struggles between the Papacy and the Empire, ever be
comprehended by one who has not seen the letters of
Gregory VII., of Frederick Barbarossa, of Boniface VIII.?

And if, through reading original documents, one gains a
clearer insight into the truth itself, how much more critical
—and how much more appreciative—does one become
towards modern writers. Let one of my readers compare
a chapter of Milman's "Latin Christianity" with documents here given in the book on Church and State. Nothing
can be more instructive than such an exercise. One can
examine at leisure the materials with which the historian
worked—his methods will be clear from knowing with what
he had to deal; the documents themselves will be illumined
by his intelligence and learning. A guide book is only of
real worth to those who are, to some extent, familiar with
the scenes described.

It is necessary here to say a few words: first, as to why I
have chosen the middle ages for my field of operations; and
secondly, as to why I have selected these particular docu-

ments from the great store—we know of 40,000 papal
letters alone previous to the beginning of the fourteenth
century—that is still preserved to us.

And here let me add my voice to that of those who ob·
ject to an expression, very common twenty years ago, and
which has not yet entirely gone out of use—the dark ages.
The darkest of all, the tenth, could produce a witty and
vivid report like that of Liutprand of Cremona. There are
many people sitting in high places in the realm of England
to-day who could not begin to describe the nature of their
functions in the compact and scholarly wording in which
Richard of Ely composed his dialogue concerning the
Exchequer. And those who read the other documents
here translated will be astonished to see how clear and full
of meaning they are.

I have chosen the middle ages because, in spite of many
diversities, they have a certain great stamp of unity, and,
above all, of simplicity. The Englishman of the twelfth
century had much more in common with the Frenchman
and the German of his day than is the case now. They
were all one in one faith, and all acknowledged one
supreme spiritual head. The papal court was a common
meeting place for the best intellects from all lands. There
was one common language for all formal interchange of
thought. There was one great system which separated
all Europe into classes, and made all the members of a
given class akin. A nation, on the other hand, as such, had
little influence on its neighbour, mingled seldom in that
neighbour's quarrels. Kings went their own way, for the
most part untrammelled by fear of interference. Where do
we hear of coalitions like those of the Thirty Years' War, the
war of the Spanish Succession, or the Napoleonic struggles?
There were no permanent diplomatic relations, no resident
ministers at foreign courts, who could in a moment threaten
to break off friendly intercourse in the name of their

governments. And in each country we have only to reckon
with a sovereign, a few bishops and nobles, and a large un-
educated mass of people, not as to-day, with the most far-
reaching representation—with an emperor and a diet, a
king or queen and a parliament, a president and a senate.
And all this simplicity of the times is admirably reflected
in the documents that have come down to us. Where have
we a treaty in the middle ages that can begin to compare in
bulk, or in the number of its articles, with the peace of
Westphalia or in the acts of the congress of Vienna?
Questions since treated of in thousands of volumes of state
papers had never even been broached.

I have tried first of all in this collection to choose the
most comprehensive documents, i.e., those which were important not only for the moment, but which, during long
periods of time, were pointed to as conclusive. The Rule of
Benedict, for instance, has weathered nearly thirteen centuries, and is still observed in places. Magna Carta is, in
part, embodied among the still valid statutes of Great
Britain. The forged donation of Constantine was made
the basis of actual claims at least three hundred years after
it was fabricated, and was destined to be believed in until
as late as the seventeenth century. The golden bull of Germany was punctiliously followed for three centuries without
change.

In the second place, I have striven to give documents
which will represent as far as possible the spirit of the
time. Popes fulminating anathemas at luckless emperors,
and mustering against them the whole hierarchy of Heaven
—this is one well-known mediæval type. Another is the
priest exorcising the water for the ordeal, or blessing the
red-hot iron. Emperors bidding feuds to cease, and passing
laws for the conduct of knights and bishops, vassals and
slaves; popes calling to the crusades, and offering eternal
rewards for this and that performance; barons sitting

around the exchequer and transacting the business of the realm—all these are pictures that must find a place in any general work on the middle ages.

It remains for me to say a word of acknowledgment to those who have generously helped me in my present task. One of them, Dr. S. Löwenfeld, can, alas! no longer hear the words of thanks of his disciple. There seldom has been a man who took such unselfish interest in all his pupils. My thanks are also due to Professor Emerton, of Harvard University, who first roused in me an interest in historical studies, and in whose seminary the idea of a book like the present was first broached.

In the matter of actual assistance with the work in hand, I am bounden to no one so deeply as to Dr. F. Liebermann, of Berlin, who allowed me to presume upon his amiability to quite an unreasonable extent. He has read with me, word for word, my whole manuscript of the Dialogue concerning the Exchequer.

E. F. H.

MONTREUX, *March* 18*th*, 1892.

CONTENTS.

BOOK III.   THE CHURCH.

BOOK IV.   CHURCH AND STATE.

APPENDIX.

SELECT HISTORICAL DOCUMENTS.

BOOK I. ENGLAND.

INTRODUCTION.

T HE following short notes concerning the documents here translated, are not intended in any way to be exhaustive. They will fully answer their purpose if they prove to be suggestive, if they seem to make the pieces they refer to desirable and interesting reading. The works of Gneist and Stubbs will furnish all the general knowledge that is necessary as a ground work.

No. I., the laws of William the Conqueror, is probably the sum and substance of all the enactments made by that sovereign. Especially interesting are the reference in § 6 to the wager of battle—the first mention of that institution in English law—and the law against capital punishment in § 10. Important also is the act dividing the spiritual from the temporal courts—an act which tended to increase the independence of the clergy.

No. II., the bull of pope Adrian IV., long has been, and still is, an apple of discord among scholars. Is it a genuine document or not? The question is a weighty one, for the transaction it bears witness to was the first step towards the annexation of Ireland to England—an annexation which really took place, after a warlike expedition, sixteen years later. That a papal bull was dispatched to England about this time and concerning this matter is certain. That this was the actual bull sent is doubted by many—I myself am not among the number—from the fact that in form and wording it differs from other papal bulls of the time. The question is still being investigated, and we are promised a word from a certain Berlin professor whose authority is very great in such matters.

It is interesting to note that the claim of Adrian IV., here advanced, to jurisdiction over all islands was founded, as we learn from John of Salisbury, on the forged donation of Constantine (v. Book iii. No. iii.). Urban II. had disposed of Corsica under the same pretension. Lord Lyttleton in his still valuable History of Henry II. (vol. v. p. 67) speaks as follows concerning this whole transaction : "Upon the whole, therefore, this bull, like many before and many since, was the mere effect of a league between the papal and regal powers, to abet and assist each other's usurpations ; nor is it easy to say whether more disturbance to the world, and more iniquity, have arisen from their acting conjointly, or from the opposition which the former has made to the latter ! In this instance the best, or indeed the sole excuse for the proceedings of either, was the savage state of the Irish, to whom it might be beneficial to be conquered, and broken thereby to the salutary discipline of civil order and good laws."

No. III., is the list of articles laid before Thomas Becket in 1164, for finally refusing to sign which that prelate went into his long exile.

The custom of appealing to Rome—a custom which had begun under Henry I. whose brother was papal legate for England—had assumed alarming dimensions under Henry II. The king had almost no jurisdiction over his clerical subjects. And, to make matters worse, the clergy did not refrain from crimes which called for the utmost severity of the law. In ten years we hear of more than one hundred unpunished cases of murder among them. It was to put a stop to such lawlessness that Henry caused the constitutions of Clarendon to be drawn up by two of his justiciars. They contain nothing new, no right that did not belong by precedent to the crown. It was the way in which the struggle with Becket was carried on, not the weakness of the King's standpoint that caused the latter to fail in his endeavours. Public sympathy turned against him and, in 1174, he was obliged to expressly permit appeals to Rome. Papal influence was to increase in England until it reached its zenith under Innocent III.—liege lord and collector of tribute.

Of No. IV., the Assize of Clarendon, Stubbs says (Charters, p. 141): "It is a document of the greatest importance to our legal history, and must be regarded as introducing changes into the administration of justice which were to lead the way to self government at no distant time."

It is interesting to note (in § 21) the comparative mildness of the measures against heretics. Half a century later heresy and apostasy were alike punished with death.

No. V., the Dialogue concerning the Exchequer, is one of the few actual *treatises* of the middle ages. It is a most learned essay concerning all that went on at the bi-yearly meetings of the exchequer officials, and branches out into a description of all the sources of revenue of the English crown, and of the methods of collecting them. The value of this essay for early English history cannot be over-estimated; in every direction it throws light upon the existing state of affairs.

According to Brunner, Gneist, Pauli, and F. Liebermann[1] the Dialogue was completed in the winter of 1178-9.

[1] "Einleitung in den Dialogus de Scaccario." Göttingen. 1875.

Stubbs thinks—or has thought—that it was composed after 1181, perhaps as late as 1188. The author of the work, whose name is not mentioned in the two existing manuscripts, has been proved by Madox to be Richard, son of Bishop Nigel of Ely. Richard, as well as his father, was for many years a high official at the exchequer, was clear-headed and logical, and was, in addition, gifted with great literary ability. His knowledge of the classics is shown by his frequent quotations from them.

As a result of the combination of so many good qualities in its author the Dialogue is not only learned but readable and interesting. There is much to make one believe that the work has an official character, and that it was composed by order of the government. Liebermann regards it as a parallel work to Glanville's Tractatus.

In general Richard's assertions are deserving of the highest confidence. Occasionally, indeed, in the matter of derivations and of the origin of institutions, he is found to be weak.

Much of his information was gained orally, and in all cases he seems to have gone directly to the highest authority on the particular point to be treated of.

No. VI., Richard's punishments for criminal crusaders, is interesting as showing the discipline that was to be preserved on the ships going to Jerusalem. Curious is the mention of tarring and feathering. As far as I have been able to ascertain this is the first appearance in history of this peculiar punishment, still in vogue in America, though never administered except informally.

No. VII., Magna Carta, is the most valued bill of concessions ever wrested by a people from its king. It was granted by the most feeble and worthless monarch that England ever had, but strong and weak alike have since been forced to confirm it. Whenever, thereafter, a king wanted money or other favors from the people, he was

obliged to swear once more to this charter of liberties.
Thirty - eight distinct confirmations of this kind are
recorded.

John succeeded in losing all that kings ave to lose.
To France he sacrificed the great fiefs held by the English
from the French kings—he had scorned to answer before
Philip Augustus for the death of Prince Arthur, and they
were confiscated in consequence. Of the church he became the bondsman, laying the independence of England
in the hands of a papal legate, and promising a shameful
tribute.[1] To the barons he conceded the privileges here
translated. They will be seen to place legal restraint on
the king in many different ways. The death-knell of
absolutism had struck in England.

The demands that the king, as feudal lord, could make
on his subjects were distinctly regulated—what aids he
might ask, for what purposes, and when and how often.
All barriers were levelled which had prevented freemen
from obtaining justice in the county and other courts—
either in criminal or in civil cases. Fines for petty offences
were not to be inordinate, and clemency in certain cases
was guaranteed. The taxes and payments of cities as
well as of individuals were established upon a just basis.

All in all, as Hallam remarks, "Magna Carta is the
foundation stone of English freedom, and all later privileges are little more than a confirmation and commentary
upon it."

No. VIII., the Statute of Mortmain, was intended, as
Stubbs tells us, to put an end to "the fraudulent bestowal of estates on religious foundations, on the understanding that the donor should hold them as fiefs of the
church, and as so exonerated from public burdens. . .
The Statute of Mortmain bears a close relation to the
statute *Quia Emptores*, enacted eleven years later, in which

[1] See Book iv. No. v.

the feudal dues of the superior lords, the king the chief of them, are secured by the abolition of subinfeudation; as, in this act, they are secured by the limitation of ecclesiastical endowments."

No. IX., the *Quia Emptores* just mentioned, was passed by Edward I., in 1290, to prevent tenants from disposing of their holdings to others, sub-tenants, who felt themselves dependent on no one save the lord from whom they immediately held. Henceforth the feudal aids were to be paid directly to the lords in chief.

No. X. The Manner of holding Parliament. Stubbs describes this document as a " somewhat ideal description of the constitution of parliament in the middle of the fourteenth century." Its value consists in its undoubted antiquity, for it is found already in fourteenth century manuscripts. Its claim to be a relic of the times of the Conqueror seems to have been urged in answer to an inward craving for the sanction of long custom. Just so, many of the laws in the "Sachsenspiegel" are made to date back to Charlemagne.

No. XI., the Statute of Labourers, was issued after the great plague of the Black Death, which raged in Europe from 1347 to 1349. The same fields remained to be tilled, the same manual labour to be performed; but a large proportion of the labourers had died, and the rest could command what wages they pleased. Edward III., to stop this evil, issued this rather Draconian decree.

I.

STATUTES OF WILLIAM THE CONQUEROR.

(Stubbs' "Charters," p. 83-85.)

Here is shown what William the king of the English, together with his princes, has established since the Conquest of England.

1. Firstly that, above all things, he wishes one God to be venerated throughout his whole kingdom, one faith of Christ always to be kept inviolate, peace and security to be observed between the English and the Normans.

2. We decree also that every free man shall affirm by a compact and an oath that, within and without England, he desires to be faithful to king William, to preserve with him his lands and his honour with all fidelity, and first to defend him against his enemies.

3. I will, moreover, that all the men whom I have brought with me, or who have come after me, shall be in my peace and quiet. And if one of them shall be slain, the lord of his murderer shall seize him within five days, if he can; but if not, he shall begin to pay to me forty-six marks of silver as long as his possessions shall hold out. But when the possessions of the lord of that man are at an end, the whole hundred in which the slaying took place shall pay in common what remains.

4. And every Frenchman who, in the time of my relative king Edward, was a sharer in England of the customs of the English, shall pay according to the law of the English what they themselves call "onhlote" and "anscote." This decree has been confirmed in the city of Gloucester.

5. We forbid also that any live cattle be sold or bought for money except within the cities, and this before three faithful witnesses; nor even anything old without a surety and warrant. But if he do otherwise he shall pay, and shall afterwards pay a fine.

6. It was also decreed there that if a Frenchman summon an Englishman for perjury or murder, theft,

homicide, or "ran"—as the English call evident rape which can not be denied—the Englishman shall defend himself as he prefers, either through the ordeal of iron, or through wager of battle. But if the Englishman be infirm he shall find another who will do it for him. If one of them shall be vanquished he shall pay a fine of forty shillings to the king. If an Englishman summon a Frenchman, and be unwilling to prove his charge by judgment or by wager of battle, I will, nevertheless, that the Frenchman purge himself by an informal oath.

7. This also I command and will, that all shall hold and keep the law of Edward the king with regard to their lands, and with regard to all their possessions, those provisions being added which I have made for the utility of the English people.

8. Every man who wishes to be considered a freeman shall have a surety, that his surety may hold him and hand him over to justice if he offend in any way. And if any such one escape, his sureties shall see to it that, without making difficulties, they pay what is charged against him, and that they clear themselves of having known of any fraud in the matter of his escape. The hundred and county shall be made to answer as our predecessors decreed. And those that ought of right to come, and are unwilling to appear, shall be summoned once; and if a second time they are unwilling to appear, one ox shall be taken from them and they shall be summoned a third time. And if they do not come the third time, another ox shall be taken: but if they do not come the fourth time there shall be forfeited from the goods of that man who was unwilling to come, the extent of the charge against him,—"ceapgeld" as it is called,—and besides this a fine to the king.

9. I forbid any one to sell a man beyond the limits of the country, under penalty of a fine in full to me.

10. I forbid that any one be killed or hung for any fault, but his eyes shall be torn out or his testicles cut off. And this command shall not be violated under penalty of a fine in full to me.

Ordinance of William I., separating the Spiritual and Temporal Courts.

William by the grace of God King of the English, to R. Bainard and G. de Magnavilla, and P. de Valoines, and to my other faithful ones of Essex and of Hertfordshire and of Middlesex, greeting. Know all of you and my other faithful ones who remain in England, that in a common council and by the advice of the archbishops and bishops, and abbots, and of all the princes of my kingdom, I have decided that the episcopal laws, which up to my time in the kingdom of the English have not been right or according to the precepts of the holy canons, shall be emended. Wherefore I command, and by royal authority decree, that no bishop or archdeacon shall any longer hold, in the hundred court, pleas pertaining to the episcopal laws, nor shall they bring before the judgment of secular men any case which pertains to the rule of souls; but whoever shall be summoned, according to the episcopal laws, in any case or for any fault, shall come to the place which the bishop shall choose or name for this purpose, and shall there answer in his case or for his fault, and shall perform his law before God and his bishop not according to the hundred court, but according to the canons and the episcopal laws. But if any one, elated by pride, shall scorn or be unwilling to come before the judgment seat of the bishop, he shall be summoned once and a second and a third time; and if not even then he come to make amends, he shall be excommunicated; and, if it be needful to give effect to this, the power and justice of the king or the sheriff shall be called in. But he who was summoned before the judgment seat of the bishop shall, for each summons, pay the episcopal fine. This also I forbid and by my authority interdict, that any sheriff, or prevost, or minister of the king, or any layman concern himself in the matter of laws which pertain to the bishop, nor shall any layman summon another man to judgment apart from the jurisdiction of the bishop. But judgment shall be passed in no place except within the episcopal see, or in such place as the bishop shall fix upon for this purpose.

II.

THE BULL OF POPE ADRIAN IV. EMPOWERING HENRY II. TO CONQUER IRELAND.
A.D. 1155.

(Lyttleton's " Life of Henry II.," vol. v. p. 371.)

Bishop Adrian, servant of the servants of God, sends to his dearest son in Christ, the illustrious king of the English, greeting and apostolic benediction.   Laudably and profitably enough thy magnificence thinks of extending thy glorious name on earth, and of heaping up rewards of eternal felicity in Heaven, inasmuch as, like a good catholic prince, thou dost endeavour to enlarge the bounds of the church, to declare the truth of the Christian faith to ignorant and barbarous nations, and to extirpate the plants of evil from the field of the Lord. And, in order the better to perform this, thou dost ask the advice and favour of the apostolic see.   In which work, the more lofty the counsel and the better the guidance by which thou dost proceed, so much more do we trust that, by God's help, thou wilt progress favourably in the same ; for the reason that those things which have taken their rise from ardour of faith and love of religion are accustomed always to come to a good end and termination.

There is indeed no doubt, as thy Highness doth also acknowledge, that Ireland and all other islands which Christ the Sun of Righteousness has illumined, and which have received the doctrines of the Christian faith, belong to the jurisdiction of St. Peter and of the holy Roman Church.   Wherefore, so much the more willingly do we grant to them that the right faith and the seed grateful to God may be planted in them, the more we perceive, by examining more strictly our conscience, that this will be required of us.

Thou hast signified to us, indeed, most beloved son in Christ, that thou dost desire to enter into the island of Ireland, in order to subject the people to the laws and to extirpate the vices that have there taken root, and that thou art willing to pay an annual pension to St. Peter of one penny from every house, and to preserve the rights of the churches in that land inviolate and entire. We, therefore, seconding with the favour it deserves thy pious and laudable desire, and granting a benignant assent to thy petition, are well pleased that, for the enlargement of the bounds of the church, for the restraint of vice, for the correction of morals and the introduction of virtues, for the advancement of the Christian religion, thou should'st enter that island, and carry out there the things that look to the honour of God and to its own salvation. And may the people of that land receive thee with honour, and venerate thee as their master; provided always that the rights of the churches remain inviolate and entire, and saving to St. Peter and the holy Roman Church the annual pension of one penny from each house. If, therefore, thou dost see fit to complete what thou hast conceived in thy mind, strive to imbue that people with good morals, and bring it to pass, as well through thyself as through those whom thou dost know from their faith, doctrine, and course of life to be fit for such a work, that the church may there be adorned, the Christian religion planted and made to grow, and the things which pertain to the honour of God and to salvation be so ordered that thou may'st merit to obtain an abundant and lasting reward from God, and on earth a name glorious throughout the ages.

III.

CONSTITUTIONS OF CLARENDON. (1164.)

(Stubbs' " Charters," p. 135.)

In the year 1164 from the Incarnation of our Lord, in the fourth year of the papacy of Alexander, in the tenth year of the most illustrious king of the English, Henry II., in the presence of that same king, this memorandum or inquest was made of some part of the customs and liberties and dignities of his predecessors, viz., of king Henry his grandfather and others, which ought to be observed and kept in the kingdom. And on account of the dissensions and discords which had arisen between the clergy and the Justices of the lord king, and the barons of the kingdom, concerning the customs and dignities, this inquest was made in the presence of the archbishops and bishops, and clergy and counts, and barons and chiefs of the kingdom. And these customs, recognized by the archbishops and bishops and counts and barons and by the nobler ones and elders of the kingdom, Thomas Archbishop of Canterbury, and Roger archbishop of York, and Gilbert bishop of London, and Henry bishop of Winchester, and Nigel bishop of Ely, and William bishop of Norwich, and Robert bishop of Lincoln, and Hilary bishop of Chichester, and Jocelin bishop of Salisbury, and Richard bishop of Chester, and Bartholemew bishop of Exeter, and Robert bishop of Hereford, and David bishop of le Mans, and Roger elect of Worcester, did grant; and, upon the Word of Truth did orally firmly promise to keep and observe, under the lord king and under his heirs, in good faith and without evil wile, — in the presence of the following: Robert count of Leicester, Reginald count of Cornwall, Conan count of Bretagne, John count of Eu, Roger count of Clare, count Geoffrey of Mandeville, Hugo count of Chester, William count of Arundel, count Patrick, William count of Ferrara, Richard de Luce, Reginald de St. Walerio, Roger Bigot, Reginald de Warren, Richer de Aquila, William de Braiose, Richard de Camville, Nigel de Mowbray, Simon de Bello Campo, Humphrey de Bohen, Matthew de Hereford, Walter de Medway, Manassa Biseth —steward, William Malet, William de Curcy, Robert de Dunstanville, Jocelin de Balliol, William de Lanvale, William de Caisnet, Geoffrey de Vere, William de Hastings, Hugo de Moreville, Alan de Neville, Simon son of Peter, William Malduit—chamberlain, John Malduit, John Marshall, Peter de Mare, and many other chiefs and nobles of the kingdom, clergy as well as laity.

A certain part, moreover, of the customs and dignities of the kingdom which were examined into, is contained in the present writing. Of which part these are the paragraphs;

§ 1. If a controversy concerning advowson and presentation of churches arise between laymen, or between laymen and clerks, or between clerks, it shall be treated of and terminated in the court of the lord king.

§ 2. Churches of the fee of the lord king cannot, unto all time, be given without his assent and concession.

§ 3. Clerks charged and accused of anything, being summoned by the Justice of the king, shall come into his court, about to respond there for what it seems to the king's court that he should respond there; and in the ecclesiastical court for what it seems he should respond there ; so that the Justice of the king shall send to the court of the holy church to see in what manner the affair will there be carried on. And if the clerk shall be convicted, or shall confess, the church ought not to protect him further.

§ 4. It is not lawful for archbishops, bishops, and persons of the kingdom to go out of the kingdom without the permission of the lord king. And if it please the king and they go out, they shall give assurance that neither in going, nor in making a stay, nor in returning, will they seek the hurt or harm of king or kingdom.

§ 5. The excommunicated shall not give a pledge as a permanency, nor take an oath, but only a pledge and surety of presenting themselves before the tribunal of the church, that they may be absolved.

§ 6. Laymen ought not to be accused unless through reliable and legal accusers and witnesses in the presence of the bishop, in such wise that the archdean do not lose his right, nor any thing which he ought to have from it. And if those who are inculpated are such that no one wishes or dares to accuse them, the sheriff, being requested by the bishop, shall cause twelve lawful men of the neighbourhood or town to swear in the presence of the bishop, that they will make manifest the truth in this matter, according to their conscience.

§ 7. No one who holds of the king in chief, and no one of his demesne servitors, shall be excommunicated, nor shall the lands of any one of them be placed under an interdict, unless first the lord king, if he be in the land, or his Justice, if he be without the kingdom, be asked to do justice concerning him : and in such way that what shall pertain to the king's court shall there be terminated; and with regard to that which concerns the ecclesiastical court, he shall be sent thither in order that it may there be treated of.

§ 8. Concerning appeals, if they shall arise, from the archdean they shall proceed to the bishop, from the bishop to the archbishop. And if the archbishop shall fail to render justice, they must come finally to the lord king, in order that by his command the controversy may be terminated in the court of the archbishop, so that it shall not proceed further without the consent of the lord king.

§ 9. If a quarrel arise between a clerk and a layman or between a layman and a clerk concerning any tenement which the clerk wishes to attach to the church property, but the layman to a lay fee: by the inquest of twelve lawful men, through the judgment of the chief Justice of the king, it shall be determined, in the presence of the Justice himself, whether the tenement belongs to the church property, or to the lay fee. And if it be recognized as belonging to the church property, the case shall be pleaded in the ecclesiastical court; but if to the lay fee, unless both are holders from the same bishop or baron, the case shall be pleaded in the king's court. But if both vouch to warranty for that fee before the same bishop or baron, the case shall be pleaded in his court; in such way that, on account of the inquest made, he who was first in possession shall not lose his seisin, until, through the pleading, the case shall have been proven.

§ 10. Whoever shall belong to the city or castle or fortress or demesne manor of the lord king, if he be summoned by the archdean or bishop for any offence for which he ought to respond to them, and he be unwilling to answer their summonses, it is perfectly right to place him under the interdict; but he ought not to be excommunicated until the chief servitor of the lord king of that town shall be asked to compel him by law to answer the summonses. And if the servitor of the king be negligent in this matter, he himself shall be at the mercy of the lord king, and the bishop may thenceforth visit the man who was accused with ecclesiastical justice.

§ 11. Archbishops, bishops, and all persons of the kingdom who hold of the king in chief have their possessions of the lord king as a barony, and answer for them to the Justices and servitors of the king, and follow and perform all the customs and duties as regards the king; and, like other barons, they ought to be present with the barons at the judgments of the court of the lord king, until it comes to a judgment to loss of life or limb.

§ 12. When an archbishopric is vacant, or a bishopric, or an abbey, or a priory of the demesne of the king, it ought to be in his hand; and he ought to receive all the revenues and incomes from it, as demesne ones. And, when it comes to providing for the church, the lord king should summon the more important persons of the church, and, in the lord king's own chapel, the election ought to take place with the assent of the lord king and with the counsel of the persons of the kingdom whom he had called for this purpose. And there, before he is consecrated, the person elected shall do homage and fealty to the lord king as to his liege lord, for his life and his members and his earthly honours, saving his order.

§ 13. If any of the nobles of the kingdom shall have dispossessed an archbishop or bishop or archdean, the lord king should compel them personally or through their families to do justice. And if by chance any one shall have dispossessed the lord king of his right, the archbishops and bishops and archdeans ought to compel him to render satisfaction to the lord king.

§ 14. A church or cemetery shall not, contrary to the king's justice, detain the chattels of those who are under penalty of forfeiture to the king, for they (the chattels) are the king's, whether they are found within the churches or without them.

§ 15. Pleas concerning debts which are due through the giving of a bond, or without the giving of a bond, shall be in the jurisdiction of the king.

§ 16. The sons of rustics may not be ordained without the consent of the lord on whose land they are known to have been born.

Moreover, a record of the aforesaid royal customs and dignities has been made by the aforesaid archbishops and bishops, and counts and barons, and nobles and elders of

the kingdom, at Clarendon on the fourth day before the
Purification of the blessed Mary the perpetual Virgin;
the lord Henry being there present with his father the
lord king. There are, moreover, many other and great
customs and dignities of the holy mother church, and of
the lord king, and of the barons of the kingdom, which
are not contained in this writ. And may they be preserved to the holy church, and to the lord king, and to his
heirs, and to the barons of the kingdom, and may they be
inviolably observed for ever.

IV.

ASSIZE OF CLARENDON, 1166.

(Stubbs' "Charters," p. 143.)

1. In the first place the aforesaid king Henry, by the
counsel of all his barons, for the preservation of peace and
the observing of justice, has decreed that an inquest shall
be made throughout the separate counties, and throughout
the separate hundreds, through twelve of the more lawful
men of the hundred, and through four of the more lawful
men of each township, upon oath that they will speak the
truth: whether in their hundred or in their township there
be any man who, since the lord king has been king, has
been charged or published as being a robber or murderer
or thief; or any one who is a harbourer of robbers or
murderers or thieves. And the Justices shall make this
inquest by themselves, and the sheriffs by themselves.

2. And he who shall be found through the oath of the
aforesaid persons to have been charged or published as
being a robber, or murderer, or thief, or a receiver of them,
since the lord king has been king, shall be taken and shall
go to the ordeal of water, and shall swear that he was not
a robber or murderer or thief or receiver of them since the
lord king has been king, to the extent of five shillings as
far as he knows.

3. And if the lord of him who has been taken, or his
steward or his vassals, shall, as his sureties, demand him

back within three days after he has been taken, he himself, and his chattels, shall be remanded under surety until he shall have done his law.

4. And when a robber or murderer or thief, or har-bourers of them, shall be taken on the aforesaid oath, if the Justices shall not be about to come quickly enough into that county where they have been taken, the sheriffs shall send word to the nearest Justice through some intelligent man, that they have taken such men; and the Justices shall send back word to the sheriffs where they wish those men to be brought before them: and the sheriffs shall bring them before the Justices. And with them they shall bring, from the hundred or township where they were taken, two lawful men to bear record on the part of the county and hundred as to why they were taken; and there, before the Justice, they shall do their law.

5. And in the case of those who shall be taken on the aforesaid oath of this Assize, no one shall have court or justice or chattels save the king himself in his own court, before his own Justices; and the lord king shall have all their chattels. But in the case of those who shall be taken otherwise than through this oath, it shall be as it ordinarily is and ought to be.

6. And the sheriffs who take them shall lead them before the Justice without other summons than they have from him. And when the robbers or murderers or thieves, or receivers of them, who shall be taken through the oath or otherwise, are given over to the sheriffs, they also shall receive them straightway without delay.

7. And, in the different counties where there are no jails, such shall be made in the burgh or in some castle of the king from the money of the king and from his woods if they be near, or from some other neighbouring woods, by view of the servants of the king; to this end, that the sheriffs may keep in them those who shall be taken by the servitors who are accustomed to do this, and through their servants.

8. The lord king wills also that all shall come to the county courts to take this oath; so that no one shall remain away, on account of any privilege that he has, or of a court or soc that he may have, from coming to take this oath.

9. And let there be no one, within his castle or without his castle, nor even in the honour of Wallingford, who shall forbid the sheriffs to enter into his court or his land to take the view of frankpledge; and let all be under pledges: and let them be sent before the sheriffs under free pledge.

10. And, in the cities or burroughs, let no one have men or receive them in his home or his land or his soc whom he will not take in hand to present before the Justice if they be required ; or let them be in frankpledge.

11. And let there be none within a city or burroughs or castle, or without it, nor also in the honour of Wallingford, who shall forbid the sheriffs to enter into their land or soc to take those who shall have been charged or published as being robbers or murderers or thieves, or harbourers of the same, or outlawed or accused with regard to the forest, but he (the king) commands that they shall aid them (the sheriffs) to take them (the robbers, etc.).

12. And if any one shall be taken who shall be possessed of robbed or stolen goods. if he be notorious and have evil testimony from the public, and have no warrant, he shall not have law. And if he be not notorious, on account of the goods in his possession, he shall go to the water.

13. And if any one shall confess before lawful men, or in the hundred court, concerning robbery, murder, or theft, or the harbouring of those committing them, and afterwards wish to deny it, he shall not have law.

14. The lord king wishes also that those who shall be tried and shall be absolved by the law, if they be of very bad testimony and are publicly and disgracefully defamed by the testimony of many and public men, shall forswear the lands of the king, so that within eight days they shall cross the sea unless the wind detains them ; and, with the first wind which they shall have afterwards, they shall cross the sea ; and they shall not return any more to England unless by the mercy of the lord king: and there, and if they return, they shall be outlawed ; and if they return they shall be taken as outlaws.

15. And the lord king forbids that any waif, that is vagabond or unknown person, shall be entertained any where except in the burgh, and there he shall not be

entertained more than a night, unless he become ill there, or his horse, so that he can show an evident essoin.

16. And if he shall have been there more than one night, he shall be taken and held until his lord shall come to pledge him, or until he himself shall procure safe pledges ; and he likewise shall be taken who shall have entertained him.

17. And if any sheriff shall send word to another sheriff that men have fled from his county into another county on account of robbery or murder or theft, or the harbouring of them, or for outlawry, or for a charge with regard to the forest of the king, he (the sheriff who is informed) shall capture them : and even if he learn it of himself or through others that such men have fled into his county, he shall take them and keep them in custody until he have safe pledges from them.

18. And all sheriffs shall cause a register to be kept of all fugitives who shall flee from their counties ; and this they shall do before the county assemblies ; and they shall write down and carry their names to the Justices when first they shall come to them, so that they may be sought for throughout all England, and their chattels may be taken for the service of the king.

19. And the lord king wills that, from the time when the sheriffs shall receive the summonses of the itinerant Justices to appear before them with their counties, they shall assemble their counties and shall seek out all who have come anew into their counties since this assize ; and they shall send them away under pledge that they will come before the Justices, or they shall keep them in custody until the Justices come to them, and then they shall bring them before the Justices.

20. The lord king forbids, moreover, that monks or canons or any religious house, receive any one of the petty people as monk or canon or brother, until they know of what testimony he is, unless he shall be sick unto death.

21. The lord king forbids, moreover, that any one in all England receive in his land or his soc or the home under him any one of that sect of renegades who were excommunicated and branded at Oxford. And if any one receive them, he himself shall be at the mercy of the lord king ;

and the house in which they have been shall be carried
without the town and burned.   And each sheriff shall
swear that he will observe this, and shall cause all his
servitors to swear this, and the stewards of the barons, and
all the knights and free tenants of the counties.

22. And the lord king wills that this assize shall be
kept in his kingdom as long as it shall please him.

V.

THE DIALOGUE CONCERNING THE
EXCHEQUER.

(Stubbs' " Charters," p. 168.)

PREFACE.

It is necessary to subject one's self in all fear to the
powers ordained by God, and likewise to serve them.   For
every power is from God the Lord.   Nor does it therefore
seem absurd or foreign to ecclesiastics, by serving kings
who are, as it were, pre-eminent, and other powers, to uphold their rights ; especially in matters which are not contrary to divine Truth or honesty.   But one should serve
them not alone in preserving those dignities through which
the glory of the royal majesty shines forth, but also in preserving the abundance of worldly wealth which pertains to
them by reason of their station : for the former cast a halo
round them, the latter aid them.   For indeed abundance
of means, or the lack of them, exalts or humbles the power
of princes.   For those who lack them will be a prey to their
enemies, to those who have them their enemies will fall a
prey.   But although it may come about that these accrue
to kings for the most part, not by some right that has been
thoroughly examined into, but at times through paternal
customs, at times through the secret designs of their own
hearts, or occasionally through the arbitrariness of their
own sole will, nevertheless their acts are not to be discussed
or condemned by their subjects.   For the cause of those

whose hearts and the motions of whose hearts are in
the hand of God, and to whom by God Himself the sole
care of their subjects has been committed, stands and falls
before a Divine tribunal alone, not before a human one.
Let no one, therefore, no matter how rich, flatter himself
that he will go unpunished if he act otherwise, for of such
it is written, " the powerful shall powerfully suffer torments." Therefore of whatever nature the origin or manner
of acquiring may be or may seem to be, those who are
officially deputed to look after the revenues should be none
the more remiss in caring for them. But in the matter of
collecting, guarding, and distributing them, careful diligence befits those who are about to render an account, as
it were, of the state of the kingdom, which, through the
revenues, is preserved from harm. We know, indeed, that
chiefly by prudence, fortitude, temperance, and justice, and
other virtues, kingdoms are ruled and laws subsist; wherefore the rulers of the world should strive after these with
all their strength. But it happens at times that what is
conceived with sound counsel and excellent intent is carried
through by, so to say, a routine-like method. But this
is not only necessary in time of war but also in time
of peace. For at the one time it displays itself in fortifying towns, in delivering to the soldiers their pay, and
in very many other ways, according to the quality of
the persons, for the sake of keeping up the condition of the
kingdom; at the other, although the weapons are at rest,
churches are built by devout princes, Christ is fed and
clothed in the person of the poor, and, by persisting
in other acts of benevolence, it exhibits itself in charity.
But the glory of princes consists in the mighty deeds of
both seasons, but it excels in those where, instead of
temporal riches, lasting ones, with their blessed reward, are
attained. Wherefore, illustrious king, greatest of earthly
princes, inasmuch as we have often seen thee glorious
in both seasons, not sparing indeed treasures of money,
but providing for the suitable expenses according to the
place, time, and persons, we have dedicated to thy Excellency
this modest work, not written concerning great matters or
in brilliant discourse, but in rustic style, having to do with
the necessary observances of thy exchequer. We lately

saw thee somewhat concerned as to these, so that, dis-
patching discreet men from thy side, thou didst address
thyself to the then bishop of Ely in this matter. Nor was
it extraordinary that a man of such surpassing genius,
a prince of such singular power, should, among other
greater matters, also have provided for these. For the
exchequer, indeed, comes to its laws not at hap-hazard, but
through the thoughtfulness of great men ; and, if its rules
be regarded in all things, the rights of individuals can be
preserved, and what is due to the fisc will come to thee in
full; which same thy hand, which ministers to thy most
noble mind, can suitably distribute.

First Book.

In the twenty-third year of the reign of King Henry II.,
while I was sitting at the window of a tower next to the
River Thames, a man spoke to me impetuously, saying :
" master, hast thou not read that there is no use in science
or in a treasure that is hidden ? " when I replied to him,
" I have read so," straightway he said : " why, therefore,
dost thou not teach others the knowledge concerning the
exchequer which is said to be thine to such an extent, and
commit it to writing lest it die with thee ? " I answered :
" lo, brother, thou hast now for a long time sat at the
exchequer, and nothing is hidden from thee, for thou art
painstaking. And the same is probably the case with the
others who have seats there." But he, " just as those who
walk in darkness and grope with their hands frequently
stumble,—so many sit there who seeing do not perceive,
and hearing do not understand." Then I, " thou speakest
irreverently, for neither is the knowledge so great nor does
it concern such great things ; but perchance those who are
occupied with important matters have hearts like the claws
of an eagle, which do not retain small things, but which
great ones do not escape." And he, " so be it : but
although eagles fly very high, nevertheless they rest and
refresh themselves in humble places ; and therefore we beg
thee to explain humble things which will be of profit to the
eagles themselves." Then I ; " I have feared to put together a work concerning these things because they lie

open to the bodily senses and grow common by daily use ;
nor is there, nor can there be in them a description of
subtile things, or a pleasing invention of the imagination."
And he, "those who rejoice in imaginings, who seek the
flight of subtile things, have Aristotle and the books
of Plato; to them let them listen. Do thou write not
subtile but useful things." Then I; "of those things
which thou demandest it is impossible to speak except in
common discourse and in ordinary words." "But," said
he, as if aroused to ire,—for to a mind filled with desire
nothing goes quickly enough,—" writers on arts, lest they
might seem to know too little about many things, and in
order that art might less easily become known, have sought
to appropriate many things, and have concealed them
under unknown words : but thou dost not undertake to
write about an art, but about certain customs and laws of
the exchequer; and since these ought to be common,
common words must necessarily be employed, so that the
style may have relation to the things of which we are
speaking. Moreover, although it is very often allowable
to invent new words, I beg, nevertheless, if it please thee,
that thou may'st not be ashamed to use the customary
names of the things themselves which readily occur to the
mind, so that no new difficulty from using unfamiliar
words may arise to disturb us." Then I; " I see that thou
art angry; but be calmer; I will do what thou dost urge.
Rise, therefore, and sit opposite to me; and ask me concerning those things that occur to thee. But if thou shalt
propound something unheard of, I shall not blush to say
'I do not know.' But let us both, like discreet beings,
come to an agreement." And he; "thou respondest
to my wish. Moreover, although an elementary old man
is a disgraceful and ridiculous thing, I will nevertheless
begin with the very elements."

I. What the Exchequer is, and what is the reason of this name.

Disciple. What is the exchequer?

Master. The exchequer is a quadrangular surface about
ten feet in length, five in breadth, placed before those who

sit around it in the manner of a table, and all around it it
has an edge about the height of one's four fingers, lest any
thing placed upon it should fall off.   There is placed over
the top of the exchequer, moreover, a cloth bought at the
Easter term, not an ordinary one but a black one marked
with stripes, the stripes being distant from each other the
space of a foot or the breadth of a hand.   In the spaces
moreover are counters placed according to their values;
about these we shall speak below.   Although, moreover,
such a surface is called exchequer, nevertheless this name
is so changed about that the court itself which sits when
the exchequer does is called exchequer; so that if at any
time through a decree any thing is established by common
counsel, it is said to have been done at the exchequer of
this or that year.   As, moreover, one says to-day "at the
exchequer," so one formerly said "at the tallies."

D. What is the reason of this name?

M. No truer one occurs to me at present than that it
has a shape similar to that of a chess board.

D. Would the prudence of the ancients ever have called
it so for its shape alone, when it might for a similar reason
be called a table (tabularium)?

M. I was right in calling thee painstaking.   There is
another, but a more hidden reason.   For just as, in a
game of chess, there are certain grades of combatants and
they proceed or stand still by certain laws or limitations,
some presiding and others advancing: so, in this, some
preside, some assist by reason of their office, and no one is
free to exceed the fixed laws; as will be manifest from
what is to follow.   Moreover, as in chess the battle is
fought between kings, so in this it is chiefly between two
that the conflict takes place and the war is waged,—the
treasurer, namely, and the sheriff who sits there to render
account; the others sitting by as judges, to see and to
judge.

D. Will the accounts be received then by the treasurer,
although there are many there who, by reason of their
power, are greater?

M. That the treasurer ought to receive the account from
the sheriff is manifest from this, that the same is required
from him whenever it pleases the king: nor could that be

required of him which he had not received. Some say, nevertheless, that the treasurer and the chamberlains should be bounden alone for what is written in the rolls in the treasury, and that for this an account should be demanded of them. But it is believed with more truth that they should be responsible for the whole writing of the roll, as will be readily understood from what is to follow.

II. That there is a lower one and an upper one; both have the same origin however.

D. Is that exchequer, in which such a conflict goes on, the only one?

M. No. For there is a lower exchequer which is also called the Receipt, where the money is handed over to be counted, and is put down in writing and on tallies, so that afterwards, at the upper exchequer, an account may be rendered of them; both have the same origin however, for whatever is declared payable at the greater one is here paid; and whatever has been paid here is accounted for there.

III. As to the nature or arrangement of the lower one according to the separate offices.

D. What is the nature or arrangement of the lower exchequer?

M. As I see, thou canst not bear to be ignorant of any of these things. Know then that that lower exchequer has its persons, distinct from each other by reason of their offices, but with one intent devoted to the interests of the king, due regard, nevertheless, being paid to equity; all serving, moreover, not in their own names but in the names of their masters; with the exception of two knights, he, namely, who conducts the assays, and the melter. Their offices depend on the will of our king; hence they seem to belong rather to the upper than to the lower exchequer, as will be explained below. The clerk of the treasurer is there with his seal. There are also two knights of the chamberlains. There is also a certain knight who may be called the silverer, for, by reason of his office, he presides at the testing of silver. There is also the melter who tests the silver. There are also four tellers to count the money. There is also the usher of the treasury and the watchman. These, moreover, are their offices: The clerk of the treasurer, when the money has been counted and put in boxes by the hundred pounds, affixes his seal and puts down in writing how much he has received, and from whom, and for what cause; he registers also the tallies which have been made by the chamberlains concerning that receipt. Not only, moreover, does he place his seal on the sacks of money, but also, if he wishes, on the chests and on the separate boxes in which the rolls and tallies are placed, and he diligently supervises all the offices which are under him, and nothing is hidden from him. The office of the knights, who are also called chamberlains because they serve in the name of the chamberlains, is this: they carry the keys of the chests; for each chest has two locks of a different kind, that is, to neither of which the key of the other can be fitted; and they carry the keys of them. Each chest, moreover, is girded with a certain immovable strap, on which, in addition, when the locks are closed the seal of the treasurer is placed; so that neither of the chamberlains can have access except by common consent. Likewise it is their duty to weigh the money which has been counted and placed by the hundred shillings in wooden receptacles, so that there be no error in the amount; and then, at length, to put them in boxes by the hundred pounds as has been said. But if a receptacle is found to have any deficiency, that which is thought to be lacking is not made good by calculation, but straightway the doubtful one is thrown back into the heap which is to be counted. And take note that certain counties from the time of king Henry I. and in the time of king Henry II. could lawfully offer for payment coins of any kind of money provided they were of silver and did not differ from the lawful weight; because indeed, by ancient custom, not themselves having moneyers, they sought their coins from on all sides; such are Northumberland and Cumberland. Coins thus received, moreover, although they came from a farm, were nevertheless set apart from the others with some marks placed on them. But the remaining counties were accustomed to bring only the usual and lawful coin of the present money as well from farms as from pleas. But after the illustrious king whose renown shines the brighter in great matters, did, in his reign, institute one weight and one money for the whole kingdom, each county began to be bound by one necessity of law and to be constrained by the manner of payment of a general commerce. All, therefore, in whatever manner they are bounden, pay the same kind of money; but nevertheless all do not sustain the loss which comes from the testing by combustion. The chamberlains likewise make the tallies of receipts, and have in common with the clerk of the treasurer to disburse the treasure received when required by writs of the king or an order of the barons; not, however, without consulting their masters. These three, all together or by turns, are sent with treasure when it is necessary. These three have the principal care of all that is done in the lower exchequer.

D. Therefore, as I perceive, these men are allowed to disburse the treasure received, in consequence of a royal writ or of an order from those who preside—after consultation with their masters, however.

M. They are allowed, I say; in so far as they are entrusted with the payment of the servants of the lower exchequer, and with buying the small necessaries of the exchequer, such as the wooden receptacles, and other things which will be mentioned below; but not otherwise. When any one brings a writ or order of the king for money, by command of their masters that sum which is expressly named in the writ may be paid, with the understanding that, before he go out, he shall count the money received. But if anything be lacking, he who received it shall return to the exchequer and shall give an oath to this effect: that he has brought back as much as he received, adding this, *upon his conscience*, as is done in other things; and this being done the rest shall be paid him, it being first counted in the presence of all by the regular tellers. But if, the conditions being known to him, he shall have gone out of the door of the treasury, whoever the person, or however great the loss, no heed shall be paid to him. The offices of the knight silverer and of the melter are conjoined and belong rather to the upper exchequer, and therefore will be explained there with the other offices. The office of the four tellers is the following: When the money is sent to the exchequer to be counted, one of them diligently mixes the whole together, so that the better pieces may not be by themselves and the worse by themselves, but mixed, in order that they may correspond in weight; this being done, the chamberlain weighs in a scale as much as is necessary to make a pound of the exchequer. But if the number shall exceed 20 shillings by more than six pence in a pound, it is considered unfit to be received; but if it shall restrict itself to six pence or less, it is received, and is counted diligently by the tellers by the hundred shillings as has been said. But if the coins are from a farm and are to be tested, 44 shillings from the heap, being mixed together, are placed in a compartment by themselves, and on this the sheriff puts a mark; so that there may be afterwards a testing, which is commonly called assaying, of them, as will be made clear further on. It shall, moreover, be the care of those who preside over the Receipt by virtue of their masters—that is of the clerks of the treasurer and of the chamberlains—when the money is received, to put aside weights of the tested silver and coins from a farm, placing certain marks on the bags that contain them, so that, if the king wishes silver vessels to be made for the uses of the house of God, or for the service of his own palace, or perchance money for beyond seas, it may be made from this.

D. There is something in what thou hast said that strikes me.

M. Speak then.

D. Thou said'st, if I remember rightly, that sometimes money is brought to be paid into the exchequer which is judged unfit to be received, if, indeed, being weighed against a pound weight of the exchequer, a deficiency is found of more than six pence. Inasmuch, then, as all money of this kingdom ought to have the stamped image of the king, and all moneyers are bound to work according to the same weight, how can it happen that all their work is not of one weight?

M. That is a great question which thou askest, and one which requires further investigation; but it can happen through forgers and clippers or cutters of coin. Thou knowest, moreover, that the money of England can be found false in three ways: false, namely, in weight, false in quality, false in the stamping. But these kinds of falsification are not visited by an equal punishment. But of this elsewhere.

D. If it please thee, continue concerning the offices as thou hast begun.

M. It is the duty of the usher to exclude or admit as is necessary, and to be diligent in guarding every thing which is shut in by the door; wherefore, as door-money, he shall have two pence from each writ of exit. He furnishes the boxes to put the money in, and the rolls and the tallies, and the other things which become necessary during the year; and for each box he has two pence. He furnishes the whole Receipt with wood suitable for the tallies of receipts and of accounts, and once, that is at the Michael-mas term, he receives five shillings for the wood of the tallies. He furnishes the wooden receptacles, the knives, the compartments, and the straps and the other minute necessaries of the fisc. At that same term are due two shillings for furnishing the ink of the whole year to both exchequers, and this amount, by ancient right, the sacristan of the greater church of Westminster claims for himself. The office of the watchman is the same there as else-where; most diligent guarding, namely, at night, chiefly of the treasure and of all those things which are placed in the treasury building. Thus thou hast the various offices of those who serve in the lower exchequer. And they have fixed payments while the exchequer is in progress, that is from the day on which they are called together, to the day on which there is a general departure. The clerk of the treasurer who is below, has five pence a day. The scribe of the same treasurer in the upper exchequer has likewise five. The scribe of the chancellor, five. The two knights who bear the keys have each eight, by reason of their knighthood. For they claim that they are bound to be ready with the necessary horses and weapons, so that when they are sent with the treasure they may thus more readily execute what pertains to their office. The knight-silverer has twelve pence a day. The melter, five. The usher of the greater exchequer, five. The four tellers, each three pence, if they are at London; if at Winchester each one has two, since they are generally taken from there. The watchman has one penny. For the light of each night at the treasury one halfpenny.

D. For what reason does the usher of the treasury alone receive no pay?

M. I do not exactly know   But, however, perhaps he does not receive any pay because he is seen to receive something as door-money, and for furnishing the boxes and tallies; or perchance because he seems to serve, not the king, but the treasurer and the chamberlains in guard-ing the door of their building. In this way, then, has the arrangement of the lower exchequer or Receipt been made.

D. I have been so well satisfied in this regard that nothing seems to be wanting. Proceed now, if it please thee, concerning the greater exchequer.

IV. What is the competency of the Upper Exchequer, and whence it takes its origin.

M. Although the offices of those who have seats at the greater exchequer seem to differ in certain functions, the purpose, nevertheless, of all the offices is the same, to look out for the king's advantage; with due regard for equity, however, according to the fixed laws of the exchequer. The arrangement or ordering of the latter is confirmed by its antiquity and by the authority of the nobles who have their seats there. It is said to have begun with the very conquest of the kingdom made by king William, the arrangement being taken, however, from the exchequer across the seas; but they differ in very many and almost the most important points. Some believe it to have existed under the Anglo-Saxon kings, taking their argu-ment in this matter from the fact that the peasants and already decrepit old men of those estates which are called of the crown, whose memory is gray in these matters, knew very well, having been taught by their fathers, how much extra money they are bound to pay on the pound for the blanching of their farm. But this argument applies to the payment of the farm, not to the session of the exchequer. The fact also seems to be against those who say that the blanching of the farm began in the time of the Anglo-Saxon kings, that in the Domesday book, in which a diligent description of the whole kingdom is contained, and in which the value is expressed of the different estates as well of the time of king Edward as of the time of king William, under whom it was made,—there is no mention at all of the blanching of the farm: from which it seems probable that, after the time when that survey was made in the reign of the aforementioned king, the blanching of the farm was fixed upon by his investigators on account of causes which are noted below. But at whatever time it came into use, it is certain that the exchequer is confirmed by the authority of the great, so that it is allowed to no one to infringe its statutes or to resist them by any kind of rashness. For it has this in common with the Court itself of the lord king (Curia Regis), in which he in his own person administers the law, that no one is allowed to contradict a record or a sentence passed in it. The authority, moreover, of this court is so great, as well on account of the pre-eminence of the royal image, which, by a special prerogative, is kept on his seal of the treasury, as on account of those who have their seats there, as has been said; by whose watchfulness the condition of the whole kingdom is kept safe. For there sits the Chief Justice of the lord king by reason of his judicial dignity, as well as the greatest men of the kingdom, who share familiarly in the royal secrets; so that whatever has been established or determined in the presence of such great men subsists by an inviolable right. In the first place, there sits, nay also presides, by reason of his office, the first man in the kingdom,— namely, the Chief Justice. With him sit, solely by command of the sovereign, with momentary and varying authority, indeed, certain of the greatest and most discreet men in the kingdom, who may belong either to the clergy or to the court. They sit there, I say, to interpret the law and to decide upon the doubtful points which frequently arise from incidental questions. For not in its reckonings, but in its manifold judgments, does the superior science of the exchequer consist. For it is easy when the sum required has been put down, and the sums which have been handed in are placed under it for comparison, to tell by subtraction if the demands have been satisfied or if anything remains. But when one begins to make a many-sided investigation of those things which come into the fisc in varying ways, and are required under different conditions, and are not collected by the sheriffs in the same way,—to be able to tell if the latter have acted otherwise than they should, is in many ways a grave task. Therefore the greater science of the exchequer is said to consist in these matters. But the judgments on doubtful or doubted points which frequently come up can not be comprehended under one form of treatment; for all kinds of doubts have not yet come to light. Certain, however, of the matters which we know to have been brought up and settled, we shall note below in their proper place.

V. What is the office of the President, and of all those who sit there officially; and what the arrangement of the seats.

D. What is the office of this so important a member?

M. Nothing can be more truly said of him than that he looks after all things in the lower and upper exchequer, and all the lower offices are arranged according to his will; in such wise, however, that they duly turn out to the advantage of the lord king. In this, moreover, among other things, his exalted character is seen,—that he, under his own witness, can cause a writ of the lord king to be made out so that any sum may be delivered from the treasury, or that there may be computed to any one, whatever he knows ought, by command of the king, to be computed to him. Or, if he prefer, he can make his own writ, witnessed to by others, concerning these matters.

D. Great is this man to whose fidelity the care of the whole kingdom, nay, the very heart of the king is entrusted.

For, indeed, it is written : " where your treasure is, there will your heart be also." But now, if it please thee, continue concerning the others.

M. Dost thou wish me to proceed with them according to the grade of their dignities, or according to the disposition of the seats ?

D. According as each one, by reason of his office, has attained his seat. For it will be easy, I imagine, to conclude the dignities from the offices.

M. That thou may'st understand in what order they are arranged, know that at the four sides of the exchequer four seats or benches are placed. But at the head of the exchequer—that is, where the broad side is,—in the middle, not of the seat, but of the exchequer, is the place of that chief man of whom we spoke above. In the first place on his left sits, by reason of his office, the chancellor, if he should happen to be present ; after him the knight whom we call constable : after him, two chamberlains, he being first who, judging from his more advanced age, is the more venerable : after these, the knight who is commonly called the marshal. In the absence of these, others, however, are sometimes put in their place ; or perchance even when they are present, if, namely, the authority of those who are delegated by the king shall be so great that the others ought to give place to them. Such is the arrangement of the first bench. In the second, moreover, which is on the long side of the exchequer, sits, in the place at the head, the clerk or another servant of the chamberlains, with the " recauta,"—that is, with the counter-tallies from the Receipt. After him, some coming in between who do not sit there by reason of their office but are delegated by the king, is a place almost in the middle of the side of the exchequer, for him who puts down the sums by the placing of counters. After him some, not by reason of their office, but nevertheless necessary. At the end of that bench sits the clerk who presides over the scriptorium, and he by reason of his office. Thus thou hast the arrangement of the second bench. But at the right of the presiding Justice sits in the first place the now Bishop of Winchester, the former arch-dean of Poictiers,—not, indeed, by reason of his office, but by a new decree ; in order, namely, that he may

be next to the treasurer and may diligently give his attention to the writing of the roll.   After him, at the head of
the third seat, on the right, sits the treasurer, who has to
attend most carefully to everything which is done there,
being bound to give an account, as it were, of all these
things, if there shall be need of it.   After him sits his
clerk, the scribe of the roll of the treasury: after him,
another scribe, of the roll of the chancery : after him, the
clerk of the chancellor, who with his own eyes always sees
to it that his roll corresponds to the other in every point,
so that not one jot is lacking and that the order of writing
does not differ: after him, almost at the end of that bench,
sits the clerk of the constable, great, indeed, and busy at
the court of the lord king, and having, indeed, here an
office which he performs in person or, if the king shall
seem to have more use for him elsewhere, through a discreet clerk.   This, then, is the description of the third
bench. On the fourth bench, which is opposite the Justice,
Master Thomas, who is called Brunus, sits at the head
with a third roll which has been added as a new institution, that is, by our lord king ; for it is written, "and a
threefold cord is not quickly broken."   After him the
sheriffs and their clerks, who sit there to render account
with tallies and other necessaries. This then is the arrangement of the fourth bench.

D. Has then the scribe of Master Thomas his seat in
the same range with the other scribes, and not rather
above the others ?

M. He does indeed have his seat not with the others
but above the others.

D. Why is this so?

M. Inasmuch as, from the beginning, the seats were so
arranged that the scribe of the treasurer should sit at his
side lest anything should be written which should escape
his eye ; and in like manner the scribe of the chancery at
the side of the scribe of the treasurer, that he might faithfully take down what the latter wrote ; and likewise the
clerk of the chancery was of necessity next to that scribe,
lest he might err: there was no place left in the order of
the bench where Master Thomas's scribe might sit, but a
raised place was given him that he might be above and

overlook the scribe of the treasurer, who is the first to write, and may take down from him what is necessary.

D. He would need to have the eyes of a lynx so as not to err; for an error in these things is said to be dangerous.

M. Although, on account of being far off, he sometimes makes a mistake, yet, when the rolls are corrected, a comparison being made of all three, it will be easy to correct the mistakes.

D. Enough has thus far been said concerning the order of seating. Now proceed, if it please thee, concerning their offices, beginning on the left of the president.

As to the Chancellor.

M. In that order the chancellor is first; and as in the court, even so is he great at the exchequer; so that without his consent and advice nothing great is done or may be done. But this is his office when he sits at the exchequer: to him pertains the custody of the royal seal which is in the treasury, but it does not leave there except when, by order of the Justice, it is borne by the treasurer or chamberlain from the lower to the upper exchequer, for the sole purpose of carrying on the business of the exchequer. This having been performed, it is put in its box and the box is sealed by the chancellor and is given thus to the treasurer to be guarded. Likewise, when it becomes necessary, it is proffered sealed to the chancellor before the eyes of all; it is never to be proffered, by him or by another, in any other way. Likewise to him, through a substitute, pertains the custody of the roll of the chancery; and, since it so seemed good to great men, the chancellor is equally responsible with the treasurer for all the writing on the roll, except alone what has been written down as having been received in the treasury: for although he may not prescribe how the treasurer writes, nevertheless, if the latter shall have erred, it is allowed to him or to his clerk with modesty to chide the treasurer and suggest what he shall do. But if the treasurer persevere, and be unwilling to change, being himself confident,—the chancellor can accuse him, but only before the barons, so that by them shall be declared what ought to be done

D. It seems probable that the guardian of the third roll, also, is bound by the same responsibility as to the writing.

M. It is not only probable but true: for those two rolls have an equal authority in the matter of the writing; for so it pleased the originator.

As to the Constable.

The office of the constable at the exchequer is, in the case of royal writs concerning the issue of treasure or concerning any accountings to be made, to be witness, together with the president, for those who make the account. For in all such writs it is necessary, according to ancient custom, that two witnesses shall be inscribed. It is likewise his office, when the king's soldiers come to the exchequer for their pay, whether they reside in the castles of the king or not, taking with him the clerk of the constabulary—whose duty it is to know their terms of payment—and the marshall of the exchequer,—to compute their payments and to take their oath concerning arrears, and to cause the rest to be paid. For every payment of all persons whatever, whether of hawkers, or falconers, or bear-wardens, pertains to his office if he be present; unless, perchance, the lord king shall have previously assigned some one else to this duty: for the constable can not easily be torn from the king, on account of greater and more urgent business. It is to be noted that the marshall of the exchequer takes from the payments of native knights what belongs to him by reason of his office; not however from alien ones. It is likewise common to him with the other greater barons, that no great measure shall be taken without consulting him.

As to the Chamberlains.

The office of the chamberlains is akin to the office of the treasurer, for they are known to serve under one and the same mantle of honour or loss; and they have one will with regard to the king's honour; so that what has been done by one may not be declared invalid by any of them.

For the treasurer receives the accounts for himself and for them ; and, according to the qualities of the items, furnishes the wording for the writing of the roll; in all of which things they are bound by an equal bond of union. And it is the same with regard to all other things which are done by him or by them—saving their fealty to the lord king—whether in the matter of writing, of receipts, of tallies or of expenses.

As to the Marshal.

It is the duty of the marshal to put aside in his box the tallies of the debtors which the sheriff hands in, which, all the same, are put down on the roll ; also the writs of the king concerning the computing or remitting or giving of those things which are demanded of the sheriff through the summons.   On that box is placed the name of the county to which these belong, and it is necessary that, for the separate counties, separate boxes should be furnished to the marshal by the sheriff who renders his account.

D. There is something here that troubles me.

M. I quite foresaw it.   But wait a little.   Everything will be plain from what follows.   Likewise if any debtor, not giving satisfaction for the amount of his summons, shall have deserved to be siezed, he is handed over to the marshal to be guarded, and when the exchequer of that day is dissolved, the latter shall, if he wish, send him to the public jail ; he shall not, however, be chained or thrust into the dungeon, but shall be apart by himself or above the subterraneous jail.   For although he be not solvent, he has not, nevertheless, on this account deserved to be put with the criminals ; that is, provided he is not a knight ; for concerning knights held for debt there is an illustrious decree of the king which will be noticed below in treating of the sheriff.   It is likewise the marshal's concern, when the account of the sheriff, or administrator, or whatever person sits to render account, is finished, to take an oath from him in public to the effect that, upon his conscience, he has rendered a true account.   But if the sheriff, or he who has accounted, is bound by any debt he shall add that he will not depart from the exchequer, that is, from the banlieu of the town in which it is, without permission of the barons, unless he is going to return on the same day. Likewise the marshal shall receive, numbered, the writs of summons made out against the term fixed for the next exchequer, sealed with the royal seal; and shall distribute them with his own hand to the usher of the upper exchequer to be carried throughout England. Thus thou hast the different offices of those who sit on the first bench.

As to the Maker of Tallies.

Now at the head of the second seat the serjeant of the chamberlains comes first, a clerk or a layman, whose office can briefly be disposed of; in word, however, not in deed. He brings forth from the treasury the tallies against the sheriff or against him who renders account; and, when it is necessary, according as the manner of accounting demands, he changes or diminishes or adds to the tally, comparing it with the counter tally of the sheriff. This having been done at the Easter term, he gives back the longer one to the sheriff to bring again at the Michaelmas term. But at the Michaelmas term, when the amount of it shall have been put down in writing in the roll, he hands this same longer one to the marshal to put in his box.

D. I wonder at thy saying that a tally once offered for an account, should again be offered for another account.

M. Do not wonder; for with regard to whatever has been exacted, or paid by the sheriff at the Easter term, he must again be summoned; not, indeed, in order that what has been paid should be paid again, but that the sheriffs shall present themselves to give account, and that the tally offered for the payment previously made may be reduced to writing in the roll, and that thus he may be absolved from his debt. For so long as he has the tally in his possession, he will not be acquitted but will always be liable to be summoned.

D. And all this seems necessary. But proceed, if it please thee, concerning the offices.

M. Nay, since we have made mention of tallies, learn in a few words what the process is in which the matter of tallying consists. There is, then, one kind of tally which is called simply tally; another, which we call memoranda tally. The length of an ordinary tally is from the top of the forefinger to the top of the extended thumb; there it is perforated with a moderate borer. But a memoranda which is always accustomed to be made for a blank farm is a little shorter; for when the assay is made through which the farm is blanched, that first one is broken, and the tally of combustion being added to it, it then first merits the length of a tally. The incision, moreover, is made in this way : At the top they put 1000£, in such way that its notch has the thickness of the palm; 100£, of the thumb; 20£, of the ear; the notch of one pound, about of a swelling grain of barley; but that of a shilling, less; in such wise, nevertheless, that, a space being cleared out by cutting, a moderate furrow shall be made there; the penny is marked by the incision being made, but no wood being cut away. On the side where the 1000 is cut thou dost not put another number, unless, perhaps, the middle part of it; in such wise that thou in like manner dost take away the middle part of its notch and dost place it below.[1] Just so if 100£ is to be cut in, and thou hast no thousands, thou shalt do the same; and if 20£, the same; and if 20 shillings, which we call a pound. But if many thousands or hundreds or twenties of pounds are to be cut in, the same law shall be observed, so that on the more open side of the tally, that is, that which is placed directly before thee, a mark being made, the greater number shall be cut; but on the other, the lesser; but on the obverse side, is always the greater number at the top, but on the converse always the lesser, that is, the pence. For a mark of silver there is no special notch at the exchequer, but we designate it in shillings. But a mark of gold thou dost cut in the middle of the tally as though it were one pound. But one gold piece is not cut altogether like a silver piece, but by drawing the knife directly through the middle of the tally; not obliquely, as in the case of

---

[1] The meaning of this passage is obscure. The Latin reads : " Ex qua vero parte millenarius inciditur, alium non pones numerum; nisi forte mediam ejus partem; sic ut mediam similiter incisionis ejus demas, et infra constituas."

the silver piece. Thus, therefore, both, the arrangement of the positions and the difference of cut, determines what is gold and what is silver. But thou shalt learn all this more conveniently by looking at it than by hearing of it.

D. What remains of this will be made clear by ocular demonstration. Now, if it please thee, proceed concerning the offices.

M. After him, as we said above, a few discreet men who are delegated by the king coming in between, sits he who, by command of the king makes computations by the placing of coins used as counters. This office indeed is perplexing and laborious enough; and, without it, seldom or never could the business of the exchequer be carried on; but it belongs officially to none of those who sit there, but to him to whom the king or the Justice shall give it to fill. Laborious, I say, for other offices are filled by the tongue or the hand, this by both; in it " the hand, the tongue and the eye, and the mind are unwearied in labour."

As to the Calculator.

This is his business: according to the usual course of the exchequer, not according to arithmetical laws. Thou wilt remember, I presume, my saying that on the exchequer was placed a cloth divided by stripes, in the spaces of which heaps of cash are placed. Now the calculator sits in the middle of the side, that he may be visible to all, and that his busy hand may have free course. He has placed already at his right hand, in the lower space, a heap of pennies from 11 down; in the second, of shillings from 19 down; but in the third, of pounds. And this heap, indeed, ought to be opposite and directly facing him, for in the ordinary accounts of the sheriff it is the medium; in the fourth is the heap of the twenties; in the fifth, of the hundreds; in the sixth, of the thousands; in the seventh, but rarely, of the ten thousands of pounds; rarely, I say, that is when, through the king or his mandate, the account for the receipts of the whole kingdom is received by the nobles of the kingdom from the treasurer and the chamberlains. Moreover, it is lawful for the calculator to put a silver piece in place of ten shillings, or a gold obol in place of ten pounds, so that the account may be more quickly made. He must take care, however, lest his too hasty hand proceed before his tongue, or the reverse; but at the same time that he counts he shall place the counter and designate the number, lest there be an error in the number. The sum, therefore, which is required from the sheriff being arranged in heaps, those sums which have been paid in, either to the treasury or otherwise, are arranged below, likewise in heaps. But if it be a farm by tale which is required of him, or any other debt which can be satisfied by tale only, there shall simply be made a deduction of the lower from the upper sum, and he shall be bounden for the rest; it shall be done otherwise, however, if he be about to pay a blank farm; as will be more fully shown when we treat of the sheriff's business.

D. Spare a moment thy running pen that I may be allowed to say a few words.

M. It is thy turn to throw the die, nor may speech be denied thee.

D. It seems to me as if I were given to understand that, by means of calculation, the same coin being placed for a counter shall signify now a penny, now a shilling, now a pound, now a hundred, now a thousand.

M. So it is, but only, however, if it is placed with coins corresponding to those values; or, if it is taken away from them, it can, at the pleasure of the calculator, be brought about that the one which signifies a thousand, by gradually descending, shall signify one.

D. Thus it happens when one of the people, since he is a man and can not be any thing else, ascends from the depths to the summit, temporal benefits being bestowed on him by the will of the President; and then, according to Fortuna's law, is thrust back into the depths, remaining what he was although he seemed by reason of his dignity and standing to have been changed from himself.

M. Know that thy words do not apply in all respects. But, however it may seem to others, I am well pleased that from these matters thou dost infer others; indeed it is praiseworthy to seek the flowers of mystic meaning in the winnowings of mundane affairs. And not alone in these things that thou dost mention, but in the whole description of the exchequer there are hiding places, as it were, of holy truths. For the diversity of officials, the authority of the judicial power, the impression of the royal image, the sending out of summonses, the writing of the rolls, the account of land rents, the exaction of debts, the condemnation or absolution of the accused, are a symbol of the strict examination that will be made when the books of all shall be opened and the gates closed. But so much for these things. Now let us proceed concerning the offices; after him who has charge of the counters, first, by reason of his office, sits the clerk who presides over the scriptorium of the king.

As to the Clerk who presides over the scriptorium.

To him it pertains to find suitable scribes for the roll of the chancery, and for the writs of the king which are made in the exchequer, also for writing summonses; and to see to it that they are well done: which offices, although they are expressed in a few words, can scarcely be fulfilled even with infinite pains; as those know who have learnt by experience in such matters. Thus thou hast the offices of those who are placed on the second bench.

As to the Archdean of Poictiers, now Bishop of Winchester.[1]

D. If I remember well, first at the right of the president sits the Bishop of Winchester, whose office at the exchequer I should like straightway to find out. For he is great and ought not to be busied save with great things.

M. He is great, without doubt; and, intent on great things, he is drawn in many directions, as is more fully shown in the Tricolumnis. He, before the time of his promotion, when he was serving a little lower in the court of the king (Curia Regis), seemed, by reason of his fidelity and industry, necessary to the business of the king, and very ready and officious in computations and in the writing of

---

[1] Richard of Ilchester.

rolls and writs. Wherefore the place was given him at the side of the treasurer, so that with the latter, indeed, he might attend to the writing of the rolls and to all of these things. The treasurer, indeed, is distracted by so many and such great cares and ·solicitudes for all things, that necessarily at times slumber creeps over such great labours. For in human affairs hardly anything is entirely perfect.

D. What dost thou say ? For I do not even know what the Tricolumnis is.

M. It is a book, indeed, composed by us although in the time of our youth, concerning the three-fold history of the kingdom of England, under the illustrious king of the English, Henry the Second. And this, because we have treated it all through in three columns, we have called the Tricolumnis. In the first, indeed, we have treated of many matters concerning the English church, and of some rescripts of the apostolic see. But in the second, of the distinguished deeds of the aforesaid king, which exceed human belief. But in the third many public as well as private matters are treated of, and also sentences of the court. If this by chance should fall into thy hands, see that it do not escape thee; for it may be useful in future times and entertaining to those who shall be interested in the state of the kingdom under the aforesaid prince. For although this king is descended from ancestral kings, and has spread his kingdom with triumphant victory throughout long spaces of land : it is nevertheless a great thing, that, by his mighty deeds, he has surpassed the title of fame so prodigal towards him. But enough of this. Now let us continue the matter begun.

D. So be it, if it so please thee. It may be that due reverence for the treasurer is observed : here it seems derogatory to his dignity that in all things his sole faith is not trusted.

M. God forbid; nay rather, in this way his labours are spared and indemnity is assured to him; for it is not that he or another—so many and so great they are who sit at the exchequer—is not trusted : but that for such great matters and affairs of the kingdom, under so great a prince, it is fitting that great men and many of them be chosen; not, however, that they may look out for their own advantage, but that they may serve the glory and honour of the king.

D. Proceed, if it please thee, concerning the offices.

As to the Treasurer.

M. The office of the treasurer, or his care and business, could hardly be expressed in words, even though mine were the pen of a ready writer. For in all things, and concerning all things which are carried on either in the lower or the upper exchequer, his careful diligence is necessary. From what has been said before, nevertheless, it will be in great part clear in what things his principal care consists, so that he can not be torn from these so long as the exchequer lasts: namely, in receiving the accounts of the sheriff, and in the writing of the roll. For he furnishes the words, according to the nature of the matters, for the writing of his roll,—from which afterwards that same wording is taken by the other rolls as has been said above; and he must take care that there be no mistake either in the number, or the cause, or the person,—lest he be cancelled who is not quit, or he be summoned again who ought to be acquitted. For so great is the authority of his roll that it is permitted to no one to contradict it or to change it; unless, perchance, there be so manifest an error that it is clear to all: nor may it even then be changed unless by the common counsel of all the barons, and in their presence, the exchequer of that day being still in session. But a writing of the roll made in the year gone by, or even one of the current year, after the exchequer has been dissolved, may lawfully be changed by no one except the king, to whom, with regard to these matters, every thing is lawful that pleases him. Likewise it is the treasurer's duty to be associated in all great matters with his superiors, and to let nothing be hidden from him.

As to the Scribe of the Treasurer.

The office of the scribe who is next to the treasurer is to prepare the rolls for writing, from sheep-skins, not without cause. Their length, moreover, is as much as results from two membranes; not from random ones, but from large ones, prepared with care for this purpose: but the breadth is a little more than that of one and a half. The rolls, therefore, being ruled from the top almost to the bottom, and on both sides, the lines being suitably distant from each other, the counties and bailiwicks of which an account is below rendered are marked at the top: but a moderate interval being left, the space as it were of three or four fingers, in the middle of the line is written the name of the county which is treated of in the first place. Then at the head of the following line is written the name of the sheriff, followed by this form of words: "that or that sheriff renders account of the farm of that or that county." Then a little further on in the same line is written "in the treasury," and nothing else is added until the account is completed, for an important reason which is explained in the chapter on the sheriff. Then at the head of the following line is put down what part of the farm of the county is expended in alms and in the fixed tithes, what, also, in liveries. After these, at the head of the lower line are noted, among the lands given away, those which the generosity of the kings has conferred on churches or on those who did military service for them; among the estates called crown lands, which are blank, which by tale.

D. It surprises me, what thou sayest, that some estates are given blank, some by tale.

M. Let us proceed at present concerning the office of the scribe; and, when we are treating of the sheriff, ask me concerning this if thou wilt. After the lands given away, a space being left of one line so that the things by their very nature may seem separate, those things are noted which were ordered to be expended from the farm by a writ of the king; for these are not fixed, but casual. Some also which are without writs are accounted for as by custom of the exchequer, concerning which we will speak later: and thus the account for the body of the county is terminated. After this, a space being left of about six or seven lines, an account is made of the purprestures and escheats under this form of words: "the same sheriff renders account of the farm of purprestures and escheats"; but also of all the farms of manors and of the rent of woods which are annually due and paid. After these the accounts are put down in their order, excepting some cities and towns and bailiwicks of which the accounts are greater because they have fixed alms or liveries or lands given; and to the administrators of such lands special summonses are sent concerning their dues to the king. Their accounts, moreover, are made up after the account of the county in which they are is altogether finished. Such are Lincoln, Winchester, Mienes (?), Berchamstead, Colchester, and very many others.

D. I wonder at thy saying that some fixed revenues are called farms, but some, rents.

M. Farms are of manors; rents, however, only of woods. For the things that come from manors are rightly called firm and immutable, because, through agriculture, they are every year renewed and return, and besides this constitute in themselves sure revenues by the perpetual law of custom. But what by a yearly law is due from woods which are daily cut down and perish—for which there is not so firm or fixed a demand, but which are subject to rises and falls, though not yearly, yet frequent—is called rent: and so, by elision, they say that these revenues are rented. Some nevertheless believe that what is paid by individuals is called rent; but a farm, what results from these rents; so that farm is a collective name like crowd: wherefore, as is believed, it is thus called rent to indicate a yearly payment and show that it is not firm. After these fixed payments, a space again being left, an account is made of the debts concerning which the sheriff has been summoned; the names, however, being first put down of those judges who have apportioned these debts. But lastly an account is made of the chattels of fugitives or of those mutilated for their offences. And all this being completed, the account of that county is terminated. The scribe must take care not to write anything of his own accord in the roll, except what he has learned from the treasurer's dictation. But if, perhaps, through negligence or any other chance he should happen to err in writing the roll, either in the name or the amount or in the matter—in which the greater force of the writing consists,—he shall not presume to erase, but shall cancel by drawing, underneath, a thin line, and shall write directly following what is necessary. For the writing of

the roll has this in common with charters and other letters
patent, that it may not be erased : and for this reason
care has been taken to make them of sheep-skins ; for they
do not easily yield to erasure without the blemish becoming
apparent.

D. Does that scribe furnish the rolls at his own expense
or at that of the fisc ?

M. At the Michaelmas term he receives five shillings
from the fisc, and the scribe of the chancery likewise
another five ; from which they procure the membranes for
both rolls and for the summonses and receipts of the lower
exchequer.

As to the Scribe of the Chancery.

The care, the labour, the zeal of the remaining scribe sitting at his side consists chiefly in this, namely, that he shall
take down from the other roll word for word ; as we said
before, the same order being observed. Likewise it pertains
to him to write the writs of the king concerning outlays of
the treasury, but only for those payments which, in the
judgment of the barons, while the exchequer is in session,
ought to be made by the treasurer and chamberlains :
likewise he writes the writs of the king concerning the
computing or remitting of those things which the barons
have decreed should be computed or remitted at the exchequer. It is his duty also, when the accounts of the
sheriff have been gone through, and the dues of the king
for which the summonses are made, estimated, to write
out the latter, with diligent and at the same time laborious
discretion, to be sent throughout the whole kingdom : for
by them, and on account of them, the exchequer of the
following term is called together.

*VI. What the tenor is of Writs of the King made at the
Exchequer, whether concerning outlays of the Treasury,
or computings or remittings.*

D. Under what form of words are writs of the king concerning outlays of the treasury drawn up ?

M. The treasurer and chamberlains do not expend the money received, unless by express mandate of the king or of the presiding justice: for when the general account is demanded from them, they must have the authority of a rescript of the king concerning the money distributed; moreover this is the wording under which they are drawn up: "H. king, etc., to N. the treasurer and to this man and that man, chamberlains, greeting. Pay from my treasury to that or that man, this or this sum. These being witnesses before N. at the exchequer." Moreover "at the exchequer" is added that thus there may be a difference from the writs that are made in the curia regis. It is also necessary, when a writ is made concerning an outlay from the treasury, as we have said, that that same scribe shall make a copy of it, which is commonly called counter-writ; and this the clerk of the chancery shall reserve in his own possession, in testimony of the payment made through the original writ of the king, which the treasurer and chamberlains have. Also writs of computing or remitting those things which the barons shall have decreed should be computed or remitted—the will of our lord king having previously become known—are drawn up under this tenor of words: "H. by the grace of God, etc., to the barons of the exchequer, greeting. Compute to that or that man this or this sum, which he expended for this or that affair of mine. These being witness there at the exchequer." Likewise: "The king to the barons of the exchequer, greeting. I remit to that man, or quit-claim to this or that one this or that. These being witnesses there at the exchequer." Copies of all these writs shall remain with the aforesaid clerk, as a proof that the writs were made out. For the original writs of computations or remissions are enclosed in the boxes of the marshall when the accounts of the sheriffs are made up; for the rest, unless a dispute arise concerning them, they are not to be shown. Moreover, what we have said of the writs of the king is likewise to be understood of the writs of the presiding justice; but only when the king is absent and, with the impress of his seal, the laws of the kingdom are established and the cases are called, so that they who are summoned before the court are condemned or acquitted. But so long as the king shall be in the kingdom of England, the writs of the exchequer shall be made in the royal name, under the witness of this same president and of some other magnate. What the tenor is, moreover, of those writs which are called summonses, will be more fully told below in the chapter on summonses.

As to the Clerk of the Chancellor.

The clerk of the chancellor, who is next to the latter, although he serves not in his own but in another's name, is, nevertheless, busied about great things, and is called in many directions : so that from the very beginning of the accounts to the end he can not be torn thence ; unless perchance he is lenient to himself, a discreet representative being meanwhile substituted for him. He has the first care after the treasurer in all these things which are done there ; principally, however, in the matter of writing the rolls and writs ; for in these things he is chiefly versed. And he looks out lest the pen of his scribe, while he follows the other with equal steps, should commit an error. Likewise he looks diligently at the roll of the former year placed before him, until satisfaction shall have been given by the sheriff for those debts which are there marked, and for which he is summoned. Likewise when the sheriff sits to render account, the fixed payments from the county having been computed and put in writing, he takes from the sheriff the writ of summons to which the king's seal is appended, and presses the sheriff for those debts which are there written down, speaking in public, and saying ; "render for this, so much ; and for that, so much." The debts, moreover, which are paid entirely, and for which satisfaction is given, the same clerk cancels by a line drawn through the middle ; so that there may thus be a distinction between what is paid and what is to be paid. He also guards the counter-writs of those drawn up at the exchequer. He also corrects and seals the summonses made, as has been said before ; and he has infinite labour and is the greatest after the treasurer.

D. Here Argus would be more useful than Polyphemus.

As to the Clerk of the Constabulary.

M. The clerk of the constabulary is great, and busied at the curia regis ; at the exchequer also he is called in, together with the magnates to all the most important affairs, and with his consent matters concerning the king are carried on.   He is, moreover, sent by the king to the exchequer with the counter-writs against the terms of the exchequer, but only concerning those things which are done at the curia.   He also, with the constable, sees to the payments of the knights, or of certain of them as has been said ; and at times his office is laborious enough, although it is expressed in few words.   Nevertheless he fills it very often through a substitute as does the chancellor ; for the higher officials can not easily absent themselves from the presence of the king.   Thus thou hast, to some extent, the distribution of offices of those placed on the third bench at the right of the president.

As to Brunus.

Now at the head of the fourth seat which is placed opposite the justices sits Master Thomas, called Brunus. His authority at the exchequer is not to be despised.   For it is a great and mighty proof of his faithfulness and discretion that he was chosen by a prince of such excellent talents to have, contrary to the ancient custom, a third roll in which he may write the prerogatives of the realm and the secrets of the king, and which, keeping it in his own charge, he may carry wherever he wishes.   He also has his clerk in the lower exchequer, who, sitting next to the clerk of the treasury, has free opportunity to write what is received and expended in the treasury.

D. Is, then, his faith and discretion so well known to the king that, for this work, no one else is considered equal to him in merit ?

M. He was great at the court of the great king of Sicily, provident in his counsels, and almost first in the privy council of the king.   Meanwhile a new king arose who ignored him, one who, having evil men around him, perse-

cuted his father in the persons of the latter's adherents.
That man, therefore, his good fortune having changed,
was compelled to flee for his life, and although access was
open to him with the greatest honour to very many kingdoms, nevertheless, being frequently invited by Henry the
illustrious king of the English, whose fame is less than the
truth itself, he preferred to go to his native soil and to his
hereditary and incomparable master. Being received therefore by him as befitted both, because in Sicily he had been
concerned with great matters, here also he is deputed to
the great affairs of the exchequer. Thus, therefore, he
attained an abiding place and an office of dignity. He is
called in, also, with the magnates to all the great matters
of the exchequer. The above, then, are the different prerogatives of all those who, by reason of their office, sit at
the greater exchequer. It is next in order, if I mistake
not, that we proceed to tell what their dignities are by
reason of their sitting at the exchequer.

D. Nay, if it please thee, the office is still to be explained
of the knight whom thou dost call the silverer, and also
the office of the melter; for they have been put off thus
far since they are akin to each other and pertain to the
greater exchequer.

M. I see that the memory of the things promised does
not escape thee, whence the sure hope is conceived that
forgetfulness will not defraud thee of what I have already
said. I thought, indeed, that I had satisfied thee concerning the offices because I had omitted no one of those
who have seats at the exchequer. But those of whom thou
dost remind me have not fixed seats allotted them ; nay,
they fulfil their office according to the command of the
president or treasurer.

As to the Knight Silverer.

The knight silverer, then, carries from the lower to the
upper exchequer the box of money to be tested, of which
we spoke above; when he has brought this in, signed with
the seal of the sheriff, he pours out in the exchequer, under
the eyes of all, forty four shillings, which, when he took
them from the heap, he had previously marked ; and mix-

ing them together so that they may correspond in weight, he puts in one scale of the balance a pound weight, in the other as many of the coins as shall be necessary; this being done, he counts them, so that it may be evident from the number if they are of legal weight. But of whatever weight they are found to be, he puts apart into a cup one £, that is, twenty shillings, of which a test shall be made; but the remaining twenty four shillings he puts into a box. Likewise, besides the £ to be tested, two pence are given to the melter, not from the fisc, but on the part of the sheriff; as a reward, so to speak, for his labour. Then there are chosen by the president, or, if he be absent, by the treasurer, two other sheriffs; so that they, together with the knight silverer and also the sheriff against whom the test is to be made, shall proceed to the fire; there the melter, warned before and having made the necessary preparations, awaits their coming. There again, in the presence of the melter and of those who have been sent by the barons, they are diligently counted and handed over to the melter.

As to the Melter.

He, receiving them, counts them with his own hand, and thus places them on a vessel of burning embers which is in the furnace. Then, therefore, obeying the law of the art of melting, he reduces them to a mass, blowing upon, and cleansing, the silver. But he must take care lest it stand longer than necessary, or lest by excessive boilings he trouble and consume it; the former on account of the risk of loss to the king; the latter, to the sheriff; but he shall in every way, with all the industry possible, provide and procure that it be not troubled, but that it be boiled only so as to be pure. Those, moreover, who are sent there by the greater officials, should also see to this same thing. When the test, then, has been made, the others accompanying, the knight silverer carries the silver to the barons; and then, before the eyes of all, he weighs it with the aforesaid pound weight. Moreover he then supplies what the fire has consumed, putting in coin out of that same box, until that which has been tested is in equilibrium with the weight; then the result of that test is inscribed

above with these words: "Yorkshire.   The pound burnt with
so and so many pence loss"; and then that is called an assay;
for it is not inscribed unless it be previously agreed that it
ought to stand that way.   But if the sheriff from whom it
comes shall claim that more has been consumed than is
just,—by the heat of the fire, perhaps, or by the infusion
of lead ; or if the melter himself shall confess that, for
some reason or other, the test was imperfect ;—again
twenty shillings—those which remain in the aforesaid box
—shall be counted before the barons, as has been described ; so that, the same process being observed, a test
may be made of them.   Hence it must be clear to thee for
what reason, from the great heap of money placed there
originally, forty four shillings are, from the first, put aside
in a box, on which is placed the seal of the sheriff.   It is to
be noted, indeed, that the melter receives two pence for
the testing, as has been said.   But if, by any chance, he
should go through it again—or even if he test it a third
time—he shall not receive anything, but shall be content
with the two pence which he has once received.

D. I wonder that by such great men such diligence
should be applied to the testing of one pound, since neither
great gain nor much loss can come from it.

M. This is gone through with not on account of this
pound alone, but on account of all those which, together
with this, are paid by the same sheriff under the name of
the same farm.   For as much as, through the purging fire,
falls off from this pound, so much the sheriff knows is to
be subtracted from each other pound of his sum : so that
if he pays a hundred pounds by tale, and twelve pence
have fallen off the test pound, only ninety five are computed to him.

D. Now I seem to see that, from these things, no small
gain can arise; but to whom it ought to go I am ignorant.

M. It has been said, and it is always meant, that the
advantage of the king alone is served in all these matters.
Although, moreover, the combustion is subtracted from the
tally of the sheriff, it is nevertheless placed apart on
another, shorter tally, so that the treasurer and chamberlains may answer for the the total of it.   But thou must
know that, through this tally of combustion the farm of

the sheriff is blanched; wherefore, in testimony of this, it always remains hanging to the greater tally.

D. A question strikes me here which I remember to have propounded when we were treating of the lower exchequer: why, namely, one pound should fall off more than another, since the condition ought to be the same of all those who have to do with coining money.

M. To this question, as to that former one, it is sufficient to reply that this can be done through forgers and clippers of coin. Some, moreover, have believed—and I do not differ from them—that the money of this kingdom was not lawful if the tested pound decreased more than six pence from the weight to which it corresponds when counted; and also that money of this kind, brought to the exchequer, ought to fall to the fisc,—unless, perhaps, the coins are new and not customary, and the inscription upon them betrays their producer; for then that moneyer shall be strictly called to account for his work, and, according to the established laws, shall be condemned or absolved without loss to the sheriff. But if, the coin being proved and re-proved by testing, the moneyer shall have been condemned and punished, the coins shall be reduced to a mass by the melter of the exchequer—others skilled in this art being present—and its weight shall be computed to the sheriff. But all this is almost abolished now and much relaxed; since, with regard to money, all sin in common; when, however, the money shall come to be of the right measure, and the one fixed by law, it will become necessary to keep the law as originally established. On the other hand, if any sheriff should have brought coins, a pound of which, when burned, kept within five or four or less, and they seemed to have been newly made, not usual or current,— they were likewise called not lawful: exceeding, as it were, the common standard; whence, like the others, they also could be confiscated.

There are likewise at the exchequer fixed payments which are made at stated terms without a writ of the king: such is the salary of the "nauclerus," *i.e.*, the master, of the king's ship which we call "esnecca," who receives twelve pence daily. For this, and for similar payments, tallies are made by the chamberlains, since they do not have writs for them. The knight silverer, moreover, has the " recauta" of these, *i.e.*, the counter-tallies. Likewise he and the melter—when it becomes necessary, and the great quantity of money brought in burdens the tellers—may, on being requested by the chamberlains, aid them in counting ; it is, however, optional on their parts, not compulsory. Thus thou hast the offices of the knight silverer and the melter.

D. What are the signs of a test completed or of one not completed ?

M. I do not sufficiently know ; nor have I troubled myself about these things. But so long as over the already liquid silver a sort of little black cloud is seen to hover, it is called incomplete. But when, as it were, certain minute grains ascend from the bottom to the top and there dissolve, it is a sign that the test is done.

VII. By whom, or for what purpose, the testing of silver was instituted.

D. By whom, and on what account, was this testing or combustion instituted ?

M. In order that it may be clear to- thee concerning these things, I must begin a little further back. In the primitive state of the kingdom after the Conquest, as we have learned from our fathers, not weights of gold or silver, but solely victuals were paid to the kings from their lands ; from which the necessaries for the daily use of the royal household were furnished. And those who had been appointed for this purpose knew how much came from the separate estates. But from the pleas of the kingdom and from feudal reliefs, and from the cities or castles by which agriculture was not practised, cash money for the stipends or gifts of the soldiers, and for other necessary things came in. This arrangement, however, continued during the whole time of king William I., and up to the time of king Henry, his son ; so that I myself saw some people who had seen victuals carried at stated times from the estates of the crown to the court : and the officials of the royal household knew from which counties corn and from which different kinds of meat, or fodder for horses,

or any other necessary things, were due. These being paid
according to the measure fixed upon of each thing, the
royal officials put them to the account of the sheriff,
reducing them to a total of money: for a measure, namely,
of grain enough for the bread of a hundred men, one
shilling; for the body of a fattened ox, one shilling;
for a ram or a sheep, 4d.; for the fodder of twenty
horses, likewise 4d. But as time went on, when the
same king was occupied across the channel and in
remote places, in calming the tumults of war, it came
about that the sum necessary for meeting these expenses
was paid in ready money. Meanwhile there kept coming
to the court of the king a complaining multitude of
peasants; or, what seemed to him worse, they frequently
came in front of him as he passed, proffering their ploughs
as a sign of the defective agriculture; for they were
oppressed by innumerable burdens on account of the
victuals, which, having to traverse great distances in
the realm, they brought from their lands.   Yielding,
therefore, to their complaints, the opinion of the nobles
having been ascertained, he sent out throughout the
kingdom the men most prudent and discreet in these
matters. These, going around and examining with their
own eyes the different estates, and estimating the victuals
that were paid from them, reduced them to a sum of
money.   They decreed, moreover, that for the sum of the
sums which was arrived at from all the estates in one county,
the sheriff of that county should be bounden to the exchequer; adding that he should pay by scale,—that is, besides
each cash pound, 6d. For they thought that, in course of
time, it might easily come about that money, then good,
might fall from its condition. Nor did their opinion
prove false. Therefore they were compelled to decree that
the farm of manors should be paid, not alone by scale, but
by weight; which could not be done without adding a
great deal.   This rule of payment was observed for many
years in the exchequer: whence, frequently, in the old
yearly rolls of that king, thou wilt find written: "in the
treasury 100 pounds according to scale," or, "in the
treasury 100 pounds according to weight." Meanwhile
there came into prominence a prudent man, provident in

his plans, discreet in discourse, and, by the grace of God, most remarkably adapted especially for great matters; thou would'st say that in him was fulfilled what is written, "the grace of the Holy Spirit knows no tardy delays." He being called to court by this same king, although unknown, yet not ignoble, taught by his example,

> How poverty,[1] e'en when extreme, can be most fruitful of heroes!

He therefore, increasing in favour with his prince, with the clergy, and with the people, being made bishop of Salisbury, enjoyed the highest honours in the kingdom, and had a great knowledge of the exchequer; so that, as is not doubtful, but is manifest from the rolls themselves, it flourished greatly under him. And from his troughs we, also, have received by tradition that little which we possess. Upon this point, at present, I omit to say much; because, as was due to the greatness of his position, he left a memory to survive him which gives proof of a most noble mind. He afterwards, by order of the prince, came to the exchequer; and after having sat there for some years, he learned that by the kind of payment described above the fisc did not fully get its dues: for although it seemed to get its dues in number and weight, it did not, nevertheless, in material. For it did not follow, when for one pound he paid twenty shillings in cash, even if they corresponded to a pound in weight, that he consequently paid a pound of silver: for he could have paid one mixed with copper or with any ore, since no test was made. In order therefore that the royal and the public advantage might at the same time be provided for, the advice of the king himself having been heard on this matter, it was decreed that the burning or testing of the farm should take place in the aforesaid manner.

D. Why do you say "the public advantage"?

M. Because the sheriff, feeling himself wronged by the combustion of the deteriorated money, when he is about to pay his farm, takes careful heed that the moneyers placed

---

[1] This is a play upon words. The name of the distinguished man in question was Roger the Poor (le Poer). He was the granduncle of the author of this present treatise.

under him do not exceed the bounds of the established standard; and when he has found them out, they are so punished that others may be frightened by their example.

D. Ought then a blank farm to be paid by all the counties, or should a test be made in the case of all the counties?

M. No; but those which by ancient right are said to belong to the royal crown pay thus. Those, however, which pay the fisc for some incidental causes, render their dues by tale alone; such are Shropshire, Sussex, Northumberland and Cumberland. It is open to the sheriff, instead of a blank farm, to pay the weight of tested silver; and thus he will escape the loss by combustion; provided, nevertheless, that the melter of the king shall decree that the same is worthy to be received. Thou knowest now what thou did'st ask about, namely, by whom and for what cause the testing was instituted.

D. I see that, by this, is fulfilled to the letter what is written: "each man's work shall be tried by fire." But now may it please thee to go on with what thou hast begun.

M. So be it. It is in order, I believe, in accordance with the arrangement of the plan laid down, that we proceed to treat of the prerogatives of those who sit at the exchequer, whether officially, or by order of the king.

D. I wonder very much for what reason, when thou wert treating of the offices, thou did'st either refrain on purpose from speaking of the usher of the upper exchequer and his office, or else did'st pass it by, the evil of forgetfulness coming in the way.

M. I congratulate thee on thy memory of what has gone before; for, indeed, the glory of the teacher is in the proficiency of his pupil. Thou knewest that the already mentioned usher received his pay with the other officials, and therefore thou dost rightly ask what is his office. It is then as follows:

As to the Usher of the Upper Exchequer.

That usher, alone, without an associate, guards the door of the exchequer building: unless when, from his own home, he takes servants for the burdensome part of his office. Likewise the same man guards the door of the chamber of secrets, which is situated next to the exchequer building. Thither go the barons when a doubtful question is propounded to them in the exchequer, concerning which they prefer to deliberate by themselves rather than in the hearing of all. But it is chiefly on this account that they go apart by themselves,—lest, namely, the accounts which are being made up at the exchequer should be impeded; and while they are delaying in private council, the usual course of the accounts goes on. But if any question should arise, it would be referred to them. It is also free to the usher, with impunity, to preclude ingress when he wishes, to any men—even if great in authority—who are not necessary to the matter in hand. To those alone, who sit at the exchequer by reason of their office or by mandate of the king, is voluntary ingress to either chamber permitted. But if they are persons vouched for, who can not suitably go in when alone, one or two may be shown into the outer building of the exchequer; but into the chamber of secrets only the officials enter, others being excluded; unless when they are called by their masters to perform some matters for the king. Likewise the usher receives the summonses, made out and signed by the marshall. When the exchequer of that term has been dissolved, he bears them in his own person, or by means of a faithful messenger, throughout England, as has been said above. He also, by command of the president, calls into the latter's presence, when he needs them, the sheriffs, who are dispersed in all directions outside the building. Likewise it pertains to him to see to any of the small matters which are necessary in the exchequer building—such as placing and preparing the seats around the exchequer and the like. From the foregoing it is clear to thee, as we believe, concerning the offices of those who sit at the exchequer. We will now show what are their rights or prerogatives by reason of their sitting at the exchequer.

VIII. What are the rights and prerogatives of those sitting at the Exchequer, by reason of their sitting there.

Still further, indeed, the tongue of the detractor must continue to spare us, and the tooth of envy, lest it leap upon us and tear us to pieces ; for scarcely any of these things would come to thy knowledge if we saw fit to insist, not on the customary names of things, but on some exquisite scheme of words or on made-up appellations.

D. A novelty of words was the one thing I warned thee to shun from the beginning, and I obtained from thee that thou should'st use common and customary words with regard to common things, lest unaccustomed novelty should disturb the rudimentary teachings. So, therefore, as thou hast begun, may it please thee again to continue thy undertaking. But if, when thou dost thus advance, the emulous mind or tongue of a detractor should overtake thee, thou may'st obtain this from him, that he who in his writings is without sin shall cast the first stone at thee.

M. I willingly obey so long as that rule is observed. The pre-eminence of those sitting at the exchequer consists in many things. For whether they who sit there by his mandate are of the clergy or of the curia regis,—from the day on which they come together, up to the general departure, they are not called to any other cases under any judges whatever; and if, by chance, they shall have been summoned, they are excused by reason of their public function. But if those who sit there are the accusers and not the accused, and have suits elsewhere,—it shall be at their option either to have the case tried by a procurator, or to postpone the day without any detriment to their rights. But if the judge under whom their case is being tried, whether he be ecclesiastical or lay, being ignorant of this law, shall, after the already mentioned day of convocation to the exchequer, have cited any one of them, and shall, perhaps, by a judgment have despoiled the absent one of his possession or of some right,—by authority of the prince and by reason of the session, his case shall be recalled to that state in which it was before the citation. But the judge has not, on this account, merited punishment; for he has followed out what belonged to his duty ; although, by reason of the public function, it does not take effect. But if he shall have been so cited that the decisive day, fixed for him and determined by the law, shall come before the day of the convocation to the exchequer, he shall not be able to excuse himself on that account, or to evade the sentence of the judge, or to make it vain when declared against him ; even though the one day be so near to the other that he be compelled to start on his journey. He shall, in that case, obtain for himself a procurator or sponsor, and shall himself, bent on the king's business, without guile, hasten to the court. The barons, moreover, who sit at the exchequer shall pay nothing under the name of customs for the victuals of their household bought in the cities and burroughs and ports. But if an officer of the revenues shall have compelled one of them to pay anything for these,—if only one of his servants is present who is willing to prove by taking an oath that the things have been bought for his master's use : to the baron, indeed, the money exacted shall be restored entire, and the scoundrel of a collector shall pay a pecuniary punishment according to the quality of the person. Likewise if any one, even if great in the kingdom, shall, with inconsiderate heat of mind, injure any one who sits at the exchequer, through taunts or insults,—an excess of this kind shall, if the president himself is present, at once receive a vindicating pecuniary punishment. But in the president's absence if the man constantly denies the injury done and those sit- ting there call out that he has said what he is charged with, he shall nevertheless straightway be judged guilty to the extent of a fine to the king whom he serves, unless he hastens to anticipate judgment by begging mercy. But if those who sit at the exchequer shall have mutually molested each other with any sort of contumelious attack, they shall make peace again ; the others of their rank who serve with them acting as mediators, in such wise that satisfaction shall be rendered by him who, in their estima- tion, has injured an innocent person. But if he be un- willing to acquiesce, but rather persevere in his rashness, the matter shall be laid before the president ; and after- wards, from him each one shall receive justice. But if, through the devil, the instigator of evil, who does not look with unmoved eyes on the joyous happiness of fraternal peace, it should happen that occasion for discord should come up among the greater officials themselves; and thence —which God forbid—a war of insults should arise; and, Satan adding goads, peace can not be restored by the other colleagues in those labours:—the knowledge of all these things shall be reserved for the prince himself; who, according as God, in whose hand it is, inspires his heart, shall punish the offence; lest those who are set over others should seem to be able to do with impunity what they decree should be punished in others.

D. From this is manifest what Solomon says: "death and life are in the power of the tongue," and likewise James; "the tongue is a little member and boasteth great things."

M. So it is; but let us proceed concerning the prerogatives. Common assessments are held at times, throughout the counties, by itinerant justices whom we call deambulatory or wandering judges; the assessments are called common because, when the sum is known which is required in common from those who have estates in the county, it is distributed according to the hides of land, so that when the time comes for payment at the exchequer, nothing of it is lacking. From all these payments all those who, by mandate of the king, sit at the exchequer are entirely free, so that not only are none of them exacted from their domains, but also none from all their fiefs. If, however, one who sits there has an estate either in farm or in custody, or also as a pledge for money, he shall not be exempt, but rather more subject for these to the common law. In addition to and besides these exemptions, moreover, he shall be free at the exchequer from murder-fines, scutages and Danegeld. Moreover what pertains to him shall be deducted from the fixed total, and shall be placed to the account of the sheriff in these words: "remitted by writ of the king, to him or him this or that sum"; although, in fact, he has no writ of the king concerning this. Moreover he to whom anything has been remitted by the prince must see to it lest afterwards he require, from those in turn subject to him, the amount which has been remitted; he had the rather better be mindful of that word, "forgive and be forgiven"; for if this shall have been found out, the prince, emulating the teaching of the Gospel, will neither let him go nor forgive his debt, but perhaps will punish him a hundred fold; for he is seen to abuse the favour bestowed on him, when he irreverently exacts from others what has been freely forgiven to himself.

D. It has been said, if I remember aright, that whoever, by precept of the king, sits at the exchequer is free, by reason of his sitting there, from certain things determined by the law. It was added also, if I recollect well, that the exchequer sits at the Easter term; that, however, the things that are done then are not entirely terminated, but that their consummation is reserved for the Michaelmas term. Since, now, it is possible, nay, frequently happens, that some one by mandate of the king is called to it at the Easter term, who at the Michaelmas term has either paid his debt to fate, or is transferred by order of the king to other business of the realm, or, what seems more weighty with some, having in the meantime become hateful to the king, is judged unworthy to perform such important duties: I ask does he who is quit at the Easter term, in which few things are terminated but all things renewed by repeating the summons,—does such a one deserve to be absolved at the Michaelmas term, even when he has ceased to deserve his seat at the exchequer and the favour itself of his prince?

M. Probably an abundance of reasons can be found for taking either side of this question; but know that the choice of the royal munificence, after the favour of absolution has once been indulged, is always, even with pecuniary loss, more prone to the better part: indeed, the principle of the gifts and of the remissions of the king is the same, that just as his gifts cannot be recalled or re-demanded, so also the acquittals of the king, which are commonly called pardons, can not be invalidated. He therefore is free and absolved at the term of consummation who in any way merited to be absolved at the preceding one.

D. Some things which have been said give me concern. First, that thou dost say that anything is remitted to any one under this tenor of words: "in pardons by writ of the king, to him or him, this or that," when, nevertheless, he has obtained no writ of remission from the king. For how it can happen that such writing of the roll is not found to be false, I do not see.

M. It gives thee concern not without cause; for it has long concerned me; ·and, as I believe, the reason of thus writing is not yet clear to all; wherefore, although it is no great matter that thou askest about, nevertheless it is unusual and does seem absurd that that is said to be remitted by writ of the king, which is always to be remitted without a writ. For which reason I once attacked on this very matter the bishop of Ely, as the man most skilled in this branch—blessed be his memory for ever. He, the illustrious treasurer of that king of the English, Henry I., and the nephew of him of Salisbury whom we mentioned above, had a knowledge of the exchequer incomparable in his time: for being supreme in those things which pertained to the dignity of his standing, he made the fame of his name wide-spread; so that almost alone in the kingdom he so lived and died that no envious tongue dares to blacken his glory. He, moreover, being frequently requested by the illustrious king, Henry the Second, reformed the knowledge of the exchequer which, the time of warfare having lasted for many years, had almost entirely died out; and, like another Esdras, sedulous restorer of the Bible, renewed the form of its whole arrangement. The prudent man, indeed, thought it better to mark down for posterity the laws constituted by the ancients, rather than, by his silence, to bring it about that new ones should be made. For modern times, in the matter of gaining money, have scarcely dictated laws gentler than the former ones. From him, therefore, in this matter, this is the kind of answer I received; " brother, he who has ears eager to hear, easily finds the tongue of a detractor; even he who has them not, will not easily escape the same. It was thus that there came to king Henry I. a certain man having the tongue of a serpent, saying to him : ' your barons who sit at the exchequer, why do they not pay the dues that arise from their lands? For some have fixed payments at the exchequer for sitting there; some also, on account of their office, have estates and their fruits; hence, therefore, a heavy loss falls on the fisc." When, therefore, he, urging the gain that it would be to the prince, repeatedly returned to the attack, these words at length possessed the latter's mind to such an extent, that he ordered all the established dues to be paid by all and to be remitted to no one, unless someone should have obtained from him an express mandate concerning this : and it was done accordingly. But as time went on, when the prince remembered the counsel of Achitopel, he repented of having acquiesced. He decreed, therefore, that all the aforesaid payments should be computed to those who served there, considering the loss of a small sum of money as nothing in comparison with the great honour gained. And so he despatched his writ to the exchequer, to the effect that those sitting there should, by a perpetual law, be free from these payments. From this writ, therefore, it was said then and is said now, "remitted by the king's writ"; and so it came about that what was granted to the fathers should even now continue in the case of their posterity. We remember ourselves in modern times to have seen a similar payment to this, which, after all this time was computed to those who deserved to be absolved under a similar tenor of words. For our lord king Henry II., at the Michaelmas term of the 24th year of his reign, ordered that the knights of the Temple, and the brothers Hospitallers, and the monks of the Cistercian order, to whom, by the privileges in their charter, he had long since indulged quittance of all things pertaining to money—jurisdiction over life and members being excepted,—should really now be quit of all things pertaining to money throughout the different counties; so that henceforth they should not be compelled to bring their charters to the exchequer. And the authority of the royal piety decreed this—that thus once for all, in the consideration of the barons they should be freed of all these things lest those who have gone over to the enjoyment of a better life, and are obliged the more to have freedom for prayer, should be compelled for such a cause to make a tedious and useless delay with their charters at the exchequer. By the counsel, therefore, and the deliberation of the barons who were present, a writ of the lord king was drawn up under this tenor: "I quit claim the knights of the Temple of five marks which are exacted from their vassals for default, and I prohibit that now from them or their vassals or their lands anything be exacted or received which pertains to money. These being witnesses, there." And in like manner as to the brothers Hospitallers and to the aforesaid monks. By the authority of this mandate, therefore, they will henceforth be quit, throughout the several counties of all things which pertain to money : so that that which we mentioned above may rightly be spoken of in the yearly roll as " remitted by writ of the king."

D. I have understood very well what has been said. Now, if it please thee, do not delay to make clear what are scutage, murdrum and Danegeld. They seem, indeed, to be something barbarous; but they concern me the more for the reason that, as thou sayest, those who minister at the exchequer are free from them.

IX. *What Scutage is, and why it is so called.*

It happens sometimes that, when the machinations of enemies threaten or attack the kingdom, the king decrees that, from the different knights' fees, a certain sum shall be paid,—a mark, namely, or a pound ; and from this come the payments or gifts to the soldiers. For the prince prefers to expose mercenaries, rather than natives to the fortunes of war. And so this sum, which is paid in the name of the shields, is called scutage. From this, moreover, they who sit at the exchequer are quit.

X. *What Murder is, and why so called.*

Murder (murdrum), indeed, is properly called the secret death of somebody, whose slayer is not known. For " murdrum " means the same as " hidden " or " occult." Now in the primitive state of the kingdom after the Conquest those who were left of the Anglo-Saxon subjects secretly laid ambushes for the suspected and hated race of the Normans, and, here and there, when opportunity offered, killed them secretly in the woods and in remote places : as vengeance for whom—when the kings and their ministers had for some years, with exquisite kinds of tortures, raged against the Anglo-Saxons; and they, nevertheless, had not, in consequence of these measures, altogether desisted,—the following plan was hit upon, that the so called " hundred," in which a Norman was found killed in this way—when he who had caused his death was not to be found, and it did not appear from his flight who he was—should be condemned to a large sum of tested silver for the fisc ; some, indeed, to 36, some to 44£, according to the different localities and the frequency of the slaying. And they say that this is done with the following end in view, namely, that a general penalty of this kind might make it safe for the passers by,—and that each person might hasten to punish so great a crime and to give up to justice him through whom so enormous a loss fell on the whole neighbourhood. Know that from such payments, as we have said, those who sit at the exchequer are free.

D. Ought not the occult death of an Anglo-Saxon, like that of a Norman, to be reputed murder ?

M. By the original institution it ought not to, as thou hast heard : but during the time that the English and Normans have now dwelt together, and mutually married and given in marriage, the nations have become so intermingled that one can hardly tell to-day—I speak of freemen—who is of English and who of Norman race ; excepting, however, the bondsmen who are called " villani," to whom it is not free, if their lords object, to depart from the condition of their station. On this account almost always when any one is found thus slain to-day, it is punished as murder ; except in the case of those who show certain proofs, as we have said, of a servile condition.

D. I wonder that this prince of singular excellence, and this man of most distinguished virtue, should have shown such mercy towards the race of the English, subjugated and suspected by him, that not only did he keep the serfs by whom agriculture could be exercised, from harm, but left even to the nobles of the kingdom their estates and ample possessions.

M. Although these things do not pertain to the matters undertaken and concerning which I have bound myself, I will nevertheless freely expound what I have heard on these matters from the natives themselves. After the conquest of the kingdom, after the just overthrow of the rebels, when the king himself and the king's nobles went over the new places, a diligent inquiry was made as to who there were who, contending in war against the king had saved themselves through flight. To all of these, and even to the heirs of those who had fallen in battle, all hope of the lands and estates and revenues which they had before possessed was precluded : for it was thought much for them even to enjoy the privilege of being alive under their enemies. But those who, having been called to the war, had not yet come together, or, occupied with family or any kind of necessary affairs had not been present,—when, in course of time, by their devoted service they had gained the favour of their lords, they began to have possessions for themselves alone ; without hope of hereditary possession, but according to the pleasure of their lords. But as time went on, when, becoming hateful to their masters, they were here and there driven from their possessions, and there was no one to restore what had been taken away,—a common complaint of the natives came to the king to the effect that, thus hateful to all and despoiled of their property, they would be compelled to cross to foreign lands. Counsel at length having been taken on these matters, it was decided that what, their merits demanding, a legal pact having been entered into, they had been able to obtain from their masters, should be conceded to them by inviolable right : but that, however, they should claim nothing for themselves by right of heredity from the time of the conquest of the race. And it is manifest with what discreet consideration this provision was made, especially since they would thus be bound to consult their own advantage in every way, and to strive henceforth by devoted service to gain the favour of their lords. So, therefore, whoever, belonging to the conquered race, possesses estates or any thing of the kind,—he has acquired them, not because they seemed to be due to him by reason of heredity, but because his merits alone demanding, or some pact intervening, he has obtained them.

D. I do not exactly know what is a " centuriata " or hundred.

M. Wait a little ; thou wilt know later in its proper place ; that is, in the chapter on the Domesday book. Now let us proceed concerning Danegeld, and pay a little attention, so that the reason of this name may be clear to thee.

XI. What is Danegeld, and why so called.

Our island, content with its own, does not need the goods of the
    stranger ;
Therefore, with very good right, our predecessors have called it,
Truly the lap of riches ; the home, too, of every delight.

On account of this she has suffered innumerable injuries from outsiders; for it is written : " marked jewels attract the thief." For the robbers of the surrounding islands, making an irruption and depopulating the shores, carried off gold and silver and all sorts of precious things. But when the king and the natives, drawn up in warlike array, pressed on in defence of their race, they betook themselves to flight by sea. Now among these robbers almost the first, and always the most ready to do harm, was that warlike and numerous race of the Danes ; who, besides possessing the common avarice of plunderers, pressed on the more eagerly because they claimed, of ancient right, some part in the domination of that kingdom, as the history of the Britons more fully relates. In order, therefore, to ward these off, it was decreed by the English kings that, from each " hide " of the kingdom, by a certain perpetual right, two shillings of silver should be paid for the use of the brave men who, patrolling and carefully watching the shores, kept off the attack of the enemy. Therefore, since principally on account of the Danes this revenue was instituted, it is called " Danegeldum " or " Danegeldus." This, therefore, under the native kings, was paid yearly, as has been said, until the time of king William I. of the race and people of the Normans. For in his day the Danes as well as the other robbers by land and by sea restrained their hostile attacks, knowing to be true that which is written, " when a strong man armed keepeth his palace his possessions are in peace." For they also knew, indeed, that men of surpassing valour do not suffer injuries to go unpunished. When, therefore, the land had long been

quiet under the rule of this king, he became unwilling that
that should be paid as a yearly tax which had been exacted
by the urgent necessity of a time of war ; nor yet, however,
on account of unforeseen cases, did he wish it to be entirely omitted.   It was occasionally paid, therefore, in his
time and in that of his successor : that is, when, from outside nations, wars or rumours of wars arose.   But whenever it is paid, those who sit at the exchequer, are free from
it, as has been said.   The sheriffs too, although they are
not counted under the barons of the exchequer, are quit of
this for their domains on account of the labour of collecting the tax.   Know, moreover, that the domains of any
one are called those which are cultivated at his own
expense or labour, and likewise those which are possessed
by his serfs in his name.   For the serfs, according to the
law of the kingdom, not only may be transferred by their
lords from those places which they now possess to others ;
but they themselves also are sold or sundered in every
possible way ; with right they themselves, as well as the
lands which they cultivate in order to serve their masters,
are considered domains.   Likewise it is said by those to
whom the ancient dignity of the exchequer was known
from what they had seen with their own eyes, that its
barons are free, for their domains, of essarts (clearance-
fines) of the forests.   With whom we also agree ; adding
the reservation, that they may be called quit of those
essarts which had been made before the day on which the
illustrious king Henry I. bade farewell to human affairs.
For if they were quit of all, whenever made or to be made,
the barons would seem to be free with impunity, according
to their own will and judgment, to cut down their woods,
in which the royal forest consists ; which they can, in fact,
by no means do with impunity, unless the consent of the
king or of the chief forester has first been gained.   Nay,
those who have their domicile in the forest may not take
from their own woods what they want for the necessary
uses of their homes, unless by view of those who are deputed to guard the forest.   But there are many who wish
to prove by their arguments that no one, by reason of his
seat at the exchequer, is free from these essarts. If any one
at all of those sitting there should, by any misfortune,

commit a fault against the king for which he would merit to be punished with a pecuniary fine, he would not be freed from that punishment except by special mandate of the king. Since, therefore, a clearance is a fault committed against the forest of the king, he who thus errs and on this account receives a penalty, ought not, as they say, to be acquitted unless by express mandate of the king. Now although this reasoning is subtle and seems to some almost sufficient, it is to be said, in objection to it, that the penalty for clearance is fixed and common to those who err in this way; so that, namely, for the clearance of one acre of wheat land one shilling is paid; but for an acre in which oats are sown, six pence, by a perpetual law. Moreover from these items a certain total sum arises, for which the sheriff is compelled to account to the exchequer; just as from the established two shillings or one from the different "hides," one sum arises which is called the common assessment. Since, therefore, in these respects, the essart has an express similitude with the common assessment, as has been said, it would seem as if the barons, not without justice, should be considered quit from the essarts, just as from the other common assessments. Likewise the authority, not to be despised, of custom and long usage is against them (the cavillers). For those whose memory is hoary call to mind that it was so in past times. I myself, who speak with thee, have, in modern times, looked upon Robert, earl of Leicester, a discreet man, learned in letters and versed in matters of the law. He, while having an inborn virtue of mind, became also an emulator of his father's prudence: his industry examined into many matters under our prince Henry the Second, whom neither fictitious prudence nor dissimulated folly deceives; so that, by the king's order, not only at the exchequer did Robert obtain the dignity of president, but also throughout the whole kingdom. He once, when the visitation of the forests which they commonly call the "view" (reguarda), and which takes place every third year, was at hand, obtained a writ of the king to the effect that he should be quit of whatever might be demanded from his land for essarts, the sum being stated to which these amounted: and when this writ was brought and publicly read before the exchequer, all were amazed and wondered, saying: "does not this earl invalidate our privileges?" And while those who sat there mutually regarded each other, Nigel of blessed memory, the whilom bishop of Ely, began, speaking thus with modesty: "My lord earl, thou dost seem to have invalidated, by this writ, the prerogative of the exchequer, since thou hast obtained a mandate of the king for those things from which thou, by reason of thy seat at the exchequer, art free; and if one may logically draw an inference by deduction from the major term, whoever does not obtain a writ of the king concerning his essarts, will soon become answerable for their payment; but, with all due reverence, this mode of absolution is pernicious on account of the example it sets." When, therefore, as happens in doubtful cases, some were of one opinion, others of another, there was brought in, as a valid argument in this matter, the yearly (pipe) roll of the time of that great king of whom we spoke above, under whom the dignity and the knowledge of the exchequer are said to have flourished in a high degree; and something was found which seemed to justify the bishop who made the assertion concerning the prerogative of those sitting there. Having heard these things, the earl, after deliberating a little with himself, said: I confess that in this matter I obtained a writ of the king, not that I might invalidate your right, but that thus, without trouble, I might avoid the too importunate exaction—unknown, however, to the king—of the collectors. Abandoning his writ, therefore, he chose to be absolved on account of the prerogative of his seat. Some time after, when the aforesaid bishop, detained by infirmity could not be present, and I myself supplied, as well as I could, his place at the exchequer, it happened that essarts were paid; when, therefore, what had been exacted from his domain had been paid, I complained publicly, alleging the right of exemption. By the common counsel and verdict of all, therefore, the sum which had been already paid was restored to me. Reserving, therefore, what had been raised from his domain, I restored to his serfs, in its entirety, what had been exacted from each one, so that the memory might survive and be witness in this matter.

D. With all due reverence, one should not use examples but reasons in these matters.

M. That is so; but it happens, at times, that the causes of things and the reasons of sayings are secret, and then it suffices to bring up examples relating to them; especially if they are taken from the cases of prudent men, whose deeds are circumspect and are not done without reason. But whatever we have said about these things, taking part for this privilege or against it, thou may'st be sure that in this matter we have called nothing certain, unless what the authority of the king decreed should be observed. But the account of the forests and also the punishment or absolution of those who transgress with regard to them, whether it be a pecuniary or a corporal one, is kept separate from the other judgments of the kingdom, and is subjected to the will of the king alone or to that of some one of his intimates specially deputed for this purpose. It subsists by its own laws, which, they say, are not subject to the common law of the kingdom, but to the voluntary decree of the princes; so that whatever has been done according to its law may be said to be not absolutely just, but just according to the law of the forest. The forests, moreover, are the sanctuaries of kings and their greatest delight; thither they go for the sake of hunting, having laid aside their cares for a while, so that they may be refreshed by a short rest. There, the serious, and at the same time natural uproars of the court having ceased, they breathe in for a while the boon of pure liberty; whence it comes that they who transgress with regard to the forest are subject to the royal displeasure alone.

D. From my earliest youth I have learned that it is wrong for a prudent person to prefer to suffer ignorance rather than to demand the causes of things that have been said; in order, therefore, that the foregoing may more fully be made clear, do not put off revealing what a forest is, and what an essart.

XII. What is the Forest of the King, and what the reason of this name.

M. The forest of the king is the safe dwelling-place of wild beasts; not of every kind, but of the kinds that live in woods; not in all places, but in fixed ones, and ones suitable for the purpose; whence it is called "foresta," the " e " being changed into " o," as if it were " feresta " —*i.e.*, an abiding place for wild beasts.

D. Is there a forest of the king in each county?

M. No; but only in the wooded ones, where the wild beasts can have their lairs and ripe nourishment: nor does it matter to whom the woods belong, whether to the king, or to the nobles of the kingdom,—the wild beasts can none the less run around everywhere free and unharmed.

XIII. What is an Essart, and why so called.

Essarts are commonly called what are named " occationes " in the works of Isidor; that is, when any groves or thickets in the forest, which are fit for pasture and for lairs, are cut down; after which same cutting down and tearing up by the roots, the land is dug up and cultivated. But if groves are so cut that anyone standing still, leaning against the remaining stump of an oak, or any other tree that has been cut down, shall, on looking round, perceive five that have been cut down, they consider this a wilderness (vastum)—that is, a place laid waste (vastatum)—so called by syncope. Such an excess, moreover, even if committed in one's own groves, is considered so grave that a man may never be acquitted of it by reason of his seat at the exchequer; but he ought rather to be pecuniarily punished according to the power of solvency of his rank. Thus far I have expounded, to some extent figuratively, what succint brevity has permitted, and what has at short notice offered itself to my mind, concerning the dignities of those sitting at the exchequer. But in these matters I have constituted for the munificence of the kings no bounds of which they may not overstep; they are all inclined, moreover, on account of the grace entrusted to them to promote the glory of their prerogative, especially those who are truly wise. But he most of mundane princes, the very great and illustrious king of the English, Henry the Second, strives always to increase the dignities of those serving under him; knowing for certain that benefits bestowed on his followers purchase, with titles of immortal fame, the glory of his name. Now then, let us turn our flowing pen to other things.

D. It is in order, if I mistake not, as I seem to have gathered from the foregoing, that thou should'st proceed concerning the king's seal and the doomsday book, of which the first, if I remember aright, is kept in the treasury and not allowed to leave it.

M. Nay, both of them, and also very many other things.

XIV. That " Thesaurus " sometimes means the money itself; sometimes the place where it is kept.

Know, moreover, that "thesaurus" sometimes means the money in cash itself, as well as gold or silver vessels of different kinds, and changes of vestments. According to this acceptation it is said, " where thy treasure is, there will thy heart be also." For " thesaurus " is called the place in which it reposes, therefore " thesaurus " = " auri thesis," namely, the place of gold, So that if one asks about some one where he is, it may not incongruously be replied : " he is in the 'thesaurus,'" that is, in the place where the " thesaurus " is kept. Cash money, indeed, or the other things mentioned, having once been put in a safe place, are not taken away except when, by mandate of the king, they are sent to him to be distributed for his necessary uses. But there are many things in the repository vaults of the treasury which are carried around, and they are shut up and guarded by the treasurer and the chamberlains, as has been more fully shown above : such are the seal of the king concerning which thou dost ask, the doomsday book, the so-called exactory roll, which some name the writ of farms. Likewise the great yearly (pipe) rolls, the rolls of accounts, a numerous multitude of privileges, counter-tallies of receipts, and rolls of receipts, and writs of the king concerning outlays of the treasury, and many other things which, when the exchequer is in session, are necessary to its daily uses.

XV. What use is made of the Royal Seal which is in the Treasury.

What ought to be the use of the royal seal is clear from the foregoing: for with it are sealed the summonses that are made out, and the other mandates which pertain solely to the exchequer of the king; nor is it carried elsewhere; but, as has been said above, is guarded by the chancellor through a representative. It has, moreover, stamped upon it, exactly the same image and inscription as the deambulatory seal of the court, so that both may be known to have the same authority of commanding, and that he who acts counter may be similarly judged guilty according to the one or the other. Then that book about which thou dost ask is the inseparable companion of the royal seal in the treasury. From Henry, formerly bishop of Winchester, I have heard as follows the cause of this institution.

XVI. What is the Doomsday Book, and for what purpose composed.

When that distinguished conqueror of England, a relative by blood of this same prelate, had subdued the utmost limits of the island to his rule, and had tamed the minds of the rebels by examples of terrible things,—he decreed, lest a free opportunity of erring should again be given, that the people subject to him should submit to written custom and laws. The English laws, therefore, being laid before him according to their triple distinction, that is, Mercian law, Dane law, and West Saxon law,— some he rejected; others, moreover, approving, he added to them the transmarine laws of Neustria which seemed most efficacious for protecting the peace of the kingdom. At length, lest anything should seem to be wanting to the sum of all his forethought, having taken counsel, he despatched from his side the most discreet men in circuit throughout the kingdom. By these men, in this way, a diligent description of the whole land was made with regard to its woods as well as its pastures and meadows, also its agriculture; and this description having been noted down in common words, it was collected into a book; in order, namely, that each one, content with his own right, should not with impunity usurp that of another. Moreover the survey is made by counties, by hundreds and by hides,—the name of the king being marked at the very head, and then, in turn, the names of the other lords being placed according to the dignity of their standing; that is to say, those who are tenants in chief of the king. Moreover against the separate names thus arranged in order are placed numbers by means of which, below, in the course of the book itself, whatever concerns these persons is more easily found. This book is called by the natives Domesday; that is, by metaphor, the day of judgment; for just as a sentence of that strict and terrible last trial cannot possibly be eluded by any art of tergiversation : so when, in the kingdom, contention shall arise concerning those things that are there noted,—when the book is appealed to its sentence can not be scorned or avoided with impunity. On this account we have named this book the book of dooms; not that, in it, a sentence is given concerning any doubtful matters that come up, but that from it, as from a judgment that has been given, it is not allowed in any way to depart.

D. If it please thee, explain what is a county, what a hundred, what a hide; otherwise the things that have been said will not be clear.

XVII. What is a Hide, what a Hundred, what a County, according to the common opinion.

M. The country people know this better; but, as we have heard from them, a hide, from its primitive institution, consists of a hundred acres : but a hundred, of several hundred hides—the number not being a fixed one, however; for one consists of many, another of fewer hides. Hence thou wilt frequently find that, in the old privileges of the Anglo-Saxon kings, a hundred (hundredus) is frequently called a centuriate (centuriata). The county, moreover, consists in like manner of hundreds; that is, some of more, some of less, according as the land has been divided by discreet men. The county, then, is called from the count, or the count from the county. It is the count, moreover, who receives the third portion of what comes from the pleas in each county. For that sum, which, under the name of a farm, is required from the sheriff, does not all arise from the revenues of estates, but in great part from pleas; and of these the count (comes) receives the third part; he is therefore said to be so called because he shares with the fisc, and is a companion (comes) in receiving. Then the sheriff (vice-comes) is so called because he supplies the place of the count in those pleas in which the count shares by reason of his dignity.

D. Do the counts receive those payments from each and all the counties ?

M. By no means : those alone receive them whom the munificence of the kings, in view of service rendered, or of distinguished probity, has made counts, and on whom this same munificence has decided, by reason of this dignity, to confer them; on some as hereditary, on others for their own persons only.

XVIII. *What is the Exactory Roll.*

The exactory roll is that in which, distinctly and diligently enough, are marked the farms of the king which arise from the separate counties, and the sum of which may not, indeed, be diminished, but is frequently increased by the laborious diligence of the justice. The reason of the remaining rolls, such as the yearly one and the others which we mentioned above, which are in the treasury and do not leave it, is clear enough from the foregoing. It remains, therefore, for us to turn to the greater and more necessary institutions of the exchequer, in which, as has been said, consists the more excellent, the more useful, and from many the more occult knowledge of the exchequer.

Book Second.

Hear me, brother, and, with the ears of one hearing, understand what I say unto thee. Thou wilt not repent of thy willingness to spend a short portion of time snatched from idleness upon matters of business. For there are some who do not blush to say in their hearts, " he who lays up knowledge lays up also grief " : to these learning is a burden, and it is a pleasure to play the fool. Therefore the truth is far removed from those who, fearing the pleasant labour of a pursuit, fall into error. They become blind of heart, therefore, and, not seeing the dangers of the way, fall headlong down a precipice. But thee, oh brother, let no day find idle ; lest, perchance that condition of human infirmity which is most prone to evil subject thee, off thy guard, to certain of the worst things. But if, by chance, thou hast no affairs, nevertheless invent some honest ones, that thy mind, always exercised, may be more open to learning. Attend, therefore, a little to those matters in which thou hast involved us ; not that from them thou wilt harvest great fruits of labour, but only lest thou be idle.

D. I fear lest the twilight of approaching night may put a sudden end to the matters in hand, and lest, omitting many necessary things, thou wilt so hasten that thou will'st free thyself of the importunity of an interrogator.

M. Nay, I rather feared lest, after thy long silence, a long suppressed laugh might be shaking thee on account of my rustic style ; or lest, perchance, thou wert silently cogitating how, without hurting me, thou mightest pluck thyself from these matters to which thou hast forced me. Therefore I confess that I had almost put an untimely end to what I was saying : but, nevertheless, since thou art docile and the zeal of attention has not yet grown tepid in thee, I will continue on the path begun. For the purpose, therefore, of complying with the order of business laid down, we must speak, in the first place, concerning summonses : for what debts they are made out namely, and how, and for what purpose. And that these matters may be more fully clear to thee, let the last of these three

things be shown before the first,—that is, for what purpose they are made.

*I. Summonses, indeed, are made in order that the Exchequer
may be held.*

A writ of summons, which is sealed by the image of
the royal authority, having previously been sent out, those
who are necessary are called together to the place named ;
for they are not obliged to come unless a summons is first
sent.   Some, moreover, come in order that they may
sit and judge, some that they may pay and be judged.
The barons, of whom we spoke above, sit and judge by
reason of their office, or by mandate of their prince.   But
the sheriffs and many others in the kingdom pay and are
judged ; of whom some are bound to voluntary offerings,
some to necessary payments; concerning which we shall
speak more fully below in treating of the sheriff.   Now
since there is a great number of these throughout all the
counties, it ought to be expressed in order in the summons
sent out, in the case of each one, how much ought to be
paid at the next term, the cause also being added ; as if it
were said, " thou shalt have, from this man, this or that
sum for this or this cause."   Furthermore if, when the
sheriff sits rendering his account, anything is required of
any debtor in his county, of which, however, no mention
was made in the summons, he will not be compelled to
answer; but will rather be excused because a summons of
this thing has not gone before.   Summonses are made,
therefore, for this purpose, that the farms of the king, and
the debts which are to be required for different reasons,
may flow into the fisc.   But there are some things which
must necessarily come through the hand of the sheriff,
even though no summons concerning them is made out:
but these are rather casual than fixed or certain, as will
appear from what follows.

How Summonses are made out.

I must first tell how, or in what order, they are made
out, and lastly, for what debts.   Know then, that when

the exchequer of that term in which the summonses are made is dissolved, the debts due the king throughout the different counties are taken by the clerks of the treasury from the great roll of that year and are written down, together with the causes, on smaller rolls; this being done, those whom we call the greater barons go apart, and, each county being mentioned in turn, they decree, concerning its different debtors, for how much each ought to be summoned; consideration being had for the quality of the person, and for the nature of the matter and for the cause for which he is bounden to the king. The authentic yearly roll, also, from which the debts are taken, lies before the treasurer or his clerk, lest there might, perchance, in some way, have been an error in making the abstract of them. There is also another clerk who studiously puts down what they have agreed upon in the matter of the debts of which the abstract has been made; and concerning these a summons is made in these words: " H. king of the English, to that or that sheriff, greeting. See to it as thou lovest thyself and all thy possessions, that thou art at the exchequer in such or such a place, on the day after St. Michael's day, or on the day after the close of Easter, and that thou hast there with thee whatever thou owest of the farm of former years or of this year, and these debts mentioned here by name: from that man 10 marks, for that reason, and so on." Moreover, when all the debts which are contained in the greater yearly roll, with their causes, have thus been marked down there in order, the lesser rolls, those of the itinerant justices, are brought forth; from these are taken what things are, by their labour and industry, owing to the lord king in the different counties; and these being assessed by the greater barons, they are put down in the summonses; these things having been arranged in order, the summons terminates with these words: " and thou shalt have a l these with thee in money, tallies and writs and quittances, or they shall be taken from thy farm; witness, that or that person, there, at the exchequer." Some have believed that one ought to say: " in money, *or* (vel) tallies, *or* writs, *or* quittances "; not understanding that *vel* is sometimes used subdisjunctively. Moreover, a contention of this kind concerning words is superfluous, since their meaning is clear: for whether thou sayest " in money and (vel) writs, and quittances," or "in money and (et) writs and quittances," the meaning is the same ; so, namely, that in all these things, or some of them, he renders satisfaction for what is contained in the summons.   Moreover, since a new disease should be met by new remedies, this addition was made in the summonses by a new statute— since the time of king Henry I., namely : that " if by chance thou art summoned for the debt of any one who has not land or chattels in thy bailiwick, and thou knowest in whose bailiwick or county he has them : thou thyself shalt signify to such sheriff or bailiff this same fact by thy writ, —some one bearing it who has been sent by thee, and who shall deliver thy writ to him in the county court if he can, or in the presence of many people."   A ridiculous and dangerous enough subterfuge of certain people compelled the addition of this which we have stated.   For when it became known to which addresses the summonses were sent out, before the summons concerning his debt came to the county, a man, sitting empty handed in his home, awaited with confidence the advent of the sheriff and other officials, having emptied his barns and having put his money somewhere away from him, or having transferred it to a safe place ; and, by this device, for many years the authority of a royal summons seemed to be eluded, not without loss.   For the other sheriff to whose district a man, fearing such summons, had gone over with his property, did not dare to lay hands on his possessions, since he had no mandate to this effect.   For this reason, therefore, the clause which we have mentioned was put in the summonses for some years ; nor after that did any one have any ground of subterfuge for every debtor not rendering satisfaction in every way; saving, alone, him whom the most extreme want excuses.   When, moreover, it had already become clear to all sheriffs and debtors that, in this way, their sophistical impudence could be put an end to, it became unnecessary any longer to add that clause, nor is it added now.   The method described, however, of coercing debtors wherever they may have betaken themselves, continues among the sheriffs, and is kept up, being instituted, as it were, by a certain perpetual law.

D. I have heard already, being told by many, that the exchequer is called together twice in the year, namely at the Easter term and at the Michaelmas term. Thou hast also said, if I remember aright, that the exchequer was not held unless the summonses had previously been sent out. Since, therefore, summonses are made out for each term, I ask thee please to reveal whether the same rule is observed in both summonses; or, if there is a difference in the tenor of the words, what it is and why it is so.

II. How the Summonses differ according to the term.

M. It is a great proof of thy advancement that thou hast already known enough to doubt of these things. To be sure it is as certain as possible that the exchequer is convoked and held twice in the year; being preceded, nevertheless, as has been said, by summonses. Thou dost remember very well the terms of both sessions. But mark that, in the Easter term, not accounts, but certain views of accounts are made by the sheriff; wherefore almost nothing of the things that are there done at that time is committed to writing; but the whole is reserved for the other term; and then, in the great yearly roll, the separate items are marked in order; some memoranda, however, which frequently occur, are written apart by the clerk of the treasury; so that, when the exchequer of that term is dissolved, the greater barons may decide concerning them; which things, indeed, on account of the number of them, would not easily be recalled unless they were committed to writing. Furthermore there is written what part of his farm the sheriff pays into the treasury; and then, if he fulfil his obligation, in the same line : " and is quit "; if not, his debt is distinctly put down on the lower line, so that he shall know how much of the total of that term is wanting; and straightway he shall render satisfaction according to the judgment of those presiding. For each sheriff is to pay at that term the half of that farm which accrues from his county in a year. Know, moreover, that in these summonses the tenor of words is not changed unless so far as concerns the term or the place; when for instance, the greater barons have decreed that the exchequer of Easter is to be held in one place and the exchequer of Michaelmas in another. But although the same virtue of words is regarded in both summonses, the marking of the debts set down is different. For in the summons made out against the Easter term, since the year is said to commence then, it shall simply read: "from such a one thou shalt have 10£." And from this summons he shall not be absolved unless he pay then or render satisfaction for 10£. But when the summons is to be made out against the Michaelmas term, in which that same year is closed and terminated and the yearly roll is made up, there shall be added to the aforesaid 10£ other 10£ or more, according as it shall seem fit to those presiding; and it shall read: "from such a one thou shalt have 20£." He, however, who had at the Easter term paid 10 of this sum, but now pays 10£ in money and offers a tally for the 10 already paid, shall merit to be absolved from the summons: for it says in the summons, "thou shalt have all these in money and writs and tallies." Know moreover, that, when a summons is made out, if, when it is corrected, an error shall be found, it ought not to be cancelled by drawing a line under it, and also not to be erased, because the writing is patent: nay rather the summons in which the error was made ought to be entirely obliterated, so that what had been written will be visible to no one; the reason for which, if thou reflectest upon these things, may readily occur to thee.

D. Since, as thou sayest, that writing is patent, and is sent thus to the sheriff, and remains for a long time with him and his people, the safety of the summons is committed to his sole faith. He could, then, with impunity wipe out, change or diminish what he likes, since no copy of it remains with the barons.

M. Perhaps he could if he wished; but it would be a proof of an insane head if, of his own will, he were to subject himself to so great dangers; especially since he could not thus do away with his indebtedness to the king, and scarcely even defer it. For all the debts, for which summonses are made out, are kept diligently noted elsewhere; so that no one could by this device be freed from his debt even if the sheriff tried to bring it about. But for a greater safeguard in this affair we ourselves have seen how, by the archdean of Poictiers, now bishop of Winchester, copies of all summonses were made. Nor were at any time the originals sent out, unless copies of them had been made and diligently corrected. When, moreover, the sheriff sitting to render account, the summons was read by the clerk of the chancellor, the clerk of the archdean, looking at his copy, observed him lest he swerved from the truth. But as time went on, when the number of debts increased immensely, so that the length of one membrane did not suffice for one summons, this manifold and laborious labour was put an end to, and they were content, as formerly, with the original summons alone. Thus thou hast, I think, as well as brevity permits, an explanation as to how and for what reason summonses are made. We are now free to examine by whom they ought to be made, although, from what has been said, this, too, is already clear for the most part.

For what Debts Summonses are made out.

Henry, the illustrious king of the English, is called the second of those kings sharing in this name ; but, with regard to administration, he is believed to have been second in ability of mind to no one of modern times : for, from the very beginning of his reign, he directed his whole mind to this, that by many an overthrow he should destroy malcontents and rebels, and should mark in the hearts of men in every way the benefits of peace and faith. Although now, among all people, a wide-spread fame has made commonly known the great deeds of this man, so that it may now seem superfluous to insist on expounding them,—yet there is one thing which I cannot pass over in silence, by which alone his singular probity and unheard-of piety is established.

This was no work of man, but rather of pitying Godhead
That, with a few, himself—nay, the whole world—he resisted.

D. How it can be called a great deed to resist himself, I do not see, unless thou make it plain.

M. Although these things do not belong to the work

begun or intended, nevertheless, mindful of that high-souled king, I have not been able to pass them over and keep my peace of mind. Thou may'st see, therefore, how miraculously that man resisted himself, against the sons, indeed, of his own flesh, nay, further, the sole hope and singular glory of his soul after God. When they were young and, by reason of their age, waxen beyond measure, and prone to every emotion of the soul, the pertinacious little foxes were carried away by wicked counsels, and, at length, turned their bowels against their father as against an enemy; "and a man's enemies have become they of his own household, and those who guarded his side have taken counsel against him; saying"—to his sons and his enemies —" persecute him and take him for there is none to deliver him"; thou would'st say that in them the word of the prophet was fulfilled: "I have nourished and brought up children and they have rebelled against me." When, therefore, the wife was raging against the husband, the sons against their father, the servants, without cause, against their master,—would'st thou not say with the best of reasons that a man was warring against himself? But, against the numerous multitude of his enemies, the magnitude of the Divine grace alone aided him; and, as though God were fighting for him, he so in a short time got hold of almost all the rebels, that he was by far more strongly confirmed in the kingdom than before, by means of that very thing which was to have weakened him.

For those who had conspired against him, in all his strength, came to know through this, most plainly, that the club can not be extorted from the hand of Hercules except by force. Moreover, when they were taken, an unheard-of clemency spared the enemies, the inciters of such a tremendous crime; so that few of them sustained the loss of their goods—none, however, of their rank or their bodies. If thou should'st read the revenge which David visited on the overthrowers of his son Absalom, thou would'st say that Henry had been far more gentle than he: although it is written of him, "I have found a man after mine own heart." Although, then, the great king had an abundant number of precedents, and might have exercised against them even the most shameful revenge,—he preferred,

nevertheless, to spare rather than to punish those whom
he had beaten ; in order that, even against their will, they
should see his kingdom grow great.   May that king, therefore, long live glorious and happy, and for the grace
granted may he merit grace from on High.   May his
noble offspring also live, subject to their father and not
unlike to him : and, since they are born to rule over
nations, may they learn, by their father's and by their own
example, how glorious it is " to spare the subjugated and
to vanquish rebels."   But let us proceed with what we
have undertaken.   But if thou dost wish to be more fully
instructed concerning these and other mighty acts of his,
examine, if it please thee, the book of which we spoke
above (Tricolumnis).   When, therefore, after the ship-
wrecked condition of the kingdom, peace had been re-
established, the king strove to renew again the times of
his grandfather ; and, choosing discreet men, he divided
the kingdom into six parts, so that the chosen justices
whom we call itinerant might go through it and restore
the laws which had been abandoned.   His envoys, therefore, being ready with their advice in the different
counties, and exhibiting the fulness of justice to those who
considered themselves wronged, assuaged the labours and
expenses of the poor.   It came about, moreover, in the
case of these people, that the different misdemeanours
were, for the most part, punished in different ways according to the nature of the matters, so that some made corporal, others, pecuniary amends.   The pecuniary penalties
of the delinquents, then, are carefully noted in the rolls of
the itinerant justices, and when the exchequer sits they are
handed over to the treasury in the presence of all.   The
justices, moreover, must see to it that they deliver to the treasurer correct rolls and ones arranged in order; for, having
once handed them over, it will not be lawful even for the
justices themselves to change one iota, even in a matter
on which all the justices are of one mind.

D. In so far it is to be wondered at that, since they are
the authors of their writings, and nothing is collected
except by their own industry and labour, they may not,
even when they consent together as to anything, change
their own writing.

M. Inasmuch as the time for correction has been given them, and they knew the fixed rule, they have themselves to thank; for the total of the offerings will be required either from the debtors, if they are condemned to this, or from the justices themselves. So that if in the roll they have put any one down as condemned to pay 20, and, after the pledge has already been handed over to the treasurer, they shall remember that he may not be held but for ten: the judges themselves shall render satisfaction for the rest; for their writing, made and corrected with deliberation, may not be recalled after its surrender. The treasurer causes the debts of the rolls received to be diligently and distinctly marked by counties in the great yearly roll, together with the reasons: the names of the justices, as has been said, being first put down; so that, in this way, there may be clearness with regard to the things exacted. From these, therefore, the summonses shall be made out as follows: " according to the pleas of these or those men N. N., from this man so much,"—according as those presiding have formerly estimated the debts. Thou hast learnt from the aforesaid, as we believe, so much as is necessary as to for what debts and how, and for what purpose, summonses are made out: now let us pass on to the duties of the sheriff. It is fitting, moreover, that thou should'st give alert attention to what is to be said; for, as was said in the beginning, in these things consists the higher science of the exchequer.

III. *Manifold concerning the duties of the Sheriff.*

All the sheriffs, therefore, and the bailiffs, to whom summonses are directed, are bound by the same necessity of the law; that is, by the authority of the royal mandate; that, namely, on the day mentioned and at the place designated, they shall come together and render satisfaction for their debts. In order that this may be clearer to thee, look more closely at the tenor of the summons itself, for it reads: " See to it, as thou dost love thyself and all thy belongings, that thou art at the exchequer of such and such a time and place; and that thou hast with thee whatever thou owest of the old farm and the new, and these debts written below." Pay attention, then, for two things are said which fit in with the two which follow ; for this, " see to it as thou dost love thyself," refers to " that thou art there and there at such and such a time and place " ; that expression, however, " and as thou dost love all thy belongings," seems to refer to this : " and that thou hast with thee these debts written below " ; as if it were openly said, " thy absence, whoever thou art that receiveth a summons, unless it can be excused by causes necessary and defined by law, will redound to the peril of thy head ; for thou wilt seem thus to have spurned the royal mandate, and to have acted irreverently in contempt of the royal majesty, if, being summoned concerning the matters for which thou art bounden to the king, thou dost neither come nor send one to excuse thee. But if thou have been the cause that the appended debts were not paid, then, from the farm which thou art about to pay, the other debts for which thou art summoned shall be taken ; but the farm shall be completed from thy chattels and the revenues of thy estate ; thou thyself, meanwhile, if the barons have decreed it, being placed in a safe place in liberal custody." When, therefore, the aforesaid summons shall have been received by the sheriff, on the very day named he shall come and show himself to the president, if he happen to be there, or to the treasurer if the president himself should not be present. Then, having saluted the greater barons, he shall have that day to himself, being about to return to the exchequer both on the morrow and on each day thereafter. But if, by chance, he shall neither come nor send in advance a just excuse, on the first day he shall be condemned to pay to the king one hundred shillings of silver for each county ; on the next, ten £ of silver ; likewise on the third, as we have heard from those who were our predecessors, whatever movable goods he possesses shall be at the disposal of the king ; but on the fourth, since now from this he is convicted of contempt for the royal majesty, he shall lie at the sole mercy of the king not only as to his property, but also as to his own person. There are those, nevertheless, who think that for the whole total a pecuniary punishment alone will suffice ; in such wise, namely, that on the first day those absenting themselves should be punished to the extent of a hundred shillings; on the second, likewise to a hundred shillings; and so on for each day to the extent of another hundred. I do not disagree with them; that is, however, if he against whom the wrong has been done consents to this; it is probable enough, moreover, that the king would be willing to admit this kind of punishment, since his remarkable grace is slow to punish and swift to reward.

D. It is the part of an imprudent and alike impudent hearer to interrupt the flowing pen before an end has been reached of the things which are being said; and so I have borne it, revolving in my mind what in part disturbs me: for thou hast said that if it rested with the sheriff that the debts appended were not paid, then they should be taken from the farm which he is about to pay. If, therefore, the sheriff shall have distributed by writ of the king, either in public works or otherwise, all that he was about to have paid in,—what will be done?

M. When, by mandate of the king, he shall have expended the farm of the county either for the expenses of the court, or in works or on anything else, if he is found to be backward in paying his debts, he shall be detained, on his oath, where the greater barons shall decree, until he give satisfaction for them as he would have done for his farm.

D. Since upon a sheriff summoned, and not coming or excusing himself, there falls a heavy loss both to his movable and his immovable property and to his own person, unless he explain away his absence as not voluntary but necessary: I ask, if it please thee, that thou delay not to reveal what causes, when summoned, he can allege as sufficient for his absence.

IV. *For what causes the absence of the Sheriffs is considered condoned.*

M. There are many kinds of excuses by which the absence of the sheriff is considered condoned, provided, nevertheless, that, the reason or excuse having been sent in before, he shall, on the day named, send ahead through lawful men the money of the king previously collected;

and they, handing to the president the letters of excuse, and alleging the necessary causes of their master's absence, shall confirm the same, even by an oath taken in their own persons, if it shall please the president. But if the sheriff or any servant who has been summoned, detained by infirmity, can not be present, he shall add in his letters of excuse which are sent to the exchequer : " and since I am unable to come, I send to you these my servants N. and N., that they may take my place and do what pertains to me ; I being ready to ratify what they shall do."

He who excuses himself, moreover, shall provide that one or the other of those sent shall be a knight or other layman, joined to him by reason of blood or otherwise; that is, one to whose faith and discretion he may not hesitate to commit himself and his interests : for clergy alone should not be taken for this purpose; because, if they act wrongly, it will not be fitting to seize them for money or for the rendering of accounts. But if a sheriff who has been summoned shall happen to be absent, being hindered, not indeed through sickness, but for some other cause, he can, perhaps, even then be freed from the punishment established : but no one shall be received for him to render his account except his first-born son ; not his general steward, even though he himself have sent his writ saying that he would ratify what such and such a one should do for him. But solely by the authority of a mandate of the king, or indeed of the president if the king be absent, can another be substituted to render his account. If, however, he shall be doing other business assigned to him by the lord king, he himself shall name some one present in his own person at the exchequer, who, according to what has been said above, can and ought to transact the business of the absent sheriff. That writ, moreover, of the king or the president or of the sheriff sending an excuse shall be kept in the box of the marshall, of which we spoke above, in testimony of this matter. But if the sheriff, being needed elsewhere by the king, shall have been called by him outside of the kingdom ; or, having received permission for family affairs, shall have arranged to leave the country,—he shall first go to the president, and with his own lips shall delegate his functions at the exchequer to whatever lawful man he wishes; this being done, when he is absent he is neither compelled to send a writ nor to excuse his absence. But where the sheriff excuses himself on account of infirmity, when they shall come to write his account in the yearly roll, it shall read: "William, sheriff of London; Robert, his son, for him, renders account for the farm of London." But if, by mandate of the king, another is substituted for him, or he with his own lips, as has been said, shall have designated to the president some one in his place, then in all respects it is to read as if he himself, in his own person, were sitting and rendering an account.

D. Is illness the sole sufficient excuse by which one who absents himself after having been summoned can be preserved from harm?

M. Far from it; for there are many at the exchequer; but this in trials, as well as in other ecclesiastical and judicial matters, is the most usual. Thou must, however, be mindful of the things that have been said, in order to understand that no excuse brings it about that the money of the king which has been collected from a county is detained with impunity in the sheriff's keeping, or is not, on the day named, sent to the exchequer. Having sent the money, therefore, he may be excused through illness as has been said. Likewise if his first-born son, whom he has declared to be his future heir, should be considered nigh unto death, he will be excused. Likewise if his wife have begun to be in danger with the pangs of child-birth, or for any other cause lie nigh unto death, —since she is a portion of his flesh, he can be excused. Likewise if his lord who is commonly called liege—that is, he to whom alone, by reason of his dominion, he is so bound that as against him he owes nothing to any one except alone the king—shall summon him to aid him, he being proceeded against in court for his own fief or for the greater part of it, or for any other reason which seems to redound to the detriment of that lord's standing or of his body,—he can be excused; provided, however, that that lord is not able further to do without him, or otherwise to avoid the litigation. But if that same lord have entered a suit against another in an affair of this kind, and

it is in his power without great harm to postpone the day,
—if he have summoned a sheriff of the lord king in
the person of his vassal, indeed, the latter shall not be
bound to come, for he can not then be excused from the
exchequer.   Likewise if that same lord, oppressed by the
weight of illness, wishes to make a will in the presence of
his people, and have called him in for this purpose with his
other faithful men, he shall be excused.   Likewise if his
lord or his wife or his son shall have paid the debt of the
flesh, and he shall have seen to the necessary funeral
arrangements, he shall merit to be excused.   There are
also many other excuses for the absence of a sheriff,
necessary, indeed, and determined by rule, which we do
not deny or exclude ; nay, when they shall seem sufficient
to the greater barons, we willingly receive them ; but, for
the sake of example, we have given those which at present
have occurred to our mind, they being, as it were, the more
frequent ones.

D. I seem to gather from the aforesaid that a knight or
other discreet person may be made a sheriff or other bailiff
by the king, even though he hold nothing from the king,
but only from others.

M. This prerogative belongs to the dignity of a public
function, that no matter whose vassal any man in the
kingdom is, no matter for whom he may do military
or other service,—if he be found necessary to the king,
he can be   eely taken and deputed to the royal service.

D. From this, indeed, I can see that that is true which
is said :

    " Dost thou not know that of kings the hands are extremely
        lengthy ? "

But now already, if it please thee, do not delay putting thy
hand to the occupations of the sheriff ; for on these matters,
warned by thee, I have concentrated the whole zeal of
my attention ; knowing that in them, as has been said,
the higher knowledge of the exchequer should be sought.

M. I congratulate thee on being mindful of what has
been said ; by which, I confess, thou hast added a stimulus
to my almost languishing pen.   Know, then, that the
sheriff, unless a test has first been made and the debts for

which he was summoned have been paid, is not allowed to take his seat for the account; but that when he shall have come and already taken his seat, the other sheriffs are excluded; and he shall sit alone with his people, about to reply to the interrogations. He shall see to it, moreover, that on the day itself, or on the day preceding, it shall have become known to the debtors of his county on what day he is going to sit and render account; and also, around the building of the exchequer and the village or the town, he shall, by the voice of a herald, make known to them that he is to sit then or there. Then when all are seated and listening, the treasurer, who, as has been said, by reason of his office sits opposed to him, asks him if he is ready to render an account; he replying, "I am ready," the treasurer goes on: "say, therefore, first, if the alms, if the tithes, if the fixed liveries, if the lands given are the same this year as they have been in the past." But if he reply that they are the same, then the scribe of the treasurer shall, in writing down these fixed payments, follow diligently the roll of the past year; the treasurer looking on the while, lest by chance the hand of the scribe should err. And since, in the chapter on the office of the scribe of the treasurer, I remember to have said enough concerning the order of writing, I pass these things over at present.

D. Speak then, if it please thee, concerning those things which thou long since did'st put off until treating of the duties of the sheriffs; how it is, namely, that some lands are given by the king blank, some by tale; for this has troubled me from the beginning.

M. It is clear enough to thee, I believe, from the foregoing, how it is that certain farms are paid blank, others by tale. A farm, indeed, is paid blank when it has been blanched by testing.

V. How it is that some estates are given blank, some by tale.

Who, indeed, was the author of this institution, and what the reason for starting it, is well enough known. We say, then, that a farm is paid by tale, when satisfaction is given for it by counting alone, and not by testing. When,

therefore, the king 'has conferred on any one any estate,
together with the hundred court and the pleas which come
from this, they say that that estate was conferred on that
man blank : and when, retaining for himself the hundred
court through which the farm is said to have been
blanched, the king has simply given the estate, not decreeing that it shall be with the hundred court, or blank,
it is said to have been given by tale.   Moreover, it is necessary that he on whom it has been conferred shall, at
the Michaelmas term, bring to the exchequer the writ of
the king, or his charter, for the estate conferred, so that it
may be computed to the sheriff; otherwise it will not be
written in the great yearly roll, nor will it be computed to
the sheriff; it shall be written, moreover, thus : after the
alms and tithes and fixed liveries of both kinds, at the
head of the line : "to lands given to such a one N. 20£
blank, in such a place; and to such a one N. 20£ by
tale, in such a place."   Remark also, that if, perchance,
among the lands given, thou findest : " to such a one or
such a one 10£, blank or by tale, from a loan of the
king,"—when he who rejoiced in the benefit of the accom-
modation or loan shall pay the debt of fate, no opportunity is given to his wife or his children or to any one of
his name, of making reclamation on account of that loan,
unless by favour of the king ; just as if it had been said,
" to such a one 10 so long as it shall please the king."

VI. *What are the fixed payments that are to be computed to
the Sheriff ; alms, namely, and tithes, and liveries of
both kinds, and lands given.*

D. What is what thou did'st speak of as liveries of both
kinds ?

M. Some of the liveries are of poor people ; as when,
solely from the promptings of charity, one penny a day, or
two or more, are accorded to some one by the king for
food and clothing. But some are of people who do service,
so that they receive them as wages ; such are the custo-
dians of the palaces, the guardians of the royal temples,
the pipers, the seizers of wolves, and the like. These, then,
are liveries of different kinds which are paid for different

reasons, but are counted among the fixed payments. And
mark that, although the king is free to confer these liveries
on any poor people whatever, they nevertheless, by ancient
custom, are usually assigned to those who minister at
court, and who, having no income, fall into bodily sickness
and become unfit for labour. All of these things having
been put down in order, the treasurer asks the sheriff if,
in addition to the fixed payments, he have expended anything by writ of the king. Then, one by one, the sheriff
hands over to the clerk of the chancellor the writs of the
king which have been sent to him. He, having read them
in public, delivers them to the treasurer, so that the latter,
according to the form in which the writs have been drawn
up, may furnish appropriate words for the writing of his
roll: for he, as has been said, prescribes, and the others
who write with him take down from his roll. This being
done, the sheriff shows if, not through writs but through
the fixed rule of the exchequer, he have expended any
thing which ought to be computed to him; such are the payments of the king's approvers, and likewise those things
which are spent in carrying out sentences and judgments.

*VII. What things are to be computed through custom of the
Exchequer alone,—that is, without a writ.*

Remark, moreover, that sentences are here usually called
executions of the law carried out against any men; but
judgments, the ordeals of the glowing iron or of boiling
water. The liveries of approvers, therefore, are made on
this basis. On account of the innumerable riches of this
kingdom, and likewise on account of the inclination to
drunkenness inborn in the natives—which lust always
follows as a companion,—it happens that, in it, thefts, open
or secret, and also homicides and crimes of different kinds,
are frequently committed; the harlots adding incentives,
so that there is nothing which those who subject themselves
to their counsels will not dare or attempt. When, therefore, any one one notoriously guilty of these things is
taken by the royal servants who look out for the peace of
the kingdom,—on account of the great number of scoundrels and in order that, even in this way, the land may be

purged from the miscreants, the judges at times agree
upon this: that if any one of this kind, confessing his
crime, be willing to challenge the accomplices in that crime,
and be able, by engaging in a duel, to prove the crime of
which he charges the other or others,—he shall escape the
death which he merited, and, with safety to his body, departing, nevertheless, beyond the boundaries of the entire
kingdom, shall be dismissed and swear not to return.
Some, moreover, having previously made an agreement
with the judges, even though they prove their charges do
not, nevertheless, go away in safety, but escaping hanging
or some other disgraceful kind of death, which, by their
own confession, they have merited, being punished however with mutilation of their members, become a miserable
spectacle among the people and restrain rash undertakings
by their terrible examples. Since, therefore, the charge of
that crime being brought up against him and proved, he
can save his life; and likewise, since whatever seems to
promote the peace of the kingdom is, without doubt, to
the advantage of the king, he is called a king's approver.
From the day, moreover, on which he is received for the
purpose of proving, until his promise has been fulfilled, or
until he fails, he shall receive from the fisc each day one
penny for his support, which penny is computed to the
sheriff solely by custom of the exchequer. But if that
approver shall have been ordered to be removed to another
place, so that, it being easier for the judges to assemble
there, he may fulfil his promise—or perhaps, failing, may
receive the condign punishment of his crimes: only the
sum which he provides for taking vehicles thither and for
furnishing him with victuals, shall be computed to the
sheriff by custom; but the rest, not unless by writ of the
king. There are, moreover, in certain counties, many who,
as a privilege of their estates, lay avenging hands upon
the condemned; so that they punish some by hanging,
others by mutilation of the members, or in other ways,
according to the measure of the crime perpetrated. There
are, on the other hand, counties in which those who are
thus to be condemned are only punished when cash has first
been paid by the fisc. Whatever, therefore, in order to
put into effect these judgments or sentences, is paid by

the sheriff to men of detestable avarice who receive this for the effusion of blood, it is computed to him as by custom of the exchequer; that is, not by writ of the king. And there is another thing which ought to be computed to the sheriff by custom alone: when the treasure of the king, being about to be borne by decree of the greater barons from one place to another has need of vehicles and minor things of the kind, the sheriff, by order of the treasurer, or the chamberlains, or their servants sent for this purpose, pays from his farm what is necessary, and this is computed to the sheriff without a writ,—the treasurer himself, however, or any one of the aforesaid who has ordered this to be done, bearing witness concerning this matter in the presence of the greater barons; and then it shall read in the roll: "for these or these necessaries of the treasury, this or that, through such and such a one." Likewise if a royal fish is taken, a turbot or a whale or another of the kind, what is paid out by the sheriff for salting it and for furnishing other necessaries is computed without a writ. Likewise what is spent in cultivating the vines on the domains of the king, and in vintaging them, or in furnishing receptacles and other necessaries, is computed without a writ, on the oath of the sheriff; concerning which oath, how it is taken, whether once or oftener, we shall speak below. These, therefore, are the things which occur to us at present which are to be placed to the account of the sheriff by custom alone. Now let us continue concerning the other things which pertain to the account from the body of the county.

VIII. In what order those things are to be computed to the sheriff which were spent in public works by a writ of the king not specifying the amount.

It happens sometimes that the king gives orders to the sheriff by his writ, that for fortifying castles or for building edifices and the like, he shall furnish from his farm what is necessary, by view of two or three men whose names are expressed in that writ; and that he adds at the end a short clause, but one necessary for those making up the accounts: "and it shall be computed to thee at the exchequer." When, therefore, the time shall have arrived for the account of the sheriff, those who were chosen as overseers of the works come together, and having taken an oath in public that, to the best of their knowledge, the sum named has been expended to the king's advantage on that public work, a writ of the king shall there be made out at the exchequer, under the witness of the president and of another whom he shall name, in which that sum concerning which they have testified, and likewise the names of the overseers, shall be expressed ; and then at length it shall be computed to the sheriff. But if, through these expenditures, the work of the king shall have been completed, that first writ, concerning the furnishing of the necessary amounts, which was sent to the sheriff, and this last one which is made at the exchequer, are placed in the marshal's box for the accounts rendered. If, however, something remains to be done on that work, the sheriff shall keep by him the writ that was sent him, until that same work is completed; so that from it he may have authority to furnish the amounts necessary for completing the work; but the other one shall be closed up in the box which has been mentioned. For when it is written in the yearly roll, " to that work 100£," there should consequently be added: "by writ of the king and by view of these N." But if there were no writ of the king containing the amount and the names of the overseers, the writing of the roll which says " by writ of the king " might seem to be false.

D. By this discourse I have been so thoroughly satisfied that I willingly omit those things about which I had already opened my mouth to inquire. For when a writ of the king is brought to the sheriff concerning the payment of the necessary sums for this or that work, and it is added: "and it will be computed to thee at the exchequer," or this : " spend from thy farm,"—which is almost of the same authority,—it seemed superfluous that he should be put to the trouble of another writ; but I did not, indeed, understand that in such writ the amount was to be expressed, so that thus it might correspond to the authentic yearly roll, the tenor of words being the same.

IX. That no one is absolved from a debt by a writ of the king which does not express the amount, even though it give the cause.

M. Know likewise that in the affairs of the exchequer it is different than in other ones: for it is said in very many cases that what is expressed does harm, and what is not expressed does no harm: but here what is expressed helps and what is not expressed harms one. For example, if any one is bounden to the king for a hundred £, and brings to the exchequer his writ, that he is to be quit of the debt which he owes him, and even adds " the whole," and likewise expresses the reason but not the amount: he shall not be absolved on this account, but rather, through this, shall merit delay until another summons. For it should have been written in the roll: " remitted by writ of the king, to such a one N. one hundred pounds "; but since that is seen to be not altogether cancelled which is not yet expressed in the writ, he is compelled with much labour to seek the means by which he may merit to be absolved: therefore, in these matters, what is not expressed harms.

D. With all due reverence to the president and those who sit with him, it does not seem as if the mandate of the king were here fulfilled in all regards; for he is not quit whom the king, adding also the cause for which he was bounden to him, ordered to be quit.

M. Nay, a truce in these matters to the subtlety of thy scrupulous mind. Thou should'st have known, indeed, that ignorance of a law does not excuse the very men who have most to do with the law. He, therefore, who is bounden to the king, must diligently inquire how he can be fully absolved from this—that is, according to the fixed law concerning these things; but if he have not done so, he shall lay it to the charge not of the president but of himself; for the president is not allowed to change one iota of that which he brought him in the writ: since, therefore, he is not quit through this, he shall hasten to obtain what is needful.

D. I perceive that these things are observed principally on this account, that they may not be contradictory to the writing of the roll.   But now let us proceed concerning the other matters.

M. When, therefore, all those things shall have been noted down which are either fixed or are to be computed by writ of the king, or by custom of the exchequer,—then the account is left unfinished, as it were, and they turn to other things ; for " and is quit " or "and he owes," by which, indeed, the acccount is said to be finished, is not written in the yearly roll until satisfaction shall have been given for every thing that is contained in the summons ; the cause of which proceeding will be clear enough from what is to follow.   After the account for the body of the county—that is, for the principal farm, which, as has been said, is left unfinished until the end,—a moderate space being left, the account is put down of the old farm of the county ; that is, whatever by any chance had remained over from the previous year : but it shall only be thus if the sheriff who then served shall have been changed.   But if the same one continue also in this year, he shall make satisfaction for the old farm before beginning an account of the new ; and the old one shall be distinctly and diligently written down in the beginning, and afterwards the new one.   For these things, know that the changed sheriff of the old farm is to be summoned like any other of the debtors ; not for a part of it but for the whole, because it is a farm the payment of which ought not to be put off. But it suffices to send a summons for a debt of the old farm, for which he is bounden who is still serving, under this form of words : "whatever thou dost owe from the old farm and the new."   Concerning which enough has been said above in the chapter on summonses.

X. *Concerning escheats and trespass-lands, or, as we more generally say, concerning purprestures and escheats.*

After these things, moreover, a space of about six lines being left, there follows the account concerning escheats and trespass-lands, or, as we more usually say, " concerning purprestures and escheats."   In the middle of the line, indeed, is made a heading in capital letters, " concerning purprestures and escheats " ; but at the beginning of the lower one is written thus: "this same sheriff renders account for the farm of purprestures and escheats; namely for 40£ from this and for 20£ from that"; and then afterwards, according as, from the roll of the itinerant justices, it has previously been put down in the yearly one, "total 100£." Then, at the end of that line where the total is, is written: in the treasury 20£ in so many tallies, and owes four times 20£; or "paid in the treasury and is quit." But thou wilt learn the order of writing these things better by ocular demonstration than by a verbal description, however detailed.

D. What these escheats and trespass-lands are, and for what reason they flow into the fisc, I cannot see unless thou wilt explain it more fully.

M. It happens sometimes through the negligence of the sheriff or his servants, or also on account of a season of warfare continued for a long time, that those dwelling near the estates which are called crown-lands, usurp for themselves some portion of them and join it to their own possessions. When, therefore, the itinerant justices, through the oath of lawful men, shall have seized these, they shall be appraised separately from the farm of the county, and handed over to the sheriffs that they may answer for them separately; and these we call purprestures or trespass-lands. And when they are seized they are taken, as has been said, from their possessors, and henceforth go to the fisc. But if he from whom the trespass-land is taken be the author of the deed, then, in addition, unless the king spare him, he shall be pecuniarily most severely punished; but if he be not the author, but the heir of the author, then the revocation of that estate alone suffices for punishment. From which, indeed, as from many other things, the mercy of the king is proved; inasmuch as so enormous an excess of the father is not punished on the son, who, until the inquest was made, was enriched at a loss to the public power.

Escheats, to proceed, are commonly called what falls to the fisc when those who are tenants in chief of the king die, and there does not remain an heir by blood. Concerning these, moreover, together with the purprestures, the accounts are made under one rubric; so, however, that the

names of the separate items are expressed in order. But
when the father of the family, be he knight or serjeant,
who holds from the king in chief, shall have paid his debt
to fate, leaving children, however, of which the eldest is a
minor, his revenues, indeed, revert to the fisc ; but in this
case it is not simply called escheat but escheat with heir.
And thus neither is the heir taken from the inheritance
nor the inheritance from him ; but, being placed, together
with his inheritance, under the guardianship of the king
for the time of his pupillary age, both he and the other
children shall receive from that inheritance, through the
officials of the king, what is necessary. The remaining
sums, however, which come from it, go to the royal uses.
The accounts for them, moreover, are made separately ; for
not by perpetual, but by a certain temporary right, are they
due to the fisc. For when the heir who is now a minor,
having attained the benefits of a lawful age, shall know
how to make disposition for himself and those belonging
to him, he shall receive from the royal munificence what is
due to him by paternal right ; some, free, as it were by the
sole favour of the prince ; some, on promising a certain
sum ; concerning which, when the account shall be made,
it shall read in the yearly roll : " that or that person renders account for 100£ for the relief of the land of his
father ; in the treasury so much, and he owes so much."
Concerning this, moreover, no further account shall be
made in the yearly roll ; for henceforth it does not revert
any more to the fisc. But so long as it is in the hand of
the king, it shall be written of thus in the yearly roll :
" such a sheriff renders account for the farm of such
an honour "—if it is a barony ;—" in the treasury so
much, and, for the care of the children of such a one,
so much by writ of the king " ;—and this shall be made
out there at the exchequer by custom—" and he owes
so much," or " and he is quit." But if this be a minor
holding, so that there are one or two or three estates,
it shall read thus : " that sheriff " or " that person N."—
he to whom the king chanced to have deputed the care of
that matter—" renders account for the farm of that land
N., which belonged to that man N., which the king holds
in his hand," or, " which is in the hand of the king with the

heir "; " in the treasury so much, and owes so much "; or
" and he is quit." Notice, moreover, that so long as that
honour or estate shall be in the hand of the king, with the
heir, all the alms and payments of the poor which were established by the former lords out of sole regard for charity,
shall be paid in their entirety to those to whom they are
due, and shall be computed to the administrator at the exchequer: but the wages of servants, who may have seemed
necessary to the lords for the performing of any services,
and have received their position for this purpose, shall be
paid at will while the king has possession. When, moreover, the heritage shall have come into the hand of the heir
he should inhere in the footsteps of his father; so that, indeed, as long as those shall live for whom these payments
were established to be enjoyed during life, he shall satisfy
them; and after this, if he wish, he shall use or not use
their services.

D. Thou did'st say, if I remember aright, that if any one
holding in chief from the king should die and leave a
minor as heir, he who was left receives at length, after
attaining his majority, what is due him from the king,
some without payment, some on promising money. Moreover, what is thus paid thou dost call a relief. Say, therefore, if, from every estate which is held of the king in chief,
the relief ought to be exacted to the same amount,—or if not
to the same amount, wherefore this?

M. I seem to have armed thee to my own ruin. For,
conjecturing others from the things that have been said,
thou dost vex me with armed questions. Know, then, that
a different amount arises from the reliefs that are due to
the king according to the different ranks of the possessors;
for some, indeed, hold in chief from the king crown fiefs
—greater, namely, or lesser baronies. If, therefore, a father
having a possession of this kind die, leaving an heir who
is already adult, the latter shall give satisfaction for these
things, not according to a fixed sum, but according to what
he can obtain from the king. But if the heir be a minor,
being placed in wardship, he shall await his majority; then,
moreover, either gratis as has been said, or, like the adult,
at the good pleasure of the king, he shall obtain his
paternal heritage. But if any one should die, holding at

the time a knight's fee from the king—not, indeed, a crown
fief, but rather one belonging to some barony which, for
some reason, had lapsed into the hand of the king; such as
a bishopric when the see is vacant: the heir of the dead
man, if he be an adult, shall pay for a knight's fee 100
shillings; for two 10£, and so on, according to the number of knights which the heritage had owed to the lord
before it had lapsed to the fisc.   But if an heir is left who
is a minor, what comes from his heritage shall, by reason
of the wardship, fall to the fisc for the time that he is
under age, as has been said; if he have been left by his
father an adult already, he shall pay for each knight's fee
100 shillings, or even proportionately less; that is, 50
shillings if he possess a half of a knight's fee, and so on.
Nor may it be hidden from thee that, from him whom,
together with the fruit of his possession, thou dost have in
custody for several years, thou wilt not be able to ask a
relief when he comes to his majority.

D. In this matter the law judges for the wards, decrees
as well becomes pious minds.

M. Thus it is; but let us continue concerning what we
have undertaken.   There is likewise also a third kind of
escheats which comes to the exchequer by perpetual right.
When any tenant in chief of the king, conscious to himself
of a crime committed, whether he be accused of it or not,
nevertheless leaving all that he has, seeks to save his life
by flight: or if, being convicted of that of which he is
accused, or confessing the same, he is judged unworthy at
the same time of his land and of his life: all things which
were his by right are straightway confiscated; and all his
revenues by a yearly, nay, also by a perpetual right, are
paid into the exchequer by the sheriff, and what comes
from the sale of what is movable among them goes to the
king.   Likewise if a man of whatsoever condition, or the
slave or freeman of whatsoever lord, through fear of the
more rigid law which the king has established on account
of criminals, shall flee from his home, and, during the
terms fixed and defined by law, shall not have presented
himself or excused himself,—or also if, the neighbourhood
raising a hue against him, being suspected and afterwards
taken, he shall be convicted by the fixed law of the assize

as guilty of the crime: all his movable goods go to the fisc, the immovable, however, to the lords. The prices, however, of his movable goods shall be handed in by the sheriff to the exchequer, and shall be marked thus in the yearly roll: " the same sheriff renders account of the chattels of fugitives and of those mutilated by the assize of such a place ; namely, from this one 5, from that one 10," and so on through the separate headings, their names being expressed and the sums which arise from the chattels of the different ones.   At the end, moreover, shall be put down the total of all, and near the end of that same line in which the total is shall be written : " in the treasury 40£ in so and so many tallies, and he owes 10£," or " and he is quit." These, oh brother, are the things which we mentioned above which are to be carried to the exchequer by the sheriff even though no summons shall have preceded.   Such is also treasure dug out of the ground, or otherwise found.   Likewise, when any one having a lay estate, or also a citizen, practises public usury, if he die intestate ;—or also if, not giving satisfaction to those whom he has defrauded, he is seen to have made a will concerning his unrighteous acquisitions, but has not distributed these, nay rather has kept them by him ;—since, thus intent on gain, the desire of possessing is not believed to have left him : his money and all his movables are straightway confiscated, and, without a summons, are carried by officials to the exchequer.   The heir of the deceased, moreover, may rejoice that he still has the paternal estate and the movable property, which were all but withdrawn from him.

D. With regard to the foregoing remarks which have been made about usurers, a grave question strikes my mind, which, if it please thee, I should like to have more fully explained ; for thou did'st say : " when any one having a lay estate, or also a citizen, practises public usury, etc." ; from which words it seems that a certain distinction of persons can be made among those who are thus delinquent, and that the condition of clergy is one, that of laymen another, when they are equal in crime. Likewise from that which is added, " practises public usury," I presume that there can be a kind that is not public, and I am altogether ignorant whether any one who continues in it is subject to the law concerning that which is public.

M. In vain did I think to satisfy thee with short answers and commonplaces, since from such thou dost elicit a question, the explanation of which has hitherto been hidden from some of the skilled. But what thou sayest : "from thy words the condition of the clergy and of laymen who are thus delinquent seems to be unequal, when they are equal in crime," I do not approve of ; for, as in their grades, so do they differ in their guilt ; according to that saying : "the loftier the grade, the more grave the fall." Likewise, also, as it has seemed to some, they are unequal in good and meritorious works, for laymen, who are less bound by the restraint of a vow, seem to merit ampler grace ; just as, in perverse acts, those who are under a vow of religion offend more gravely. But so much for these matters. Thou hast, indeed, from what precedes, a means of answering the first part of thy question. For inasmuch as a clerk practising usury deserves to lose the privilege of his dignity, he merits for himself a like punishment with a layman who is thus delinquent, namely, that, when he himself dies, all his movable goods are due to the fisc. In fact we have heard from prudent persons that it is so. Against a clerk or a lay Christian thus delinquent, the royal power has no claim so long as they are alive, for there remains time for repentance ; but he is the rather reserved for an ecclesiastical tribunal, to be condemned according to the quality of his rank. When, moreover, he shall have fulfilled the decree of fate, all his goods, the church having no claim on them, go to the king: unless, as has been said, while life remained he have worthily repented and, his will being made, he have entirely alienated from himself what he shall have decided to will away. It remains now for us to explain what we call public usury, and what not public; then, whether those who err in either are within the scope of the same law. We call it, therefore, public and common usury when, after the manner of the Jews, one is about to receive in kind, by convention, more than one has lent,—as a pound for a mark, or, for a pound of silver two pence a week of gain, besides the principal :—not public, indeed, but none the less to be condemned, when one receives any estate or church in return for a loan, and, the principal remaining intact, takes for himself the fruits of it until that principal have been paid. This kind, on account of the labour and expense which are usually bestowed upon agriculture, seems to be more allowable; but, beyond a doubt, it is sordid and rightly to be counted as usury. But if the creditor, avaricious and prone to the ruin of his soul, have seen fit to have the matter so expressed in writing that it shall read: "be it known to all, that I, N., owe N. one hundred marks of silver; and for these hundred marks I have pledged to him such a piece of land for £10, until I or my heir shall pay to him or his heir the aforesaid hundred marks": when, after the death of the creditor, the tenor of this infamous charter shall come to the notice of the king or the chief justice,—first, the foul pursuit of usury shall be condemned, and the creditor, betrayed by his writing, shall be judged a usurer, unworthy of his movable goods. But if he, whose estate it is, shall in some way have obtained from the king that that which was thus alienated shall be restored to him, he shall be bounden to the king for the whole principal, even if the creditor shall have possessed the estate for two years or more; the munificence of the king, however, usually enters into an agreement concerning the amount of that total, chiefly on account of the gift of especial grace which imposes on him the duty of preferring those who are faithful; and, furthermore, because in the name of the public power he is about to receive all the goods of that creditor or usurer who had grown rich to the enormous detriment of a faithful subject. There are also many other things which pertain separately to the fisc, which cannot easily be brought under one rubric; for they are not fixed but casual. The accounts of the escheats of this third kind, however, are made out not above, after the farms, but below, after all the pleas and before the chattels of fugitives: so that they, by their actual position, may be seen to pertain to the fisc on account of the enormous faults of the delinquents.

D. I wonder at the things that thou hast said; for they do not seem to be able to agree with what goes before. For since it is free to the lords of bondsmen not only to transfer them but also to alienate them in every kind of way, as has been said above; and since they are rightly considered lords, not only of their chattels but also of their bodies: it is to be wondered at why, when the lord of the goods and of the guilty man has committed no offence against the law, he should be deprived of his possession. For it would seem just that the decree of the king should punish an excess in the person of the one who committed it, but that the movable goods, together with the estates themselves, should go to the use of the lords.

M. What troubles thee troubles me also; but I think it superfluous to delay long over these things, since they are foreign to the matters undertaken.   But to satisfy thee: know that it is so on account of the law of the king alone; nor is there, indeed, anyone who may presume to act counter to a royal decree, which is made for the good of the peace.   But if the chattels of their servants who were condemned by law came to the lords,—perchance because the fervid thirst of human cupidity had a place in their midst,—some would revel, on account of a small gain, in the slaughter of their servants even when innocent: therefore the king himself, to whom, even by God, the general care of his subjects is entrusted, decreed this to be so, in order that thus the guilty, satisfying the law, may be punished in the body, and that, their movable goods being retained by himself, they may not be exposed to their domestic enemies—that is, to their lords.   But, as we have said, the law of the king alone, made at the voice of necessity for the good of the peace, is the principal solution of this question.

D. I see that it does not happen without reason.   Now, if it please thee, continue.   But there remains something in the foregoing which I should wish, if it please thee, to have more thoroughly explained.   For thou did'st say that the movable goods of fugitives and those mutilated by law, in consequence of a summons are brought to the exchequer and are written in the yearly roll in the proper place : thou hast not said, however, what ought to be done with the chattels of robbers and thieves; whether, namely, they pertain to the king, or to whom they ought by right to go.

M. The condition is different of robbers, who are also

called manifest thieves, and of those who steal in secret. Furthermore, of these as well as of those there are two kinds, from each of which the chattels go to different persons in a different way. Some robbers, indeed, as well as some thieves, are lawless—outlaws, as we more usually call them,—some not: they become outlaws or lawless, moreover, when, being lawfully summoned, they do not appear, and are awaited and even sought for during the lawful and fixed terms, and do not present themselves before the law. Of these, therefore, the chattels and also the lives are known to be in the hands of those who seize them, nor can they for any reason pertain to the king: of robbers, however, who have not yet sunk to this depth of misery, the goods, if they are seized, go to the fisc; but of thieves, to the sheriff under whom they are seized and punished. But if the sheriff have deemed the case of a thief worthy to be brought to court, to be there judged, nothing which that thief possessed is due to him, but all to the king. But if any one have pursued the man who robbed him, and have brought him up in the first court of the lord king, or also in the county court,—and, according to the form of proof decreed by the judge, shall have proved him guilty of theft: that which was taken shall first be restored to the injured person from the chattels of the thief, if they are sufficient for that purpose; the affidavit or oath of him who claims it being first taken, if it so please the justice of the lord king. Afterwards, moreover, by the provident institution of those eager for peace, the same man is to receive, as a solace for his labour and expense, as much again as he had at first lost by the wiles of the thief. This double and prudently procured payment was called by the ancients, not without reason, "solta" and "persolta" or "prosolta": first, indeed, what had been taken is also paid, and on account of this is called "solta"; then that which is added for the charge of labour or expense is called "pro-" or "persolta." These things having been thus carried out, the remainder of the goods of the accused shall go to the fisc.

D. These things also seem necessary; but now, according to thy promise, proceed, if it please thee, concerning the rents of woods.

M. I congratulate thee since I see that thou hast held in memory as well the worth of what has been said, as the order of what is to be said. It remains, therefore, that I do not omit to satisfy thy wishes according to my powers.

XI. *Concerning the Rents of woods.*

After the account of the purprestures and escheats, there follows the account for wood-rents, very short and · clear, under this tenor of words: "the same sheriff, or such another one N., renders account of 20£ from the rent of such a wood or forest of Northamptonshire; he has paid in the treasury and is quit." There are, however, some forests from which the tenth part of the fixed rents are paid to the head churches; so from Wiltshire and from Hampshire to Salisbury cathedral, but from Northampton-shire to Lincoln cathedral: the cause of which payment I have heard to be this, almost the whole or the greater part of what is paid for the forests comes from pleas and exactions; thus then, by giving the tenths, illicit gains seem to be to some extent redeemable. Of these, more-over, the accounts are made thus: "such or such a one renders account for 20£ from the rent of such a forest; in the treasury 18£"; and at the head of the next line below, thus: "and in fixed tithes to such a church 40*s.*"; then at the end of that same line, a little apart from the rest of the writing, thus: "and is quit." Remark also that it has once been said to thee that all debts, and likewise those payments which shall have been made to the treasury, are to be placed apart from the rest of the writing; so that to the eye running over them and the mind assisting they may more readily occur; for summonses are made out for what is due, and quittances for what has already been paid. After the diligent account of the principal farm, the old or the new, and likewise after the account of the purprestures and escheats and of the wood-rents—all of which, as has been said, are paid on a yearly basis—there follows the account for the pleas and covenants; in which first, after a moderate space, a note is made in the middle of the line as to the justices to whom these belong.

XII. Concerning Pleas and Covenants: in what order the accounts for them are made when the required amounts are paid.

We call pleas, indeed, the pecuniary penalties which delinquents call down upon themselves, but covenants, spontaneous offerings.   When, therefore, the exaction of these is at hand, the summons is then first given over to the clerk of the chancellor ; he attacks the sheriff for the separate items in order, saying: " render from such a one 10£, for such a reason " ; but if what is required is paid in the treasury, it shall be written thus in the yearly roll : " N. renders account for 10£ for such a cause " ; and then shall be written in order, " has paid in the treasury and is quit."   But if it is by writ of the king that he is quit, provided, as we have said, that the amount is expressed in the writ, it shall read : " N. renders account for 10£," adding the cause ; then, a little lower, in the same line : " by writ of the king to that same N., 10£, and he is quit."   But if he be summoned for 100s., when, nevertheless, the total of the debt is, in the yearly roll, 10£, and have paid 100s. in money, or have obtained for 100s. a writ of the king, it shall read : " N. renders account for 10£., in the treasury 100 shillings and owes 100 shillings " ; or " remitted by writ of the king, to N. himself 100 shillings and he owes 100 shillings."   And mark that, in all accounts concerning pleas and covenants, individuals shall respond for themselves, so that each one, namely, shall receive in his own name the burden of the debt if he do not give satisfaction for it, or the absolution if he pay the whole ; with the exception of common assizes, Danegeld and murder fines,—for, concerning these, the sheriff renders account, and, with reference to them, is himself written down in the yearly roll as either quit or in debt.   But if the sheriff shall have been changed, he, nevertheless, who succeeds him shall answer for the same and be summoned concerning them ; and, unless he render satisfaction, shall be coerced through the farm which he is about to pay.   For whoever, when the sheriff is changed, succeeds to the burden of that office, receives from him rescripts of the debts of the king

in that county; so that he may be able to know by this,
when he shall receive the summons brought to him, from
what persons what they owe is to be demanded. To the
sheriff, therefore, pertains the general account, to him
alone belongs the coercion of individuals; and he who shall
have been sheriff when the account was made, shall be
written down in this manner as quit or in debt.

D. I retain in my memory what ought to happen when
any one, summoned concerning any debt, brings a writ of
the king which expresses the required amount. But if he
bring to the exchequer a charter of quittance for things of
the same kind, so that it reads thus: " I will, therefore, that
he hold all of these free and quit of pleas and murder
fines," and of this and that and the like, will he not be
pardoned?

M. He will be, as a matter of fact; but it will not
read: " remitted by charter of the king," or " by liberty
of a charter " this or that; but rather, " by writ of the
king ": but if the charter, not specifying, contains this:
" he shall possess the foregoing free and quit of all exaction and secular service," he is not then quit through this
of those things which are required of him, nor will it be
written down among the pardons: for those who sit there
are not willing that a special debt should be done away
with by a general absolution.

D. That subtlety is pernicious enough; for he who is
free from the whole of the parts, deserves also to be absolved from the parts of the whole.

M. It is true what thou sayest, nor do we disagree;
but, nevertheless, we are explaining what takes place, not
what perhaps ought to take place. When, therefore, for
all these things which are contained in the summons,
satisfaction shall have been rendered either in cash or by
writs of the king, this rule of writing which is explained
above is always to be employed: but when any one has not
paid the whole of what is required of him, but a part of it,
or perhaps none of it, the cause is straightway to be inquired from the sheriff as to why he was not solvent. But
if the sheriff shall reply that he have diligently sought the
chattels of the man in question, and could not find them,
the treasurer shall say: " be on thy guard, for by person-

ally taking an oath thou shalt confirm the truth of this matter,"—namely, that thou have sought and not been able to find that by which the demands might be satisfied. If he replies, "I am ready to do so," the taking of the oath shall be deferred until the account is finished; when, being once given, it shall suffice for many like cases. Concerning this oath, indeed, much has already been said near the beginning, and something remains to be said in its proper place.

XIII. Concerning the different kinds of persons who are not solvent; with regard to what persons an oath is offered by the Sheriff, and under what tenor of words the oath shall be given.

Here, indeed, we must first distinguish with regard to debtors and debts; so that it may be clear to thee in the case of whom the oath offered shall be allowable, and in the case of whom, not. For if a knight or other freeman, or a bondsman, or any such person of whatever condition or sex, is bound to the king for any debt—which, indeed, must be a punishment for a misdemeanour, not a spontaneous offering,—the treasurer shall be content with that proferred oath of the sheriff which is to be taken at the end; and the man or woman, the action against whom, by reason of their poverty, has become void, shall again be written as debtor in this yearly roll as in the last. But it is otherwise if that debtor from whom the debt is sought is a citizen or burgher; if, namely, he is a citizen by birth, or if he have subjected himself of his own will to the laws of his fellow-citizens, necessity bringing it about. For it does not suffice for the sheriff that of these, if any do not render satisfaction for the sum required, he pay in, in order to thus be quit at the exchequer, the movable goods alone, or that he offer an oath as to his having sought and not found any: he must confiscate their homes and their estates and any revenues from the cities, and place them in the hands of others; so that, even in this way, the money due to the king may be forthcoming; but if none be found who will receive them, since men of the same condition mutually spare each other, he shall fasten up their houses with bolts and shall cause their estates to be diligently cultivated. But if in the meantime they pay what is required, by the hand of the sheriff what belongs to them shall be restored to the rightful owners without damage.

D. I cannot wonder enough, when the fault does not differ,

Why more severely our law should oppress this species of mortals.

M. The greatest part of the possession of those who have estates and live by agriculture, consists in flocks, in cattle and in crops, and in like things which can not easily escape the notice of the neighbours. But to those who deal with wares, and who, sparing expense, press on with all their strength and in every way to multiply their possessions, money is the goal that they strive for. For, by means of this, commerce is more easily carried on, and this can readily be placed in safe and secret places : whence it happens that often he who is rich, when that which is hidden does not appear, will be reputed poor. For this reason, therefore, that law decrees more severely against those persons; for a superabundant well of wealth does not seem to be easily exhausted..

D. What a common assessment is, and who responds for it and in what order, is in great part plain from the foregoing. Now, if it please thee, explain about the aids or gifts of cities or burroughs ; how accounts are made of them, and who chiefly are to be convened or coerced concerning them ; for the manner of coercion is now plain from the foregoing.

M. I rejoice that thou art mindful of what has been said ; and by this, I confess, thou dost encourage me the more. Know then that it makes a great difference whether the gift or aid of a city is fixed by the Justices according to the separate individuals dwelling in it, or if the citizens offer to the justices some amount which seems worthy of the prince, and it is accepted by them : for in these two cases the manner of coercion is different. For if the gift is fixed by the judges according to individuals, and any one of them be not solvent, the aforesaid law concerning insolvent citizens is observed ; namely, that he shall be deprived of his houses and revenues until payment is made.   But if it has been said by the citizens : " we will give to the king a thousand pounds," and this sum is judged worthy to be received, they themselves must provide that at the stated terms the same is paid.   But if, by chance, they commence to make excuses, alleging the poverty of some of those who were bound to supply some part of such sum,—then diligently, that is by oath of the sheriff, inquiry is to be made if, at the time that the gift or aid was settled upon by those citizens, these persons had been incapable of paying. But if it shall be found to be thus, they shall provide others by whom the previous sum shall be paid, or the remainder shall be distributed in common.   If, however, at the time it was settled upon, they were rich, but by the law of fortune, changeable by nature, they are now in want,—patience is to be had with them until, by the grace of God, they shall grow rich again.

D. I perceive that in all things, keeping within due bounds, you always take the side of the king's advantage.

M. Thou dost retain in memory what is to be done concerning citizens or burghers who are not solvent.   But if, by chance, any knight or other freeman, degenerating— which God forbid—from the dignity of his standing, proceed to multiply his money by public trade or by the most disgraceful kind of gain—that is, by usury, and do not voluntarily pay what is demanded of him : the sheriff shall not be absolved by an oath alone as to having found nothing, but when he shall have imparted this to the president, he shall obtain a strict mandate from him that, for the sum which is required from him, that man shall find sponsors within a fixed time ; but if he will not, all his revenues shall be confiscated, since in this respect he may rightly be considered

> Like to those who increase, whatever the means be, their
>   fortunes.

D. It is indeed fitting that a degenerate knight or other freeman who loses his standing through disgraceful gain, should be punished beyond the common measure of freemen.   But now, at length, if it please thee, explain what the things are which may be reckoned among the chattels of him who is bounden to the king, and whether from all, until the sum required is raised, all things are to be taken by the sheriff; when, namely, the original debtor does not of his own will pay what is required.

XIV. What chattels of debtors, when they do not pay of their own free will, are not to be sold, and what order is to be observed in selling.

M. Thou dost drive me into a sea of questions; God knows, I do not, where I am about to emerge. Know then that here again a distinction of persons is necessary —as will be clear from what follows. I should wish thee, nevertheless, to spare me in this regard, and not compel me to say what will be displeasing to many.

D. So long as thou dost not stray from the path of the established law, thou wilt not merit the just anger of the prudent man; but if that which the law has decreed shall seem burdensome to any one, let him be angry at him who made it, not at thee.

M. From the beginning, by my promise, I became thy debtor. Hence it is that I am willing and bound to obey thee when thou dost wish or ask anything. The chattels which are lawfully sold, then, of debtors who do not of their own will pay what is demanded of them, are those goods which are movable and which move themselves: such are gold, silver, and vessels composed of the same; also precious stones, and changes of vestments and the like; also both kinds of horses, the ordinary ones, namely, and the untamed ones; herds also of oxen and flocks of sheep, and other things of the kind. The nature of fruits also and of some victuals is movable, so that, namely, they may be freely sold; deducting only the necessary expenses of the debtor for his victuals—so that, namely, he may provide for his needs, not his extravagance, and likewise may satisfy nature, not gluttony. Nor are these necessaries furnished to the debtor alone, but to his wife and children and to the household, which he was seen to have had while he was living at his own expense.

D. Why dost thou say " of some " victuals?

M. Victuals which are prepared by them for daily use, and which without essential change are suitable for eating —such as bread and drink—may by no means be sold. Of victuals, then, only those are lawfully sold which, aside from necessary uses, had been reserved by the masters themselves that they might be for sale,—such as meats laid in salt, cheeses, honey, wines, and the like. And mark that if that debtor who is not solvent have once obtained the belt of knighthood, though the other things are sold, nevertheless a horse, not any one but the one he uses, shall be reserved for him; lest he who, by rank, has become a knight, may be compelled to go on foot. But if he be a knight who

> Delights in the glory of arms, finds pleasure in using his
>   weapons,

and who, his merits demanding, ought to be reckoned among the brave, all the armature of his body, together with the horses necessary to carry it, shall be left entirely free by the sellers; so that, when it is necessary, equipped with arms and horses, he can be called to the service of king and kingdom.

> If, however, this man whom the law has partially favoured,

hearing of the need of the king or kingdom, shall conceal and absent himself, or, being summoned for this purpose, do not come—provided he serve not at his own expense, but at the king's,—and have not given a plain excuse for his absence, the sellers shall not refrain from these arms, etc., either; but, content with the one single horse left to him on account of the dignity of knighthood, he shall be subject to the general rule. The sheriff, moreover, shall take care to warn his sellers that, with regard to the things to be sold, they observe this order: the movable goods of any one shall first be sold, but they shall spare, as much as possible, the plough oxen, by which agriculture is wont to be carried on; lest, that failing him, the debtor be still further reduced to want in the future. But if even thus, indeed, the sum required is not raised, the plough oxen are not to be spared. When, therefore, all the saleable things that belong especially to him have been sold, if the amount is still not made up, they shall approach the estates of his bondsmen and lawfully sell their chattels, observing at the same time the aforesaid order and rule; for these are known to belong to the lord, as has been said above. This being done, whether the required sum is thus made up or not, our law orders the sellers to quit; unless, perhaps, it be scutage which is required from a lord; for if the chief lord who is bounden to the king for scutage do not pay, not only his own, but also the chattels of his knights and bondsmen everywhere are sold, for the matter of scutages regards his knights in great part; for they are not due to the king except by knights and by reason of military service. I myself, indeed, whose memory is not yet hoary, have seen how, for the personal debts of those who did not render satisfaction, not only their own, but also the chattels of their knights and bondsmen were lawfully sold. But the law of the illustrious king has decreed that this is to be observed only in the matter of scutages, the order being regarded that first their own, then the goods of others are to be sold. But if the knights have paid to the lord the produce of their fiefs, and are willing to prove this by offering a pledge, the law forbids that their chattels be sold for those payments which are required from the lords.

XV. That the Sheriff may take from the debtors of that debtor who does not pay the king, the debt due to the king.

Likewise the sheriff is to be warned that he diligently and carefully investigate, as well as he can, if there is any one in his county in debt to that debtor for the payment of money lent to him or deposited with him. But if it be found that there is, the sum which is required from his creditor, the man bounden to the king, shall be exacted from that debtor, and he shall be prevented by authority of the public law from being answerable for it to that creditor.

XVI. That the Sheriff may take from the estates of him who does not pay, that which is required, even if, after the time when he commenced to be bounden to the king, he have alienated them in any way.

Likewise if a debtor, from the time when he began to be bounden to the king, shall have rented his estate or revenue to another, or have given it as a pledge for money, or even—which, perhaps, will seem absurd to thee—have transferred his domain from himself by sale: if means can not otherwise be found to give satisfaction to the king, whoever the person be or by whatever title he may have gained possession,—nevertheless what belongs to the king shall be taken from him; saving the proprietorship of the lord who has commenced to possess it with a just title. Unless, perchance, that debtor shall, in the beginning, of his own will pay to the king the price of the estate sold. For, in that case, the right of possession of the buyer shall remain undisputed. The cause of this, moreover, although it seems to be somewhat wrong and to serve too much the advantage of the king, thou wilt see to be evident, nevertheless, and just enough according to the laws of the country. For whoever is found to have committed an offence against the royal majesty is at the mercy of the king in one of three ways, according to the quality of his crime. For he is sentenced, for lesser faults, either to the extent of all his movable goods, or of all his immovable—that is, his estates and revenues,—so that he shall be deprived of his heritage; but if for greater faults, or for any very great or enormous crimes, to the extent of his life or members. When, therefore, any one is condemned to the mercy of the king as to his movable goods, and the sentence is passed upon him by the judges in these words: "such a man is at the mercy of the king as regards his money," it is the same as if they said: "all his money." For the indefinite sentences of laymen have their signification not according to the interpretation of those for whom it is more safe that they should be so interpreted—that is, of individuals,—but are equal for all. Since, therefore, the chattels of that estate which the debtor afterwards alienated had been condemned as at the good pleasure of the king, and he had not given satisfaction for the required sum, it is unjust that he should have alienated a thing that was not his own at a loss to the fisc.

XVII. That a Sheriff is not allowed to receive money due to himself from those who do not pay the king : and what is to be done if he should happen to receive it.

Likewise the sheriff is to be warned on account of the oath, concerning those who do not pay, which is required of him—nay, which he himself is seen to have offered of his own free will, in order that thus he might be absolved from the summons made against him,—that he do not receive from any debtor who does not pay the king, anything, in the meantime, that was justly due to himself. For it is not likely that the sheriff could not find enough to pay the sum due the king among the chattels of him who, willingly or unwillingly, has paid what is required to the sheriff himself. But if, before taking the oath, the sheriff has remembered of himself or through another that he has received something from such persons ;—or even after taking it, provided the exchequer of that day is nevertheless not yet dismissed ; that is, while his account is fresh ;— and if, coming in public, he be willing to prove with querulous voice—taking an oath concerning these things—that he had forgotten at that time having received anything : he shall be acquitted on paying in the name of the debtor the money received. But if—which God forbid—after giving his oath, and after the exchequer is dissolved, this should become known through another,—he shall not then be released simply on payment of what he had received, but, being declared at the good pleasure of the king on account of his offence, he shall be pecuniarily punished. Finally, let it suffice to have warned the sheriff that after receiving the summons he shall diligently inquire in the neighbourhood if the man who was not solvent, by taking a wife, or the woman by marrying some one richer, or in any other way, has grown rich, so that he or she may give satisfaction for what is required. If this be found to be so, upon the oath of the sheriff he or she shall be obliged to pay. But if none of these things be found to be so, the sheriff can then, with a clear conscience, give an oath concerning this, and avoid the imminent loss of his possessions.

XVIII. How a husband is to be called to account for a wife or a wife for a husband, if he or she be not solvent.

D. Should a husband, indeed, be called to account for a wife who was bounden to the king and who has already died, or ought a woman who survives her husband to be called to account for him?

M. Thou hast heard often enough, that "he who cleaves to a woman is made one flesh," in such way, however, that he is her head. With right, therefore, he is to be called to account for her, for the woman has not power over herself, but the man over her. But if the husband have had off-spring by her, to which offspring, by reason of the wife, the heritage is due, and, the wife being already dead, the money due to the king has not yet been paid: then that husband is to be called to account in the name of the heir, and coerced; but otherwise not. A woman, on the other hand, who survives her husband, and has offspring, and remains in widowhood with it, is to be called to account and coerced by reason of the offspring to whom the heritage is due; in such manner, however, that her dowry shall be spared, since it is the price of her virginity. But if, leaving her children, the woman cleave to another husband, the lawful heir is to be called to account for the debt of his father. If, however, a woman who has committed an offence and is bounden to the king, her former husband being dead without children, shall transfer herself and her heritage to another, her debt is to be required from the new husband. This is, then, what thou did'st ask. And in this way a man is to be summoned on account of the wife and a wife on account of the husband. Thou may'st be sure also that the lawful heir who succeeds to a debtor is to be called to account for him: so that he may succeed to the burdens as well as to the emolument. The bondsman alone, and he who dies without heritage, are, after their chattels have been sold, freed from their debt by death's last throw. They are, however, not cancelled from the yearly roll in which these debts are entered, unless by writ of the king; when, namely, it is suggested to the king concerning these by the treasurer, that it is useless to write them in the roll, since by no arrangement could it come about that the money due from them should be forthcoming.

XIX. That there is not the same mode of coercion for the king's barons and for others, in the matter of pecuniary penalties.

In addition it is fitting thou should'st know that, in the matter of requiring debts due to the king and of coercing debtors, the conditions do not apply equally to the chief barons of the king and to others who here and there are punished for their offences by fines to the king. Concerning those, then, who hold nothing in chief from the king, the foregoing rule is observed. But if one who holds a barony from the king, having heard the summons, shall, either in his own person or at the hand of his general steward, whom people ordinarily call seneschal, give a pledge into the hand of the sheriff to the effect that, on the day of his account, he will give security to the barons of the exchequer for this sum and for this summons: then the sheriff may rest content.

XX. What is to be done when the steward, who has pledged himself to render satisfaction, does not appear.

If, however, being summoned by the voice of the herald, he do not come on the day of the account, and do not render satisfaction of himself or through another, the sheriff shall be considered to have done what pertained to him; but the case being carefully jotted down separately, at the treasurer's dictation, in the memoranda of the exchequer, shall be reserved for the end of the session; when, counsel having been taken, he who thus offended may be more severely punished. But if, after the account of the sheriff is ended, he shall come and render satisfaction,— by the favour of those in session and by the indulgence of the law he may be absolved. But it is necessary that the sheriff receive his oath in the county court, before the eyes of all; because if, by chance, he who gave it wishes to do evil and to deny that he gave it, the recollection of the county will suffice for the whole burden of proof against him. But if the sheriff shall confess that it was given him in any other manner, he shall be considered to have done nothing. Therefore the required sum shall straightway be taken from his farm, so that he shall satisfy the summons which says in this regard: "or they shall be taken from thy farm."

XXI. *What if he comes and does not give satisfaction, if he is a knight. What if he is not a knight.*

But if one who does not deny that he gave an oath shall come on the day named and do not render satisfaction, he shall, if he is a lord, be detained at the exchequer as long as it shall be in session, taking an oath to the marshal, as we said above, that he will not go beyond the banlieu of the town unless by permission of the barons. But when the exchequer of that term is dissolved, if he have not yet rendered satisfaction, he shall be put in a safe place, in free custody, until the king himself, if he be present, or the president with the others in session shall decree what is to be done with a man who confesses that he promised on oath to render satisfaction, and has in no wise done so. But if a knight or other person who is his steward come and do not render satisfaction, he shall be seized for breaking his oath and shall be given over to the custody of the marshal, being lawfully liable to be bound when the exchequer is dissolved, and to be put in prison whether he be a knight or no. But a knight who does not render satisfaction for his own debt, when, nevertheless, he has taken an oath that he would do so, shall be kept in liberal custody after the exchequer is dissolved—not in a prison, but within the enclosure of the prison building,—giving an oath personally that he will not go away from there without the king's or the president's permission. For the illustrious king of memorable nobility decreed that whoever is resplendent with the dignity of knighthood may not be sent to prison for his own debt, when he is considered a pauper by the sheriff and the neighbourhood alike; but he shall be kept apart, at large, within the enclosure of the prison building. But whoever, by order of his lord, has given an oath to the sheriff, as has been said, and comes but does not pay: the law decrees that such a one shall be seized and put in prison when the exchequer dissolves, whether he be a knight or no. And since any baron is free to set up the oath of his official for the debt that is required of himself, so that he may in the meantime be free from the importunity of the sheriff and may himself arrange his affairs more conveniently : lest thus the authority of the king's mandate be eluded to an infinite extent, it is decreed that, when he is seized who, by not rendering satisfaction, has brought judgment upon himself as being guilty of a broken oath,—straightway servants shall be sent by the sheriff who, going through the estates of the chief lord, selling his chattels as best they can, shall bring the sum required to the exchequer of that term. And, finally, he who was seized for breaking his oath shall pay a pecuniary fine according to his means, and shall not, even though the lord order it, be any more permitted to give an oath concerning that debt.

XXII. How a lord shall be punished who has voluntarily exposed a knight so that he himself may in the meantime be free.

Furthermore, lest the chief lord may presume upon this with impunity, if he should, by chance, be again summoned for that debt, he shall not again merit the benefit of delay through the oath of a substitute, but solely through his own. Some, indeed, believe that he may not any more, even through his own oath, obtain from the sheriff a delay until the exchequer meets—which benefit or delay, indeed, they who are bounden to the exchequer consider great, for they can in the meantime dispose more favourably of their possessions and prepare what is needed for a payment that is put off for a while,—but they say rather that, having received the summons, the sheriff may be allowed to lay hands at once upon their chattels, according to the common law regarding others. I do not altogether disagree with such people, I confess ; but nevertheless there should be many evidences and proofs to make it seem probable that the lord allowed his knight to be exposed to such hazards in order that, even thus, he himself might in the meantime go free. The most valid proof, moreover, against the lord in this matter is if he is considered, by the sheriff and the neighbourhood alike, well to do, abounding in possessions, able to pay.

D. It is indeed fitting that he should cease to merit a favour granted to him who has abused the same to the detriment of him who granted it.

M. Thou hast from the foregoing to some extent a distinction as to which chattels may be sold and which not, and also with regard to what persons discretion is to be used and to what persons not;—that is, in the case where debtors who are bounden to the king for pecuniary punishments are not solvent. It remains for us to show what ought to be done concerning voluntary oblations when they likewise do not pay them.

XXIII. *What is to be done concerning those who make voluntary offerings when they too do not pay.*

Know then that of the oblations to the king some are offered for a present benefit, some for a prospect. We say that one offers for a present benefit, when the offering is accepted by the king, and he who offers it receives from the king in proportion to what he has offered: as when any one, for some liberty, for an estate or for a farm, or for the wardship, to be enjoyed until he is of age, of some one who is a minor, or for any thing else which seems to add to his convenience or honour, offers of his own accord to the king £100 or 100 marks, and, the king consenting, immediately after the offer receives what he wished for. Concerning those, therefore, who bind themselves of their own will, and who, after having made an agreement with the prince, have already begun to hold possession, our law decrees that, so long as they pay, they may enjoy and make use of the benefits indulged to them. But if, after having been summoned for the debt of the king, they cease to pay, they shall straightway be deprived of what they had obtained; in such manner, however, that

if while the exchequer lasts they render satisfaction for
the same, without damage that which was taken away
shall be restored. And note that any person, of whatever
condition or sex, will always be subject to this rule concerning voluntary offerings,—that, namely, he shall satisfy
the summons or do without what he had obtained ; unless
the king himself, out of regard for a service rendered or
for his poverty, indulge him something beyond the ordinary. So it is, when, on behalf of the offerer of a large
sum at any exchequer he decrees that a certain portion
shall be paid by himself, and makes this known through
his writ to the barons. On the other hand, offerings are
said to be made for a prospect when any one, for the sake
of having justice done him concerning a certain estate or
revenue, offers a certain sum to the king ; not, however,
in order that justice be done—do not burst out upon us
and say that justice is venal with us—but that it be done
without delay. Know, however, that not every thing thus
offered is accepted by the king, not even though it seem to
be immeasurably great. For to some, solely out of regard
for a service rendered, or out of charity, he exhibits gratis
the plenitude of justice ; to others, moreover, according to
the law of human nature, he is willing neither for prayer
nor for price to show favour, the merits of those who are
meanwhile known to be in possession coming in the way.
Or perchance the merits of those themselves who make
the demand by no means call for this, they being accused
of having committed some offence either against the state
or against the king himself. Concerning such persons,
moreover, the illustrious king has thus decreed : that,
before they have justice—that is, before they obtain it by
a sentence,—or if, the matter being settled altogether contrary to them, they have abandoned all hope, they shall
pay nothing in the way of offerings, but it shall suffice for
the sheriff to reply concerning such persons : " they have
not yet had justice." The sheriff shall, nevertheless, take
care lest it happen through the debtor himself that his
case does not come up for action, if, namely, he be unwilling to bring the matter before the law, so that, in this
way, the king shall be defrauded of the money promised
to him. For when this has been found out the subterfuge

shall not avail him, but he shall be coerced in all things as though he had obtained justice through a sentence. It is a sign, moreover, of such wilful delay, when, keeping by him the writ of the king, he does not use it. However, through the compassion of the prince, they usually proceed rather gently with those who, after promising the money, let the case fall; lest, frustrated in their hope, being deprived also of their possessions without having gained any thing, they be reduced to despair by a double misfortune.

XXIV. *As to Reliefs not voluntarily paid.*

There are likewise payments of a third kind which do not seem altogether fit to be counted under offerings, but are rather called fines to the exchequer. They are made, namely, when one holding a barony in chief from the king dies and leaves an heir, and that heir compounds with the king for what sum he can, in order that he may merit to enter upon his father's privileges; which fine we commonly call a relief. If it is a barony, indeed, it is at the good pleasure of the king what the amount of the relief ought to be; if, however, it is a question of an escheat which has fallen into the hands of the king through default of an heir or otherwise, for one knight's fee he shall pay under the name of a relief to the king only so much as he would have been about to pay to his lord; that is, one hundred shillings. Some think, moreover, that those who are bounden to the king for reliefs, and do not pay when summoned, are subject to the rules regarding free-will offerings, namely, that when they do not pay they shall be deprived of the favours obtained. But it can be more truly said that it shall be proceeded in the case of reliefs as in the case of pecuniary penalties; for the heritage due to the children by reason of their succession seems to exclude them from the rule concerning voluntary payments.

XXV. *What is to be done concerning birds offered, and at what time a summons is to be sent for them.*

It likewise happens at times that, for some reason or other, there are promised to the king royal birds; hawks, namely, or falcons. But if he who promises says in explanation, "a hawk of the present year," or 'one that has already moulted," or also expresses the origin, saying, "I will give an Irish one," "a Spanish," "a Norwegian one," he shall render satisfaction accordingly. But if neither he who promises, nor he to whom it is promised shall specify, it shall rest with the discretion of the promiser whether he shall pay one that has moulted or not. But if it shall be judged sound and healthy by the hawk-keepers of the king, it shall be received no matter what its extraction. But if, having been summoned, he shall carry to the exchequer one worthy to be received, and there be no one there to receive it, he cannot, even if, after this, the summons is put off for a year, or two years or more, be compelled to pay any other than the one he prefers : one that has moulted, namely, or one of the present year. But if, having been summoned, he shall procure in some way that the payment be deferred, he shall, according to the number of years during which the delay is granted to him—two years, namely, or three, or so on, pay one that has moulted. Concerning these birds, moreover, a summons is not made out against the Easter term, for their use is rare in the summer time ; for then they are diligently guarded, being shut up in mews, so that, their old ones being laid aside, the glory of their feathers may return, and their youth be renewed like that of the eagle. But those that are due to the king shall be called for against the Michaelmas term ; so that, as the winter approaches, they may be fitted for the service of the king. In coercing those, moreover, who thus bind themselves of their own accord and who do not pay, the aforesaid rule concerning voluntary offerings shall be observed.

XXVI. *Concerning the Queen's gold.*

Besides this, those should know who voluntarily bind themselves to the king for a sum of ready cash, that they are likewise bounden to the queen, although it has not been expressed. Although not expressed, indeed, it is, nevertheless, comprised in the promise: so that when he shall have promised one hundred or two hundred marks to the king, he is in like manner bounden to the queen to the extent of one mark of gold for a hundred marks of silver promised to the king, two marks of gold for two hundred, and so on. In collecting these, moreover, the sheriff shall in all things observe the same rule which he observed with regard to the debts of the king, not, however, before, but after the latter have been collected. When, therefore, summonses are made out concerning debts to the king, a clerk of the queen, appointed for this, is present, and adds in the summons: "from such a one thou shalt have a hundred marks for such a cause, and one mark of gold for the queen." The amounts called for, moreover, are received separately at the exchequer by her officials constituted for this purpose. Know also that even though the king relinquish the half or the whole of the money promised to himself, or even put off sending a summons for it,—nevertheless, as to what pertains to the queen it shall be done in all things according as it seems good to her; so that, if she be unwilling, what is due to her may neither be remitted nor put off, but the amount of the summons shall be paid, and those who do not pay shall be coerced in the aforesaid manner.

D. Is anything due to the queen from sums under one hundred marks promised to the king?

M. To some it seems right that it should hold good for as low as ten marks—so, namely, that he who has promised 10 to the king is bounden to the queen for one ounce of gold;—to others, not unless for a hundred or more promised in the beginning. Concerning these things, therefore, wait with modesty for the present; for, the matter not being ended yet, the clearing up of it is suspended. On the part of the queen, indeed, litigation concerning this is being carried on with the debtors, and as yet the case is in the hands of the judge. From the amercements of the Jews, moreover, and from the redemption of moneyers her portion is due to the queen in the aforesaid form, just as we have said that it is from voluntary offerings.

D. With regard to pecuniary fines, and voluntary offerings, does the same law coerce clergy and laymen without a difference?

M. With regard to voluntary offerings one law is observed for all : that, whether he who does not pay be clerk or layman, he shall be deprived of the benefit until he render satisfaction. The same observance is regarded likewise in the case of every thing else that is due to the king, through any agreement, from the clergy—if, namely, they have neglected to announce the privilege of their standing and of free possession. Concerning those, moreover, who do announce it, learn what ought to be done, if it please thee, from discreet and God-fearing laymen; for I omit these things on purpose at present, lest I be said to have dictated to the men of my condition my own rules and more gentle laws.

D. Thou did'st say, if I remember aright, that baronies or estates frequently come into the king's hands; I should wish thee, therefore, please to explain in what manner the income of escheats flows into the fisc; whether in one way or in different ways.

XXVII. That farms are to be answered for in one way and wardships in another, and that the oath is to be given in different wording.

M. When a barony or any great holding falls into the hands of the king, by his or by the president's mandate there are sent to it discreet men of both orders, who going through the different localities reduce the revenues of the same to a total, and agree that for this total the sheriff or some one else shall be bounden at the exchequer. When, therefore, he who has been appointed for this purpose renders satisfaction for this total in money, or writs and tallies, afterwards giving an oath that it is a true account, he deserves to be acquitted. And concerning it there shall be written this in the yearly roll: "such and such a one renders account for the farm of such an honour; in the treasury so much, and he is quit"; or "and he owes." But when the king has committed the custody of his escheat to the faith of some one in such wise, namely, that the latter is to pay the income from it into the exchequer, then, after the account has been made, the oath shall not be given in the aforesaid tenor of words; but rather to the effect that, as much as he has received from it in money or in any other things whatever, so much, upon his conscience, he has paid into the exchequer: excepting alone such victuals as have been brought to him, he not extorting them under the semblance of voluntary contributions.

D. Does that administrator, then, receive the necessaries of life from these revenues?

M. Although it is written: "Thou shalt not muzzle the ox when he treadeth out the corn," nevertheless, except by express mandate of the king, he receives nothing from them; for, whoever he be, he shall serve the king at his own expense in these matters. Concerning such a one, moreover, it shall be written thus in the yearly roll: "such and such a one renders account for the income from such an honour on his affirmation." When, therefore, satisfaction has been rendered for all the aforesaid fixed or casual payments, and the separate items have, in due form, been written down in order in the roll, all those who have seats there are called together to complete the account of the principal farm, he whose name is marked at the head of the roll returns, and the account is completed in the following order. The farm paid this term by the sheriff, concerning which a test has been made, shall first be distributed by the calculator in coin heaps in the spaces marked by the stripes; then, deducting for the combustion, as has been said, the same is blanched, and the little tally of combustion being appended to it, though not being computed to the sheriff,—the sum which is left is put on a tally. Likewise, also, what had been paid at the Easter term, and blanched, is put on the same tally. Likewise, also, the amount of combustion for that term is placed together with the combustion of the final term; so that there may be one tally for both payments, and, in the same way, one for combustion. This having been done, the treasurer, bringing forth the exactory roll which we mentioned above, causes the total for that county to be arranged above in heaps and in order. From this, then, is deducted what was paid into the treasury and blanched; after this, whatever the king has conferred on any one blank from the farm of the county. After this, again, the amount of the other payments made by writ of the king, or otherwise, is arranged in heaps, and is reckoned as blanched by the sub-

traction of twelve pence from each pound, just as that
which is paid in the treasury is blanched by combustion.
Then, indeed, a subtraction is made of the expenses below
from the total above ; and, if he have deserved to be altogether absolved, there is written at the end of that account
in large letters : " and he is quit " ; or below, at the head
of the lower line : " and he owes." Then, at length, the
account being ended, the amount of the payments actually
in the treasury is put down where we said some time since
" in the treasury " was written—where a blank had been
left on purpose, lest the scribe might, perhaps, be obliged
to erase ; which, especially with regard to numbers and
names and causes, is, as we said long since, to be avoided.

*XXVIII. That an oath as to the truth of an account, being
once given, suffices once and for all.*

The account for the body of the county being settled, as
has been said, the oath of the sheriff is taken by the marshall once, under the aforesaid form ; and, after being thus
absolved he is dismissed. Some, however, believed that
the sheriff should give a separate oath for each separate
item that needed confirmation,—so that he should give his
oath as often as he said that anything was so which could
be confirmed by his oath alone. But this was seen to be a
very pernicious subtlety by prudent men and ones skilled in
the divine Law, because when once he had given his oath, he
had, upon his conscience, made a lawful account for everything. Therefore, after a while, this opinion together with
its author came to be rightly despised, and they were content with one oath—that is, with an oath once given ;
for they are one body in the confession of one faith.

D. I perceive by the already languishing pen that the
end of speaking is at hand. But, although the twilight of
approaching night, and the more extended labour of a
more lengthy task call us to other things and compel us to
breathe a little,—I should like thee, nevertheless, if it can
be done, to give certainty to the mind of thy pupil which is
in suspense and fluctuating at present by reason of thy
words, by showing, namely, how it is, as I remember thee
to have said in the beginning, that the whole description of

the exchequer is a sort of hiding place for sacred truths, which are to be revealed when the books of all are opened and the gates closed.

M. It is great what thou askest and needs further investigation; nor, by my promise, did I become thy debtor to the extent of explaining these things. I pass them over, then, at present, reserving them for the disputation of another day. I fear, indeed, lest if I should impose a new burden on one who is already charged with so many, thou would'st give way under the weight; and, likewise, if to that already said and which is to be committed to memory, I should add the study of something new, I should drive thee to hate both. Be content, therefore, with the things that have already been said, and to which thou did'st drive me; for thou hast in them, as much as could offer itself to a fresh memory, an explanation, as it were from the first principles, of whatever seemed best to thee relating to the science of the exchequer. But as to explaining exactly the different things which in the course of time must necessarily come up,—for that, neither a man's strength, nor perhaps his life would suffice. For from varied and unusual cases either no system at all can be formed, or one hitherto unknown. But for this reason I shall be rather exposed to the tongues of detractors when, as time goes on, many doubtful and hitherto unheard of points shall happen to be brought up. And when they find nothing here concerning these or similar points, they will commence to mock, saying: this man began to build and could not or did not know how to finish. I do not differ from them. I have followed, indeed, myself as the worst of masters; but have nevertheless, thou compelling me, done what I could without a leader and without a model. For I put my axe to a rude and untouched forest, cutting wood for royal edifices, to be planed by the tool of a more skilful builder. When, therefore, from this material the structure of the royal palace shall have arisen, let him who made the beginning merit the first, even though not the chief thanks.

Farewell, illustrious king.

THE END.

VI.

LAWS OF RICHARD I. (COEUR DE LION) CONCERNING CRUSADERS WHO WERE TO GO BY SEA. 1189 A.D.

("Roger of Hoveden," III. p. 36 [Rolls Series].)

Richard by the grace of God king of England, and duke of Normandy and Aquitaine, and count of Anjou, to all his subjects who are about to go by sea to Jerusalem, greeting. Know that we, by the common counsel of upright men, have made the laws here given. Whoever slays a man on shipboard shall be bound to the dead man and thrown into the sea. But if he shall slay him on land, he shall be bound to the dead man and buried in the earth. If any one, moreover, shall be convicted through lawful witnesses of having drawn a knife to strike another, or of having struck him so as to draw blood, he shall lose his hand. But if he shall strike him with his fist without drawing blood, he shall be dipped three times in the sea. But if any one shall taunt or insult a comrade or charge him with hatred of God: as many times as he shall have insulted him, so many ounces of silver shall he pay. A robber, moreover, convicted of theft, shall be shorn like a hired fighter, and boiling tar shall be poured over his head, and feathers from a cushion shall be shaken out over his head,—so that he may be publicly known; and at the first land where the ships put in he shall be cast on shore. Under my own witness at Chinon.

VII.

MAGNA CARTA.

(Stubbs' "Charters," pp. 296 ff.)

John, by the grace of God king of England, lord of Ireland, duke of Normandy and Aquitaine, count of Anjou: to the archbishops, bishops, abbots, earls, barons, justices, foresters, sheriffs, prevosts, serving men, and to all his bailiffs and faithful subjects, greeting. Know that we, by the will of God and for the safety of our soul, and of the souls of all our predecessors and our heirs, to the honour of God and for the exalting of the holy church and the bettering of our realm: by the counsel of our venerable fathers Stephen archbishop of Canterbury, primate of all England and cardinal of the holy Roman church; of Henry archbishop of Dublin; of the bishops William of London, Peter of Winchester, Jocelin of Bath and Glastonbury, Hugo of Lincoln, Walter of Worcester, William of Coventry and Benedict of Rochester; of master Pandulf, subdeacon and of the household of the lord pope; of brother Aymeric, master of the knights of the Temple in England; and of the noble men, William Marshall earl of Pembroke, William earl of Salisbury, William earl of Warren, William earl of Arundel, Alan de Galway constable of Scotland, Warin son of Gerold, Peter son of Herbert, Hubert de Burgh seneschal of Poictiers, Hugo de Neville, Matthew son of Herbert, Thomas Basset, Alan Basset, Philip d'Aubigni, Robert de Roppelay, John Marshall, John son of Hugo, and others of our faithful subjects:

1. First of all have granted to God, and, for us and for our heirs forever, have confirmed, by this our present charter, that the English church shall be free and shall have its rights intact and its liberties uninfringed upon. And thus we will that it be observed. As is apparent from the fact that we, spontaneously and of our own free will, before discord broke out between ourselves and our barons, did grant and by our charter confirm—and did cause the lord pope Innocent III. to confirm—freedom of elections, which is considered most important and most necessary to the church of England. Which charter both we ourselves shall observe, and we will that it be observed with good faith by our heirs forever. We have also granted to all free men of our realm, on the part of ourselves and our heirs forever, all the subjoined liberties, to have and to hold, to them and to their heirs, from us and from our heirs:

2. If any one of our earls or barons, or of others holding from us in chief through military service, shall die; and

if, at the time of his death, his heir be of full age and owe a relief: he shall have his inheritance by paying the old relief;—the heir, namely, or the heirs of an earl, by paying one hundred pounds for the whole barony of an earl; the heir or heirs of a baron, by paying one hundred pounds for the whole barony; the heir or heirs of a knight, by paying one hundred shillings at most for a whole knight's fee; and he who shall owe less shall give less, according to the ancient custom of fees.

3. But if the heir of any of the above persons shall be under age and in wardship,—when he comes of age he shall have his inheritance without relief and without fine.

4. The administrator of the land of such heir who shall be under age shall take none but reasonable issues from the land of the heir, and reasonable customs and services; and this without destruction and waste of men or goods. And if we shall have committed the custody of any such land to the sheriff or to any other man who ought to be responsible to us for the issues of it, and he cause destruction or waste to what is in his charge: we will fine him, and the land shall be handed over to two lawful and discreet men of that fee who shall answer to us, or to him to whom we shall have referred them, regarding those issues. And if we shall have given or sold to any one the custody of any such land, and he shall have caused destruction or waste to it,—he shall lose that custody, and it shall be given to two lawful and discreet men of that fee, who likewise shall answer to us, as has been explained.

5. The administrator, moreover, so long as he may have the custody of the land, shall keep in order, from the issues of that land, the houses, parks, warrens, lakes, mills, and other things pertaining to it. And he shall restore to the heir when he comes to full age, his whole land stocked with ploughs and wainnages, according as the time of the wainnage requires and the issues of the land will reasonably permit.

6. Heirs may marry without disparagement; so, nevertheless, that, before the marriage is contracted, it shall be announced to the relations by blood of the heir himself.

7. A widow, after the death of her husband, shall straightway, and without difficulty, have her marriage

portion and her inheritance, nor shall she give any thing in return for her dowry, her marriage portion, or the inheritance which belonged to her, and which she and her husband held on the day of the death of that husband. And she may remain in the house of her husband, after his death, for forty days; within which her dowry shall be paid over to her.

8. No widow shall be forced to marry when she prefers to live without a husband; so, however, that she gives security not to marry without our consent, if she hold from us, or the consent of the lord from whom she holds, if she hold from another.

9. Neither we nor our bailiffs shall seize any revenue for any debt, so long as the chattels of the debtor suffice to pay the debt; nor shall the sponsors of that debtor be distrained so long as that chief debtor has enough to pay the debt. But if the chief debtor fail in paying the debt, not having the wherewithal to pay it, the sponsors shall answer for the debt. And, if they shall wish, they may have the lands and revenues of the debtor until satisfaction shall have been given them for the debt previously paid for him; unless the chief debtor shall show that he is quit in that respect towards those same sponsors.

10. If any one shall have taken any sum, great or small, as a loan from the Jews, and shall die before that debt is paid,—that debt shall not bear interest so long as the heir, from whomever he may hold, shall be under age. And if the debt fall into our hands, we shall take nothing save the chattel contained in the deed.

11. And if any one dies owing a debt to the Jews, his wife shall have her dowry, and shall restore nothing of that debt. But if there shall remain children of that dead man, and they shall be under age, the necessaries shall be provided for them according to the nature of the dead man's holding; and, from the residue, the debt shall be paid, saving the service due to the lords. In like manner shall be done concerning debts that are due to others besides Jews.

12. No scutage or aid shall be imposed in our realm unless by the common counsel of our realm; except for redeeming our body, and knighting our eldest son, and

marrying once our eldest daughter. And for these purposes there shall only be given a reasonable aid. In like
manner shall be done concerning the aids of the city of
London.

13. And the city of London shall have all its old liberties
and free customs as well by land as by water. Moreover
we will and grant that all other cities and burroughs, and
towns and ports, shall have all their liberties and free
customs.

14. And, in order to have the common counsel of the
realm in the matter of assessing an aid otherwise than in
the aforesaid cases, or of assessing a scutage,—we shall
cause, under seal through our letters, the archbishops,
bishops, abbots, earls, and greater barons to be summoned
for a fixed day—for a term, namely, at least forty days
distant,—and for a fixed place. And, moreover, we shall
cause to be summoned in general, through our sheriffs and
bailiffs, all those who hold of us in chief. And in all
those letters of summons we shall express the cause of the
summons. And when a summons has thus been made,
the business shall be proceeded with on the day appointed
according to the counsel of those who shall be present,
even though not all shall come who were summoned.

15. We will not allow any one henceforth to take an aid
from his freemen save for the redemption of his body, and
the knighting of his eldest son, and the marrying, once, of
his eldest daughter; and, for these purposes, there shall
only be given a reasonable aid.

16. No one shall be forced to do more service for a
knight's fee, or for another free holding, than is due from
it.

17. Common pleas shall not follow our court but shall
be held in a certain fixed place.

18. Assizes of novel disseisin, of mort d'ancestor, and of
darrein presentment shall not be held save in their own
counties, and in this way : we, or our chief justice, if we
shall be absent from the kingdom, shall send two justices
through each county four times a year; they, with four
knights from each county, chosen by the county, shall
hold the aforesaid assizes in the county, and on the day
and at the place of the county court.

19. And if on the day of the county court the aforesaid assizes can not be held, a sufficient number of knights and free tenants, from those who were present at the county court on that day, shall remain, so that through them the judgments may be suitably given, according as the matter may have been great or small.

20. A freeman shall only be amerced for a small offence according to the measure of that offence. And for a great offence he shall be amerced according to the magnitude of the offence, saving his contenement; and a merchant, in the same way, saving his merchandize. And a villein, in the same way, if he fall under our mercy, shall be amerced saving his wainnage. And none of the aforesaid fines shall be imposed save upon oath of upright men from the neighbourhood.

21. Earls and barons shall not be amerced save through their peers, and only according to the measure of the offence.

22. No clerk shall be amerced for his lay tenement except according to the manner of the other persons aforesaid; and not according to the amount of his ecclesiastical benefice.

23. Neither a town nor a man shall be forced to make bridges over the rivers, with the exception of those who, from of old and of right ought to do it.

24. No sheriff, constable, coroners, or other bailiffs of ours shall hold the pleas of our crown.

25. All counties, hundreds, wapentakes, and trithings— our demesne manors being excepted—shall continue according to the old farms, without any increase at all.

26. If any one holding from us a lay fee shall die, and our sheriff or bailiff can show our letters patent containing our summons for the debt which the dead man owed to us, —our sheriff or bailiff may be allowed to attach and enroll the chattels of the dead man to the value of that debt, through view of lawful men; in such way, however, that nothing shall be removed thence until the debt is paid which was plainly owed to us. And the residue shall be left to the executors that they may carry out the will of the dead man. And if nothing is owed to us by him, all the chattels shall go to the use prescribed by the

deceased, saving their reasonable portions to his wife and children.

27. If any freeman shall have died intestate his chattels shall be distributed through the hands of his near relatives and friends, by view of the church ; saving to any one the debts which the dead man owed him.

28. No constable or other bailiff of ours shall take the corn or other chattels of any one except he straightway give money for them, or can be allowed a respite in that regard by the will of the seller.

29. No constable shall force any knight to pay money for castle-ward if he be willing to perform that ward in person, or—he for a reasonable cause not being able to perform it himself—through another proper man. And if we shall have led or sent him on a military expedition, he shall be quit of ward according to the amount of time during which, through us, he shall have been in military service.

30. No sheriff nor bailiff of ours, nor any one else, shall take the horses or carts of any freeman for transport, unless by the will of that freeman.

31. Neither we nor our bailiffs shall take another's wood for castles or for other private uses, unless by the will of him to whom the wood belongs.

32. We shall not hold the lands of those convicted of felony longer than a year and a day ; and then the lands shall be restored to the lords of the fiefs.

33. Henceforth all the weirs in the Thames and Medway, and throughout all England, save on the sea-coast, shall be done away with entirely.

34. Henceforth the writ which is called *Praecipe* shall not be served on any one for any holding so as to cause a free man to lose his court.

35. There shall be one measure of wine throughout our whole realm, and one measure of ale and one measure of corn—namely, the London quart ;—and one width of dyed and russet and hauberk cloths—namely, two ells below the selvage. And with weights, moreover, it shall be as with measures.

36. Henceforth nothing shall be given or taken for a writ of inquest in a matter concerning life or limb ; but it shall be conceded gratis, and shall not be denied.

37. If any one hold of us in fee-farm, or in socage, or in burkage, and hold land of another by military service, we shall not, by reason of that fee-farm, or socage, or burkage, have the wardship of his heir or of his land which is held in fee from another. Nor shall we have the wardship of that fee-farm, or socage, or burkage unless that fee-farm owe military service. We shall not, by reason of some petit-serjeanty which some one holds of us through the service of giving us knives or arrows or the like, have the wardship of his heir or of the land which he holds of another by military service.

38. No bailiff, on his own simple assertion, shall henceforth put any one to his law, without producing faithful witnesses in evidence.

39. No freeman shall be taken, or imprisoned, or disseized, or outlawed, or exiled, or in any way harmed—nor will we go upon or send upon him—save by the lawful judgment of his peers or by the law of the land.

40. To none will we sell, to none deny or delay, right or justice.

41. All merchants may safely and securely go out of England, and come into England, and delay and pass through England, as well by land as by water, for the purpose of buying and selling, free from all evil taxes, subject to the ancient and right customs—save in time of war, and if they are of the land at war against us. And if such be found in our land at the beginning of the war, they shall be held, without harm to their bodies and goods, until it shall be known to us or our chief justice how the merchants of our land are to be treated who shall, at that time, be found in the land at war against us. And if ours shall be safe there, the others shall be safe in our land.

42. Henceforth any person, saving fealty to us, may go out of our realm and return to it, safely and securely, by land and by water, except perhaps for a brief period in time of war, for the common good of the realm. But prisoners and outlaws are excepted according to the law of the realm; also people of a land at war against us, and the merchants, with regard to whom shall be done as we have said.

43. If any one hold from any escheat—as from the

honour of Wallingford, Nottingham, Boloin, Lancaster, or the other escheats which are in our hands and are baronies —and shall die, his heir shall not give another relief, nor shall he perform for us other service than he would perform for a baron if that barony were in the hand of a baron; and we shall hold it in the same way in which the baron has held it.

44. Persons dwelling without the forest shall not henceforth come before the forest justices, through common summonses, unless they are impleaded or are the sponsors of some person or persons attached for matters concerning the forest.

45. We will not make men justices, constables, sheriffs, or bailiffs, unless they are such as know the law of the realm, and are minded to observe it rightly.

46. All barons who have founded abbeys for which they have charters of the kings of England, or ancient right of tenure, shall have, as they ought to have, their custody when vacant.

47. All forests constituted as such in our time shall straightway be annulled; and the same shall be done for river banks made into places of defence by us in our time.

48. All evil customs concerning forests and warrens, and concerning foresters and warreners, sheriffs and their servants, river banks and their guardians, shall straightway be inquired into in each county, through twelve sworn knights from that county, and shall be eradicated by them, entirely, so that they shall never be renewed, within forty days after the inquest has been made; in such manner that we shall first know about them, or our justice if we be not in England.

49. We shall straightway return all hostages and charters which were delivered to us by Englishmen as a surety for peace or faithful service.

50. We shall entirely remove from their bailiwicks the relatives of Gerard de Athyes, so that they shall henceforth have no bailiwick in England: Engelard de Cygnes, Andrew Peter and Gyon de Chanceles, Gyon de Cygnes, Geoffrey de Martin and his brothers, Philip Mark and his brothers, and Geoffrey his nephew, and the whole following of them.

51. And straightway after peace is restored we shall remove from the realm all the foreign soldiers, crossbowmen, servants, hirelings, who may have come with horses and arms to the harm of the realm.

52. If any one shall have been disseized by us, or removed, without a legal sentence of his peers, from his lands, castles, liberties or lawful right, we shall straightway restore them to him. And if a dispute shall arise concerning this matter it shall be settled according to the judgment of the twenty five barons who are mentioned below as sureties for the peace. But with regard to all those things of which any one was, by king Henry our father or king Richard our brother, disseized or dispossessed without legal judgment of his peers, which we have in our hand or which others hold, and for which we ought to give a guarantee: we shall have respite until the common term for crusaders. Except with regard to those concerning which a plea was moved, or an inquest made by our order, before we took the cross. But when we return from our pilgrimage, or if, by chance, we desist from our pilgrimage, we shall straightway then show full justice regarding them.

53. We shall have the same respite, moreover, and in the same manner, in the matter of showing justice with regard to forests to be annulled and forests to remain, which Henry our father or Richard our brother constituted; and in the matter of wardships of lands which belong to the fee of another—wardships of which kind we have hitherto enjoyed by reason of the fee which some one held from us in military service;—and in the matter of abbeys founded in the fee of another than ourselves—in which the lord of the fee may say that he has jurisdiction. And when we return, or if we desist from our pilgrimage, we shall straightway exhibit full justice to those complaining with regard to these matters.

54. No one shall be taken or imprisoned on account of the appeal of a woman concerning the death of another than her husband.

55. All fines imposed by us unjustly and contrary to the law of the land, and all amerciaments made unjustly and contrary to the law of the land, shall be altogether remitted, or it shall be done with regard to them according

to the judgment of the twenty five barons mentioned below as sureties for the peace, or according to the judgment of the majority of them together with the aforesaid Stephen archbishop of Canterbury, if he can be present, and with others whom he may wish to associate with himself for this purpose. And if he can not be present, the affair shall nevertheless proceed without him ; in such way that, if one or more of the said twenty five barons shall be concerned in a similar complaint, they shall be removed as to this particular decision, and, in their place, for this purpose alone, others shall be substituted who shall be chosen and sworn by the remainder of those twenty five.

56. If we have disseized or dispossessed Welshmen of their lands or liberties or other things without legal judgment of their peers, in England or in Wales,—they shall straightway be restored to them. And if a dispute shall arise concerning this, then action shall be taken upon it in the March through judgment of their peers—concerning English holdings according to the law of England, concerning Welsh holdings according to the law of Wales, concerning holdings in the March according to the law of the March. The Welsh shall do likewise with regard to us and our subjects.

57. But with regard to all those things of which any one of the Welsh was, by king Henry our father or king Richard our brother, disseized or dispossessed without legal judgment of his peers, which we have in our hand or which others hold, and for which we ought to give a guarantee : we shall have respite until the common term for crusaders. Except with regard to those concerning which a plea was moved, or an inquest made by our order, before we took the cross. But when we return from our pilgrimage, or if, by chance, we desist from our pilgrimage, we shall straightway then show full justice regarding them, according to the laws of Wales and the aforesaid districts.

58. We shall straightway return the son of Llewelin and all the Welsh hostages, and the charters delivered to us as surety for the peace.

59. We shall act towards Alexander king of the Scots regarding the restoration of his sisters, and his hostages, and his liberties and his lawful right, as we shall act towards

our other barons of England; unless it ought to be otherwise according to the charters which we hold from William, his father, the former king of the Scots. And this shall be done through judgment of his peers in our court.

60. Moreover all the subjects of our realm, clergy as well as laity, shall, as far as pertains to them, observe, with regard to their vassals, all these aforesaid customs and liberties which we have decreed shall, as far as pertains to us, be observed in our realm with regard to our own.

61. Inasmuch as, for the sake of God, and for the bettering of our realm, and for the more ready healing of the discord which has arisen between us and our barons, we have made all these aforesaid concessions,—wishing them to enjoy for ever entire and firm stability, we make and grant to them the following security: that the barons, namely, may elect at their pleasure twenty five barons from the realm, who ought, with all their strength, to observe, maintain and cause to be observed, the peace and privileges which we have granted to them and confirmed by this our present charter. In such wise, namely, that if we, or our justice, or our bailiffs, or any one of our servants shall have transgressed against any one in any respect, or shall have broken some one of the articles of peace or security, and our transgression shall have been shown to four barons of the aforesaid twenty five: those four barons shall come to us, or, if we are abroad, to our justice, showing to us our error; and they shall ask us to cause that error to be amended without delay. And if we do not amend that error, or, we being abroad, if our justice do not amend it within a term of forty days from the time when it was shown to us or, we being abroad, to our justice: the aforesaid four barons shall refer the matter to the remainder of the twenty five barons, and those twenty five barons, with the whole land in common, shall distrain and oppress us in every way in their power,—namely, by taking our castles, lands and possessions, and in every other way that they can, until amends shall have been made according to their judgment. Saving the persons of ourselves, our queen and our children. And when amends shall have been made they shall be in accord with us as they had been previously. And whoever of the land wishes to do so,

shall swear that in carrying out all the aforesaid measures he will obey the mandates of the aforesaid twenty five barons, and that, with them, he will oppress us to the extent of his power. And, to any one who wishes to do so, we publicly and freely give permission to swear; and we will never prevent any one from swearing. Moreover, all those in the land who shall be unwilling, themselves and of their own accord, to swear to the twenty five barons as to distraining and oppressing us with them : such ones we shall make to swear by our mandate, as has been said. And if any one of the twenty five barons shall die, or leave the country, or in any other way be prevented from carrying out the aforesaid measures,—the remainder of the aforesaid twenty five barons shall choose another in his place, according to their judgment, who shall be sworn in the same way as the others. Moreover, in all things entrusted to those twenty five barons to be carried out, if those twenty five shall be present and chance to disagree among themselves with regard to some matter, or if some of them, having been summoned, shall be unwilling or unable to be present: that which the majority of those present shall decide or decree shall be considered binding and valid, just as if all the twenty five had consented to it. And the aforesaid twenty five shall swear that they will faithfully observe all the foregoing, and will cause them to be observed to the extent of their power. And we shall obtain nothing from any one, either through ourselves or through another, by which any of those concessions and liberties may be revoked or diminished. And if any such thing shall have been obtained, it shall be vain and invalid, and we shall never make use of it either through ourselves or through another.

62. And we have fully remitted to all, and pardoned, all the ill-will, anger and rancour which have arisen between us and our subjects, clergy and laity, from the time of the struggle. Moreover we have fully remitted to all, clergy and laity, and—as far as pertains to us—have pardoned fully all the transgressions committed, on the occasion of that same struggle, from Easter of the sixteenth year of our reign until the re-establishment of peace. In witness of which, moreover, we have caused to be drawn up for

them letters patent of lord Stephen, archbishop of Canterbury, lord Henry, archbishop of Dublin, and the aforesaid bishops and master Pandulf, regarding that surety and the aforesaid concessions.

63. Wherefore we will and firmly decree that the English church shall be free, and that the subjects of our realm shall have and hold all the aforesaid liberties, rights and concessions, duly and in peace, freely and quietly, fully and entirely, for themselves and their heirs, from us and our heirs, in all matters and in all places, forever, as has been said. Moreover it has been sworn, on our part as well as on the part of the barons, that all these above mentioned provisions shall be observed with good faith and without evil intent. The witnesses being the above mentioned and many others. Given through our hand, in the plain called Runnimede between Windsor and Stanes, on the fifteenth day of June, in the seventeenth year of our reign.

VIII.

STATUTE OF MORTMAIN (1279).

(Stubbs' "Charters," p. 457.)

The king to his Justices of the Bench, greeting. Whereas of late it was provided that religious men should not enter into the fees of any without the will and licence of the lords in chief of whom these fees are held immediately; and such religious men have, notwithstanding, later entered as well into their own fees as into those of others, appropriating them to themselves, and buying them, and sometimes receiving them from the gift of others, whereby the services which are due of such fees, and which at the beginning, were provided for the defence of the realm, are unduly withdrawn, and the lords in chief do lose their escheats of the same; we, therefore, to the profit of our realm, wishing to provide a fit remedy in this matter, by advice of our prelates, counts and other subjects of our realm who are of our council, have provided, established, and ordained, that no person, religious or other, whatsoever he be, shall presume to buy or sell any lands or tenements, or under colour of gift or lease, or of any other term or title whatever to receive them from any one, or in any other way, by craft or by wile to appropriate them to himself, whereby such lands and tenements may come into mortmain; under pain of forfeiture of the same. We have provided also that if any person, religious or other, do presume either by craft or wile to offend against this statute, it shall be lawful for us and for other immediate lords in chief of the fee so alienated, to enter it within a year from the time of such alienation and to hold it in fee as an inheritance. And if the immediate lord in chief shall be negligent and be not willing to enter into such fee within the year, then it shall be lawful for the next mediate lord in chief, within the half year following, to enter that fee and to hold it, as has been said; and thus each mediate lord may do if the next lord be negligent in entering such fee, as has been said. And if all such chief lords of such fee, who shall be of full age and within the four seas and out of prison, shall be for one year negligent or remiss in this matter, we, straightway after the year is completed from the time when such purchases, gifts, or appropriations of another kind happen to have been made, shall take such lands and tenements into our hand, and shall enfief others therein by certain services to be rendered thence to us for the defence of our kingdom; saving to the lords in chief of the same fees their wards, escheats and other things which pertain to them, and the services therefrom due and accustomed. And therefore we command you to cause the aforesaid statute to be read before you, and from henceforth to be firmly kept and observed. Witness myself at Westminster, the 15th day of November, the 7th year of our reign.

IX.

STATUTE OF 1290 CONCERNING THE BUYING AND SELLING OF LAND (*Quia emptores*).

Forasmuch as purchasers of lands and tenements of the fees of magnates and others, have many times previously entered into their fees to the prejudice of the same (lords), since to them (the purchasers) the free tenants of these same magnates and others have sold their lands and tenements to be held in fee for themselves and their heirs from the subinfeudators and not from the lords in chief of the fees, whereby the same lords in chief have often lost the escheats, marriages and wardships of lands and tenements belonging to their fees, which thing indeed seemed very hard and extreme to the magnates and other lords, and moreover, in this case, manifest disinheritance ; the lord king in his parliament at Westminster after Easter in the 18th year of his reign, viz., in the Quinzime of St. John the Baptist, at the instance of his magnates, did grant, provide and decree that henceforth it shall be lawful for any free man to sell at will his lands or tenements or a part of them ; in such manner, however, that the infeudated person shall hold that land or tenement from the same lord in chief and by the same services and customs by which his infeudator previously held them. And if he shall have sold to any one any part of those his lands or tenements, the infeudated person shall hold that (part) directly of the lord in chief, and shall straightway be charged with as much service as pertains or ought to pertain to that lord for that parcel, according to the quantity of the land or tenement sold ; and so in this case there shall fall away from the lord in chief that part of the service which is to be performed by the hand of the infeudator, from the time when the infeudated person ought to be attendant and answerable to that same lord in chief, according to the quantity of the land or tenement sold, for that parcel of service thus due. And it must be known that by the said sales or purchases of lands or tenements, or any part of them, those lands or tenements in part or in whole, may not come into mortmain, by art or by wile, contrary to the statute recently issued on this point. And it is to be known that that statute concerning lands sold holds good only for those holding in fee simple, etc. ; and that it extends to future time ; and it shall begin to take effect at the feast of St. Andrew next coming.

X.

THE MANNER OF HOLDING PARLIAMENT.

(Stubbs' "Charters," p. 502.)

Here is described the manner in which the parliament of the king of England and of his English was held in the time of king Edward, son of king Ethelred. Which manner, indeed, was expounded by the more discreet men of the kingdom in the presence of William, duke of Normandy, and Conqueror and king of England, the Conqueror himself commanding this; and was approved by him, and was customary in his times and also in the times of his successors, the kings of England.

The Summoning of Parliament.

The summoning of parliament ought to precede the first day of parliament by forty days.

To the parliament ought to be summoned and to come, by reason of their tenure, each and all the archbishops, bishops, abbots, priors, and, by reason of such tenure, the other greater clergy who are holders of a county or a barony; and none of the lesser, unless their presence and coming is required otherwise than on account of their tenures: that is, if they belong to the king's council, or if their presence is thought useful or necessary to the parliament. And the king is required to furnish their outlays and expenses in coming to and remaining at the parliament. Nor should such lesser clergy receive a summons to parliament; but the king usually sent his writs at the proper time, requesting that they might be present at his parliament.

Likewise the king used to send his summons separately to the archbishops, bishops and other exempt persons—such as the abbots, priors, deans and other ecclesiastical persons who have jurisdictions through such exemptions and privileges—to the effect that they, for each deanery and archdeanery of England, should, through the deaneries and archdeaneries themselves, cause to be elected two skilled and suitable representatives for their own archdeanery, who should come to and be present at the parliament in order to submit to, to assert and to do, the same thing as every one and all the persons of those deaneries and archdeaneries would have done, had they there been personally present.

And such representatives should come with their warrants duplicated, signed with the seals of their superiors, to the effect that they, as members of the clergy, are sent to be such representatives; of which letters one shall be given over to the clerks of parliament to be enrolled, and the other shall remain with the representatives themselves. And thus, under these two forms, the whole clergy ought to be summoned to parliament.

Concerning Lay Members.

Likewise each and all the earls and barons and their peers ought to be summoned and to come; that is, those who have lands and revenues of the value of a county— twenty knights' fees, namely, each fee being computed at yearly twenty pounds' worth, which makes four hundred pounds worth in all: or of the value of one whole barony —thirteen fees, namely, and the third part of one knight's fee; each fee being computed at twenty pounds' worth, which makes in all four hundred marks. And no lesser laymen ought to be summoned, or to come to parliament by reason of their tenure, unless their presence be useful or necessary to the parliament from other causes; and then it should be done concerning them as has been said is done concerning the lesser clergy, who are not at all bound by reason of their tenure to come to parliament.

Concerning the Barons of the Ports.

Likewise the king is bound to send his writs to the warden of the Cinque Ports, to the effect that he shall cause to be elected from each port, through the port itself, two suitable and skilled barons to come and be present at his (the king's) parliament; in order to answer, to submit to, to assert and to do the same thing as their baronies; just as if, from those baronies, each and every man were there in person. And such barons shall come with their warrants duplicated, signed with the common seals of their ports, to the effect that they were duly elected for this purpose, and were given their powers and were sent for those baronies. Of which warrants one shall be given to the clerks of the parliament, and the other shall remain with the barons themselves. And when such barons of the ports, having obtained permission, had made their retreat from the parliament, then they were accustomed to have a writ under the great seal of the warden of the Cinque Ports, to the effect that he would cause to be paid the reasonable outlays and expenses of such barons, by the community of the port in question, from the first day on which they started towards the parliament, until the day when they returned to their home; express mention, moreover, being made, in that writ, of the stay which they had made at parliament, of the day on which they arrived, and that on which they had been given permission to return. And, sometimes, they used to make mention in the writ of how much such barons ought to receive daily from those communities; some, namely, more, some less, according to the capacities, distinction, and reputation of the persons. Nor was there usually expended for the two barons daily more than twenty shillings—consideration being had for their habits, labours and expenses. Nor are such expenses usually paid for certain by the court, without regard to whom the persons thus elected and sent by the communities may be; unless the persons themselves have been honest and of good conduct in parliament.

Concerning the Knights.

Likewise the king was accustomed to send his writs to all the sheriffs of England, to the effect that they should each cause to be elected from their county, by the county itself, two suitable honest and skilled knights to come to his parliament; in the same manner as has been described with regard to the barons of the ports. And it shall be the same concerning their warrants. But for the expenses of two knights from one county, it is not usual to pay more than one mark a day.

Concerning Citizens.

In the same way he was accustomed to send an order to the mayor and sheriffs of London, and to the mayor and bailiffs, or the mayor and citizens, of York and the other cities: to the effect that they, for their cities as a whole, should elect two suitable, honest and skilled citizens, to come to, and be present at parliament; in the same manner as has been described concerning the barons of the Cinque Ports and the knights of the shires. And the citizens were accustomed to be on the same footing, and equal, with the knights of the shires, as regards the expenses of coming, remaining, and returning.

Concerning Burgesses.

Likewise, in the same manner, there used to be, and should be, an order sent to the bailiffs and trustworthy men of the burroughs, to the effect that they, from themselves and for themselves, shall elect two suitable, honest and skilled burgesses to come and be present at parliament; in the same manner as has been described concerning the citizens. But two burgesses did not usually receive for their expenses for one day more than ten shillings, and sometimes more than half a mark; and this was usually estimated, by the court, according to the magnitude and power of the burrough, and according to the distinction of the persons sent.

Concerning the principal Clerks of Parliament.

Likewise two principal clerks of parliament shall sit in the midst of the justices, and shall enroll all the pleas and transactions of parliament.

And be it known that those two clerks are not subject to any justices whatever; nor is there any justice of England in parliament. Nor have justices of themselves the right of recording in parliament, unless a new power has been assigned or given them in parliament through the king or the peers of parliament: as when they are assigned, with other members of parliament, to hear and dispose of different petitions and complaints put forth in parliament. And those two clerks are directly subject to the king and to his parliament in common, unless it happens that one or two justices are assigned to them to examine and correct their enrollments. And when peers of parliament have been assigned to hear and examine, apart by themselves, any petitions: then, when they shall have become united and concordant in rendering judgment concerning such petitions, they shall both explain the proceedings that have taken place concerning them, and shall render their judgments in full parliament;—chiefly so that those two clerks may enroll all pleas and all judgments in the principal roll of parliament, and may surrender those same rolls to the treasurer of the king before parliament shall be dismissed; so that those rolls shall, by all means, be in the treasury before the breaking up of parliament; excepting however a transcript therefrom, or a counter-roll, belonging to those same clerks if they wish to have it. Those two clerks, unless they have another office under the king, and hold fiefs from him so that they can live respectably therefrom, shall receive from the king daily one mark, in equal portions, for their expenses. Unless they are at the table of the lord king; in which case they shall receive, besides their meals, a half a mark in equal portions daily, throughout the whole of parliament.

Concerning the Five Clerks.

Likewise the king shall assign five skilled and approved clerks; of whom the first shall minister to, and serve, the bishops; the second, the representatives of the clergy; the third, the counts and barons; the fourth, the knights of the shires; the fifth, the citizens and burgesses. And each of them, unless he be with the king and receive from him such a fee, or such wages, that he can honestly live from them, shall receive from the king daily two shillings. Unless they are at the table of the lord king; in which case they shall receive daily ten pence. And these clerks shall write down the objections and responses which they (the bishops, clergy, etc.) make to the king and the parliament; and shall be present at their councils whenever they wish to have them. And, when they (the clerks) are at leisure, they shall aid the principal clerks with their enrollments.

Concerning difficult Cases and Judgments.

When a dispute, a doubt, or a difficult case, whether of peace or war, comes up in the kingdom or out of it,—that case shall be drawn up in writing and read in full parliament; and shall be treated of and disputed there among the peers of parliament; and, if it be necessary, it shall be enjoined—through the king, or on the part of the king if he be not present—on each of the grades of peers, that each grade shall go apart by itself; and that that case shall be delivered to their clerk in writing; and that they, in a fixed place, shall cause that case to be read before them, so that they may ordain and consider among themselves how, in that case, they shall best and most justly proceed; according as they themselves are willing to answer before God for the person of the king, and for their own persons, and also for the persons of those whose persons they represent. And they shall draw up in writing their replies and views; so that when all their responses, plans and views, on this side and on that, have been heard, it may be proceeded according to the better and more healthful plan, and according as, at length, the majority of the parliament shall agree. And if, through discord between them and the king and some magnates—or, perhaps, between the magnates themselves—the peace of the kingdom is endangered, or the people or the country troubled; so that it seems to the king and his council to be expedient that that matter shall be treated of and emended through the attention of all the peers of his kingdom; or if, through war, the king or the kingdom are in trouble; or if a difficult case come up before the chancellor of England; or a difficult judgment be about to be rendered before the justices, and so on: and if perchance, in such deliberations, all, or at least the majority, can not come to an agreement;—then the earl seneschal, the earl constable, the earl marshall, or two of them, shall elect twenty five persons from all the peers of the realm—two bishops, namely, and three representatives for the whole clergy; two counts, and three barons; five knights of the shires; five citizens, and five burgesses;—which make twenty five. And those twenty five can elect from themselves twelve and resolve themselves into that number; and those twelve, six, and resolve themselves into that number; and those who were hitherto six, three, and resolve themselves into that number. And those three can not resolve themselves into fewer, unless by obtaining permission from our lord the king. And, if the king consent, those three can resolve into two; and of those two, one into the other; and so at length that man's decision shall stand above the whole parliament. And thus, by resolving from twenty five persons into one single person,—if a greater number cannot be concordant and make a decision,—at last one person alone, as has been said, who cannot disagree with himself, shall decide for all; it being allowed to our master the king, and to his council, to examine and amend such decisions after they have been written out—if they can and will do this. In such manner that this same shall then be done in full parliament, and with the consent of the parliament, and not behind the parliament.

Concerning the Business of Parliament.

The matters for which parliament has been summoned ought to be deliberated upon according to the calendar of parliament, and according to the order of the petitions delivered and filed; no respect being had for the persons of any one; but he who first made a proposition shall act first. In the calendar of parliament all the business of parliament should be called up in this order: first what concerns war, if there is war, and what concerns other matters relating to the persons of the king, the queen and their children; secondly, what concerns the common affairs of the kingdom, such as the making of laws against defects of original laws, judicial and executive, after the judgments have been rendered—which things, most of all, are common affairs; thirdly, there should be called the separate matters, and this according to the order of the petitions filed, as has been said.

Concerning the Days and Hours for Parliament.

Parliament ought not to be held on Sundays, but it can be held on all other days; that day always being excepted, and three others, viz.: All Saints', and Souls', and the nativity of John the Baptist. And it ought to begin each day in the middle of the first hour; at which hour the king is bound to be present in parliament, together with all the peers of the kingdom. And parliament ought to be held in a public place, and not in a private nor in a secret place. On feast days parliament ought to begin at the first hour, on account of the Divine Service.

Concerning the Grades of Peers.

The king is the head, beginning and end of parliament; and thus he has no peer in his grade, and the first grade consists of the king alone. The second grade consists of the archbishops, bishops, abbots, priors, who hold by barony. The third grade consists of the representatives of the clergy. The fourth, of earls, barons, and other magnates and chiefs, whose holding is of the value of a county and barony—as has been explained in the clause concerning laymen. The fifth is of knights of the shires. The sixth, of citizens and burgesses. And thus parliament consists of six grades. But it must be known that even though any one of the said grades except the king be absent—provided, however, that all have been forewarned by reasonable summonses of parliament—nevertheless, it shall be considered as a full parliament.

Concerning the Manner of Parliament.

Having first shown under what form and at what time the summons of parliament ought to be made to each one; and who ought to come by summons and who not; we must, in the second place, tell who they are who ought to come by reason of their offices, and who are bound to be present through the whole parliament, without summons. Wherefore it is to be noted that these officials, the two principal clerks of parliament elected by the king and his council, and the other secondary clerks—of whom and whose offices we shall speak more especially hereafter,—and the chief crier of England with his sub-criers, and the chief usher of England—which two offices, that is, the office of the crier and of the usher, used to belong to one and the same person:—are bound to be present on the first day. The chancellor of England, the treasurer, the chamberlain, and the barons of the exchequer, the justices, all the clerks and knights of the king, together with those who serve the king with regard to the pleas, and who are of the king's council: are bound to be present on the second day, unless they have reasonable excuses for not being present; and then they ought to send good excuses.

Concerning the Opening of Parliament.

The lord king shall sit in the middle of the greater bench, and shall be bound to be present on the first and sixth day of parliament. And the chancellor, the treasurer, the barons of the exchequer, and the justices, were accustomed to record the defaults made in parliament, in the following order. On the first day the burgesses and citizens of all England shall be called; on which day if they do not come the burrough shall be fined a hundred marks and the city a hundred pounds. On the second day, the knights of the shires of all England shall be called; on which day if they do not appear, the county whence they are shall be fined a hundred pounds. On the third day of parliament shall be called the barons of the Cinque Ports, and after that the barons, and after that the earls; whereupon if the barons of the Cinque Ports do not appear, that barony whence they are shall be fined a hundred marks. In like manner an ordinary baron shall be fined a hundred marks, and an earl a hundred pounds. And in like manner shall be done in the case of those who are the peers of earls and barons; that is, who have lands and revenues to the value of one county or one barony; as has been explained before in the chapter concerning the summoning. On the fourth day shall be called the representatives of the clergy; on which day, if they do not come, their bishops shall be fined a hundred marks for each archdeanery that has made default. On the fifth day shall be called the deans, priors, abbots, bishops, and, at length, the archbishops. And if they do not come, each archbishop shall be fined a hundred pounds; a bishop holding a whole barony a hundred marks; and it shall be done likewise with regard to the abbots, priors, and others. On the first day a proclamation should be made —first in the hall, or monastery, or in any public place where the parliament is held, and afterwards publicly in the city or town,—to the effect that all those who wish to deliver petitions and complaints to the parliament, should deliver them within the five days immediately following the first day of parliament.

Concerning the Preaching to the Parliament.

An archbishop, or bishop, or one of the greater clergy who is discreet and eloquent, and who is chosen by the archbishop in whose province the parliament is held, should preach, on one of those first five days of parliament; in full parliament and in the presence of the king; and this, when parliament shall have been for the most part united and assembled together. And, in his discourse, he shall suitably enjoin on the whole parliament with him, humbly to supplicate God, and adore Him, for the peace and tranquillity of the king and kingdom; as will be more specially explained in the following chapter on the announcement to the parliament.

Concerning the Announcement in Parliament.

After the preaching, the chancellor of England or the chief justice of England—that is, he who holds the pleas before the king,—or another suitable honest and eloquent justice or clerk, chosen by the chancellor and chief justice themselves; should announce the cases of parliament, first in general and afterwards in particular, standing. And here be it made known that each of the members of parliament, whoever he be, excepting the king, shall stand when speaking, so that all the members of parliament may be able to hear him ; and if he speak obscurely, or too low, he shall repeat what he is saying and shall speak more loudly, or another shall speak for him.

Concerning the Address of the King after the Announcement.

The king, after the announcement, ought, on behalf of the parliament, to ask the clergy and laity, naming all their grades—namely the archbishops, bishops, abbots, priors, archdeacons, representatives and others of the clergy, counts, barons, knights, citizens, burgesses, and other laymen—that they diligently, studiously and heartily labour to treat of and deliberate upon the business of parliament : according as they shall learn and feel, in the first place that this is. principally and chiefly, according to the will of God ; and secondly, that such things will be of advantage to his (the king's) and their own honour.

Concerning the Absence of the King from Parliament.

The king is in every way bound to be personally present in parliament, unless he be detained by bodily sickness ; and then he can keep his room, provided it do not lie beyond the manor, or at least the town, where the parliament is held ; in which case he ought to send for twelve of the greater and more illustrious men who have been summoned to parliament : two bishops, namely, two earls, two barons, two knights of the shires, two citizens and two burgesses,—to view his person and testify about his condition. And, in their presence, he ought to enjoin upon the archbishop of the place, the seneschal, and his chief justice, that they together and separately shall begin and continue the parliament in his name ; express mention being made then, in that commission, of the cause of his absence : which proceedings ought to suffice and, together with the clear testimony of the said twelve men their peers, to convince the other nobles and magnates of parliament. The reason for all this is, that there used to be a clamour and a murmur in parliament on account of the absence of the king; for it is hurtful and dangerous to the whole community of the parliament, and even of the kingdom, when the king is absent from parliament; nor should he nor may he absent himself, unless only in the aforesaid case.

Concerning the Position and Seatings in Parliament.

First, as has been said, the king shall sit in the middle place of the chief bench; and on his right side shall sit the archbishop of Canterbury, and on his left side the archbishop of York; and directly after them the bishops abbots and priors in a line: always in such manner, with regard to the aforesaid grades and their positions, that no one shall be seated except among his peers. And the seneschal of England shall be bound to see to this, unless the king appoint another. At the foot of the king, on the right, shall sit the chancellor of England and the chief justice of England; and their companions and their clerks who belong to the parliament.

Concerning the Usher of Parliament.

The principal usher of parliament shall stand within the great door of the monastery, hall or other place where the parliament is held, and shall guard the door; so that no one shall enter parliament unless he whose duty it is to be present at and attend the parliament, or he who shall have been summoned on account of some matter which is going on in parliament. And it ought to be so that that usher has knowledge of the persons who ought to enter; so that to no one at all shall ingress be denied, who is bound to be present at the parliament. And that usher may, and ought to, if it be necessary, have several ushers under him.

Concerning the Crier of Parliament.

The crier of parliament shall stand without the door of the parliament, and the usher shall announce to him what

he is to cry. The king usually sent his men-at-arms to
stand in the great space before the door of parliament, to
guard the door, so that no one should make attacks against
the door or disturbances before it, through which the parliament might be impeded, under penalty of bodily capture. For according to law the door of parliament may
not be closed, but shall be guarded by the usher and the
men-at-arms of the king.

Concerning the Standing of those who speak.

All the peers of parliament shall sit, and no one shall
stand except when he speaks ; and he shall so speak that
every one in parliament may hear him. No one shall
enter the parliament, or go out from parliament, unless
through the one door ; and whenever any one says something that is to be deliberated upon by the parliament, he
shall always stand when he speaks ; the reason is that he
may be heard by his peers, for all his peers are judges and
justices.

Concerning Aid to the King.

The king does not usually ask aid from his kingdom
unless for imminent war, or for knighting his sons, or for
marrying his daughters ; and then such aids ought to be
sought in full parliament ; and to be delivered in writing
to each grade of the peers of parliament ; and to be replied to in writing. And be it known that if such aids
are to be granted, all the peers of parliament ought to
consent. And be it known that the two knights who come
to parliament for the shire, have a greater voice in parliament, in granting and refusing, than a greater earl of
England ; and, likewise, the representatives of the clergy
of one bishopric have a greater voice in parliament, if they
are all of one mind, than the bishop himself. And this is
the case in all matters which ought to be granted, refused
or done through the parliament. And this is evident, that
the king can hold parliament with the commonality of his
kingdom, without the bishops earls and barons, provided
they have been summoned to parliament, even though no

bishop, earl or baron, answer to his summons. For, formerly, kings held their parliaments when no bishop, earl or baron was present. But it is another matter, on the contrary, if the commonality—the clergy and laity— have been summoned to parliament, as they have a right to be, and are not willing to come for certain causes ; as if they were to maintain that the lord king did not rule them as he ought to, and were to signify in what especial respect he did not do so ; then it would not be a parliament at all, even though the archbishops, bishops, counts and barons and all their peers, were present with the king. And so it is necessary that all things which are to be affirmed or cancelled, granted or denied, or done by the parliament, should be granted by the commonality of the parliament, which consists of the three grades or divisions of parlia- ment : viz. of the representatives of the clergy, the knights of the shires, the citizens and burgesses, who represent the whole commonality of England ; and not by the magnates. For each of them is in parliament for his own person alone, and not for any one else.

Concerning the Dismissal of Parliament.

Parliament ought not to be dismissed so long as any petition remains undiscussed ; or, at least, any to which the reply has not been determined on. And, if the king permits the contrary, he is perjured. No single one of the peers of parliament can or may retire from parliament, un- less permission to that effect has been obtained from the king, and from all his peers ; and this in full parliament. And of such permission a memorandum shall be made in the roll of parliament. And if any one of the peers, while parliament is in session, shall become ill, so that he can not come to parliament, then for three days he shall send excusers to the parliament. And if he do not then come there shall be sent to him two of his peers, to view and testify to such infirmity ; and if there be suspicion, those two peers shall swear that in this matter they tell the truth. And if it shall be found that he has been feigning, he shall be fined as if for default. And if he have not been feigning, then he shall, in their presence, empower some suitable person to be present in parliament for him ; nor can a healthy man be excused if he be of sound mind.

The dismissal of parliament is, by custom, managed thus :—First it should be asked and publicly proclaimed in parliament, and within the confines of parliament, if there is any one who has handed in a petition to the parliament, and has not yet received a reply. But, if no one calls out, it is to be supposed that every one has been satisfied, or at least a reply given as far as there lawfully can. And then at length, indeed, when no one who has handed in his petition this term calls out, we shall dismiss our Parliament.

Concerning Copies of Records in Parliament.

The clerks of parliament shall not deny to any one a copy of his process, but shall deliver it to whoever seeks it ; and they shall receive always for ten lines one penny ; unless, indeed, an oath is made of insolvency ; in which case they shall receive nothing. Rolls of parliament shall measure in width ten inches. Parliament shall be held in whatever place of the kingdom it pleases the king.

Here ends the Manner of holding Parliament.

XI.

THE STATUTE OF LABORERS.

("Statutes of the Realm," vol. i. p. 307.)

Edward by the grace of God etc. to the reverend father in Christ William, by the same grace archbishop of Canterbury, Primate of all England, greeting. Because a great part of the people and especially of the workmen and servants has now died in that pestilence, some, seeing the straights of the masters and the scarcity of servants, are not willing to serve unless they receive excessive wages, and others, rather than through labour to gain their living, prefer to beg in idleness : We, considering the grave inconveniences which might come from the lack especially of ploughmen and such labourers, have held deliberation

and treaty concerning this with the prelates and nobles
and other learned men sitting by us; by whose consentient
counsel we have seen fit to ordain: that every man and
woman of our kingdom of England, of whatever condition,
whether bond or free, who is able bodied and below the
age of sixty years, not living from trade nor carrying on
a fixed craft, nor having of his own the means of living, or
land of his own with regard to the cultivation of which he
might occupy himself, and not serving another,—if he,
considering his station, be sought after to serve in a suitable service, he shall be bound to serve him who has seen
fit so to seek after him; and he shall take only the wages,
liveries, meed or salary which, in the places where he
sought to serve, were accustomed to be paid in the twentieth
year of our reign of England, or the five or six common
years next preceding. Provided, that in thus retaining
their service, the lords are preferred before others of their
bondsmen or their land tenants: so, nevertheless that
such lords thus retain as many as shall be necessary and
not more; and if any man or woman, being thus sought
after in service, will not do this, the fact being proven by
two faithful men before the sheriffs or the bailiffs of our
lord the king, or the constables of the town where this
happens to be done,—straightway through them, or some
one of them, he shall be taken and sent to the next jail,
and there he shall remain in strict custody until he shall
find surety for serving in the aforesaid form.

And if a reaper or mower, or other workman or servant,
of whatever standing or condition he be, who is retained in
the service of any one, do depart from the said service
before the end of the term agreed, without permission or
reasonable cause, he shall undergo the penalty of imprisonment, and let no one, under the same penalty, presume to
receive or retain such a one in his service. Let no one,
moreover, pay or permit to be paid to any one more wages,
livery, meed or salary than was customary as has been
said; nor let any one in any other manner exact or receive
them, under penalty of paying to him who feels himself
aggrieved from this, double the sum that has thus been
paid or promised, exacted or received; and if such person
be not willing to prosecute, then it (the sum) is to be given

to any one of the people who shall prosecute in this matter;
and such prosecution shall take place in the court of
the lord of the place where such case shall happen. And
if the lords of the towns or manors presume of themselves
or through their servants in any way to act contrary to this
our present ordinance, then in the Counties, Wapentakes
and Trithings suit shall be brought against them in
the aforesaid form for the triple penalty (of the sum) thus
promised or paid by them or their servants; and if perchance, prior to the present ordinance any one shall have
covenanted with any one thus to serve for more wages, he
shall not be bound by reason of the said covenant to pay
more than at another time was wont to be paid to such
person; nay, under the aforesaid penalty he shall not presume to pay more.

Likewise saddlers, skinners, white-tawers, cordwainers,
tailors, smiths, carpenters, masons, tilers, shipwrights,
carters and all other artisans and labourers shall not take
for their labour and handiwork more than what, in the
places where they happen to labour, was customarily paid
to such persons in the said twentieth year and in the other
common years preceding, as has been said; and if any man
take more, he shall be committed to the nearest jail in the
manner aforesaid.

Likewise let butchers, fishmongers, hostlers, brewers,
bakers, pulters and all other vendors of any victuals, be
bound to sell such victuals for a reasonable price, having
regard for the price at which such victuals are sold in the
adjoining places: so that such vendors may have moderate
gains, not excessive, according as the distance of the places
from which such victuals are carried may seem reasonably
to require; and if any one sell such victuals in another
manner, and be convicted of it in the aforesaid way,
he shall pay the double of that which he received to
the party injured, or in default of him, to another who
shall be willing to prosecute in this behalf; and the mayor
and bailiffs of the cities and burroughs, merchant towns
and others, and of the maritime ports and places shall have
power to enquire concerning each and every one who shall
in any way err against this, and to levy the aforesaid
penalty for the benefit of those at whose suit such delin-

quents shall have been convicted; and in case that the same mayor and bailiffs shall neglect to carry out the aforesaid, and shall be convicted of this before justices to be assigned by us, then the same mayor and bailiffs shall be compelled through the same justices, to pay to such wronged person or to another prosecuting in his place, the treble of the thing thus sold, and nevertheless, on our part too, they shall be grievously punished.

And because many sound beggars do refuse to labour so long as they can live from begging alms, giving themselves up to idleness and sins, and, at times, to robbery and other crimes—let no one, under the aforesaid pain of imprisonment presume, under colour of piety or alms to give anything to such as can very well labour, or to cherish them in their sloth,—so that thus they may be compelled to labour for the necessaries of life.

BOOK II. THE EMPIRE.

INTRODUCTION.

OF all the German stem-tribes that descended upon the Roman provinces and took possession of them either by treaty or by conquest, none was destined to play a lasting *rôle* in European history except the Franks. Eastern and Western Goths, Vandals and Burgundians were to lose their power after a brief space and to vanish from their new settlements. But the Franks were to become the leading people in Europe, the patrons of the church, the founders of an almost universal monarchy.

In nothing is the civilizing effect of the conquered Romans on the conquering Germans so clearly to be seen as in the fact that, within half a century after the Franks had settled in Gaul, they proceeded to draw up a code of written laws. Not that the laws themselves contain much that is Roman—the conditions of life were too dissimilar—but it is easy to see in them the Roman desire for order and discipline. There is an effort to assimilate the old institution with the new, to adopt a new *modus vivendi* under completely changed circumstances. Tribes that remained on purely German soil—take the Saxons for instance—needed no such rules and regulations; they managed for centuries to live without them.

No. I. of our documents—the Salic Law—is particularly interesting from the fact that it illustrates a period concerning which we have almost no other contemporary information. A few charters, the scanty notes for this time of Gregory of Tours and the Roman writers, the contents of a few graves—the most important that of Childerich, father of Clovis (481-511), found at Tournay in 1653—are all that we would otherwise have had to show the extent of civilization under the earliest Merovingian kings.

The Salic Law was composed under Clovis. It concerns itself, as will be seen from the extracts here given, with the most manifold branches of administration. The system of landholding, the nature of the early village community, the relations of the Germans to the Romans, the position of the king, the classes of the population, family life, the disposal of property, judicial procedure, the ethical views of the time, are all illustrated in its sixty-five articles. Directly and indirectly we can gather from it a great mass of information. How clearly, for instance, does the title on insults (p. 181) show the regard paid for personal bravery and for female chastity! The false charge of having thrown away one's shield was punished as severely as assault and battery—and the person who groundlessly called a woman unclean paid a fine second only in severity to that imposed for attempted murder!

No. II., the Capitulary of 802, is, in reality, nothing more nor less than the foundation charter of that long-lived institution, the Holy Roman Empire. The latter, as will be remembered, began its existence on Christmas-day, 800, and ended it on August 6th, 1806. Already in Voltaire's time it had ceased to be "either holy, or Roman, or an empire," but its pretensions were kept up until all Germany fell asunder before the wars and the wiles of Napoleon.

This capitulary of Charlemagne is the programme, so to speak, of the young empire. It is the ideal—an ideal never once to be fulfilled—of what that empire should have been. At the head of all things stands the emperor, whose greatest duty it is to provide for the welfare of his subjects. Every male being in his realm who is over twelve years of age has to plight his troth to him. In his hands are justice, morality, and religion. His realm is to be a haven of rest where all discords are to cease and no one to infringe on the rights of another. In his care are all the churches of God, all widows, orphans, and strangers, "for the emperor himself, after God and His saints, has been constituted their protector and defender."

Quite new, in the present document, is the introduction of the "missi dominici"—regular envoys who were to radiate from the emperor as a centre, and bring peace and justice to all parts of the realm. They were to overlook all the different officials, and to listen to complaints against them. So excellent was the institution that one similar to it was adopted in England, where in the time of Henry II. the itinerant justices formed an important feature of the administration.

It is worth while to notice how completely, at this time, the clergy were under the rule of the emperor. The new empire was to be as much of a theocracy as the kingdom of that David whose name Charlemagne bore in the intimate circle of his learned friends. But too soon, alas, the elements of disruption were to make themselves felt. The clergy were to assert their allegiance to a King higher than any earthly monarch, whose commands, as issued and tampered with by His representative on earth, were to be at variance with all the best interests of the emperor. Nationality was to war with universalism, the accepted principles of heredity with the desire for the necessary unity; and with the death of the last Carolingian emperor the empire itself was irretrievably to be cleft and riven.

No. III. is the document by which Louis the Pious

decreed the division of the empire among his three sons, one of whom, however, was to bear the title of emperor and exercise a supervision over the other two. This was a compromise between the unity of the indivisible imperial power and the received principles of heredity.

The greatest advocates of unity had been the clergy, who looked upon the original establishment of the empire as the work of their head, the pope. It was, therefore, from them that the greatest opposition came when, twelve years later, a new son having in the meantime been born to him, Louis tried to nullify the document here given and to undo his own work. Again and again did the luckless emperor have to suffer for trying to disregard an agreement, drawn up and sanctioned, as this had been, by the nobles, the higher clergy and the pope. It is scarcely necessary to remind the reader of how the latter used his personal influence in favour of the elder sons, and of how on the Field of Lies, he successfully exercised his powers of seduction on the troops of the emperor.

After Louis's death the principles of heredity conquered at last the spirit of unity. By the treaty of Verdun (843)— of which unfortunately no authentic document remains— the three separate kingdoms were called into being which afterwards developed into France, Italy and Germany. The empire waned away, but did not die, although for a time the emperors were little more than petty local potentates. It was reserved for Otto the Great to restore it to its pristine glory.

No. IV. is a treaty, entered into in 870, regarding the subdivision of the central one of the three kingdoms founded by the treaty of Verdun. It is given here as showing the beginning of the thousand years' struggle between France and Germany for the possession of the border provinces. It was preliminary to the treaty of Mersen.

No. V. is the so-called Truce of God (Treuga Dei) pub-

lished by the emperor Henry IV. in 1085 to put bounds
to the numerous feuds which were looked upon—much as
the duel is still looked upon by the German nobility—as
the only possible means for wiping away the shame of
certain real or fancied wrongs. To forbid such feuds absolutely was not feasible; no attempt was made to do so
until the year 1495. The present effort to restrict them
met with no success—certainly not in the reign of the unfortunate monarch who made it, and who was finally
deposed, ostensibly because he was unable to restore peace
and quiet to his land.

No. VI. is a similar document issued eighty years later
by Frederick Barbarossa. It will be seen from § 10 that
knights of good family might still engage in wager of
battle against their equals, although, in other respects a
breach of the peace was to be severely punished.

No. VII. concerns the establishment of the Duchy of
Austria in 1156. Austria had hitherto been simply a
margravate and been comprised in the duchy of Bavaria.
The act was performed by Fred. Barbarossa as a compromise. There were two claimants for Bavaria—one the
son of that Henry the Proud who had expected to be made
king in 1137, and who had been rejected for the apparently
paradoxical reason that he already was the most powerful
noble in Germany. Conrad III. had been made king
in his stead and had soon found cause to quarrel with his
powerful rival, conferring Bavaria on his own half brother
the margrave Liutpold. After the death of Henry the
Proud there had been concessions and reconciliations with
regard to Bavaria—but at the end of Conrad's reign the
young Henry the Lion still considered himself the heir,
while the duchy was actually held by the king's brother
Henry of Austria. Frederick Barbarossa in 1156, intent
on the Italian expedition which was to gain him the
imperial crown, hastened to heal the discord between his

two powerful subjects. Henry the Lion received Bavaria, and, in order to appease Henry Jasomirgott, a new duchy was carved out for him. As will be seen from the charter it was enriched with almost unheard of privileges. But great as these were they did not satisfy one of the later dukes of Austria; and some of the most successful of mediæval forgeries distorted in the 14th century the original terms of Frederick's grant.

No. VIII. is the charter issued by Frederick Barbarossa at Gelnhausen in 1180. It commemorates a most important event in German constitutional history. The partition of Saxony was a death blow to the old ducal influence in Germany. There was, henceforth to be a new nobility, basing its claims on its services to the crown and not on its hereditary territorial power.

No. IX. is an interesting decision of a Nuremburg diet rendered in the year 1274. The election of Rudolf of Hapsburg after the long interregnum signified a renewal of the empire even though Rudolf never bore any title but king of the Romans. But how curtailed were his prerogatives compared to those of his predecessors! Future candidates were to be bound more and more by engagements and promises, to submit more and more to the arrogant assumptions of the electoral college. And in certain questions the Count Palatine of the Rhine, and not the King of the Romans was to speak the decisive word.

No. X., the Golden Bull of 1356, was issued for the purpose of determining the form for the election and coronation of the emperor, and also of regulating the duties, rights and privileges of the elector princes. It distinctly defines to whom the electoral rights belong. There had been no doubt about the three archbishoprics or about Bohemia, but disputes had arisen between rival lines both in Saxony and Brandenburg, and the seventh vote was claimed alike by Bavaria and by the Palatinate.

To the electors the Golden Bull gave sovereign rights within their districts. No one could appeal from their decisions; tolls, coinage and treasure trove were to be their perquisites, and offences against their persons were to be punished as high treason. They were to have an important share in the government of the empire.

The Golden Bull is not a law which introduced new features into the constitution. It determined, however, a number of questions that had long been wavering and became an unquestioned authority that was appealed to for centuries. The election of an emperor took place according to its articles so long as the empire lasted. It is important to note that nothing is said concerning the right of the pope, which had been recognized by Louis of Bavaria, to confirm the election.

The Golden Bull was oppressive to the lesser nobility as well as to the cities. The princes who were not electors were now only of secondary rank, and it was probably at this time that one of them, Rudolf IVth, Duke of Austria, took the opportunity of forging privileges to raise his sinking prestige (see above, No. VII.). The regulations concerning Pfalburgers and confederations were a severe blow to civic pride—however expedient they may have been,— and the cities were driven into permanent opposition to the crown. Thus the Golden Bull served to further a process of disintegration which was to lead almost to anarchy and to deaden all feeling of loyalty for the empire.

No. VI. is the formal charter which commemorates the founding of Heidelberg. The Elector of the Palatinate, Ruprecht I., had sent large sums of money to Rome to induce the Pope to confirm the foundation. This papal confirmation was not received until 1385 although the actual work of founding the university had long been in progress. It was the pope who commanded that the arrangement should be that of the Paris university, also that the chancellor should regularly be the prevost of the cathedral at Worms.

Ruprecht was unwearying in his care for his new creation and often spoke of it as his "beloved daughter." The university was consecrated on the 18th of October 1386, and, on the 19th, Marsilius began to lecture on logic, Reginald on the epistle to Titus, Heilmann on the natural philosophy of Aristotle.

Up to the year 1390, when Ruprecht died, 1050 students had attended the university.

I.

THE SALIC LAW.

(Gengler, "Germanische Rechtsdenkmaeler," p. 267.)

Title I. Concerning Summonses.

1. If any one be summoned before the "Thing" by the king's law, and do not come, he shall be sentenced to 600 denars, which make 15 shillings (solidi).

2. But he who summons another, and does not come himself, shall, if a lawful impediment have not delayed him, be sentenced to 15 shillings, to be paid to him whom he summoned.

3. And he who summons another shall walk with witnesses to the home of that man, and, if he be not at home, shall bid the wife or any one of the family to make known to him that he has been summoned to court.

4. But if he be occupied in the king's service he can not summon him.

5. But if he shall be inside the hundred seeing about his own affairs, he can summon him in the manner explained above.

Title II. Concerning Thefts of Pigs, etc.

1. If any one steal a sucking pig, and it be proved against him, he shall be sentenced to 120 denars, which make three shillings.

2. If any one steal a pig that can live without its mother, and it be proved on him, he shall be sentenced to 40 denars—that is, 1 shilling.

14. If any one steal 25 sheep where there were no more in that flock, and it be proved on him, he shall be sentenced to 2500 denars—that is, 62 shillings.

Title III. Concerning Thefts of Cattle.

4. If any one steal that bull which rules the herd and never has been yoked, he shall be sentenced to 1800 denars, which make 45 shillings.

5. But if that bull is used for the cows of three villages in common, he who stole him shall be sentenced to three times 45 shillings.

6. If any one steal a bull belonging to the king he shall be sentenced to 3600 denars, which make 90 shillings.

Title IV. Concerning Damage done among Crops or in any Enclosure.

1. If any one finds cattle, or a horse, or flocks of any kind in his crops, he shall not at all mutilate them.

2. If he do this and confess it, he shall restore the worth of the animal in place of it, and shall himself keep the mutilated one.

3. But if he have not confessed it, and it have been proved on him, he shall be sentenced, besides the value of the animal and the fines for delay, to 600 denars, which make 15 shillings.

Title XI. Concerning Thefts or Housebreakings of Freemen.

1. If any freeman steal, outside of the house, something worth 2 denars, he shall be sentenced to 600 denars, which make 15 shillings.

2. But if he steal, outside of the house, something worth 40 denars, and it be proved on him, he shall be sentenced, besides the amount and the fines for delay, to 1400 denars, which make 35 shillings.

3. If a freeman break into a house and steal something worth 2 denars, and it be proved on him, he shall be sentenced to 15 shillings.

4. But if he shall have stolen something worth more than 5 denars, and it have been proved on him, he shall be sentenced, besides the worth of the object and the fines for delay, to 1400 denars, which make 35 shillings.

5. But if he have broken, or tampered with, the lock, and thus have entered the house and stolen anything from it, he shall be sentenced, besides the worth of the object and the fines for delay, to 1800 denars, which make 45 shillings.

6. And if he have taken nothing, or have escaped by flight, he shall, for the housebreaking alone, be sentenced to 1200 denars, which make 30 shillings.

Title XII. Concerning Thefts or Housebreakings on the Part of Slaves.

1. If a slave steal, outside of the house, something worth two denars, he shall, besides paying the worth of the object and the fines for delay, be stretched out and receive 120 blows.

2. But if he steal something worth 40 denars, he shall either be castrated or pay 6 shillings. But the lord of the slave who committed the theft shall restore to the plaintiff the worth of the object and the fines for delay.

Title XIII. Concerning Rape committed by Freemen.

1. If three men carry off a free born girl, they shall be compelled to pay 30 shillings.

2. If there are more than three, each one shall pay 5 shillings.

3. Those who shall have been present with boats shall be sentenced to three shillings.

4. But those who commit rape shall be compelled to pay 2500 denars, which make 63 shillings.

5. But if they have carried off that girl from behind lock and key, or from the spinning room, they shall be sentenced to the above price and penalty.

6. But if the girl who is carried off be under the king's protection, then the " frith " (peace-money) shall be 2500 denars, which make 63 shillings.

7. But if a bondsman of the king, or a leet, should carry off a free woman, he shall be sentenced to death.

8. But if a free woman have followed a slave of her own will, she shall lose her freedom.

9. If a freeborn man shall have taken an alien bondswoman, he shall suffer similarly.

10. If any body take an alien spouse and join her to himself in matrimony, he shall be sentenced to 2500 denars, which make 63 shillings.

Title XIV. *Concerning Assault and Robbery.*

1. If any one have assaulted and plundered a free man, and it be proved on him, he shall be sentenced to 2500 denars, which make 63 shillings.

2. If a Roman have plundered a Salian Frank, the above law shall be observed.

3. But if a Frank have plundered a Roman, he shall be sentenced to 35 shillings.

4. If any man should wish to migrate, and has permission from the king, and shall have shown this in the public " Thing: " whoever, contrary to the decree of the king, shall presume to oppose him, shall be sentenced to 8000 denars, which make 200 shillings.

Title XV. *Concerning Arson.*

1. If any one shall set fire to a house in which men were sleeping, as many freemen as were in it can make complaint before the " Thing ; " and if any one shall have been burned in it, the incendiary shall be sentenced to 2500 denars, which make 63 shillings.

Title XVII. Concerning Wounds.

1. If any one have wished to kill another person, and the blow have missed, he on whom it was proved shall be sentenced to 2500 denars, which make 63 shillings.

2. If any person have wished to strike another with a poisoned arrow, and the arrow have glanced aside, and it shall be proved on him: he shall be sentenced to 2500 denars, which make 63 shillings.

3. If any person strike another on the head so that the brain appears, and the three bones which lie above the brain shall project, he shall be sentenced to 1200 denars, which make 30 shillings.

4. But if it shall have been between the ribs or in the stomach, so that the wound appears and reaches to the entrails, he shall be sentenced to 1200 denars—which make 30 shillings—besides five shillings for the physician's pay.

5. If any one shall have struck a man so that blood falls to the floor, and it be proved on him, he shall be sentenced to 600 denars, which make 15 shillings.

6. But if a freeman strike a freeman with his fist so that blood does not flow, he shall be sentenced for each blow—up to 3 blows—to 120 denars, which make 3 shillings.

Title XVIII. Concerning him who, before the King, accuses an innocent Man.

If any one, before the king, accuse an innocent man who is absent, he shall be sentenced to 2500 denars, which make 63 shillings.

Title XIX. Concerning Magicians.

1. If any one have given herbs to another so that he die, he shall be sentenced to 200 shillings (or shall surely be given over to fire).

2. If any person have bewitched another, and he who was thus treated shall escape, the author of the crime,

who is proved to have committed it, shall be sentenced to 2500 denars, which make 63 shillings.

Title XXIV. *Concerning the Killing of little children and women.*

1. If any one have slain a boy under 10 years—up to the end of the tenth—and it shall have been proved on him, he shall be sentenced to 24000 denars, which make 600 shillings.

3. If any one have hit a free woman who is pregnant, and she dies, he shall be sentenced to 28000 denars, which make 700 shillings.

6. If any one have killed a free woman after she has begun bearing children, he shall be sentenced to 24000 denars, which make 600 shillings.

7. After she can have no more children, he who kills her shall be sentenced to 8000 denars, which make 200 shillings.

Title XXX. *Concerning Insults.*

3. If any one, man or woman, shall have called a woman harlot, and shall not have been able to prove it, he shall be sentenced to 1800 denars, which make 45 shillings.

4. If any person shall have called another "fox," he shall be sentenced to 3 shillings.

5. If any man shall have called another "hare," he shall be sentenced to 3 shillings.

6. If any man shall have brought it up against another that he have thrown away his shield, and shall not have been able to prove it, he shall be sentenced to 120 denars, which make 3 shillings.

7. If any man shall have called another "spy" or "perjurer," and shall not have been able to prove it, he shall be sentenced to 600 denars, which make 15 shillings.

Title XXXIII. *Concerning the Theft of hunting animals.*

2. If any one have stolen a tame marked stag (-hound?), trained to hunting, and it shall have been proved through witnesses that his master had him for hunting, or had

killed with him two or three beasts, he shall be sentenced to 1800 denars, which make 45 shillings.

Title XXXIV. Concerning the Stealing of Fences.

1. If any man shall have cut 3 staves by which a fence is bound or held together, or have stolen or cut the heads of 3 stakes, he shall be sentenced to 600 denars, which make 15 shillings.

2. If any one shall have drawn a harrow through another's harvest after it has sprouted, or shall have gone through it with a waggon where there was no road, he shall be sentenced to 120 denars, which make 3 shillings.

3. If any one shall have gone, where there is no way or path, through another's harvest which has already become thick, he shall be sentenced to 600 denars, which make 15 shillings.

Title XLI. Concerning the Murder of Free Men.

1. If any one shall have killed a free Frank, or a barbarian living under the Salic law, and it have been proved on him, he shall be sentenced to 8000 denars.

2. But if he shall have thrown him into a well or into the water, or shall have covered him with branches or anything else, to conceal him, he shall be sentenced to 24000 denars, which make 600 shillings.

3. But if any one has slain a man who is in the service of the king, he shall be sentenced to 24000 denars, which make 600 shillings.

4. But if he have put him in the water or in a well, and covered him with anything to conceal him, he shall be sentenced to 72000 denars, which make 1800 shillings.

5. If any one have slain a Roman who eats in the king's palace, and it have been proved on him, he shall be sentenced to 12000 denars, which make 300 shillings.

6. But if the Roman shall not have been a landed proprietor and table companion of the king, he who killed him shall be sentenced to 4000 denars, which make 100 shillings.

7. But if he shall have killed a Roman who was

obliged to pay tribute, he shall be sentenced to 63 shillings.

9. If any one have thrown a free man into a well, and he have escaped alive, he (the criminal) shall be sentenced to 4000 denars, which make 100 shillings.

Title XLV. Concerning Migrators.

1. If any one wish to migrate to another village and if one or more who live in that village do not wish to receive him,—if there be only one who objects, he shall not have leave to move there.

2. But if he shall have presumed to settle in that village in spite of his rejection by one or two men, then some one shall give him warning. And if he be unwilling to go away, he who gives him warning shall give him warning, with witnesses, as follows : I warn thee that thou may'st remain here this next night as the Salic law demands, and I warn thee that within 10 nights thou shalt go forth from this village. After another 10 nights he shall again come to him and warn him again within 10 nights to go away. If he still refuse to go, again 10 nights shall be added to the command, that the number of 30 nights may be full. If he will not go away even then, then he shall summon him to the "Thing," and present his witnesses as to the separate commands to leave. If he who has been warned will not then move away, and no valid reason detains him, and all the above warnings which we have mentioned have been given according to law : then he who gave him warning shall take the matter into his own hands and request the "comes" to go to that place and expel him. And because he would not listen to the law, that man shall relinquish all that he has earned there, and, besides, shall be sentenced to 1200 denars, which make 30 shillings.

3. But if anyone have moved there, and within 12 months no one have given him warning, he shall remain as secure as the other neighbours.

Title XLVI. Concerning Transfers of Property.

1. The observance shall be that the Thunginus or Centenarius shall call together a "Thing," and shall have his

shield in the "Thing," and shall demand three men as witnesses for each of the three transactions. He (the owner of the land to be transferred) shall seek a man who has no connection with himself, and shall throw a stalk into his lap. And to him into whose lap he has thrown the stalk he shall tell, concerning his property, how much of it—or whether the whole or a half—he wishes to give. He in whose lap he threw the stalk shall remain in his (the owner's) house, and shall collect three or more guests, and shall have the property—as much as is given him—in his power. And, afterwards, he to whom that property is entrusted shall discuss all these things with the witnesses collected afterwards, either before the king or in the regular " Thing," he shall give the property up to him for whom it was intended. He shall take the stalk in the " Thing," and, before 12 months are over, shall throw it into the lap of him whom the owner has named heir ; and he shall restore not more nor less, but exactly as much as was entrusted to him.

2. And if any one shall wish to say anything against this, three sworn witnesses shall say that they were in the " Thing " which the " Thunginus " or " Centenarius " called together, and that they saw that man who wished to give his property throw a stalk into the lap of him whom he had selected. They shall name by name him who threw his property into the lap of the other, and, likewise, shall name him whom he named his heir. And three other sworn witnesses shall say that he in whose lap the stalk was thrown had remained in the house of him who gave his property, and had there collected three or more guests, and that they had eaten porridge at table, and that he had collected those who were bearing witness, and that those guests had thanked him for their entertainment. All this those other sworn witnesses shall say, and that he who received that property in his lap in the " Thing " held before the king, or in the regular public " Thing," did publicly, before the people, either in the presence of the king or in public " Thing "—namely on the Mallberg, before the " Thunginus "—throw the stalk into the lap of him whom the owner had named as heir. And thus 9 witnesses shall confirm all this.

Title L. Concerning Promises to Pay.

1. If any freeman or leet have made to another a promise to pay, then he to whom the promise was made shall, within 40 days or within such term as was agreed when he made the promise, go to the house of that man with witnesses, or with appraisers. And if he (the debtor) be unwilling to make the promised payment, he shall be sentenced to 15 shillings above the debt which he had promised.

2. If he then be unwilling to pay, he (the creditor) shall summon him before the " Thing " and thus accuse him : " I ask thee, 'Thunginus,' to bann my opponent who made me a promise to pay and owes me a debt." And he shall state how much he owes and promised to pay. Then the " Thunginus " shall say : " I bann thy opponent to what the Salic law decrees." Then he to whom the promise was made shall warn him (the debtor) to make no payment or pledge of payment to any body else until he have fulfilled his promise to him (the creditor). And straightway on that same day, before the sun sets, he shall go to the house of that man with witnesses, and shall ask if he will pay that debt. If he will not, he (the creditor) shall wait until after sunset ; then, if he have waited until after sunset, 120 denars, which make 3 shillings shall be added on to the debt. And this shall be done up to 3 times in 3 weeks. And if at the third time he will not pay all this, it (the sum) shall increase to 360 denars, or 9 shillings : so, namely, that, after each admonition or waiting until after sunset, 3 shillings shall be added to the debt.

3. If any one be unwilling to fulfil his promise in the regular assembly,—then he to whom the promise was made shall go the count of that place, in whose district he lives, and shall take the stalk and shall say : oh count, that man made me a promise to pay, and I have lawfully summoned him before the court according to the Salic law on this matter ; I pledge thee myself and my fortune that thou may'st safely seize his property. And he shall state the case to him, and shall tell how much he (the debtor) had agreed to pay. Then the count shall collect

7 suitable bailiffs, and shall go with them to the house of him who made the promise and shall say: thou who art here present pay voluntarily to that man what thou didst promise, and choose any two of those bailiffs who shall appraise that from which thou shalt pay; and make good what thou dost owe, according to a just appraisal. But if he will not hear, or be absent, then the bailiffs shall take from his property the value of the debt which he owes. And, according to the law, the accuser shall take two thirds of that which the debtor owes, and the count shall collect for himself the other third as peace money; unless the peace money shall have been paid to him before in this same matter.

4. If the count have been appealed to, and no sufficient reason, and no duty of the king, have detained him—and if he have put off going, and have sent no substitute to demand law and justice: he shall answer for it with his life, or shall redeem himself with his "wergeld."

Title LIV. Concerning the Slaying of a Count.

1. If any one slay a count, he shall be sentenced to 2400 denars, which make 600 shillings.

Title LV. Concerning the Plundering of Corpses.

2. If any one shall have dug up and plundered a corpse already buried, and it shall have been proved on him, he shall be outlawed until the day when he comes to an agreement with the relatives of the dead man, and they ask for him that he be allowed to come among men. And whoever, before he come to an arrangement with the relative, shall give him bread or shelter—even if they are his relations or his own wife—shall be sentenced to 600 denars which make xv shillings.

3. But he who is proved to have committed the crime shall be sentenced to 8000 denars, which make 200 shillings.

Title LVI. Concerning him who shall have scorned to come to Court.

1. If any man shall have scorned to come to court, and shall have put off fulfilling the injunction of the bailiffs, and shall not have been willing to consent to undergo the fine, or the kettle ordeal, or anything prescribed by law: then he (the plaintiff) shall summon him to the presence of the king. And there shall be 12 witnesses who—3 at a time being sworn—shall testify that they were present when the bailiff enjoined him (the accused) either to go to the kettle ordeal, or to agree concerning the fine; and that he had scorned the injunction. Then 3 others shall swear that they were there on the day when the bailiffs enjoined that he should free himself by the kettle ordeal or by composition; and that 40 days after that, in the "mallberg," he (the accuser) had again waited until after sunset, and that he (the accused) would not obey the law. Then he (the accuser) shall summon him before the king for a fortnight thence; and three witnesses shall swear that they were there when he summoned him and when he waited for sunset. If he does not then come, those 9, being sworn, shall give testimony as we have above explained. On that day likewise, if he do not come, he (the accuser) shall let the sun go down on him, and shall have 3 witnesses who shall be there when he waits till sunset. But if the accuser shall have fulfilled all this, and the accused shall not have been willing to come to any court, then the king, before whom he has been summoned, shall withdraw his protection from him. Then he shall be guilty, and all his goods shall belong to the fisc, or to him to whom the fisc may wish to give them. And whoever shall have fed or housed him—even if it were his own wife—shall be sentenced to 600 denars, which make 15 shillings; until he (the debtor) shall have made good all that has been laid to his charge.

Title LVII. Concerning the "Chrenecruda."

1. If any one have killed a man, and, having given up all his property, has not enough to comply with the full

terms of the law, he shall present 12 sworn witnesses to the effect that, neither above the earth nor under it, has he any more property than he has already given. And he shall afterwards go into his house, and shall collect in his hand dust from the four corners of it, and shall afterwards stand upon the threshold, looking inwards into the house. And then, with his left hand, he shall throw over his shoulder some of that dust on the nearest relative that he has. But if his father and (his father's) brothers have already paid, he shall then throw that dust on their (the brothers') children—that is, over three (relatives) who are nearest on the father's and three on the mother's side. And after that, in his shirt, without girdle and without shoes, a staff in his hand, he shall spring over the hedge. And then those three shall pay half of what is lacking of the compounding money or the legal fine ; that is, those others who are descended in the paternal line shall do this.

2. But if there be one of those relatives who has not enough to pay his whole indebtedness, he, the poorer one, shall in turn throw the "chrenecruda" on him of them who has the most, so that he shall pay the whole fine.

3. But if he also have not enough to pay the whole, then he who has charge of the murderer shall bring him before the " Thing," and afterwards to 4 Things, in order that they (his friends) may take him under their protection. And if no one have taken him under his protection —that is, so as to redeem him for what he can not pay— then he shall have to atone with his life.

Title LIX. *Concerning private Property.*

1. If any man die and leave no sons, if the father and mother survive, they shall inherit.

3. If the father and mother do not survive, and he leave brothers or sisters, they shall inherit.

3. But if there are none, the sisters of the father shall inherit.

4. But if there are no sisters of the father, the sisters of the mother shall claim that inheritance.

5. If there are none of these, the nearest relatives on the father's side shall succeed to that inheritance.

6. But of Salic land no portion of the inheritance shall come to a woman: but the whole inheritance of the land shall come to the male sex.

Title LXII. Concerning Wergeld.

1. If any one's father have been killed, the sons shall have half the compounding money (wergeld); and the other half the nearest relatives, as well on the mother's as on the father's side, shall divide among themselves.

2. But if there are no relatives, paternal or maternal, that portion shall go to the fisc.

II.

CAPITULARY OF CHARLEMAGNE ISSUED IN THE YEAR 802.

(From "Mon. Germ. hist." [Quarto Series] LL. II., p. 91-99; also to be found in "Altmann u. Bernheim," p. 4.)

CHAPTER I. CONCERNING THE EMBASSY SENT OUT BY THE LORD EMPEROR.

The most serene and most Christian emperor Charles did choose from among his nobles the most prudent and the wisest men—archbishops as well as other bishops, and venerable abbots, and pious laymen—and did send them over his whole kingdom; and did grant through them, by means of all the following provisions, that men should live according to law and right. He did order them, moreover, that, where anything is contained in the law that is otherwise than according to right and justice, they should inquire into this most diligently, and make it known to him: and he, God granting, hopes to better it. And let no one, through his cleverness or astuteness—as many are accustomed to do—dare to oppose the written law, or the sentence passed upon him, or to prevail against the churches of God, or the poor, or widows, or minors, or any Christian man. But all should live together according to the precept of God, in a just manner and under just judgment ; and each one should be admonished to live in unity with the others in his occupation or calling.　The monastic clergy should altogether observe in their actions a canonical mode of living, far removed from turpid gains; nuns should keep diligent guard over their lives; laymen and secular clergy should make proper use of their privileges without malicious fraud ; all should live together in mutual charity and perfect peace.　And let the messengers diligently investigate all cases where any man claims that injustice has been done to him by any one, according as they themselves hope to retain for themselves the grace of omnipotent God, and to preserve the fidelity promised to Him.　And thus, altogether and everywhere and in all cases, whether the matter concerns the holy churches of God, or the poor, or wards and widows, or the whole people, let them fully administer law and justice according to the will and to the fear of God. And if there should be any matter such that they themselves, with the counts of the province, could not better it and render justice with regard to it : without any ambiguity they shall refer it, together with their reports, to the emperor's court.　Nor should anyone be kept back from the right path of justice by the adulation or the reward of any man, by the obstacle of any relationship, or by the fear of powerful persons.

2. CONCERNING THE FEALTY TO BE PROMISED TO THE LORD EMPEROR.

And he ordained that every man in his whole kingdom —ecclesiastic or layman, each according to his vow and calling—who had previously promised fealty to him as king should now make this promise to him as emperor; and that those who had hitherto not made this promise should all, down to those under 12 years of age, do likewise.　And he ordained that it should be publicly told to all—so that each one should understand it—what important things and how many things are comprehended in

that oath: not alone, as many have hitherto believed,
fidelity to the emperor as regards his life, or the not
introducing an enemy into his kingdom for a hostile purpose, or the not consenting to the infidelity of another, or
the not keeping silent about it. But all should know that
the oath comprises in itself the following meaning:

3. Firstly, that every one of his own accord should
strive, according to his intelligence and strength, wholly
to keep himself in the holy service of God according to the
precept of God and to his own promise—inasmuch as the
emperor can not exhibit the necessary care and discipline
to each man singly.

4. Secondly, that no one, either through perjury or
through any other wile or fraud, or on account of the
flattery or gift of any one, shall refuse to give back, or
dare to abstract or conceal a slave of the emperor, or a
district or territory or anything that belongs to his pro-
prietary right; and that no one shall presume to conceal
or abstract, through perjury or any other wile, fugitive
fiscaline slaves who unjustly and fraudulently call themselves free.

5. That no one shall presume through fraud to plunder
or do any injury to the holy churches of God, or to widows,
orphans or strangers; for the emperor himself, after God
and his saints, has been constituted their protector and
defender.

6. That no one shall dare to devastate a fief of the
emperor or to take possession of it.

7. That no one shall presume to neglect a summons to
arms of the emperor; and that no count be so presump-
tuous as to dare to release—out of regard for any relationship, or on account of flattery or of any one's gift—any
one of those who owe military service.

8. That no one at all shall dare in any way to impede a
bann or precept of the emperor, or delay or oppose or
damage any undertaking of his, or in any way act contrary
to his will and precepts. And that no one shall dare to
interfere with his taxes and with what is due to him.

9. That no man shall make a practice of unjustly carrying
on the defence of another in court, whether from any
cupidity, being not a very great pleader; or in order, by

the cleverness of his defence, to impede a just judgment;
or, his case being a weak one, by a desire of oppressing.
But each man, with regard to his own case, or tax, or debt,
must carry on his own defence; unless he be infirm or
ignorant of pleading—for which sort of persons the
" missi," or those who preside in that court, or a judge
who knows the case for the defendant, shall plead before
the court.   Or, if necessary, such a person may be granted
for the defence as shall be approved by all, and well versed
in that case.   This, however, shall be done altogether
according to the pleasure of those who preside, or of the
" missi " who are present.   And all this shall be done in
every way according to law, so that justice shall be in no
way impeded by any gift, payment, or by any wile of evil
adulation, or out of regard for any relationship.   And that
no man shall make any unjust agreement with another, but
that all shall be prepared, with all zeal and good will to
carry out justice.

For all these things here mentioned should be observed
as being comprised in the oath to the emperor.

10. That bishops and priests should live according to
the canons and should teach others to do likewise.

11. That bishops, abbots and abbesses, who are placed in
power over others, should strive to surpass in veneration
and diligence those subject to them; that they should not
oppress them with severe and tyrannous rule, but should
carefully guard the flock committed to them, with simple
love, with mercy and charity, and by the example of good
works.

12. That abbots should live where the monks are, and
wholly with the monks, according to the rule; and that
they should diligently teach and observe the canons; and
that abbesses shall do the same.

13. That bishops, abbots and abbesses, shall have bailiffs
and sheriffs and judges skilled in the law, lovers of justice,
peaceful and merciful: so that, through them, more profit
and gain may accrue to the holy church of God.   For on
no account do we wish to have harmful or greedy prevosts
or bailiffs in a monastery; for, from them, the greatest
blasphemies or evils may arise for us.   But let them be
such as the decree of the canons or of the rule bids them

to be,—submissive to the will of God, and always ready to do justice in every way, wholly observing the law without malice or fraud, always exercising a just judgment in all things: such prevosts, in short, as the holy rule recommends. And they shall altogether observe this, that they shall on no account [1] . . . . depart from the model of the canons or the rule, but shall practise humility in all things. If they presume to act otherwise they shall feel the discipline prescribed in the rule; and, if they be unwilling to amend their ways, they shall be removed from their prevostship, and others who are worthy shall be chosen in their stead.

14. That bishops, abbots and abbesses, and counts shall be mutually in accord, agreeing, with all charity and unity of peace, in wielding the law and in finding a right judgment; and that they shall faithfully live according to the will of God, so that everywhere and always, through them and among them, just judgments may be carried out. The poor, widows, orphans and pilgrims shall have consolation and protection from them; so that we, through their good will, may merit, rather than punishment, the rewards of eternal life.

15. We will, moreover, and decree, that abbots and all monks shall be subject in all obedience to their bishops, as the canonical institutions require. And all churches and chapels shall remain in the protection and power of the church. And no one shall presume to divide or cast lots for the property of the church. And what is once offered (for sale?) shall go no further, but shall be sanctified and reclaimed. And if any one presume to act counter to this, he shall pay and make good our royal fine. And the monks of that province shall be admonished by the bishop; and, if they do not amend their ways, then the archbishop shall call them before the synod; and, if they do not thus better themselves, then they, together with the bishop, shall come to our presence.

16. In the matter of choosing candidates for ordination, the emperor has confirmed this now to the bishops and abbots just as he formerly conceded it to them under the

Frankish law. With this restriction, however, that a bishop or abbot shall not prefer the more worthless men in a monastery to the better ones; nor endeavour, on account of relationship, or through any flattery, to advance them over the better ones; nor bring such a one before us to be ordained, when he has a better man whom he conceals and oppresses. We absolutely will not allow this, for it seems to be done out of derision and deceitfulness towards us. But let there be prepared for ordination in the monasteries men of such kind that, through them, gain and profit will accrue to us and to those who recommend them.

17. That the monks, moreover, shall live firmly and strictly according to the rule; since we know that whoever is lukewarm in carrying out His will, is displeasing to God. As John, in the Apocalypse, bears witness: "I would that thou wert cold or hot. So then, because thou art lukewarm, I will spue thee out of my mouth." They shall on no account take upon themselves secular occupations. They shall not be permitted to go outside of the monastery unless great necessity compels them; and the bishop in whose diocese they are shall take great care that they do not gain the habit of wandering round outside of the monastery. But if it be necessary for any one, as an act of obedience, to go outside, this shall be done by the advice and with the consent of the bishop; and such persons shall be sent out, provided with a certificate of character, who are not evil-minded, and about whom no evil opinion is held. As to the outlying estates or property of the monastery, the abbot, by the advice and with the permission of the bishop, shall decree who shall look after them; not a monk, unless subject to another monastery. They shall in every way avoid earthly pursuit of gain, or a desire for worldly things. For avarice and concupiscence are to be avoided by all Christians in this world, but chiefly by those who have renounced the world and its desires. Let no one presume to start a quarrel or dissension either within or without the monastery. Whoever shall have presumed to do so, shall be punished by the most severe discipline of the rule, so that others shall have fear of doing likewise. Let them altogether avoid

drunkenness and feasting; for it is known to all that chiefly through them one comes to be polluted by lust. For the very pernicious rumour has come to our ears that many, in the monasteries, have been taken in fornication, in abomination and uncleanness. And most of all it saddens and disturbs us that it can be said without error that from those things whence the greatest hope of salvation for all Christians is believed to arise—namely, the manner of living and the chastity of the monks—the evil has arisen that some of the monks are found to be sodomites.

18. Monasteries for women shall be firmly ruled, and the nuns shall by no means be permitted to wander about, but shall be kept with all diligence. Nor shall they be permitted to quarrel or contend among themselves, or in any way to be disobedient and refractory towards their masters and abbesses. Where they live under the rule, they shall observe all things altogether according to the rule. They shall not be given to fornication, drunkenness, or cupidity; but in all ways they shall live justly and soberly. And let no man enter into their cloister or monastery, unless a priest, with testimonials, enter it for the sake of visiting the sick, or for the mass alone; and straightway thereafter he shall go out again. And let no one enroll his daughter among the congregation of the nuns without the knowledge and consideration of the bishop to whose diocese that place pertains; and let the latter himself diligently ascertain that she is desirous of remaining in the holy service of God, and there confirm the stability of her vow. Moreover, the handmaids of other men, and such women as are not willing to live according to the manner of life in the holy congregation, shall all be altogether ejected from the congregation.

19. That no bishops, abbots, priests, deacons—no one, in short, belonging to the clergy—shall presume to have hunting dogs or hawks, falcons or sparrow-hawks; but each one shall keep himself wholly in his proper sphere, according to the canons, or according to the rule. Any one who presumes to do this (have hunting dogs, etc.) shall know that he loses his standing. Furthermore he shall suffer such punishment for this, that others shall fear to wrongfully do likewise.

20. That abbesses and their nuns shall, with one mind and diligently, keep themselves within their cloister-walls, and by no means presume to go outside of their cloister-walls. But the abbesses, when they propose to send out any of the nuns, shall by no means do this without the permission and advice of their bishop. Likewise when any ordinations are to take place in the monasteries, or any persons to be received into the monasteries, this also they shall first fully talk over with their bishops. And the bishops shall announce to the archbishop what they consider the best and most advantageous course of proceeding; and with his advice they shall carry out what is to be done.

21. That priests and the other lesser clergy, whom they have to help them in their ministry, shall altogether show themselves subject to their bishops, as the canons demand. As they desire our favour and their own advancement, let them consent fully to be taught in sacred subjects by these their bishops.

22. The secular clergy, moreover, ought to lead a completely canonical life, and be educated in the episcopal palace, or also in a monastery, with all diligence according to the discipline of the canons. They shall by no means be permitted to wander at large, but shall live altogether apart, not given to disgraceful gain, not fornicators, not thieves, not homicides, not rapers, not quarrelsome, not wrathful, not proud, not drunken; but chaste in heart and body, humble, modest, sober, merciful, peaceful; that, as sons of God they may be worthy to be promoted to sacred orders: not, like those who are called sarabaites, living in towns and villages near or adjoining the church, without master and without discipline, revelling and fornicating, and also doing other wicked deeds the consenting to which is unheard of.

23. Priests shall carefully pay heed to the clergy whom they have with them, that they live according to the canons; that they be not given to vain sports or worldly feastings, or songs or luxuries, but that they live chastely and healthfully.

24. Moreover, any priest or deacon who after this shall presume to have women in his house without permission

of the canons, shall be deprived at once of his position and of his inheritance until he shall be brought into our presence.

25. That counts and centenars shall see to it that justice is done in full; and they shall have younger men in their service in whom they can securely trust, who will faithfully observe law and justice, and by no means oppress the poor; who will not, under any pretext, induced by reward or flattery, dare to conceal thieves, robbers, or murderers, adulterers, magicians and wizards or witches, or any godless men,—but will rather give them up that they may be bettered and chastised by the law: so that, God permitting, all these evils may be removed from the Christian people.

26. That judges shall judge justly, according to the written law and not according to their own judgment.

27. We decree that throughout our whole realm no one shall dare to deny hospitality to the rich, or to the poor, or to pilgrims: that is, no one shall refuse shelter and fire and water to pilgrims going through the land in God's service, or to any one travelling for the love of God and the safety of his soul. If any one shall wish to do further kindness to them, he shall know that his best reward will be from God, who said Himself : "And whoso shall receive one such little child in my name, receiveth me." And again: "I was a stranger and ye took me in."

28. **Concerning embassies coming from the lord emperor.**—That the counts and centenars, as they desire to obtain the emperor's favour, shall provide with all care for the envoys sent, so that they may go through their districts without delay. And he altogether recommends to all to arrange all that shall be required, in such manner that there shall nowhere be delay; but they shall speed them on their way with all haste, and shall provide for them as they, our envoys, may arrange.

29. That our judges, counts, or envoys shall not have a right to extort payment of the remitted fine, on their own behalf, from those destitute persons to whom the emperor has, in his mercy, forgiven what they ought to pay by reason of his bann.

30. As to those whom the emperor wishes by Christ's

favour to have peace and defence in his kingdom—that is, those who, whether Christians or pagans, hasten to his presence desiring to announce something, or those who seek alms on account of indigence or hunger—let no none dare to constrain them to do him service, or take possession of them, or alienate or sell them : but where they remain of their own will, there they, under the protection of the emperor, shall have alms from his bounty. If any one shall presume to transgress this, he shall know that he shall atone for it with his life, for having so presumptuously despised the commands of the emperor.

31. And let no one presume to contrive injuries or insults against those who announce a judgment of the emperor, or to show hostility to them in any way. Whoever shall have presumed to do this shall pay the king's bann ; or, if he deserve a greater punishment, it is ordered that he be brought into the king's presence.

32. With every kind of protestation we command that men leave off and shun murders, through which many of the Christian people perish. If God forbids hatred and enmity to his followers, much more does he forbid murders. For how can any one hope to be pleasing to God who has slain His son who is nearest to Him ? Or how can any one believe that Christ will be gracious to him who has slain his brother. It is a great and inevitable risk to arouse the hatred of men besides incurring that of God the Father and of Christ the ruler of Heaven. By hiding, one can escape them for a time; but, nevertheless, one falls by some chance into the hands of his enemies. And where can one flee God to whom all secrets are manifest ? by what rashness can any one hope to evade His wrath ? Therefore we have taken care to avoid, by every possible regulation, that the people committed to us to be ruled over perish by this evil. For he who has not feared that God will be angry with him, will by no means find us gentle and gracious ; we wish rather to punish with the greatest severity him who dares to commit the crime of murder. Lest, then, crime increase, and in order that very great discord may not arise among men,—wherever under the devil's suasion, a murder has occurred, the guilty one shall straightway hasten to make his amends, and shall, with all

celerity, compound worthily with the relatives of the dead man for the evil done. And this we firmly decree under our bann, that the relatives of the dead man shall by no means dare to carry further their enmity on account of the evil inflicted, or refuse to make peace with him who seeks it; but, pledging their faith, they shall make a lasting peace, and the guilty man shall make no delay in paying the wergeld. When, moreover, through the influence of sin, this shall have happened, that any one shall have slain his brothers or his relative, he shall straightway submit himself to the penance imposed, according as his bishop decides, and without any circumvention. But by the help of God he shall strive to work out his atonement; and he shall pay the fine for the slain man according to the law, and shall fully be reconciled to his relatives. And, having pledged their faith, let no one thenceforth dare to start hostilities. And whoever shall scorn to make proper amends shall be deprived of his inheritance until we shall have rendered our judgment.

33. We altogether prohibit the crime of incest. If any one be contaminated by sinful adultery, he shall not be released without grave severity, but shall so be punished for this that others may have fear of doing the same: so that uncleanness may be altogether removed from the Christian people, and that the guilty man may fully atone by such penance as shall be imposed on him by his bishop. And that woman shall be placed in the hands of her relatives until we pass sentence. But if the man be unwilling to submit to the sentence of the bishop concerning what amends he shall make, then let him be brought before our presence, mindful of the example which was made in the case of the incest committed by Fricco in the temple.

34. That all shall be fully and well prepared whenever our order or announcement shall come. If any one then say that he be not prepared, and avoid our mandate let him be brought to the palace; and not only he, but likewise all who presume to transgress our bann or command.

35. That all men shall at all times, in the service and will of God, venerate with all honour their bishops and priests. Let them not dare to pollute themselves and others by incestuous nuptials; let them not presume to be

wedded until the bishops and priests, together with the elders of the people, shall diligently inquire into the degree of blood-relationship between those being joined together. And then, with a benediction, let them be wedded. Let them avoid drunkenness, shun greed, commit no theft. Let strife and contentions and blasphemy, whether at feasts or assemblies, be altogether avoided; but let them live in charity and concord.

36. Also that, in carrying out every sentence, all shall be altogether of one mind with our envoys. And they shall not at all permit the practice of perjury, which most evil crime must be removed from Christian people. If any one henceforth shall be proved a perjurer, he shall know that he shall lose his right hand; and he shall, in addition, be deprived of his inheritance until we have judged his case.

37. As to patricides or fratricides, or those who have slain their mother's or their father's brother, or any relation,—if they have been unwilling to obey and agree to the sentence of the bishops and other priests: for the safety of their souls and that they may pay a just penalty, let our envoys and counts keep them in such custody until they are brought into our presence, that they may be safe and may not infect other people. And they shall, in the meantime, be deprived of their property.

38. And let the like be done to those who have been reprimanded and corrected for unlawful and incestuous unions, and who art not willing to obey their bishops and priests, and who presume to despise our bann.

39. Let no one in our forests dare to rob our game, which we have already many times forbidden to be done. And now again we firmly decree that no one shall do this any more. Each one shall keep guard on himself as he hopes to keep the fealty sworn to us. But if any count or centenar or lower official of ours, or any one of our serving-men, shall have stolen our game, he shall without fail be brought to our presence and called to account. Any other common man who may have stolen our game, shall compound for it to the full extent of the law; and by no means shall any allowance be made for such persons in this matter. If any one knows that this evil deed has been perpe-

trated by another, let him not, by the fealty which he has promised and must now promise to us, dare to conceal it.

40. Lastly, then, we wish our decrees to be known, through the envoys whom we now send, by everyone in our whole realm—by ecclesiastics, viz.: bishops, abbots, priests, deacons, canons, all monks and nuns;—so that they, each one in his office or calling, may keep our bann and decree either in cases where it shall be necessary to thank those subject to them for their good will, or to lend them aid, or in cases where there may be need of applying a remedy. Likewise we wish our decrees to be known by laymen and in all places—whether they concern the protection of churches or widows, or orphans or the weak; or the plundering of them; or the fixing of the assembling of the army, or any other matters: in order that they may be obedient to our command to our will, and that each one may strive in all things to keep himself in the sacred service of God. And thus may all these things be good and to the praise of omnipotent God, and may we give thanks where they are due; but when we think that any thing needs vengeance, may we strive with all our will and all our zeal to better it,—so that, with God's aid, we may succeed in bettering it, to the eternal gain of ourselves and all our followers. Likewise we wish that all the above decrees be made known to our counts and centenars and officials.

III.

DIVISION OF THE EMPIRE OF THE YEAR 817.

(Altmann und Bernheim, "Ausgewählte Urkunden," p. 12. Berlin, 1891.)

In the name of the Lord God and of our Saviour Jesus Christ. Louis, the divine power ordaining, august emperor. While we in the name of God, in the year 817 of the incarnation of the Lord, in the tenth indiction, and in the fourth year of our reign, in the month of July, had assembled in our palace at Aix in our accustomed manner a sacred synod and the generality of our people to treat of ecclesiastical needs and the needs of our whole

empire, and were intent upon these,—suddenly, by divine
inspiration, it came about that our faithful ones warned
us that, while we still remained safe and peace on all
sides was granted by God, we should, after the manner of
our forefathers, treat of the condition of the whole kingdom
and of the case of our sons. But although this admonition
was devoutly and faithfully given, nevertheless it seems
good neither to us nor to those who know what is salutary,
that for the love or for the sake of our sons the unity of
the empire preserved to us by God should be rent by
human division ; lest by chance from this cause a scandal
should arise in the holy church and we should incur the
offending of Him in whose power are the laws of all kingdoms.   Therefore we thought it necessary that by fastings
and prayers and the giving of alms we should obtain from
Him that which our infirmity did not presume. Which
being duly performed for three days, by the will of
Almighty God, as we believe, it was brought about that
both our own wishes and those of our whole people con-
curred in the election of our beloved first-born Lothar.
And so it pleased both us and all our people that he, thus
manifested by the divine dispensation, being crowned in
solemn manner with the imperial diadem, should, by common wish, be made our consort and successor to the empire
if God should so wish. But as to his other brothers,
Pippin, namely, and Louis our namesake, it seemed good
by common counsel to distinguish them by the name of
kings, and to fix upon the places named below, in which
after our decease they may hold sway with regal power
under their elder brother according to the clauses mentioned
below, in which are contained the conditions which we
have established among them.   Which clauses, on account
of the advantage of the empire, and of preserving perpetual
peace among them, and for the safety of the whole church,
it pleased us to deliberate upon with all our faithful ones ;
and having deliberated, to write down ; and having written
down, to confirm with our own hands : so that, God lending
His aid, as they had been passed by all with common consent, so by common devotion they should be inviolably
observed by all, to the perpetual peace of themselves and
of the whole Christian people ; saving in all things our

imperial power over our sons and our people, with all the subjection which is exhibited by a father to his sons and to an emperor and king by his people.

1. We will that Pippin shall have Aquitania and Gascony, and all the March of Toulouse, and moreover four counties: namely, in Septimania Carcassone, and in Burgundy Autun, l'Avalonnais and Nevers.

2. Likewise we will that Louis shall have Bavaria and Carinthia, and the Bohemians, Avars, and Slavs, who are on the eastern side of Bavaria; and furthermore, two demesne towns to do service to him, in the county of Nortgau, Lauterburg and Ingolstadt.

3. We will that these two brothers, who are called by the name of king, shall possess power of themselves to distribute all honours within the range of their jurisdiction; provided that in the bishoprics and abbeys the ecclesiastical order shall be held to, and in giving other honours, honesty and utility shall be observed.

4. Likewise we will, that once a year, at a fitting time, either together or individually, according as the condition of things allows, they shall come to their elder brother with their gifts, for the sake of visiting him, and seeing him, and treating with mutual fraternal love of those things which are necessary, and which pertain to the common utility and to perpetual peace. And if by chance one of them, impeded by some inevitable necessity, is unable to come at the accustomed and fitting time, he shall signify this to his elder brother by sending legates and gifts; so, nevertheless, that at whatever suitable time it may be possible for him, he shall not avoid coming through any feigned excuse.

5. We will and order that the elder brother, when one or both of his brothers shall come to him, as has been said, with gifts, shall, according as to him, by God's will, greater power has been attributed, likewise himself remunerate them with pious and fraternal love, and a more ample gift.

6. We will and order that the elder brother shall, either in person, or through his faithful envoys and his armies, according as reason dictates and time and occasion permit, send help to his younger brothers when they shall rea-

sonably ask him to come to their aid against external nations.

7. We likewise will that without the counsel and consent of their elder brother they by no means presume to make peace with, or engage in war against, foreign nations, and those that are hostile to this empire, which is in the care of God.

8. But as to envoys, if such are sent by external nations either for the sake of making peace, or engaging in war, or surrendering castles, or of arranging any other important matters, they, the younger brothers, shall by no means give them an answer without the knowledge of the elder brother, nor shall they send them away. But if envoys shall be sent to him from any place, he of the younger brothers to whom they shall first come, shall receive them with honour, and shall cause them, accompanied by faithful envoys, to come into his (the older brother's) presence. But in minor matters, according to the nature of the embassy, they may answer of themselves. But we add this warning, that in whatever condition affairs within their confines may be, they shall not neglect to keep their elder brother always informed, that he may be found always interested and ready to give his attention to whatever things the necessity and utility of the kingdom shall demand.

9. It seems best for us also to require that after our decease the vassal of each one of the brothers, for the sake of avoiding discord, shall have a benefice only in the domain of his ruler, and not in that of one of the others. But his own property and heritage, wherever it be, each one may possess according to his law, and without unjust interference, justice being observed, with honour and security; and each free man who has not a lord shall be allowed to commend himself to whichever of the three brothers he may wish.

10. But if, what God avert and what we least of all wish, it should happen that any one of the brothers, on account of desire for earthly goods, which is the root of all evils, shall be either a divider or oppressor of the churches or the poor, or shall exercise tyranny, in which all cruelty consists: first, in secret, according to the precept of God,

he shall be warned once, twice, and thrice, through faithful envoys, to amend; and if he refuse them, being summoned by one brother before the other he shall be admonished and punished with fraternal and paternal love. And if he shall altogether spurn this healthful admonition, by the common sentence of all it shall be decreed what is to be done concerning him; so that him whom a healthful admonition could not recall from his wicked ways, the imperial power and the common sentence of all may coerce.

11. But the rulers of the churches of Francia shall have such power over the possessions of the same, whether in Aquitania or in Italy, or in other regions and provinces subject to this empire, as they had in the time of our father, or are known to have in our own.

12. Whatever of tribute, moreover, and rents and precious metals can be exacted or obtained within their confines, they shall possess; so that from these they may provide for their necessities, and may the better be able to prepare the gifts to be brought to their elder brother.

13. We will, also, that if to any one of them, after our decease, the time for marrying shall come, he shall take a wife with the counsel and consent of his elder brother. This, moreover, we decree shall be guarded against, for the sake of avoiding discords and removing harmful opportunities: that any one of them shall presume to take a wife from external nations. But the vassals of all of them, in order that the bonds of peace may be drawn more closely, may take their wives from whatever places they wish.

14. But if any one of them, dying, shall leave lawful children, his power shall not be divided among them; but rather the people, coming together in common, shall elect one of them who shall be pleasing to God; and this one the elder brother shall receive as a brother and a son, and, himself being treated with paternal honour, shall observe this constitution towards him in every way. But in the matter of the other children they shall, with pious love, discuss how they may keep them and give them advice, after the manner of our parents.

15. But if any one of them shall die without lawful

children, his power shall revert to the elder brother. And if he shall happen to have children from concubines, we exhort the elder brother to act mercifully towards them.

16. But if at our death either of them shall happen not yet to be of lawful age according to Ripuarian law, we will that, until he arrive at the established term of years, just as now by us, so by his elder brother, both himself and his kingdom shall be cared for and governed. And when he shall come to be of lawful age, he shall in all things possess his power according to the manner laid down.

17. But to our son, if God will that he be our successor, the kingdom of Italy shall in the aforesaid manner be subject in all things, just as it was subject to our father, and remains subject in the present time to us, by the will of God.

18. We exhort also the devotion of our whole people, and that firmness of a most sincere faith, the fame of which has spread among almost all nations, that if our son, who by the divine will shall succeed to us, shall depart from this life without legitimate heirs, they shall, for the sake of the salvation of all, and the tranquillity of the church and the unity of the empire, follow the conditions that we have made in the matter of his election, and elect one of our sons, if they shall survive their brother ; so that in choosing him they shall seek to fulfil, not a human will, but the will of God.

IV.

TREATY AT AIX BETWEEN LOUIS II. AND CHARLES THE BALD CONCERNING THE DIVISION OF THE KINGDOM OF LOTHAR II. A.D. 870.

(Altmann u. Bernheim, " Ausgewählte Urkunden," p. 16. Berlin, 1891.)

In the year of the Incarnation of our Lord Jesus Christ 870, on the day before the Nones of March, in the 32nd year of the most glorious king Charles, in the palace at

Aix, this agreement was made between him and his
brother king Louis.

Count Ingelram on the part of king Charles:

I promise this on the part of my lord, that my lord king
Charles consents that his brother, king Louis, shall have
such portion of the kingdom of king Lothar, as either they
themselves, or their faithful followers among themselves,
shall find to be most just and most equable. Neither with
regard to that portion nor with regard to the kingdom
which he (Louis) before held will he (Charles) deceive or
ill-advise him through any fraud or wile, provided that his
brother Louis will on his part inviolably observe, as long
as he lives, the same steadfastness and fidelity to my lord
which I have promised to him on the part of that lord.

Likewise Liutfried on the part of king Louis:

I promise this on the part of my lord, that my lord king
Louis consents that his brother, king Charles, shall have
such portion of the kingdom of king Lothar, as either they
themselves, or their faithful followers among themselves,
shall find to be most just or most equable. Neither with
regard to that portion nor with regard to the kingdom
which he (Charles) before held, will he (Louis) deceive or
ill-advise him through any fraud or wile, provided that his
brother Charles will on his part inviolably observe, as
long as he lives, the same steadfastness and fidelity to my
lord which I have promised to him on the part of that lord.
In like manner count Theoderic as a third swore to these
things on the part of the glorious king Charles, and as a
fourth count Ralph on the part of king Louis.

There were present there: archbishop Liutbert, bishop
Altfrid, bishop Odo, count Adalelm, count Ingleram, count
Liutfried, count Theoderic, likewise a count Adalelm.

V.

DECREE OF THE EMPEROR HENRY IV. CONCERNING A TRUCE OF GOD (1085 A.D.).

(Doeberl, " Monumenta Germaniae Selecta," Bd. 3,
p. 49).

Whereas in our times the holy church has been afflicted beyond measure by tribulations through having to join in suffering so many oppressions and dangers, we have so striven to aid it, with God's help, that the peace which we could not make lasting by reason of our sins, we should to some extent make binding by at least exempting certain days.   In the year of the Lord's incarnation, 1085, in the 8th indiction, it was decreed by God's mediation, the clergy and people unanimously agreeing : that from the first day of the Advent of our Lord until the end of the day of the Epiphany, and from the beginning of Septuagesima until the 8th day after Pentecost, and throughout that whole day, and on every Thursday, Friday, Saturday, and Sunday, until sunrise on Monday, and on the day of the fast of the four seasons, and on the eve and the day itself of each of the apostles—moreover on every day canonically set apart, or in future to be set apart, for fasting or for celebrating,—this decree of peace shall be observed.   The purpose of it is that those who travel and those who remain at home may enjoy the greatest possible security, so that no one shall commit murder or arson, robbery or assault, no man shall injure another with a whip or a sword or any kind of weapon, and that no one, no matter on account of what wrong he shall be at feud, shall, from the Advent of our Lord to the 8th day after Epiphany, and from Septuagesima until the 8th day after Pentecost, presume to bear as weapons a shield, sword, or lance—or, in fact, the burden of any armour.   Likewise on the other days—namely, on Sundays, Thursdays, Fridays, Saturdays, and on the eve and day of each of the apostles, and on every day canonically fixed, or to be fixed, for fasting or celebrating,—it is unlawful, except for those going a long distance, to carry arms; and even then under the condition that they injure no one in any way. If, during the space for which the peace has been declared, it shall be necessary for any one to go to another place where that peace is not observed, he may bear arms; provided, nevertheless, that he harm no one unless he is attacked and has to defend himself. Moreover, when he returns, he shall lay aside his weapons again. If it shall happen that a castle is being besieged, the besiegers shall cease from the attack during the days included in the peace, unless they are attacked by the besieged, and are obliged to beat them back.

And lest this statute of peace be violated with impunity by any person, the following sentence was decreed by all present: If a freeman or a noble shall have violated it— that is, if he shall have committed murder, or shall have transgressed it in any other way,—he shall, without any payments or any friends being allowed to intervene, be expelled from within his boundaries, and his heirs may take his whole estate; and if he hold a fief, the lord to whom it belongs shall take it. But if, after his expulsion, his heirs shall be found to have given him any aid or support, and shall be convicted of it, the estate shall be taken from them and shall fall to the portion of the king. But if he wish to clear himself of the charges against him, he shall swear with 12 who are equally noble and free. If a slave kill a man he shall be beheaded; if he wound him he shall have his right hand cut off; if he have transgressed in any other way—by striking with his fist, or a stone, or a whip, or any thing else—he shall be flogged and shorn. But if the accused (slave) wish to prove his innocence, he shall purge himself by the ordeal of cold water: in such wise, however, that he himself, and no one in his place, be sent to the water. But if, fearing the sentence that has been passed against him, he shall have fled,—he shall be forever under the bann. And wherever he is heard to be, letters shall be sent there announcing that he is under the bann, and that no one may hold intercourse with him. The hands may not be cut off of boys who have not yet completed their 12th year; if boys, then, shall transgress this peace, they shall be punished with whipping only. It is not an infringement of the peace if any one order a delinquent slave, or a scholar, or any one who is subject to him in any way, to be beaten with rods or with whips. It is an exception also to this statute of peace, if the emperor shall publicly order an expedition to be made to seek the enemies of the realm, or shall be pleased to hold a council to judge the enemies of justice. The peace is not violated if, while it continues, the duke, or other counts, or bailiffs, or their substitutes hold courts, and lawfully exercise judgment over thieves and robbers, and other harmful persons. This imperial peace has been decreed chiefly for the security of all those who are at feud; but not to the end that, after the peace is over, they may dare to rob and plunder throughout the villages and homes. For the law and judgment that was in force against them before this peace was decreed shall be most diligently observed, so that they be restrained from iniquity;—for robbers and plunderers are excepted from this divine peace, and, in fact, from every peace. If any one strive to oppose this pious decree, so that he will neither promise the peace to God nor observe it, no priest shall presume to sing a mass for him or to give heed to his salvation; if he be ill, no Christian shall presume to visit him, and, unless he come to his senses, he shall do without the Eucharist even at the end. If any one, either at the present time or among our posterity forever, shall presume to violate it, he is banned by us irrevocably. We decree that it rests not more in the power of the counts or centenars, or any official, than in that of the whole people in common, to inflict the above mentioned punishments on the violators of the holy peace. And let them most diligently be on their guard lest, in punishing, they show friendship or hatred, or do anything contrary to justice; let them not conceal the crimes of any one, but rather make them public. No one shall accept money for the redemption of those who shall have been found transgressing. Merchants on the road where they do business, rustics while labouring at rustic work—at ploughing, digging, reaping, and other similar occupations,—shall have peace every day. Women, more-over, and all those ordained to sacred orders, shall enjoy continual peace. In the churches, moreover, and in the cemeteries of the churches, let honour and reverence be paid to God; so that if a robber or thief flee thither he shall not at all be siezed, but shall be besieged there until, induced by hunger, he shall be compelled to surrender. If any one shall presume to furnish the culprit with means of defence, arms, victuals, or opportunity for flight, he shall be punished with the same penalty as the guilty man. We forbid under our bann, moreover, that any one in sacred orders, convicted of transgressing this peace, be punished with the punishments of laymen—he shall, instead, be handed over to the bishop. Where laymen are decapitated, clerks shall be degraded; where laymen are mutilated, clerks shall be suspended from their positions; and, by the consent of the laity, they shall be afflicted with frequent fasts and flagellations until they shall have atoned. Amen.

VI.

PEACE OF THE LAND ESTABLISHED BY FREDERICK BARBAROSSA BETWEEN 1152 AND 1157 A.D.

(Altmann u. Bernheim, "Ausgewählte Urkunden," p. 150. Berlin, 1891.)

Frederick by the grace of God emperor of the Romans, always august, to the bishops, dukes, counts, margraves and all to whom these letters shall come: sends his favour, peace, and love.

Inasmuch as by the ordination of the divine mercy we ascend the throne of the royal majesty, it is right that in our works we altogether obey Him by whose gift we are exalted. Therefore we, desiring the divine as well as the human laws to remain in vigour, and endeavouring to exalt the churches and ecclesiastical persons, and to defend them from the incursions and invasions of every one, do wish to preserve to all persons whatever their rights, and do by the royal authority indicate a peace, long desired and hitherto necessary to the whole earth, to be observed throughout all parts of our kingdom. In what manner, moreover, this same peace is to be kept and observed, will be clearly shown from what follows.

1. If any one, within the term fixed for the peace, shall slay a man, he shall be sentenced to death, unless by wager of battle he can prove this, that he slew him in defending his own life. But if this shall be manifest to all, that he slew him not of necessity but voluntarily, then neither through wager of battle nor in any other manner shall he keep himself from being condemned to death. But if a violator of the peace shall flee the face of the judge, his movable possessions shall be confiscated by the judge and dispensed among the people; but his heirs shall receive the heritage which he held; this condition being imposed, that a promise shall be given under oath to the effect that that violator of the peace shall never, henceforth, by their will or consent receive any emolument from it. But if later the heirs, neglecting the rigour of the law, shall allow him to have his heritage, the count shall hand over that same heritage to the rule of the king and shall receive it from the king under the name of a benefice.

2. If any one wound another after the proclamation of the peace, unless he prove by wager of battle that he did this while defending his life, his hand shall be amputated and he shall be sentenced as has been explained above: the judge shall most strictly prosecute him and his possessions according to the rigour of justice.

3. If any one take another and without shedding blood beat him with rods, or pull out his hair or beard, he shall pay by way of composition 10 pounds to him on whom the injury is seen to have been inflicted, and 30 pounds to the judge. But if without striking him he shall boldly attack him "asteros hant," as it is vulgarly called, viz., with hot hand, and shall maltreat him with contumelious words, he shall compound with 10 pounds for such excess and shall pay 10 to the judge. And whoever, for an excess, shall engage to pay 20 pounds to his judge, shall hand over his estate to him as a pledge, and within four weeks shall pay the money required; and if within four weeks he neglect

to hand over his estate, his heirs, if they wish, may receive his heritage, and shall pay to the count the 20 pounds within six weeks; but if not, the count shall assign that heritage to the power of the king, shall restore the claims of those who proclaim them, and shall receive the estate from the king under the title of a benefice.

4. If a clerk be charged with violating the peace and be openly known and published as doing so, or if he keep companionship with a violator of the peace, and be convicted of these things in the presence of his bishop and by sufficient testimony: to the count in whose county this same clerk has perpetrated this he shall pay 20 pounds, and for so great an excess he shall make satisfaction to the bishop according to the statutes of the canons. If, moreover, that same clerk shall be disobedient, he shall not only be deprived of his office and ecclesiastical benefice, but also he shall be considered an outlaw.

5. If a judge through clamour of the people shall have followed any violator of the peace to the city of any lord, that same lord whose city it is known to be shall produce him to render justice; but if he shall mistrust his own innocence and shall fear to come before the face of the judge,—if he have a dwelling in the city, his lord shall, under oath, place all his movable goods at the disposition of the judge, and in future, as an outlaw, not receive him in his house; but if he have not a dwelling in his city, his lord shall cause him to be placed in security, and afterwards the judge, with the people, shall not desist from prosecuting him as a violator of the peace.

6. If two men contend for the possession of one benefice, and one of them produces the man who invested him with that benefice, his testimony, if the investor acknowledge having given the investiture, shall be received first by the count; and if the man can prove by suitable witnesses that he obtained this same benefice without plunder, the occasion for controversy being removed, he shall hold it; but if in the presence of the judge he be convicted of plunder, he shall doubly pay the plunder, and shall be deprived of the benefice, unless, justice and judgment dictating, he may in the future seek to obtain it again.

7. If three or more contend for the same benefice, each

one producing different investors, the judge in whose presence the case is carried on shall require of two men of good testimony dwelling in the province of these same litigants, that they swear by an oath which of them, without plunder, has been the possessor of that benefice; and, the truth of the matter being known from their testimony, the possessor shall quietly obtain his benefice, unless, justice and judgment dictating, another shall snatch it from his hand.

8. If a rustic charge a knight with violating the peace, he shall swear by his hand that he does this not willingly but of necessity; the knight shall clear himself by the hand of four.

9. If a knight charge a rustic with violating the peace, the rustic shall swear by his hand that he has done this not willingly but of necessity; the rustic shall choose one of two things: whether he shall show his innocence by a divine or a human judgment, or whether he shall expurgate himself by six suitable witnesses whom the judge shall choose.

10. If for violation of the peace, or in any capital matter, a knight wishes to engage in wager of battle against a knight, permission to fight shall not be granted to him unless he can prove that from of old he himself, and his parents as well, have by birth been lawful knights.

11. After the nativity of St. Mary each count shall choose for himself seven men of good testimony, and shall wisely make arrangements for each province, and shall usefully provide for what price, according to the quality, the grain is to be sold at different times; but whoever, contrary to his ruling, within the term of the year, shall presume to sell a measure for a higher price, shall be considered a violator of the peace, and shall pay as many times thirty pounds to the count as the number of measures he shall have been convicted of selling.

12. If any rustic shall carry as weapons either a lance or a sword, the judge within whose jurisdiction he shall be found to belong shall either take away the weapons, or shall receive 20 shillings for them from the rustic.

13. A merchant passing through the province on business may tie his sword to his saddle, or place it above his

vehicle, not in order to injure the innocent, but to defend himself from the robber.

14. No one shall spread his nets or his nooses, or any other instruments for taking game, except for taking bears, boars and wolves.

15. In going to the palace of the count no knight shall bear arms unless invited by the count. Public robbers and convicts shall be condemned to the old sentence.

16. Whoever shall treat his advowson or any other benefice unbecomingly, and shall have been warned by his lord and do not amend, continuing in his insolence,—he shall be deprived by a judicial order as well of his advowson as of his benefice; and if he afterwards, with bold daring, shall invade his advowson or benefice, he shall be considered a violator of the peace.

17. If any one shall have stolen 5 shillings, or its equivalent,—he shall be hung with a rope; if less he shall be flayed with whips, and his hair pulled out with a pincers.

18. If the ministeriales of any lord have a conflict among themselves, the count or judge in whose district they do this shall carry on the law and the judgments in the matter.

19. Whoever, in passing through the land, wishes to feed his horse, may with impunity take, for the refection and refreshment of his horse, as much as he can reach when he stands in a place directly adjoining the road. It is lawful for any one to take, for his convenience and necessary use, grass and green wood; but without any devastation.

VII.

THE ESTABLISHMENT OF THE DUCHY OF AUSTRIA, SEPT. 17, 1156.

(Doeberl, iv. p. 88.)

In the name of the holy and indivisible Trinity. Frederick, by favour of the divine mercy, august emperor of the Romans. Although a transfer of property may remain valid from the actual act of performing such transfer, and those things which are lawfully possessed can not be wrested away by any act of force : it is, however, the duty of our imperial authority to intervene lest there can be any doubt of the transaction. Be it known, therefore, to the present age and to future generations of our subjects, that we, aided by the grace of Him who sent peace for men from Heaven to earth, have, in the general court of Regensburg which was held on the nativity of St. Mary the Virgin, in the presence of many of the clergy and the catholic princes, terminated the struggle and controversy concerning the duchy of Bavaria, which has long been carried on between our most beloved uncle, Henry duke of Austria, and our most dear nephew, Henry duke of Saxony. And it has been done in this way : that the duke of Austria has resigned to us the duchy of Bavaria, which we have straightway granted as a fief to the duke of Saxony. But the duke of Bavaria has resigned to us the march of Austria, with all its jurisdictions and with all the fiefs which the former margrave Leopold held from the duchy of Bavaria. Moreover, lest by this act the honour and glory of our most beloved uncle may seem in any way to be diminished,—by the counsel and judgment of the princes, Vladislav, the illustrious duke of Bohemia, proclaiming the decision, and all the princes approving,—we have changed the march of Austria into a duchy, and have granted that duchy with all its jurisdictions to our aforesaid uncle Henry and his most noble wife Theodora as a fief ; decreeing by a perpetual law that they and their children alike, whether sons or daughters, shall, by hereditary right, hold and possess that same duchy of Austria from the empire. But if the aforesaid duke of Austria, our uncle, and his wife should die without children, they shall have the privilege of leaving that duchy to whomever they wish. We decree, further, that no person, small or great, may presume to exercise any jurisdiction in the governing of that duchy without the consent or permission of the duke. The duke of Austria, moreover, shall not owe any other service to the empire from his duchy, except that, when he is summoned, he shall come to the courts which the emperor shall announce in Bavaria. And he shall be bound to go on no military expedition, unless the emperor ordain one against the countries or provinces adjoining Austria. For the rest, in order that this our imperial decree may, for all ages, remain valid and unshaken, we have ordered the present charter to be written and to be sealed with the impress of our seal, suitable witnesses to be called in whose names are as follows : Pilgrim, patriarch of Aquileija, etc. etc.

VIII.

THE GELNHAUSEN CHARTER. APRIL 13 1180 A.D.

(Doeberl, iv. p. 264.)

In the name of the holy and indivisible Trinity. Frederick, by favour of the divine mercy, august emperor of the Romans. Since human memory is short and does not suffice for a crowd of things, the authority of those who preceded our age, the divine emperors and kings, has decreed that those things were to be written down which the progress of fleeting time generally removes from the knowledge of men.

A. Wherefore let the generality of the present as well as the future subjects of our empire know, that Henry the former duke of Bavaria and Westphalia, for the reason that he gravely oppressed the liberty of the churches of God and of the nobles of the empire, occupying their possessions and diminishing their rights,—on account of the urgent complaints of the princes and of very many nobles, inasmuch as being summoned he scorned to present himself before our majesty : did, both for this contumacy and for scorning the Swabian princes of his rank, incur the sentence of our proscription. Then, as he did not desist from raging against the churches of God and the rights and liberties of the princes and nobles, being cited by a lawful triple edict, according to feudal law, before our presence, as well to answer for the injury to the princes as for the repeated contempt shown to us, and, chiefly, for the evident crime of high treason :—for the reason that he absented himself and sent no one to respond for him he was judged contumacious; and, for the future, as well the duchy of Bavaria as that of Westphalia and Angaria, and also all the benefices which he has held from the empire were, in the solemn court held at Wurzburg, by unanimous sentence of the princes declared forfeited by him and adjudged to our jurisdiction and power.

B. We, therefore, after deliberating with the princes and by their common counsel, did divide in two the duchy which is called Westphalia and Angaria, and, through consideration of the merits through which our beloved prince Philip the archbishop of Cologne has deserved the privilege of the imperial favour by promoting and upholding the honour of the imperial crown, fearing neither expense nor personal danger,—we have lawfully donated to the church of Cologne, and, from the imperial bounty, have conferred on it one portion, namely, the one that extended to the Cologne bishopric and over the whole bishopric of Paderborn. We have donated it with every right and jurisdiction, namely, with the county courts, with the advowsons, escort-monies, manors, vills, benefices, serving-men, bondsmen, and all things that pertain to that duchy. And, asking an opinion from the princes as to whether this could be done, when an affirmative one had been given and approved by the common consent of the princes and of the whole court, the consent, also, of our beloved relative duke Bernard, to whom we had given the other portion of the duchy, being given publicly,—we did solemnly invest, through an imperial standard, the aforesaid archbishop Philip with that portion of the duchy conferred on his church.

We do confirm, therefore, this lawful donation and investiture of our royal majesty to the Cologne church and to our oft-mentioned prince the archbishop Philip, and to all his successors. And wishing this to remain valid for them unto all their posterity, we forbid by an imperial edict that any one, with rash daring, infringe it or in any way attempt to violate it; and we validly corroborate this our decree by the present privilege, signed by the golden seal of our Highness, the witnesses being written down who were present at this deed. They are as follows: etc. etc.

IX.

THE COUNT PALATINE AS JUDGE OVER THE KING.

Decree of the Nuremberg Diet, Nov. 19, 1274.

(Altmann u. Bernheim, p. 23.)

In public consistory, at the time of the solemn and royal court held at Nuremberg, the princes and a brilliant assembly of counts and barons being in session, and a very great multitude of nobles and commoners standing before the most serene lord Rudolph king of the Romans for the purpose of exhibiting the fulness of justice to each person, —the king first asked that it be defined by a decree who ought to be judge if the king of the Romans should have to bring any charge against any prince of the empire in the matter of imperial possessions and those belonging to the fisc, and concerning other injuries inflicted on the realm or on the king. And it was defined by all the princes and barons who were present, that the count Palatine of the Rhine has held of old, and does hold, the right of judging in processes which the emperor or king wishes to bring against a prince of the empire.

The said count Palatine, therefore, presiding over the tribunal, the king asked that it be first established by a decree what he, the king, might and should, according to law, do with the possessions which the former emperor Frederick had and held, peacefully and quietly, before the sentence of deposition was passed upon him by the princes; and also concerning possessions otherwise falling to the empire, which possessions others hold, occupying them through violence. And it was decreed that the king himself, in the matter of all such possessions, ought to assert his own claim, and bring back those same possessions into his power; and if any one should presume to oppose himself to the king in the recovering of such possessions, the king should repel with the royal power such hurtful violence. and to preserve the rights of the empire. . . . .

X.

THE GOLDEN BULL OF THE EMPEROR CHARLES IV. 1356 A.D.

(Altmann u. Bernheim, p. 39.)

Eternal, omnipotent God, in whom the sole hope of the world is,
Of Heaven the Maker Thou, of earth, too, the lofty Creator :
Consider, we pray Thee, Thy people, and gently, from out Thy
　　high dwelling,
Look down lest they turn their steps to the place where Erinis is
　　ruler ;
There where Allecto commands, Megaera dictating the measures.
But rather by virtue of him, this emperor Charles whom Thou
　　lovest,
O most beneficent God, may'st Thou graciously please to ordain it,
That, through the pleasant glades of forests ever in flower,
And through the realms of the bless'd, their pious leader may
　　bring them
Into the holy shades, where the heavenly waters will quicken
The seeds that were sown in the life, and where the ripe crops are
　　made glorious,
Cleansed in supernal founts from all of the thorns they have
　　gathered.
Thus may the harvest be God's, and great may its worth be in
　　future,
Heaping a hundred fold the corn in the barns overflowing.

In the name of the holy and indivisible Trinity felicitously amen. Charles the Fourth, by favour of the divine
mercy emperor of the Romans, always august, and king of
Bohemia ; as a perpetual memorial of this matter. Every
kingdom divided against itself shall be desolated. For its
princes have become the companions of thieves. Wherefore God has mingled among them the spirit of dizziness,
that they may grope in midday as if in darkness ; and He
has removed their candlestick from out of His place, that
they may be blind and leaders of the blind. And those
who walk in darkness stumble ; and the blind commit
crimes in their hearts which come to pass in time of discord. Tell us, pride, how would'st thou have reigned over
Lucifer if thou had'st not had discord to aid thee? Tell us,
hateful Satan, how would'st thou have cast Adam out of

Paradise if thou had'st not divided him from his obedience? Tell us, luxury, how would'st thou have destroyed Troy, if thou had'st not divided Helen from her husband? Tell us, wrath, how would'st thou have destroyed the Roman republic had'st thou not, by means of discord, spurred on Pompey and Caesar with raging swords to internal conflict? Thou, indeed, oh envy, hast, with impious wickedness, spued with the ancient poison against the Christian empire which is fortified by God, like to the holy and indivisible Trinity, with the theological virtues of faith, hope, and charity; whose foundation is happily established above in the very kingdom of Christ. Thou hast done this, like a serpent, against the branches of the empire and its nearer members; so that, the columns being shaken, thou mightest subject the whole edifice to ruin. Thou hast often spread discord among the seven electors of the holy empire, through whom, as through seven candlesticks throwing light in the unity of a septiform spirit, the holy empire ought to be illumined.

Inasmuch as we, through the office by which we possess the imperial dignity, are doubly—both as emperor and by the electoral right which we enjoy—bound to put an end to future danger of discords among the electors themselves, to whose number we, as king of Bohemia are known to belong: we have promulgated, decreed and recommended for ratification, the subjoined laws for the purpose of cherishing unity among the electors, and of bringing about a unanimous election, and of closing all approach to the aforesaid detestable discord and to the various dangers which arise from it. This we have done in our solemn court at Nuremberg, in session with all the electoral princes, ecclesiastical and secular, and amid a numerous multitude of other princes, counts, barons, magnates, nobles and citizens; after mature deliberation, from the fulness of our imperial power; sitting on the throne of our imperial majesty, adorned with the imperial bands, insignia and diadem; in the year of our Lord 1356, in the 9th Indiction, on the 4th day before the Ides of January, in the 10th year of our reign as king, the 1st as emperor.

1. *What sort of escort the electors should have, and by whom furnished.*

(1) We decree, and, by the present imperial and ever valid edict, do sanction of certain knowledge and from the plenitude of the imperial power: that whenever, and so often as in future, necessity or occasion shall arise for the election of a king of the Romans and prospective emperor, and the prince electors, according to ancient and laudable custom, are obliged to journey to such election,—each prince elector, if, and whenever, he is called upon to do this, shall be bound to escort any of his fellow prince electors or the envoys whom they shall send to this election, through his lands, territories and districts, and even as much beyond them as he shall be able; and to lend them escort without guile on their way to the city in which such election is to be held, and also in returning from it. This he shall do under pain of perjury and the loss, for that time only, of the vote which he was about to have in such election; which penalty, indeed, we decree that he or they who shall prove rebellious or negligent in furnishing the aforesaid escort shall, by the very act, incur.

(2) We furthermore decree, and we command all other princes holding fiefs from the holy Roman empire, whatever the service they have to perform,—also all counts, barons, knights, noble and common followers, citizens and communities of castles, cities and districts of the holy empire: that at this same time—when, namely, an election is to take place of king of the Romans and prospective emperor—they shall, without guile, in the manner aforesaid, escort through their territories and as far beyond as they can, any prince elector demanding from them, or any one of them, help of this kind, or the envoys whom, as has been explained before, he shall have sent to that election. But if any persons shall presume to run counter to this our decree they shall, by the act itself, incur the following penalties: all princes and counts, barons, noble knights and followers, and all nobles acting counter to it, shall be considered guilty of perjury and deprived of all the fiefs which they hold of the holy Roman empire and of any

lords whatever, and also of all their possessions no matter from whom they hold them.   All cities and guilds, moreover, presuming to act counter to the foregoing, shall similarly be considered guilty of perjury, and likewise shall be altogether deprived of all their rights, liberties, privileges and favours obtained from the holy empire, and both in their persons and in all their possessions shall incur the imperial bann and proscription.   And any man, on his own authority and without trial or the calling in of any magistrate, may henceforth with impunity attack those whom we, by the act itself, deprive, from now or from a past time on, of all their rights.   And, in attacking them, he need fear no punishment on this account from the empire or any one else; inasmuch as they, rashly negligent in so great a matter, are convicted of acting faithlessly and perversely, as disobedient and perfidious persons and rebels against the state, and against the majesty and dignity of the holy empire, and even against their own honour and safety.

(3) We decree, moreover, and command, that the citizens and guilds of all cities shall be compelled to sell or cause to be sold to the aforesaid prince electors, or to any one of them who demands it, and to their envoys, when they are going to said city for the sake of holding said election, and even when they are returning from it: victuals at the common and current price for the needs of themselves or the said envoys and their followers.   And in no way shall they act fraudulently with regard to the foregoing.   We will that those who do otherwise shall, by the act itself, incur those penalties which we, in the foregoing, have seen fit to decree against citizens and guilds.   Whoever, moreover, of the princes, counts, barons, knights, noble or common followers, citizens or guilds of cities shall presume to erect hostile barriers or to prepare ambushes for a prince elector going to hold the election of a king of the Romans or returning from it,—or to attack or disturb them or any one of them in their persons or in their property, or in the persons of said envoys sent by them or any one of them, whether they have sought escort or have not considered it worth while to demand it: we decree that he, together with all the accomplices of his iniquity, shall,

by the act itself, have incurred the above penalties; in such wise, namely, that each person shall incur the penalty or penalties which, according to what precedes, we have thought best, relatively to the rank of those persons, to inflict.

(4) But if any prince elector should be at enmity with any one of his co-electors, and any contention, controversy, or dissension should be going on between them ;—notwithstanding this, one shall be bound, under penalty of perjury and loss, for this one time, of his vote in the election, as has been stated above, to escort in said manner the other, or the envoys of the other who shall be sent in said manner to such election.

(5) But if any princes, counts, barons, knights, noble or common followers, citizens, or guilds of cities, should bear ill-will to one or more of the prince electors, or any mutual discord, or war, or dissension should be going on between them : nevertheless, all opposition and fraud being laid aside, they ought to furnish such escort to this or to these prince electors, or to his or their envoys dispatched to or returning from such election, according as they each and all desire to avoid the said punishments declared by us against them ; punishments which those who act counter shall, we decree, by the act itself incur. Moreover, for the ampler security and certitude of all the above, we command and we will that all the prince electors and other princes, also the counts, barons, nobles, cities or guilds of the same, shall confirm all the aforesaid through their writings and through their oaths, and shall efficaciously bind themselves to fulfil them with good faith and without guile. But whoever shall refuse to give writings of this kind, shall, by the act itself, incur such punishment as we, by the above, have seen fit to inflict on each person according to his rank.

(6) But if any prince elector or other prince of whatever condition or standing, or any count, baron, or noble, or the successors or heirs of such, holding a fief or fiefs from the holy empire, be not willing to fulfill our imperial constitutions and laws above and below laid down, or shall presume to act counter to them : if such a one, indeed, be an elector prince, his co-electors shall, from that time on,

exclude him from association with themselves, and he shall lose both his vote in the election and the position, dignity and privileges possessed by the other electors; nor shall he be invested with the fiefs which he shall have obtained from the holy empire. But any other prince or nobleman infringing, as we have said, these our laws, shall likewise not be invested with fiefs which he shall obtain from the holy empire or from any one otherwise, and shall, in addition, incur by the act itself all the aforesaid penalties concerning his person.

(7) Although, indeed, we have willed and decreed in general terms that all princes, counts, barons, nobles, knights, followers, and also cities and guilds of the same, are bound, as has been said, to furnish the aforesaid escort to any prince elector or his envoys: nevertheless we have thought best to designate for each one of them special escorts and conductors who will be best suited for them according to the nearness of their lands and districts, as will directly be made clearer from what follows.

(8) For first the king of Bohemia, the arch-cupbearer of the holy empire, shall be escorted by the archbishop of Mainz, the bishops of Bamberg and Wurzburg, the bur-graves of Nuremberg; likewise by those of Hohenlohe, of Wertheim, of Bruneck and of Hohenau; likewise by the cities of Nuremberg, Rothenburg, and Windesheim.

(9) Then the archbishop of Cologne, the arch-chancellor of the holy empire for Italy, shall be escorted—they being bound to furnish such escort—by the archbishops of Mainz and Treves, the count palatine of the Rhine, the landgrave of Hesse; likewise by the counts of Katzenellen-bogen, of Nassau, of Dietz; likewise of Ysenburg, of Westerburg, of Runkel, of Limburg and Falkenstein; likewise by the cities of Wetzlar, Gelnhausen and Friedberg.

(10) In like manner the archbishop of Treves, arch-chancellor of the holy empire for the Gallic provinces and for the kingdom of Arles, shall be escorted by the arch-bishop of Mainz, the count palatine of the Rhine; likewise the counts of Sponheim, of Veldenz; likewise the Rau-graves and Wiltgraves of Nassau, of Ysenburg, of Wester-burg, of Runkel, of Dietz, of Katzenellenbogen, of Eppen-stein, of Falkenstein; likewise the city of Mainz.

(11) Then the count palatine of the Rhine, arch-steward of the holy empire, ought to be escorted by the archbishop of Mainz.

(12) But the duke of Saxony, the arch-marshall of the holy empire, shall, by right, be escorted by the king of Bohemia, the archbishops of Mainz and Madgeburg; likewise by the bishops of Bamberg and Wurzburg, the margrave of Meissen, the landgrave of Hesse; likewise the abbots of Fulda and Hersfeld, the burgraves of Nuremberg; likewise those of Hohenlohe, of Wertheim, of Bruneck, of Hohenau, of Falkenstein; likewise the cities of Erfurt, Mülhausen, Nuremberg, Rothenburg and Windesheim. And all of these last named shall likewise be bound to escort the margrave of Brandenburg, arch-chamberlain of the holy empire.

(13) We will, moreover, and do expressly decree that each prince elector who shall wish to have such escort shall make known this fact and the way by which he is to pass, and shall demand this escort in such good time that those who have been deputed to furnish such escort, and from whom it shall thus have been demanded, may be able to prepare themselves for this in good time and conveniently.

(14) We declare, moreover, that the foregoing decrees promulgated concerning the matter of escort shall, indeed, be so understood that each person named above—or perhaps not expressed—from whom, in the aforesaid case, escort may happen to be demanded, shall be bound to furnish it at least through his lands and territories, and as far beyond as he can, without fraud, under the penalties contained above.

(15) Moreover we decree, and also ordain, that he who shall be archbishop of Mainz at the time shall intimate this same election to the different princes, ecclesiastical and secular, his co-electors, by letters patent, through his envoys. In which letters, indeed, the day and the term shall be expressed within which those letters may probably reach each of those princes. And letters of this sort shall state that, within three successive months from the day expressed in the letters themselves, each and all of the prince electors ought to be settled at Frankfort on the Main, or to

send their lawful envoys, at that time and to that place, with full and diverse power, and with their letters patent, signed with the great seal of each of them, to elect a king of the Romans and prospective emperor.   How, moreover, and under what form such letters ought to be drawn up, and what formality ought to be immutably observed with regard to them, and in what form and manner the prince electors should arrange what envoys are to be sent to such election, and the power, mandate, or right of procuration that they are to have: all this will be found clearly and expressly written at the end of the present document.   And we command and decree, through the plentitude of the imperial power, that the form there established be preserved unto all time.

(16) Moreover we ordain and decree that when the death of the emperor or king of the Romans shall come to be known for certain in the diocese of Mainz,—within one month of that time, counting continuously from the day of the notice of such death, the death itself and the summons of which we have spoken shall be announced by the archbishop of Mainz through his letters patent.   But if this same archbishop should chance to be negligent or remiss in carrying out this and in sending the summons,—thereupon those same princes of their own accord shall, even without summons, by virtue of the fealty which they owe to the holy empire, come together in the oft-mentioned city of Frankfort within three months after this, as is contained in the decree immediately preceding, being about to elect a king of the Romans and future emperor.

(17) Moreover any one prince elector or his envoys should, at the time of the aforesaid election, enter the said city of Frankfort with not more than two hundred mounted followers, among which number he may be allowed to bring in with himself only fifty armed men or fewer, but not more.

(18) But a prince elector, called and summoned to such election, and neither coming to it nor sending lawful envoys with letters patent, sealed with his greater seal and containing empowerment, full, free and of every kind, for the election of king of the Romans and prospective emperor; or one who comes, or perchance sends envoys, to the same,

but who, afterwards, himself—or the aforesaid embassy—
goes away from the place of election before a king of the
Romans and prospective emperor has been elected, and
does not formally substitute a lawful procurator and leave
him there : shall forfeit for that time the vote or right
which he had in that election and which he abandoned in
such a manner.

(19) We command, moreover, and enjoin on the citizens
of Frankfort, that they, by virtue of the oath which we decree they shall swear on the gospel concerning this, shall,
with faithful zeal and anxious diligence, protect and defend
all the prince electors in general and each one of them in
particular from the invasion of the other, if any quarrel
shall arise between them ; and also from the invasion of
any other person. And the same with regard to all the
followers whom they or any one of them shall have brought
into the said city among the said number of two hundred
horsemen. Otherwise they shall incur the guilt of perjury,
and shall also lose all their rights, liberties, privileges,
favours and grants which they are known to hold from the
holy empire, and shall, by the act itself, fall under the
bann of the empire as to their persons and all their goods.
And, from that time on, every man on his own authority
and without judicial sentence may, with impunity, invade
as traitors and as disloyal persons and as rebels against the
empire, those citizens whom we, in such a case, from now
or from a former time on, deprive of all their rights. And
such invaders need in no way fear any punishment from the
holy empire or from any one else.

(20) The said citizens of Frankfort, moreover, throughout all that time when the oft-mentioned election is being
treated of and carried on, shall not admit, or in any way
permit any one, of whatever dignity, condition or standing
he may be, to enter the aforesaid city : the prince electors
and their envoys and the aforesaid procurators alone being
excepted ; each of whom shall be admitted, as has been
said, with two hundred horsemen. But if, after the entry
of these same prince electors, or while they are present, any
one shall chance to be found in the said city, the citizens
themselves shall, effectually and without delay, straightway bring about his exit, under penalty of all that has

above been promulgated against them, and also by virtue of the oath concerning this that those same citizens of Frankfort must, by the terms of this present decree, swear upon the gospel, as has been explained in the foregoing.

2. *Concerning the election of a king of the Romans.*

(1) After, moreover, the oft-mentioned electors or their envoys shall have entered the city of Frankfort, they shall, straightway on the following day at dawn, in the church of St. Bartholomew the apostle, in the presence of all of them, cause a mass to be sung to the Holy Spirit, that the Holy Spirit himself may illumine their hearts and infuse the light of his virtue into their senses ; so that they, armed with his protection, may be able to elect a just, good and useful man as king of the Romans and future emperor, and as a safeguard for the people of Christ. After such mass has been performed all those electors or their envoys shall approach the altar on which that mass has been celebrated, and there the ecclesiastical prince electors, before the gospel of St. John : "In the beginning was the word," which must there be placed before them, shall place their hands with reverence upon their breasts. But the secular prince electors shall actually touch the said gospel with their hands. And all of them, with all their followers, shall stand there unarmed. And the archbishop of Mainz shall give to them the form of the oath, and he together with them, and they, or the envoys of the absent ones, together with him, shall take the oath in common as follows :

(2) " I, archbishop of Mainz, arch-chancellor of the holy empire throughout Germany, and prince elector, do swear on this holy gospel of God here actually placed before me, that I, through the faith which binds me to God and to the holy Roman empire, do intend by the help of God, to the utmost extent of my discretion and intelligence, and in accordance with the said faith, to elect one who will be suitable, as far as my discretion and discernment can tell, for a temporal head of the Christian people,—that is, a king of the Romans and prospective emperor. And my voice and vote, or said election, I will give without any

pact, payment, price, or promise, or whatever such things may be called. So help me God and all the saints."

(3) Such oath having been taken by the electors or their envoys in the aforesaid form and manner, they shall then proceed to the election. And from now on they shall not disperse from the said city of Frankfort until the majority of them shall have elected a temporal head for the world and for the Christian people; a king, namely, of the Romans and prospective emperor. But if they shall fail to do this within thirty days, counting continuously from the day when they took the aforesaid oath: when those thirty days are over, from that time on they shall live on bread and water, and by no means leave the afore-said city unless first through them, or the majority of them, a ruler or temporal head of the faithful shall have been elected, as was said before.

(4) Moreover after they, or the majority of them, shall have made their choice in that place, such election shall in future be considered and looked upon as if it had been unanimously carried through by all of them, no one dis-senting. And if any one of the electors or their aforesaid envoys should happen for a time to be detained and to be absent or late, provided he arrive before the said election has been consummated, we decree that he shall be admitted to the election in the stage at which it was at the actual time of his coming. And since by ancient approved and laudable custom what follows has always been observed inviolately, therefore we also do establish and decree by the plenitude of the imperial power that he who shall have, in the aforesaid manner, been elected king of the Romans, shall, directly after such election shall have been held, and before he shall attend to any other cases or matters by virtue of his imperial office, without delay or contradiction, confirm and approve, by his letters and seals, to each and all of the elector princes, ecclesiastical and secular, who are known to be the nearer members of the holy empire, all their privileges, charters, rights, liber-ties, ancient customs, and also their dignities and whatever they shall have obtained and possessed from the empire before the day of the election. And he shall renew to them all the above after he shall have been crowned with

the imperial adornments.   Moreover, the elected king
shall make such confirmation to each prince elector in particular, first as king, then, renewing it, under his title as
emperor; and, in these matters, he shall be bound by no
means to impede either those same princes in general or
any one of them in particular, but rather to promote them
with his favour and without guile.

(5) In a case, finally, where three prince electors in
person, or the envoys of the absent ones, shall elect as
king of the Romans a fourth from among themselves or
from among their whole number—an elector prince,
namely, who is either present or absent:—we decree that
the vote of that person who has been elected, if he shall
be present, or of his envoys if he shall chance to be absent,
shall have full vigour and shall increase the number of
those electing, and shall constitute a majority like that of
the other prince electors.

3. Concerning the seating of the bishops of Treves, Cologne and Mainz.

In the name of the holy and indivisible Trinity felicitously amen.   Charles the Fourth, by favour of the divine
mercy emperor of the Romans, always august, and king
of Bohemia.   As a perpetual memorial of this matter.
The splendour and glory of the holy Roman empire, and
the imperial honour, and the cherished advantage of the
state are fostered by the concordant will of the venerable
and illustrious prince electors, who, being the chief
columns as it were, sustain the holy edifice by the vigilant
piety of circumspect prudence; by whose protection the
right hand of the imperial power is strengthened.   And
the more they are bound together by an ampler benignity
of mutual favour, so much more abundantly will the bles-
sings of peace and tranquillity happily flow for the people
of Christ.   In order, therefore, that between the venerable
archbishops of Mainz, Cologne and Treves, prince electors
of the holy empire, all causes of strife and suspicion
which might arise in future concerning the priority or
dignity of their seats in the imperial and royal courts may
be for all time removed, and that they, remaining in a

quiet state of heart and soul, may be able, with concordant favour and the zeal of virtuous love, to meditate more conveniently concerning the affairs of the holy empire, to the consolation of the Christian people : we, having deliberated with all the prince electors, ecclesiastical as well as secular, do decree from the plenitude of the imperial power, by this law, in the form of an edict, to be forever valid,—that the aforesaid venerable archbishops can, may, and ought to sit as follows in all public transactions pertaining to the empire; namely, in courts, while conferring fiefs, when regaling themselves at table, and also in councils and in all other business on account of which they happen or shall happen to come together to treat of the honour or utility of the empire. He of Treves, namely, shall sit directly opposite and facing the emperor. But at the right hand of the emperor of the Romans shall sit he of Mainz when in his own diocese and province ; and also, outside of his province, throughout his whole arch-chancellorship of Germany, excepting alone the province of Cologne. And he of Cologne, finally, shall sit there when in his own diocese and province, and, outside of his province, throughout all Italy and Gaul. And we will that this form of seating, in the same order as is above expressed, be extended forever to the successors of the aforesaid archbishops of Cologne, Treves and Mainz; so that at no time shall any doubt whatever arise concerning these matters.

4. *Concerning the prince electors in common.*

We decree, moreover, that, as often as an imperial court shall henceforth chance to be held, in every assembly,—in council, namely, at table or in any place whatsoever where the emperor or king of the Romans shall happen to sit with the prince electors, on the right side of the emperor or king of the Romans there shall sit immediately after the archbishop of Mainz or the archbishop of Cologne—whichever, namely, shall happen at that time, according to the place or province, following the tenor of his privilege, to sit at the right hand of the emperor—first, the king of Bohemia, as he is a crowned and anointed prince, and secondly, the count palatine of the Rhine. But on the left side, immediately after whichever of the aforesaid archbishops shall happen to sit on the left, the duke of Saxony shall have the first, and, after him, the margrave of Brandenburg the second place.

But so often and whenever the holy empire shall hereafter happen to be vacant, the archbishop of Mainz shall then have the right, which he is known from of old to have had, of convoking the other princes, his aforesaid companions in the said election. And when all of them, or those who can and will be present, are assembled together at the term of the election, it shall pertain to the said archbishop of Mainz and to no other to call for the votes of these his co-electors, one by one in the following order. First, indeed, he shall interrogate the archbishop of Treves, to whom we declare that the first vote belongs, and to whom, as we find, it hitherto has belonged. Secondly, the archbishop of Cologne, to whom belongs the dignity and also the duty of first imposing the royal diadem on the king of the Romans. Thirdly, the king of Bohemia, who, rightly and duly, on account of the prestige of his royal dignity, has the first place among the lay electors. Fourthly, the count palatine of the Rhine. Fifthly, the duke of Saxony. Sixthly, the margrave of Brandenburg. Of all these the said archbishop of Mainz shall call for the votes in the aforesaid order. This being done, the aforesaid princes his companions, shall, in their turn, call on him to express his own intention and to make known to them his vote. Moreover, when an imperial court is held, the margrave of Brandenburg shall present the water for washing the hands of the emperor or king of the Romans. And the king of Bohemia shall be the first to offer drink ; but, according to the tenor of the privileges of his kingdom, he shall not be bound to offer it with his royal crown on, except of his own free will. The count palatine of the Rhine, moreover, shall be obliged to offer food, and the duke of Saxony shall perform the office of marshal, as has been the custom from of old.

5. *Concerning the right of the count palatine and also of the duke of Saxony.*

Whenever, moreover, as has been said before, the throne of the holy empire shall happen to be vacant, the illustrious count palatine of the Rhine, arch-steward of the holy empire, the right hand of the future king of the Romans in the districts of the Rhine and of Swabia and in the limits of Franconia, ought, by reason of his principality or by privilege of the county palatine, to be the administrator of the empire itself, with the power of passing judgments, of presenting to ecclesiastical benefices, of collecting returns and revenues and investing with fiefs, of receiving oaths of fealty for and in the name of the holy empire. All of these acts, however, shall, in due time, be renewed by the king of the Romans who is afterwards elected, and the oaths shall be sworn to him anew. The fiefs of princes are alone excepted, and those which are commonly called banner-fiefs: the conferring of which, and the investing, we reserve especially for the emperor or king of the Romans alone. The count palatine must know, nevertheless, that every kind of alienation or obligation of imperial possessions, in the time of such administration, is expressly forbidden to him. And we will that the illustrious king of Saxony, arch-marshal of the holy empire, shall enjoy the same right of administration in those places where the Saxon jurisdiction prevails, under all the modes and conditions that have been expressed above.

And although the emperor or king of the Romans, in matters concerning which he is called to account, has to answer before the count palatine of the Rhine and prince elector—as is is said to have been introduced by custom :— nevertheless the count palatine shall not be able to exercise that right of judging otherwise than in the imperial court, where the emperor or king of the Romans shall be present.

6. *Concerning the comparison of prince electors with other, ordinary princes.*

We decree that, in holding an imperial court, whenever in future one shall chance to be held, the aforesaid prince electors, ecclesiastical and secular, shall immutably hold their positions on the right and on the left—according to the prescribed order and manner.   And no other prince, of whatever standing, dignity, pre-eminence or condition he may be, shall in any way be preferred to them or any-one of them, in any acts relating to that court; in going there, while sitting or while standing.   And it is distinctly declared that especially the king of Bohemia shall, in the holding of such courts, in each and every place and act aforesaid, immutably precede any other king, with what-soever special prerogative of dignity he may be adorned, no matter what the occasion or cause for which he may happen to come or to be present.

7. *Concerning the successors of the princes.*

Among those innumerable cares for the well-being of the holy empire over which we, by God's grace, do happily reign—cares which daily try our heart,—our thoughts are chiefly directed to this: that union, desirable and always healthful, may continually flourish among the prince electors of the holy empire, and that the hearts of those men may be preserved in the concord of sincere charity, by whose timely care the disturbances of the world are the more easily and quickly allayed, the less error creeps in among them, and the more purely charity is observed, obscurity being removed and the rights of each one being clearly defined.   It is, indeed, commonly known far and wide, and clearly manifest, as it were, throughout the whole world, that those illustrious men the king of Bohemia and the count palatine of the Rhine, the duke of Saxony and the margrave of Brandenburg, have—the one by reason of his kingdom, the others of their principalities, —together with the ecclesiastical princes their co-electors, their right, vote and place in the election of the king of the Romans and prospective emperor. And, together with the spiritual princes, they are considered and are the true and lawful prince electors of the holy empire. Lest, in future, among the sons of these same secular prince electors, matter for scandal and dissension should arise concerning the above right, vote and power, and the common welfare be thus jeopardized by dangerous delays, we, wishing by God's help to wholesomely obviate future dangers, do establish with imperial authority and decree, by the present ever-to-be-valid law, that when these same secular prince electors, or any of them, shall die, the right, vote and power of thus electing shall, freely and without the contradiction of any one, devolve on his first born, legitimate, lay son; but, if he be not living, on the son of this same first born son, if he be a layman. If, however, such first born son shall have departed from this world without leaving male legitimate lay heirs,—by virtue of the present imperial edict, the right, vote and aforesaid power of electing shall devolve upon the elder lay brother descended by the true paternal line, and thence upon his first born lay son. And such succession of the first born sons, and of the heirs of these same princes, to their right, vote and power, shall be observed in all future time; under such rule and condition, however, that if a prince elector, or his first born or eldest lay son, should happen to die leaving male, legitimate, lay heirs who are minors, then the eldest of the brothers of that elector, or of his first born son, shall be their tutor and administrator until the eldest of them shall have attained legitimate age. Which age we wish to have considered, and we decree that it shall be considered, eighteen full years in the case of prince electors; and, when they shall have attained this, the guardian shall straightway be obliged to resign to them completely, together with his office, the right, vote and power, and all that these involve. But if any such principality should happen to revert to the holy empire, the then emperor or king of the Romans should and may so dispose of it as of a possession which has lawfully devolved upon himself and the empire. Saving always the privileges, rights and customs of our kingdom of Bohemia concerning the election, through its subjects, of a king in

case of a vacancy. For they have the right of electing
the king of Bohemia; such election to be made according
to the contents of those privileges obtained from the illustrious emperors or kings of the Romans, and according
to long observed custom; to which privileges we wish to do
no violence by an imperial edict of this kind. On the contrary we decree that, now and in all future time, they
shall have undoubted power and validity as to all their
import and as to their form.

8. *Concerning the immunity of the king of Bohemia and his
subjects.*

Inasmuch as, through our predecessors the divine emperors and kings of the Romans, it was formerly graciously
conceded and allowed to our progenitors and predecessors
the illustrious kings of Bohemia, also to the kingdom of
Bohemia and to the crown of that same kingdom; and
was introduced, without hindrance of contradiction or
interruption, into that kingdom at a time to which memory
does not reach back, by a laudable custom preserved unshaken by length of time, and called for by the character
of those who enjoy it; that no prince, baron, noble, knight,
follower, burgher, citizen—in a word no person belonging
to that kingdom and its dependencies wherever they may
be, no matter what his standing, dignity, pre-eminence, or
condition—might, or in all future time may, be cited, or
dragged or summoned, at the instance of any plaintiff
whatsoever, before any tribunal beyond that kingdom
itself other than that of the king of Bohemia and of the
judges of his royal court: therefore of certain knowledge,
by the imperial authority and from the plenitude of
imperial power, we renew and also confirm such privilege,
custom and favour; and by this our imperial forever-to-
be-valid edict do decree that if, contrary to the said privilege, custom, or favour, any one of the foregoing—namely,
any prince, baron, noble, knight, follower, citizen, burgher,
or rustic, or any afore-mentioned person whatever—at any
time be cited in any civil, criminal, or mixed case, or concerning any matter, before the tribunal of any one outside
the said kingdom of Bohemia, he shall not at all be bound

to appear when summoned, or to answer before the court.
But if it shall chance that, against any such person or
persons not appearing, by any judge outside of that kingdom of Bohemia, no matter what his authority, judicial
proceedings are instituted, a trial is carried on, or one or
more intermediate or final sentences are passed and promulgated: by the aforesaid anthority, and also from the
plentitude of the aforesaid imperial power, we declare
utterly vain, and do annul such citations, commands, proceedings and sentences, also the carrying out of them and
everything which may in any way be attempted or done in
consequence of them or any one of them. And we expressly
add and, by the same authority and from the fulness of
the aforesaid power, do decree by an ever-to-be-valid
imperial edict that, just as it has been continually observed
from time immemorial in the aforesaid kingdom of
Bohemia, so, henceforth, no prince, baron, noble, knight,
follower, citizen, burgher, or rustic—in short no person or
inhabitant of the oft-mentioned kingdom of Bohemia,
whatever be his standing, pre-eminence, dignity, or condition—may be allowed to appeal to any other tribunal from
any proceedings, provisional or final sentences, or ordinances of the king of Bohemia or of his judges, instituted
or promulgated, or henceforth to be instituted or promulgated against him, in the royal court or before tribunals
of the king, the kingdom or the aforesaid judges. Nor
may he appeal against the putting into execution of the
same Provocations or appeals of this kind, moreover, if
any, contrary to this edict, should chance to be brought,
shall of their own accord be invalid; and those appealing
shall know that, by the act itself, they have incurred the
penalty of loss of their case.

9. *Concerning mines of gold, silver and other specie.*

We establish by this ever-to-be-valid decree, and of certain knowledge do declare that our successors the kings of
Bohemia, also each and all future prince electors, ecclesiastical and secular, may justly hold and lawfully possess—
with all their rights without exception, according as such
things can be, or usually have been possessed—all the gold
and silver mines and mines of tin, copper, lead, iron and

any other kind of metal, and also of salt : the king, those which have been found, and which shall at any future time be found, in the aforesaid kingdom and the lands and dependencies of that kingdom,—and the aforesaid electors in their principalities, lands, domains and dependencies. And they may also have the Jew taxes and enjoy the tolls which have been decreed and assigned to them in the past, and whatever our progenitors the kings of Bohemia of blessed memory, and these same prince electors and their progenitors and predecessors shall have legally possessed until now ; as is known to have been observed by ancient custom, laudable and approved, and sanctioned by the lapse of a very long period of time.

10. *Concerning money.*

(1) We decree, moreover, that our successor, the king for the time being of Bohemia, shall have the same right which our predecessors the kings of Bohemia of blessed memory are known to have had, and in the continuous peaceful possession of which they remained : the right, namely, in every place and part of their kingdom, and of the lands subject to them, and of all their dependencies— wherever the king himself may have decreed and shall please—of coining gold and silver money and of circulating it in every way and manner observed up to this time in this same kingdom of Bohemia in such matters. (2) And, by this our imperial ever-to-be-valid decree and favour we establish, that all future kings of Bohemia forever shall have the right of buying or purchasing, or of receiving in gift or donation for any reason, or in bond, from any princes, magnates, counts or other persons, any lands, castles, possessions, estates or goods, under the usual conditions with regard to such lands, castles, possessions, estates or goods : that, namely, alods shall be bought or received as alods, freeholds as freeholds ; that holdings in feudal dependency shall be bought as fiefs, and shall be held as such when bought. In such wise, however, that the kings of Bohemia shall themselves be bound to regard and to render to the holy empire its pristine and customary rights over these things (lands, etc.) which they shall, in this way, have bought or received, and have seen fit to

add to the kingdom of Bohemia. (3) We will, moreover, that the present decree and favour, by virtue of this our present imperial law, be fully extended to all the elector princes, ecclesiastical as well as secular, and to their successors and lawful heirs, under all the foregoing forms and conditions.

11. *Concerning the immunity of the prince electors.*

We also decree that no counts, barons, nobles, feudal vassals, knights of castles, followers, citizens, burghers—indeed, no male or female subjects at all of the Cologne, Mainz and Treves churches, whatever their standing, condition or dignity—could in past times, or may or can in future be summoned at the instance of any plaintiff whatsoever, beyond the territory and boundaries and limits of these same churches and their dependencies, to any other tribunal or the court of any other person than the archbishops of Mainz, Treves and Cologne and their judges. And this we find was the observance in the past. But if, contrary to our present edict, one or more of the aforesaid subjects of the Treves, Mainz or Cologne churches should chance to be summoned, at the instance of any one whatever, to the tribunal of any one beyond the territory, limits or bounds of the said churches or of any one of them, for any criminal, civil or mixed case, or in any matter at all: they shall not in the least be compelled to appear or respond. And we decree that the summons, and the proceedings, and the provisional and final sentences already sent or passed, or in future to be sent or passed against those not appearing, by such extraneous judges, —furthermore their ordinances, and the carrying out of the above measures, and all things which might come to pass, be attempted or be done through them or any one of them, shall be void of their own accord. And we expressly add that no count, baron, noble, feudal vassal, knight of a castle, citizen, peasant—no person, in short, subject to such churches or inhabiting the lands of the same, whatever be his standing, dignity or condition—shall be allowed to appeal to any other tribunal from the proceedings, the provisional and final sentences, or the ordi-

nances—or the putting into effect of the same—of such
archbishops and their churches, or of their temporal officials,
when such proceedings, sentences or ordinances shall have
been, or shall in future be held, passed or made against
him in the court of the archbishops or of the aforesaid
officials.   Provided that justice has not been denied to
those bringing plaint in the courts of the aforesaid archbishops and their officials.   But appeals against this statute
shall not, we decree, be received; we declare them null and
void.   In case of defect of justice, however, it is allowed to
all the aforementioned persons to appeal, but only to the
imperial court and tribunal or directly to the presence of
the judge presiding at the time in the imperial court.
And, even in case of such defect, those to whom justice
has been denied may not appeal to any other judge, whether
ordinary or delegated.   And whatever shall have been done
contrary to the above shall be void of its own accord.   And,
by virtue of this our present imperial law, we will that this
statute be fully extended, under all the preceding forms
and conditions, to those illustrious men the count palatine
of the Rhine, the duke of Saxony, the margrave of Brandenburg,—the secular or lay prince electors, their heirs,
successors and subjects.

12. *Concerning the coming together of the princes.*

In view of the manifold cares of state with which our
mind is constantly distracted, after much consideration
our sublimity has found that it will be necessary for the
prince electors of the holy empire to come together more
frequently than has been their custom, to treat of the
safety of that same empire and of the world.   For they,
the solid bases and immovable columns of the empire,
according as they reside at long distances from each other,
just so are able to report and confer concerning the
impending defects of the districts known to them, and
are not ignorant how, by the wise counsels of their providence, they may aid in the necessary reformation of the
same.   Hence it is that, in the solemn court held by our
highness at Nuremberg together with the venerable ecclesiastical and illustrious secular prince electors, and many

other princes and nobles, we, having deliberated with
those same prince electors and followed their advice, have
seen fit to ordain, together with the said prince electors,
ecclesiastical as well as secular, for the common good and
safety: that these same prince electors, once every year,
when four weeks, counting continuously from the Easter
feast of the Lord's resurrection, are past, shall personally
congregate in some city of the holy empire; and that
when next that date shall come round, namely, in the
present year, a colloquium, or court, or assembly of this
kind, shall be held by us and these same princes in our
imperial city of Metz.   And then, and henceforth on any
day of an assembly of this kind, the place where they shall
meet the following year shall be fixed upon by us with
their counsel.   And this our ordinance is to endure just
so long as it may be our and their good pleasure.   And,
so long as it shall endure, we take them under our imperial
safe conduct when going to, remaining at, and also returning from said court.   Moreover, lest the transactions for
the common safety and peace be retarded, as is sometimes
the case, by the delay and hinderance of diversion or the
excessive frequenting of feasts, we have thought best to
ordain, by concordant desire, that henceforth, while the
said court or congregation shall last, no one may be
allowed to give general entertainments for all the princes.
Special ones, however, which do no impede the transaction
of business, may be permitted in moderation.

13. *Concerning the revocation of privileges.*

Moreover we establish, and by this perpetual imperial
edict do decree, that no privileges or charters concerning
any rights, favours, immunities, customs or other things,
conceded, of our own accord or otherwise, under any form
of words, by us or our predecessors of blessed memory the
divine emperors or kings of the Romans, or about to be
conceded in future by us or our successors the Roman
emperors and kings, to any persons of whatever standing,
pre-eminence or dignity, or to the corporation of cities,
towns, or any places: shall or may, in any way at all,
derogate from the liberties, jurisdictions, rights, honours

or dominions of the ecclesiastical and secular prince electors; even if in such privileges and charters of any persons, whatever their pre-eminence, dignity or standing, as has been said, or of corporations of this kind, it shall have been, or shall be in future, expressly cautioned that they shall not be revokable unless, concerning these very points and the whole tenor included in them, special mention word for word and in due order shall be made in such revocation.   For such privileges and charters, if, and in as far as, they are considered to derogate in any way from the liberties, jurisdictions, rights, honours or dominions of the said prince electors, or any one of them, in so far we revoke them of certain knowledge and cancel them, and decree, from the plenitude of our imperial power, that they shall be considered and held to be revoked.

14. *Concerning those from whom, as being unworthy, their feudal possessions are taken away.*

In very many places the vassals and feudatories of lords unseasonably renounce or resign, verbally and fraudulently, fiefs or benefices which they hold from those same lords. And, having made such resignation, they maliciously challenge those same lords, and declare enmity against them, subsequently inflicting grave harm upon them. And, under pretext of war or hostility, they again invade and occupy benefices and fiefs which they had thus renounced, and hold possession of them.   Therefore we establish, by the present ever-to-be-valid decree, that such renunciation or resignation shall be considered as not having taken place, unless it shall have been freely and actually made by them in such way that possession of such benefices and fiefs shall be personally and actually given over to those same lords so fully that, at no future time, shall they, either through themselves or through others, by sending challenges, trouble those same lords as to the goods, fiefs or benefices resigned; nor shall they lend counsel, aid or favour to this end.   He who acts otherwise, and in any way invades his lords as to benefices and fiefs, resigned or not resigned, or disturbs them, or brings harm upon them, or furnishes counsel, aid or favour

to those doing this : shall, by the act itself, lose such fiefs
and benefices, shall be dishonoured and shall underlie the
bann of the empire; and no approach or return to such
fiefs or benefices shall be open to him at any time in
future, nor may the same be granted to him anew under
any conditions; and a concession of them, or an investiture which takes place contrary to this, shall have no
force.   Finally, by virtue of this present edict, we decree
that he or they who, not having made such resignation as
we have described, acting fraudulently against his or their
lords, shall knowingly invade them—whether a challenge
has previously been sent or has been omitted,—shall, by
the act itself, incur all the aforesaid punishments.

15. *Concerning conspiracies.*

Furthermore we reprobate, condemn, and of certain
knowledge declare void, all conspiracies, detestable and
frowned upon by the sacred laws and conventicles, or unlawful assemblies in the cities and out of them, and asso-
ciations between city and city, between person and person
or between a person and a city, under pretext of clientship,
or reception among the citizens, or of any other reason;
furthermore the confederations and pacts—and the usage
which has been introduced with regard to such things,
which we consider to be corruption rather than any thing
else—which cities or persons, of whatever dignity, condition or standing, shall have thus far made and shall presume to make in future, whether among themselves or
with others, without the authority of the lords whose subjects or serving-men they are, those same lords being
expressly excluded.   And it is clear that such are prohibited and declared void by the sacred laws of the divine
emperors our predecessors.   Excepting alone those confederations and leagues which princes, cities and others
are known to have formed among themselves for the sake
of the general peace of the provinces and lands.   Reserving these for our special declaration, we ordain that they
shall remain in full vigour until we shall decide to ordain
otherwise concerning them.   And we decree that, henceforth, each individual person who, contrary to the tenor

of the present decree, and of the ancient law issued regarding this, shall presume to enter into such confederations, leagues, conspiracies and pacts, shall incur, besides the penalty of that law, a mark of infamy and a penalty of ten pounds of gold.   But a city or community similarly breaking this our law shall, we decree, by the act itself incur the penalty of a hundred pounds of gold, and also the loss and privation of the imperial liberties and privileges ; one half of such pecuniary penalty to go to the imperial fisc, the other to the territorial lord to whose detriment the conspiracies, etc., were formed.

16. *Concerning pfalburgers.*

Moreover since some citizens and subjects of princes, barons and other men—as frequent complaint has shown us,—seeking to cast off the yoke of their original subjection, nay, with bold daring despising it, manage, and frequently in the past have managed to be received among the citizens of other cities ; and, nevertheless, actually residing in the lands, cities, towns and estates of the former lords whom they so fraudulently presume or have presumed to desert, succeed in enjoying the liberties of the cities to which they thus transfer themselves and in being protected by them—being what is usually called in common language in Germany " pfalburgers ": therefore, since fraud and deceit ought not to shelter any one, from the plenitude of the imperial power and by the wholesome advice of all the ecclesiastical and secular prince electors, we establish of certain knowledge, and, by the present ever-to-be-valid law do decree, that in all territories, places, and provinces of the holy empire, from the present day on, the aforesaid citizens and subjects thus eluding those under whom they are, shall in no way possess the rights and liberties of those cities among whose citizens they contrive, or have contrived, by such fraudulent means to be received ; unless, bodily and actually going over to such cities and there taking up their domicile, making a continued, true and not fictitious stay, they submit to their due burdens and municipal functions in the same. But if any, contrary to the tenor of our present law, have been, or shall in future be received as citizens, their reception shall lack all validity, and the persons received, of whatever condition, dignity or standing they may be, shall, in no case or matter whatever, in any way exercise or enjoy the rights and liberties of the cities into which they contrive to be received. Any rights, privileges, or observed customs, at whatever time obtained, to the contrary notwithstanding; all of which, in so far as they are contrary to our present law, we, by these presents, revoke of certain knowledge, decreeing from the plenitude of the aforesaid imperial power that they lack all force and validity. For in all the aforesaid respects, the rights of the princes, lords and other men who chance, and shall in future chance, to be thus deserted, over the persons and goods of any subjects deserting them in the oft-mentioned manner, shall. always be regarded. We decree, moreover, that those who, against the ordering of our present law, shall presume, or shall in the past have presumed, to receive the oft-mentioned citizens and subjects of other men, if they do not altogether dismiss them within a month after the present intimation has been made to them, shall, for such transgression, as often as they shall hereafter commit it, incur a fine of a hundred marks of pure gold, of which one half shall be applied without fail to our imperial fisc, and the rest to the lords of those who have been received as citizens.

17. *Concerning challenges of defiance.*

We declare that those who, in future, feigning to have just cause of defiance against any persons, unseasonably challenge them in places where they do not have their domicile, or which they do not inhabit in common, cannot with honour inflict any harm through fire, spoliation or rapine, on the challenged ones. And, since fraud and deceit should not shelter any one, we establish by the present ever-to-be-valid decree that challenges of this kind, thus made, or in future to be made by any one against any lords or persons to whom they were previously bound by companionship, familiarity or any honest friendship, shall not be valid; nor is it lawful, under pretext of any kind

of challenge, to invade any one through fire, spoliation or
rapine, unless the challenge, three natural days before,
shall have been intimated personally to the challenged
man himself, or publicly in the place where he has been
accustomed to reside, where full credibility can be given,
through suitable witnesses, to such an intimation. Whoever shall presume otherwise to challenge any one and to
invade him in the aforesaid manner, shall incur, by the
very act, the same infamy as if no challenge had been
made ; and we decree that he be punished as a traitor by
his judges, whoever they are, with the lawful punishments.

We prohibit also each and every unjust war and feud,
and all unjust burnings, spoliations and rapines, unlawful
and unusual tolls and escorts, and the exactions usually
extorted for such escorts, under the penalties by which the
sacred laws prescribe that the foregoing offences, and any
one of them, are to be punished.

18. *Letter of intimation.*

To you, illustrious and magnificent prince, lord margrave
of Brandenburg, arch-chamberlain of the holy empire, our
co-elector and most dear friend, we intimate by these presents the election of the king of the Romans, which is
about to take place on account of rational causes. And, as
a duty of our office, we duly summon you to said election,
bidding you within three months, counting continuously,
from such and such a day, yourself, or in the person of one
or more envoys or procurators having sufficient mandates,
to be careful and come to the rightful place, according to the
form of the holy laws issued concerning this, ready to deliberate, negotiate and come to an agreement with the
other princes, yours and our co-electors, concerning the
election of a future king of the Romans and, by God's
favour, future emperor. And be ready to remain there
until the full consummation of such election, and otherwise to act and proceed as is found expressed in the sacred
laws carefully promulgated concerning this. Otherwise,
notwithstanding your or your envoys' absence, we, together
with our other co-princes and co-electors, shall take final

measures in the aforesaid matters, according as the authority of those same laws has sanctioned.

19. *Formula of representation sent by that prince elector who shall decide to send his envoys to carry on an election.*

We . . . such a one by the grace of God, etc., of the holy empire, etc., do make known to all men by the tenor of these presents, that since, from rational causes, an election of a king of the Romans is about to be made, we, desiring to watch with due care over the honour and condition of the holy empire, lest it be dangerously subjected to so grave harm, inasmuch as we have the great confidence, as it were of an undoubted presumption, in the faith and circumspect zeal of our beloved . . . and . . . , faithful subjects of ours : do make, constitute and ordain them and each one of them, completely, in every right, manner and form in which we can or may do it most efficaciously and effectually, our true and lawful procurators and special envoys—so fully that the condition of him who is acting at the time shall not be better than that of the other, but that what has been begun by one may be finished and lawfully terminated by the other. And we empower them to treat wherever they please with the others, our co-princes and co-electors, ecclesiastical as well as secular, and to agree, decide and settle upon some person fit and suitable to be elected king of the Romans, and to be present, treat and deliberate in the transactions to be carried on concerning the election of such a person, for us and in our place and name ; also, in our stead and name, to nominate such a person, and to consent to him, and also to raise him to be king of the Romans, to elect him to the holy empire, and to take, upon our soul, with regard to the foregoing or any one of the foregoing, whatever oath shall be necessary, requisite or customary. And we empower them to substitute altogether, as well as to recall, one or more other procurators who shall perform each and every act, included in and concerning the foregoing matters, that may be needful, useful, or even in any way convenient, even to the consummation of such negotiations, nomination, deliberation and impending election. Even if the said matters, or any one of them,

shall require a special mandate ; even if they shall turn out
to be greater or more especial than the above mentioned ;
provided that we could have performed them ourselves had
we been present personally at the carrying on of such
negotiations, deliberation, nomination and eventual election. And we consider, and wish to consider, and firmly
promise that we always will consider satisfactory and valid
any thing done, transacted or accomplished, or in any way
ordained, in the aforesaid matters or in any one of them,
by our aforesaid procurators or envoys, or their substitutes,
or by those whom the latter shall substitute.

20. *Concerning the unity of the electoral principalities and of
the rights connected with them.*

Since each and all the principalities, by virtue of which
the secular prince electors are known to hold their right
and vote in the election of the king of the Romans and
prospective emperor, are so joined and inseparably united
with such right of election, also with the offices, dignities
and other rights connected with each and every such principality and dependent from it, that the right, vote, office and
dignity, and all other privileges belonging to each of these
same principalities may not devolve upon any other than
upon him who is recognized as possessing that principality
itself, with all its lands, vassalages, fiefs and domains, and
all its appurtenances : we decree, by the present ever-to-be-
valid imperial edict, that each of the said principalities,
with the right and vote and duty of election, and with all
other dignities, rights and appurtenances concerning the
same, ought so to continue and to be, indivisibly and for all
time, united and joined together, that the possessor of any
principality ought also to rejoice in the quiet and free possession of its right, vote and office, and dignity, and all the
appurtenances that go with it, and to be considered prince
elector by all. And he himself, and no one else, ought at
all times to be called in and admitted by the other prince
electors, without any contradiction whatever, to the election
and to all other transactions to be carried on for the honour
or welfare of the holy empire. Nor, since they are and
ought to be inseparable, may any one of the said rights,

etc., be divided from the other, or at any time be separated, or be separately demanded back, in court or out of it, or distrained, or, even by a decision of the courts, be separated; nor shall any one obtain a hearing who claims one without the other. But if, through error or otherwise, any one shall have obtained a hearing, or proceedings, judgment, sentence or any thing of the kind shall have taken place, or shall chance in any way to have been attempted, contrary to this our present decree : all this, and all consequences of such proceedings, etc., and of any one of them, shall be void of their own accord.

21. *Concerning the order of marching, as regards the archbishops.*

Inasmuch as we saw fit above, at the beginning of our present decrees, fully to provide for the order of seating of the ecclesiastical prince electors in council, and at table and elsewhere, whenever, in future, an imperial court should chance to be held, or the prince electors to assemble together with the emperor or king of the Romans—as to which order of seating we have heard that in former times discussions often arose : so, also, do we find it expedient to fix, with regard to them, the order of marching and walking. Therefore, by this perpetual imperial edict, we decree that, as often as, in an assembly of the emperor or king of the Romans and of the aforesaid princes, the emperor or king of the Romans shall be walking, and it shall happen that the insignia are carried in front of him, the archbishop of Treves shall walk in a direct diametrical line in front of the emperor or king, and those alone shall walk in the middle space between them, who shall happen to carry the imperial or royal insignia. When, however, the emperor or king shall advance without those same insignia, then that same archbishop shall precede the emperor or king in the aforesaid manner, but so that no one at all shall be in the middle between them ; the other two archiepiscopal electors always keeping their places—as with regard to the seating above explained, so with regard to walking—according to the privilege of their provinces.

22. *Concerning the order of proceeding of the prince electors, and by whom the insignia shall be carried.*

In order to fix the order of proceeding, which we mentioned above, of the prince electors in the presence of the emperor or king of the Romans when he is walking, we decree that, so often as, while holding an imperial court, the prince electors shall, in the performance of any functions or solemnities, chance to walk in procession with the emperor or king of the Romans, and the imperial or royal insignia are to be carried: the duke of Saxony, carrying the imperial or royal sword, shall directly precede the emperor or king, and shall place himself in the middle, between him and the archbishop of Treves. But the count palatine, carrying the imperial orb, shall march in the same line on the right side, and the margrave of Brandenburg, bearing the sceptre, on the left side of the same duke of Saxony. But the king of Bohemia shall directly follow the emperor or king himself, no one intervening.

23. *Concerning the benedictions of the archbishops in the presence of the emperor.*

Furthermore, so often as it shall come to pass that the ceremony of the mass is celebrated in the presence of the emperor or king of the Romans and that the archbishops of Mainz, Treves and Cologne, or two of them, are present, —in the confession which is usually said before the mass, and in the presenting of the gospel to be kissed, and in the blessing to be said after the " Agnus Dei," also in the benedictions to be said after the end of the mass, and also in those said before meals, and in the thanks to be offered after the food has been partaken of, the following order shall be observed among them, as we have seen fit to ordain by their own advice : namely, on the first day each and all of these shall be done by the first of the archbishops, on the second, by the second, on the third, by the third. But we will that first, second and third shall be understood in this case, according as each one of them was consecrated at an earlier or later date. And, in order that they may mutually make advances to each other with worthy and becoming honour, and may give an example to others of mutual respect, he whose turn it is according to the aforesaid, shall, without regard to that fact, and with charitable intent, invite the other to officiate; and, not till he has done this, shall he proceed to perform the above, or any of the above functions.

24.

(1) If any one, together with princes, knights or privates, or also any plebeian persons, shall enter into an unhallowed conspiracy, or shall take the oath of such conspiracy, concerning the death of our and the holy Roman empire's venerable and illustrious prince electors, ecclesiastical as well as secular, or of any one of them—for they also are part of our body; and the laws have decided that the intention of a crime is to be punished with the same severity as the carrying out of it:—he, indeed, shall die by the sword as a traitor, all his goods being handed over to our fisc. (2) But his sons, to whom, by special imperial lenity, we grant their life—for those ought to perish by the same punishment as their father, whose portion is the example of a paternal, that is of a hereditary crime—shall be without share in any inheritance or succession from the mother or grandparents, or even from relatives; they shall receive nothing from other people's wills, and shall be always poor and in want; the infamy of their father shall always follow them, and they shall never achieve any honour or be allowed to take any oath at all; in a word they shall be such that to them, grovelling in perpetual misery, death shall be a solace and life a punishment. (3) Finally we command that those shall be made notorious, and shall be without pardon, who shall ever try to intervene with us for such persons. (4) But to the daughters, as many of them as there are, of such conspirators, we will that there shall go only the "falcidia"—the fourth part of the property of the mother if she die intestate; so that they may rather have the moderate alimony of a daughter, than the entire emolu-

ment or name of an heir;—for the sentence ought to be milder in the case of those who, as we trust, on account of the infirmity of their sex, are less likely to make daring attempts.   (5) Deeds of gift, moreover, made out to either sons or daughters by the aforesaid persons, after the passing of this law, shall not be valid.   (6) Dotations and donations of any possessions; likewise, in a word, all transfers which shall prove to have been made, by any fraud or by right, after the time when first the aforesaid people conceived the idea of entering into a conspiracy or union, shall, we decree, be of no account.   (7) But the wives of the aforesaid conspirators, having recovered their dowry—if they shall be in a condition to reserve for their children that which they shall have received from their husbands under the name of a gift,—shall know that, from the time when their usufruct ceases, they are to leave to our fisc all that which, according to the usual law, was due to their children.   (8) And the fourth part of such property shall be put aside for the daughters alone, not also for the sons.   (9) That which we have provided concerning the aforesaid conspirators and their children, we also decree, with like severity, concerning their followers, accomplices and aiders, and the children of these.   (10) But if any one of these, at the beginning of the formation of a conspiracy, inflamed by zeal for the right kind of glory, shall himself betray the conspiracy, he shall be enriched by us with reward and honour; he, moreover, who shall have been active in the conspiracy, if, even late, he disclose secret plans which were, in leed, hitherto unknown,— shall nevertheless be deemed worthy of absolution and pardon.   (11) We decree, moreover, that if anything be said to have been committed against the aforesaid prince electors, ecclesiastical or secular,—even after the death of the accused that charge can be instituted.[1]   (12) Likewise in such a charge, which regards high treason against his prince electors, slaves shall be tortured even in a case concerning the life of their master.   (13) We will, furthermore, and do decree by the present imperial edict, that even after the death of the guilty persons this charge can

---

[1] " Etiam post mortem rei id crimen instaurari posse."

be instituted,[1] and, if some one already convicted die, his memory shall be condemned and his goods taken away from his heirs. (14) For from the time when any one conceived so wicked a plot, from then on he has to some extent been punished mentally; but from the time when any one drew down upon himself such a charge, we decree that he may neither alienate nor release, nor may any debtor lawfully make payment to him. (15) For in this case we decree that slaves may be tortured in a matter involving the life of their master; that is, in the case of a damnable conspiracy against the prince electors, ecclesiastical and secular, as has been said before. (16) And if any one should die, on account of the uncertain person of his successor his goods shall be held, if he be proved to have died in a case of this kind.

25.

If it is fitting that other principalities be preserved in their entirety, in order that justice may be enforced and faithful subjects rejoice in peace and quiet: much more ought the magnificent principalities, dominions, honours and rights of the elector princes to be kept intact—for where greater danger is imminent a stronger remedy should be applied,—lest, if the columns fall, the support of the whole edifice be destroyed. We decree, therefore, and sanction, by this edict to be perpetually valid, that from now on unto all future time the distinguished and magnificent principalities, viz.: the kingdom of Bohemia, the county palatine of the Rhine, the duchy of Saxony and the margravate of Brandenburg, their lands, territories. homages or vassalages, and any other things pertaining to them, may not be cut, divided, or under any condition dismembered, but shall remain forever in their perfect entirety. The first born son shall succeed to them, and to him alone shall jurisdiction and dominion belong; unless he chance to be of unsound mind, or idiotic, or have some other marked and known defect on account of which he

---

[1] " Ut etiam post mortem nocencium hoc crimen inchoari possit." (13) and (15) are an awkward repetition, an explanatory one, it is true, of (11) and (12).

could not or should not rule over men. In which case, he being prevented from succeeding, we will that the second born, if there should be one in that family, or another elder brother or lay relative, the nearest on the father's side in a straight line of descent, shall have the succession. He, however, shall always show himself clement and gracious to the others, his brothers and sisters, according to the favour shown him by God, and according to his best judgment and the amount of his patrimony,—division, partition or dismemberment of the principality and its appurtenances being in every way forbidden to him.

26.

On the day upon which a solemn imperial or royal court is to be held, the ecclesiastical and secular prince electors shall, about the first hour, come to the imperial or royal place of abode, and there the emperor or king shall be clothed in all the imperial insignia; and, mounting their horses, all shall go with the emperor or king to the place fitted up for the session, and each one of them shall go in the order and manner fully defined above in the law concerning the order of marching of those same prince electors. The arch-chancellor, moreover, in whose arch-chancellorship this takes place, shall carry, besides the silver staff, all the imperial or royal seals and signets. But the secular prince electors, according to what has above been explained, shall carry the sceptre, orb and sword. And immediately before the archbishop of Treves, marching in his proper place, shall be carried first the crown of Aix and second that of Milan: and this directly in front of the emperor already resplendent with the imperial adornments; and these crowns shall be carried by some lesser princes, to be chosen for this by the emperor according to his will. The empress, moreover, or queen of the Romans, clad in her imperial insignia, joined by her nobles and escorted by her maids of honour, shall proceed to the place of session after the king or emperor of the Romans, and also, at a sufficient interval of space, after the king of Bohemia, who immediately follows the emperor.

27. *Concerning the offices of the prince electors in the solemn courts of the emperors or kings of the Romans.*

We decree that whenever the emperor or king of the Romans shall hold his solemn courts, in which the prince electors ought to serve or to perform their offices, the following order shall be observed in these matters. First, then, the emperor or king having placed himself on the royal seat or imperial throne, the duke of Saxony shall fulfil his office in this manner: before the building where the imperial or royal session is being held, shall be placed a heap of oats so high that it shall reach to the breast or girth of the horse on which the duke himself shall sit; and he shall have in his hand a silver staff and a silver measure, which, together, shall weigh 12 marks of silver; and, sitting upon his horse, he shall first fill that measure with oats, and shall offer it to the first slave who appears. This being done, fixing his staff in the oats, he shall retire; and his vice-marshal, namely, he of Pappenheim, approaching—or, in his absence, the marshall of the court,— shall further distribute the oats. But when the emperor or king shall have gone into table, the ecclesiastical prince electors—namely the archbishops,—standing before the table with the other prelates, shall bless the same according to the order above prescribed; and, the benediction over, all those same archbishops if they are present, otherwise two or one, shall receive from the chancellor of the court the imperial or royal seals and signets, and he in whose arch-chancellorship this court happens to be held advancing in the middle, and the other two joining him on either side, shall carry those seals and signets—all touching with their hands the staff on which they have been suspended—and shall reverently place them on the table before the emperor or king. The emperor or king, however, shall straightway restore the same to them, and he in whose arch-chancellorate this takes place, as has been said, shall carry the great seal appended to his neck until the end of the meal, and after that until, riding from the imperial or royal court, he shall come to his dwelling place. The staff, moreover, that we spoke of shall be of silver, equal in weight to twelve marks of silver; of which silver, and of which price, each of those same archbishops shall pay one third; and that staff afterwards, together with the seals and signets, shall be assigned to the chancellor of the imperial court to be put to what use he pleases. But after he whose turn it has been, carrying the great seal, shall, as described, have returned from the imperial court to his dwelling place, he shall straightway send that seal to the said chancellor of the imperial court. This he shall do through one of his servants riding on such a horse as, according to what is becoming to his own dignity, and according to the love which he shall bear to the chancellor of the court, he shall be bound to present to that chancellor.

Then the margrave of Brandenburg, the arch-chamberlain, shall approach on horseback, having in his hands silver basins with water, of the weight of twelve marks of silver, and a beautiful towel; and, descending from his horse, he shall present the water to the lord emperor or king of the Romans to wash his hands.

The count palatine of the Rhine shall likewise enter on horseback, having in his hands four silver dishes filled with food, of which each one shall be worth three marks; and, descending from his horse, he shall carry them and place them on the table before the emperor or king.

After this, likewise on horseback, shall come the king of Bohemia, the arch-cupbearer, carrying in his hands a silver cup or goblet of the weight of twelve marks, covered, filled with a mixture of wine and water; and, descending from his horse, he shall offer that cup to the emperor or king of the Romans to drink from.

Moreover, as we learn it to have hitherto been observed, so we decree, that, after their aforesaid offices have been performed by the secular prince electors, he of Falkenstein, the sub-chamberlain, shall receive for himself the horse and basins of the margrave of Brandenburg; he of Northemburg, master of the kitchen, the horse and dishes of the count palatine; he of Limburg, the vice-cupbearer, the horse and cup of the king of Bohemia; he of Pappenheim, the vice-marshal, the horse, staff and aforesaid measure of the duke of Saxony. That is, if these be present at such imperial or royal court, and if each one of them minister in his proper office. But if they, or any one of them, should see fit to absent themselves from the said court, then those who daily minister at the imperial or royal court shall, in place of the absent ones,—each one, namely, in place of that absent one with whom he has his name and office in common,—enjoy the fruits with regard to the aforesaid functions, inasmuch as they perform the duties.

28.

Moreover the imperial or royal table ought so to be arranged that it shall be elevated above the other tables in the hall by a height of six feet. And at it, on the day of a solemn court, shall sit no one at all except alone the emperor or king of the Romans.

But the seat and table of the empress or queen shall be prepared to one side in the hall, so that that table shall be three feet lower than the imperial or royal table, and as many feet higher than the seats of the prince electors; which princes shall have their seats and tables at one and the same altitude among themselves.

Within the imperial place of session tables shall be prepared for the seven prince electors, ecclesiastical and secular,—three, namely, on the right, and three others on the left, and the seventh directly opposite the face of the emperor or king, as has above been more clearly defined by us in the chapter concerning the seating and precedence of the prince electors; in such wise, also, that no one else, of whatever dignity or standing he may be, shall sit among them or at their table.

Moreover it shall not be allowed to any one of the aforesaid secular prince electors, when the duty of his office has been performed, to place himself at the table prepared for him so long as any one of his fellow prince electors has still to perform his office. But when one or more of them shall have finished their ministry, they shall pass to the tables prepared for them, and, standing before them, shall wait until the others have fulfilled the aforesaid duties; and then, at length, one and all shall place themselves at the same time before the tables prepared for them.

29.

We find, moreover, from the most renowned accounts and traditions of the ancients that, from time immemorial, it has been continuously observed, by those who have felicitously preceded us, that the election of the king of the Romans and future emperor should be held in the city of Frankfort, and the first coronation in Aix, and that his first imperial court should be celebrated in the town of Nuremberg. Wherefore, on sure grounds, we declare that the said usages should also be observed in future, unless a lawful impediment should stand in the way of them or any one of them. Whenever, furthermore, any prince elector, ecclesiastical or secular, detained by a just impediment, and not able to come when summoned to the imperial court, shall send an envoy or procurator, of whatever dignity or standing,—that envoy, although, according to the mandate given him by his master, he ought to be admitted in the place of him who sends him, shall, nevertheless, not sit at the table or in the seat intended for him who sent him.

Moreover when those matters shall have been settled which were at that time to be disposed of in any imperial or royal court, the master of the court shall receive for himself the whole structure or wooden apparatus of the imperial or royal place of session, where the emperor or king of the Romans shall have sat with the prince electors to hold his solemn court, or, as has been said, to confer fiefs on the princes.

30. *Concerning the rights of the officials when princes receive their fiefs from the emperor or king of the Romans.*

We decree by this imperial edict that the prince electors, ecclesiastical and secular, when they receive their fiefs or regalia from the emperor or king, shall not at all be bound to give or pay anything to anybody. For the money which is paid under such a pretext is due to the officials; but since, indeed, the prince electors themselves are at the head of all the offices of the imperial court, having also their substitutes in such offices, furnished for this by the

Roman princes, and paid,—it would seem absurd if substituted officials, under cover of any excuse whatever, should demand presents from their superiors; unless, perchance, those same prince electors, freely and of their own will, should give them something.

On the other hand, the other princes of the empire, ecclesiastical or secular,—when, in the aforesaid manner, any one of them receives his fiefs from the emperor or king of the Romans,—shall give to the officials of the imperial or royal court 63 marks of silver and a quarter, unless any one of them can protect himself by an imperial or royal privilege or grant, and can prove that he has paid or is exempt from such, or also from any other, payments usually made when receiving such fiefs. Moreover the master of the imperial or royal court shall make division of the $63\frac{1}{4}$ marks as follows: first reserving, indeed, 10 marks for himself, he shall give to the chancellor of the imperial or royal court 10 marks; to the masters, notaries, copyists, 3 marks; and to the sealer, for wax and parchment, one quarter. This with the understanding that the chancellor and notaries shall not be bound to do more than to give the prince receiving the fief a testimonial to the effect that he has received it, or a simple charter of investiture.

Likewise, from the aforesaid money, the master of the court shall give to the cupbearer, him of Limburg, 10 marks; to the master of the kitchen, him of Northemburg, 10 marks; to the vice-marshall, him of Pappenheim, 10 marks; and to the chamberlain, him of Falkenstein, 10 marks: under the condition, however, that they and each one of them are present and perform their offices in solemn courts of this kind. But if they or any one of them shall have been absent, then the officials of the imperial or royal court who perform these same offices, shall carry off the reward and the perquisites of those whose absence they make good, individual for individual, according as they fill their place, and bear their name, and perform their task.

When, moreover, any prince, sitting on a horse or other beast, shall receive his fiefs from the emperor or king, that horse or beast, of whatever kind he be, shall be the due of

the highest marshal—that is, of the duke of Saxony if he
shall be present; otherwise of him of Pappenheim, his
vice-marshall; or, in his absence, of the marshall of the
imperial or royal court.

31.

Inasmuch as the majesty of the holy Roman empire has
to wield the laws and the government of diverse nations
distinct in customs, manner of life, and in language, it is
considered fitting, and, in the judgment of all wise men,
expedient, that the prince electors, the columns and sides
of that empire, should be instructed in the varieties of the
different dialects and languages: so that they who assist
the imperial sublimity in relieving the wants of very many
people, and who are constituted for the sake of keeping
watch, should understand, and be understood by, as many
as possible.　Wherefore we decree that the sons, or heirs
and successors of the illustrious prince electors, namely of
the king of Bohemia, the count palatine of the Rhine, the
duke of Saxony and the margrave of Brandenburg—since
they are expected in all likelihood to have naturally acquired the German language, and to have been taught it
from their infancy,—shall be instructed in the grammar of
the Italian and Slavic tongues, beginning with the seventh
year of their age; so that, before the fourteenth year of
their age, they may be learned in the same according to
the grace granted them by God.　For this is considered
not only useful, but also, from the afore-mentioned causes,
highly necessary, since those languages are wont to be
very much employed in the service and for the needs of
the holy empire, and in them the more arduous affairs of
the empire are discussed.　And, with regard to the above,
we lay down the following mode of procedure to be observed:
it shall be left to the option of the parents to send their
sons, if they have any—or their relatives whom they consider as likely to succeed themselves in their principalities,
—to places where they can be taught such languages, or,
in their own homes, to give them teachers, instructors, and
fellow youths skilled in the same, by whose conversation
and teaching alike they may become versed in those
languages.

XI.

THE FOUNDATION OF THE UNIVERSITY OF HEIDELBERG, A.D. 1386.

(Emminghaus: "Corpus Juris Germanici" (1844-6), p. 73).

a. We, Rupert the elder, by the grace of God Count Palatine of the Rhine, elector of the Holy Empire and duke of Bavaria—lest we seem to abuse the privilege conceded to us by the apostolic see of founding a place of study at Heidelberg like to that at Paris, and lest, for this reason, being subjected to the divine judgment, we should merit to be deprived of the privilege granted,—do decree with provident counsel, which decree is to be observed there unto all time, that the university of Heidelberg shall be ruled, disposed and regulated according to the modes and matters accustomed to be observed in the university of Paris.   Also that, as a handmaid of the Parisian institution—a worthy one, let us hope,—the latter's steps shall be imitated in every way possible ; so that, namely, there shall be four faculties in it: the first, of sacred theology or divinity ; the second, of canon and civil law, which, by reason of their similarity, we think best to comprise under one faculty ; the third, of medicine ; the fourth, of liberal arts—of the threefold philosophy, namely, primal, natural and moral, three mutually subservient daughters.   We wish this institution to be divided and marked out into four nations, as it is at Paris ; and that all these faculties shall make one university, and that to it the individual students, in whichever of the said faculties they are, shall indivisibly belong like lawful sons of one mother.   Likewise that that university shall be governed by one rector, and that the different masters and teachers, before they are admitted to the common pursuits of our institution, shall swear to observe the statutes, laws, privileges, liberties and franchises of the same, and not reveal its secrets, to whatever grade they may rise.   Also that they will uphold the honour of the rector and the rectorship of our university, and will obey the rector in all things lawful and honest, whatever be the grade to which they may afterwards happen to be promoted. Moreover that the different masters and bachelors shall read their lectures and exercise their scholastic functions and go about in caps and gowns of a uniform and similar nature, according as that has been observed at Paris up to this time in the different faculties. And we will that if any faculty, nation or person shall oppose the aforesaid regulations, or pertinaciously refuse to obey them or any one of them—which God forbid,—from that time forward that same faculty, nation or person, if it do not desist upon being warned, shall be deprived of all connection with our aforesaid institution, and shall not have the benefit of our defence or protection. Moreover we will and ordain that as the university as a whole may do for those assembled here and subject to it, so each faculty, nation or province of it may found lawful statutes and ones suitable to its needs, provided that through them or any one of them no prejudice is done to the above regulations and to our institution, and that no kind of impediment arise from them. And we will that when the separate bodies shall have passed the statutes for their own observance, they may make them perpetually binding on those subject to them and on their successors. And as in the university of Paris the different servants of the institution have the benefit of the different privileges which its masters and scholars enjoy, so in starting our institution in Heidelberg, we grant, with even greater liberality, through these presents, that all the servants, viz.: its Pedells, librarians, lower officials, preparers of parchment, scribes, illuminators and others who serve it, may each and all, without fraud, enjoy in it the same privileges, franchises, immunities and liberties with which its masters or scholars are now or shall hereafter be endowed.

b. Lest in the new community of the city of Heidelberg, their faults being unpunished, there be an incentive to the scholars of doing wrong, we ordain with provident counsel by these presents, that the bishop of Worms, as judge ordinary of the clerks of our institution, shall have and possess, now and hereafter while our institution shall last, prisons,

and an office in our town of Heidelberg for the detention
of criminal clerks.   These things we have seen fit to grant
to him and his successors, adding these conditions: that
he shall permit no clerk to be arrested unless for a misdemeanour; that he shall restore any one detained for
such fault or for any light offence to his master or to the
rector if he asks for him, a promise having been given that
the culprit will appear in court and that the rector or
master will answer for him if the injured parties should
go to law about the matter.   Furthermore that, on being
requested, he will restore a clerk arrested for a crime on
slight evidence, upon receiving a sufficient pledge—sponsors
if the prisoner can obtain them, otherwise an oath if he
can not obtain sponsors—to the effect that he will answer
in court the charges against him; and in all these things
there shall be no pecuniary exactions, except that the clerk
shall give satisfaction, reasonably and according to the
rule of the aforementioned town, for the expenses which he
incurred while in prison.   And that he will detain honestly
and without serious injury a criminal clerk thus arrested
for a crime where the suspicion is grave and strong, until
the truth can be found out concerning the deed of which
he is suspected.   And he shall not for any cause, moreover,
take away any clerk from our aforesaid town, or permit
him to be taken away, unless the proper observances have
been followed, and he has been condemned by judicial
sentence to perpetual imprisonment for a crime.   We command our advocate and bailiff and their servants in our
aforesaid town, under pain of losing their office and our
favour, not to put a detaining hand on any master or
scholar of our said institution, nor to arrest him nor allow
him to be arrested, unless the deed be such a one that that
master or scholar ought rightly to be detained.   He shall
be restored to his rector or master, if he is held for a
slight cause, provided he will swear and promise to appear
in court concerning the matter; and we decree that a
slight fault is one for which a layman, if he had committed
it, ought to have been condemned to a light pecuniary
fine.   Likewise, if the master or scholar detained be found
gravely or strongly suspected of the crime, we command
that he be handed over by our officials to the bishop or

to his representative in our said town, to be kept in custody.

c. By the tenor of these presents we grant to each and all the masters and scholars that, when they come to said institution, while they remain there, and also when they return from it to their homes, they may freely carry with them both coming and going, throughout all the lands subject to us, all their things which they need while pursuing their studies, and all the goods necessary for their support, without any duty, levy, imposts, tailles, gabelles, or other exactions whatever. And we wish them and each one of them, to be free from all the aforesaid imposts when purchasing corn, wines, meat, fish, clothes and all things necessary for their living and for their rank. And we decree that the scholars from their stock in hand of provisions, if there remain over one or two waggonloads of wine without their having practised deception, may after the feast of Easter of that year sell it en gros without paying impost. We grant to them, moreover, that each day the scholars, of themselves or through their servants, may be allowed to buy in the town of Heidelberg, at the accustomed hour, freely and without impediment or hurtful delay, any eatables or other necessaries of life.

d. Lest the masters and scholars of our institution of Heidelberg may be oppressed by the citizens, avarice inducing them, through the extortionate price of lodgings, we have seen fit to decree that henceforth each year, after Christmas, one expert from the university on the part of the scholars, and one prudent, pious and circumspect citizen on the part of the citizens, shall be deputed to fix on the price for the students' lodgings. Moreover we will and decree that the different masters and scholars shall, through our bailiff, our judge and the officials subject to us, be defended and maintained in the quiet possession of the lodgings given to them free or of those for which they pay rent. Moreover, by the tenor of these presents, we grant to the rector and the university, or to those deputed by them, entire and total jurisdiction concerning the paying of rents for the lodgings occupied by the students, concerning the making and buying of codices, and the borrowing of money for other purposes by the scholars of our institution; also concerning the payment of assessments, together with everything that arises from, depends on and is connected with these.

—. In addition we command our officials that, when the rector requires our and their aid and assistance for carrying out his sentences against scholars who try to rebel, they shall assist our clients and servants in this matter; first, however, obtaining lawful permission to proceed against clerks from the lord bishop of Worms, or from one deputed by him for this purpose.

BOOK III. THE CHURCH.

INTRODUCTION.[1]

N O. I., the Rule of Benedict, is given here almost in its entirety, as being historically the most important of all monastic constitutions. Benedict of Nursia was born near Rome at the end of the fifth century. When a boy of fourteen he renounced the world, and, after many changes of abode, finally settled at Monte Cassino, and became the founder of that famous monastery, destroying the temple of Apollo that stood on its site. Benedict died in 543 A.D. Pope Gregory the Great (594-604), the first real organizer among the popes, pressed the monks into the service of the church. It was the Rule of Benedict that he chose for his guidance, imposing it on a monastery that he himself had founded in Rome. By the time of Charlemagne (768-814) Benedict's Rule seems to have superseded all others. It afterwards became the basis of new orders, chief among which were Cluny and Citeaux. In the thirteenth century the Benedicts were superseded in great part by the mendicant orders, the Franciscans and Dominicans. From the fourteenth century on they were famous more for their learning than for their piety. The famous

[1] For fuller information on the different documents in this Book on the Church, see the articles in Herzog and Plitt's "Real encyclopaedie der protestantischen Theologie," 17 vols., and W. Möller's "Lehrbuch der Kirchengeschichte," 2 vols., Freiburg, 1889-90. Both of these works give manifold references for further study.

congregation of St. Maur, founded in 1618, was a congregation of Benedictines, and to them we owe the editing of many most valuable historical sources.

The French Revolution almost killed the order of Benedict, and it is now kept alive only in Austria and Italy. The monks are still famous for their classical learning.

No. II., the formulas for holding ordeals,[1] are prayers, exhortations, exorcisms, etc., used by the priests in carrying out the so-called "judgments of God." Although these formulas, as here given, are first found in manuscripts of the twelfth and thirteenth centuries, they belong undoubtedly to Carolingian times.

Ordeals were already known to the Greeks, as may be seen from v. 264 of the "Antigone." The early Germans had various forms of obtaining judgments by the use of fire. One was for the accused to hold his hand in the flame for a certain time; another, for him to walk through a fire clad in a single garment. Again, one might walk nine steps with a red-hot iron in the hand, or go barefoot over nine heated ploughshares. Richardis, the wife of Charles the Fat; Kunigunde, the wife of emperor Henry II.; not to speak of Emma, the mother of Edward the Confessor, underwent this last form of the ordeal.

In the hot water ordeal the accused was compelled to put his hand in a boiling cauldron of water and extract a stone or a ring. Another, and very common form of trying by water, was to throw the accused into a pool or tank of cold water, and see whether he sank or floated. The technical expression for this tank was "fossa"; Ducange's translation of which—a place to drown women in— does great injustice to the chivalry of our ancestors. Almost every abbot had a "furca et fossa," and the number of

[1] An excellent article on ordeals is that written by Wilda in Ersch and Gruber's "Allgemeine Encyclopædie der Wissenschaften und Künste," under "Ordalien."

women drowned would have had to be considerable had each "fossa" been used even but once.

According to another form of the ordeal, the accuser and the accused stood opposite to each other with out-stretched arms—the trial of the cross it was called—until one of them could endure no longer.   All the nuns of Bis-chofsheim were once submitted to this test, the body of a new-born babe having been found in a pond near by.

The emperor Charlemagne was a firm believer in ordeals, and ordered his subjects to respect them.   Frederick II. (1215-1250), on the contrary, the most enlightened monarch of the Middle Ages, thought a person who believed in them "non tam corrigendum quam ridendum."   The fire and water trials were forbidden by the Lateran Council of 1215, and fours years later Henry III. declared them un-lawful in England.   But as late as the year 1686 a certain Jacob Rieck wrote a book in favour of the water ordeal as actually practised in his time upon witches in Cologne; and the so-called witch-bath is heard of in Prussia even in the middle of the eighteenth century.

No. III., the Constantine Donation, or Constitutum Constantini, purports to be a deed of gift made to pope Sylvester by Constantine the Great.   It is found in the manuscript containing the "Pseudo Isidorian Decretals," but is older than that collection.   Constantine grants to the pope imperial honours, the primacy over Antioch, Con-stantinople and Alexandria, makes him chief judge of the clergy, and offers him the imperial diadem.   This the pope refuses, preferring a simpler crown.   The clergy are to have the rank of senators and the privilege of riding upon white saddle-cloths.   Last, but not least, the pope was to have dominion over all Italy, including Rome.   The word-ing is *Italiae seu occidentalium regionum*, and later popes, translating "*seu*" as "*et*," claimed nothing less than all of Western Europe.

The Donation document is first quoted in the middle of the ninth century; the legend upon which it is founded is older. That Constantine really did give a great deal to the church is undoubted. There are three lists of his gifts in the " Liber Pontificalis," the earliest history of the popes. The Constantine Donation was at times doubted even in the Middle Ages. Otto III. called it a lie, as did also Arnold of Brescia. On the other hand, Urban II. claimed Corsica by virtue of it; Anselm, Gratian, and Ivo of Chartres, all received it into their collections of canon law; and, according to John of Salisbury, Adrian IV. relied on it in claiming the right to dispose of Ireland in 1155. (See above, Book I., No. II.)

In the fifteenth century the Donation began to be seriously attacked by such men as Pecock and Cusa, but it was reserved for Laurentius Valla to really prove its falseness. It has no defenders to-day even among the adherents of the papacy.

There have been many conjectures as to the date of its fabrication. Brunner tries to place it between the years 813 and 816. His argument is ingenious to say the least. It is well known that the emperor Charlemagne, in 813, himself crowned his son, Louis the Pious. The popes did not like this proceeding, and in 816 Stephen IV. comes travelling over the Alps bearing with him a crown. Brunner thinks that if Stephen increased his luggage by a bulky crown it must have been a very special one, probably the one which Sylvester had refused when it was offered by Constantine. To prove the genuineness of this crown the Constantine Donation may have been forged.

No. IV. is the foundation charter of the famous Burgundian monastery of Cluny, which became the parent of so many subordinate institutions. Cluny was founded in 910 by William the Pious, duke of Aquitaine. Berno, abbot of the Benedictine monastery of Beaume, was its first abbot. His successor, Odo, was the reformer not only of the Benedictine monasteries in general, but of the whole monastic system.

Already, in 937, there were seventeen associate monasteries under Cluny's charge, and its influence spread not only over France, but also over other countries. In the eleventh and twelfth centuries three popes, Gregory VII., Urban II., and Paschal II., went forth from its fold.

The glory of the monastery falls in the first three centuries of its existence. At the beginning of the twelfth century there were 460 monks in Cluny itself, and 314 monasteries subordinate to it. The order later fell a victim to misrule and demoralization, but lingered on until the French Revolution gave it its *coup de grâce*. Its chief building was afterwards turned into a musuem.

No. V., the summons of pope Eugene III. to a crusade, is particularly interesting, as showing the extent of papal interference in the private money affairs of Christians and in the relationships of lords and vassals. Eugene declares that debtors may put off the payment of their obligations until their return, paying no interest whatever for the time of their absence. Moreover, vassals whose lords would not advance money for their journey, might, of their own accord, pledge their estates to the church or to pious laymen.

The crusades, although the direct object for which all this blood and money was expended, was never realized, helped immeasurably to raise the prestige of the papacy. During two centuries the eyes of Europe were fixed upon the pope as the champion of the faith. The people wanted a leader, and the popes wanted to lead. And the church became richer and richer, as one crusader after another died without redeeming the lands that he had pledged.

No. VI. is a decree of the Lateran Council of 1179, declaring a two-thirds majority in the college of cardinals as necessary for the election of a pope. The measure was passed in view of the long struggle that had just been ended by the peace of Venice, and that had begun with the double election of 1160. (See Book IV., No. IV.)

No VII., the general summons of Innocent III. to a crusade in 1215, is the most exhaustive and complete appeal of the kind that was issued. For the next seventy-five years the summonses were to be simple verbal re-issues of it—small changes being made, however, as the condition of affairs became more and more despairing. Thus, for instance, it became necessary in course of time to reward by remissions of so and so many days those who would consent even to be present at the preaching of the papal legate who came to announce a crusade ; and finally, just before the fall of Acre, full remission was granted to those who would contribute anything at all to the lost cause.[1]

No. VIII. is the Rule of St. Francis, which, although Innocent III. had verbally consented to the foundation of the order, was not formally approved by the papacy until 1223. The rise of the mendicant orders is undoubtedly the most important feature in the church history of the early thirteenth century. St. Dominicus founded for him-self no new rule, simply accepting the old rule of the Augustine monks and adding to it a few new regulations.

---

[1] It is well known that the misuse of the papal power of granting indulgence for sins—a power that owes its whole development to the crusades—was one of the chief causes that brought about the Reformation. It is not generally known, however, that almost all the prominent features of the later so notorious traffic existed in their completeness nearly three hundred years earlier. I have found in an ancient chronicle (see Muratori, viii. p. 1092) an account of a papal legate who, in 1219, offered, as an inducement to all those who would prolong their stay and defend the holy land, to absolve the souls of their fathers and mothers, brothers and sisters, wives and children !

St. Francis, on the contrary, drew up the rule which is given here, and which has been called the "Magna Carta pauperitatis." It was to enforce humility and devotion in the work of nursing the sick that the name "fratres minores" was chosen for the brotherhood, and "minister generalis" for its head.

Besides the original order of St. Francis, a second and a third order soon came into being under his name. The Second Order was for women, the pious Clara of Assisi being at the head of it. The Third Order contained as members both men and women, who, while not required to renounce their family or social life, took vows to practise in the world those virtues which the brothers sought in renouncing it.

At an early period the order began to be torn by internal dissensions, and in 1517 the division into Observantists and Conventualists was formally established by a bull of Pope Leo X. Some idea of the numbers and influence of the order may be formed from the fact that, at the end of the sixteenth century, the Observantists alone had 1,400 cloisters, united in 45 provinces.

No. IX. is the bull of pope Boniface VIII. declaring the year 1300, and every hundredth year thereafter, a year of jubilee, and recommending pilgrims to visit the churches of the apostles in Rome. Boniface's festival was phenomenally successful, and probably marks the crowning moment of papal glory. One million strangers are said to have visited Rome, and so much money was thrown around the altars that priests armed with rakes could scarcely gather it in. But within three years Boniface was suffering the last indignities at the hands of the Colonna and of the emissaries of Philip the Fair, and within four more the popes were at Avignon in the service of the French kings.

The jubilee suffered the same fate as did all the other

lucrative institutions of the Roman church,—they were exploited and misused until the last shadow of a significance was taken from them.   Already, in 1343, Clement VI. declared one for 1350.   Urban VI., in 1389, reduced the intervals to 33, and Paul II., in 1470, to 25 years.   We hear of one in 1489, and another in 1500 !   Before long no price was small enough for men to pay even for "not only full and free, but the very fullest pardon of all their sins."

I.

THE RULE OF ST. BENEDICT.

(Migne, "Patrologia Latina," vol. 66, column 215 ff.)

Prologue. . . . .[1] we are about to found, therefore, a school for the Lord's service ; in the organization of which we trust that we shall ordain nothing severe and nothing burdensome. But even if, the demands of justice dictating it, something a little irksome shall be the result, for the purpose of amending vices or preserving charity ;—thou shalt not therefore, struck by fear, flee the way of salvation, which can not be entered upon except through a narrow entrance.   But as one's way of life and one's faith progresses, the heart becomes broadened, and, with the unutterable sweetness of love, the way of the mandates of the Lord is traversed.   Thus, never departing from His guidance, continuing in the monastery in His teaching until death, through patience we are made partakers in Christ's passion, in order that we may merit to be companions in His kingdom.

1. *Concerning the kinds of monks and their manner of living.*   It is manifest that there are four kinds of monks. The cenobites are the first kind ; that is, those living in a monastery, serving under a rule or an abbot.   Then the

---

The few omissions made consist almost wholly of pious expressions and exhortations.

second kind is that of the anchorites; that is, the hermits, —those who, not by the new fervour of a conversion but by the long probation of life in a monastery, have learned to fight against the devil, having already been taught by the solace of many. They, having been well prepared in the army of brothers for the solitary fight of the hermit, being secure now without the consolation of another, are able, God helping them, to fight with their own hand or arm against the vices of the flesh or of their thoughts.

But a third very bad kind of monks are the sarabaites, approved by no rule, experience being their teacher, as with the gold which is tried in the furnace. But, softened after the manner of lead, keeping faith with the world by their works, they are known through their tonsure to lie to God. These being shut up by twos or threes, or, indeed, alone, without a shepherd, not in the Lord's but in their own sheep-folds,—their law is the satisfaction of their desires. For whatever they think good or choice, this they call holy; and what they do not wish, this they consider unlawful. But the fourth kind of monks is the kind which is called gyratory. During their whole life they are guests, for three or four days at a time, in the cells of the different monasteries, throughout the various provinces; always wandering and never stationary, given over to the service of their own pleasures and the joys of the palate, and in every way worse than the sarabaites. Concerning the most wretched way of living of all of such monks it is better to be silent than to speak. These things therefore being omitted, let us proceed, with the aid of God, to treat of the best kind, the cenobites.

2. *What the Abbot should be like.* An abbot who is worthy to preside over a monastery ought always to remember what he is called, and carry out with his deeds the name of a Superior. For he is believed to be Christ's representative, since he is called by His name, the apostle saying: " Ye have received the spirit of adoption of sons, whereby we call Abba, Father." And so the abbot should not—grant that he may not—teach, or decree, or order, any thing apart from the precept of the Lord; but his order or teaching should be sprinkled with the ferment of divine justice in the minds of his disciples. Let the abbot

always be mindful that, at the tremendous judgment of
God, both things will be weighed in the balance: his
teaching and the obedience of his disciples. And let the
abbot know that whatever the father of the family finds
of less utility among the sheep is laid to the fault of the
shepherd. Only in a case where the whole diligence of their
pastor shall have been bestowed on an unruly and disobedient flock, and his whole care given to their morbid
actions, shall that pastor, absolved in the judgment of the
Lord, be free to say to the Lord with the prophet: "I have
not hid Thy righteousness within my heart, I have declared
Thy faithfulness and Thy salvation, but they despising have
scorned me." And then at length let the punishment for
the disobedient sheep under his care be death itself pre-
vailing against them. Therefore, when any one receives the
name of abbot, he ought to rule over his disciples with a
double teaching; that is, let him show forth all good and
holy things by deeds more than by words. So that to
ready disciples he may propound the mandates of God in
words; but, to the hard-hearted and the more simple-
minded, be may show forth the divine precepts by his
deeds. But as to all the things that he has taught to his
disciples to be wrong, he shall show by his deeds that they
are not to be done; lest, preaching to others, he himself
shall be found worthy of blame, and lest God may say at
some time to him a sinner: "What hast thou to do to
declare my statutes or that thou should'st take my covenant
in thy mouth. Seeing that thou hatest instruction and
casteth my words behind thee; and why beholdest thou
the mote that is in thy brother's eye, but considerest not
the beam that is in thine own eye?" He shall make no
distinction of persons in the monastery. One shall not be
more cherished than another, unless it be the one whom
he finds excelling in good works or in obedience. A freeborn man shall not be preferred to one coming from servitude, unless there be some other reasonable cause. But if,
justice demanding that it should be thus, it seems good to
the abbot, he shall do this no matter what the rank shall
be. But otherwise they shall keep their own places; for
whether we be bond or free we are all one in Christ; and,
under one God, we perform an equal service of subjection;

for God is no respecter of persons.   Only in this way is a distinction made by Him concerning us: if we are found humble and surpassing others in good works.   Therefore let him (the abbot) have equal charity for all: let the same discipline be administered in all cases according to merit.   In his teaching indeed the abbot ought always to observe that form laid down by the apostle when he says: "reprove, rebuke, exhort."   That is, mixing seasons with seasons, blandishments with terrors, let him display the feeling of a severe yet devoted master.   He should, namely, rebuke more severely the unruly and the turbulent.   The obedient, moreover, and the gentle and the patient, he should exhort, that they may progress to higher things. But the negligent and scorners, we warn him to admonish and reprove.   Nor let him conceal the sins of the erring: but, in order that he may prevail, let him pluck them out by the roots as soon as they begin to spring up; being mindful of the danger of Eli the priest of Shiloh.   And the more honest and intelligent minds, indeed, let him rebuke with words, with a first or second admonition; but the wicked and the hard-hearted and the proud, or the disobedient, let him restrain at the very beginning of their sin by castigation of the body, as it were, with whips: knowing that it is written: "A fool is not bettered by words."   And again: "Strike thy son with the rod and thou shalt deliver his soul from death."   The abbot ought always to remember what he is, to remember what he is called, and to know that from him to whom more is committed, the more is demanded.   And let him know what a difficult and arduous thing he has undertaken,—to rule the souls and aid the morals of many.   And in one case indeed with blandishments, in another with rebukes, in another with persuasion—according to the quality or intelligence of each one,—he shall so conform and adapt himself to all, that not only shall he not suffer detriment to come to the flock committed to him, but shall rejoice in the increase of a good flock.   Above all things, let him not, dissimulating or undervaluing the safety of the souls committed to him, give more heed to transitory and earthly and passing things: but let him always reflect that he has undertaken to rule souls for which he is to render account.

And, lest perchance he enter into strife for a lesser matter, let him remember that it is written: "Seek ye first the kingdom of God and His righteousness; and all these things shall be added unto you." And again: "They that fear Him shall lack nothing." And let him know that he who undertakes to rule souls must prepare to render account. And, whatever number of brothers he knows that he has under his care, let him know for certain that at the day of judgment he shall render account to God for all their souls; his own soul without doubt being included. And thus, always fearing the future interrogation of the shepherd concerning the flocks entrusted to him, while keeping free from foreign interests he is rendered careful for his own. And when, by his admonitions, he administers correction to others, he is himself cleansed from his vices.

3. *About calling in the brethren to take council.* As often as anything especial is to be done in the monastery, the abbot shall call together the whole congregation, and shall himself explain the question at issue. And, having heard the advice of the brethren, he shall think it over by himself, and shall do what he considers most advantageous. And for this reason, moreover, we have said that all ought to be called to take counsel: because often it is to a younger person that God reveals what is best. The brethren, moreover, with all subjection of humility, ought so to give their advice, that they do not presume boldly to defend what seems good to them; but it should rather depend on the judgment of the abbot; so that whatever he decides to be the more salutary, they should all agree to it. But even as it behoves the disciples to obey the master, so it is fitting that he should providently and justly arrange all matters. In all things, indeed, let all follow the Rule as their guide; and let no one rashly deviate from it. Let no one in the monastery follow the inclination of his own heart; and let no one boldly presume to dispute with his abbot, within or without the monastery. But, if he should so presume, let him be subject to the discipline of the Rule. The abbot, on the other hand, shall do all things fearing the Lord and observing the Rule; knowing that he, without a doubt, shall have to render account to God as to a most impartial

judge, for all his decisions.   But if any lesser matters for the good of the monastery are to be decided upon, he shall employ the counsel of the elder members alone, since it is written: " Do all things with counsel, and after it is done thou wilt not repent."

4. *What are the instruments of good works.*[1]

5. *Concerning obedience.*   The first grade of humility is obedience without delay.   This becomes those who, on account of the holy service which they have professed, or on account of the fear of hell or the glory of eternal life consider nothing dearer to them than Christ: so that, so soon as anything is commanded by their superior, they may not know how to suffer delay in doing it, even as if it were a divine command. Concerning whom the Lord said: " As soon as he heard of me he obeyed me."   And again he said to the learned men: " He who heareth you heareth me."   Therefore let all such, straightway leaving their own affairs and giving up their own will, with unoccupied hands and leaving incomplete what they were doing—the foot of obedience being foremost,—follow with their deeds the voice of him who orders.   And, as it were, in the same moment, let the aforesaid command of the master and the perfected work of the disciple—both together in the swift- ness of the fear of God,—be called into being by those who are possessed with a desire of advancing to eternal life.   And therefore let them seize the narrow way of which the Lord says : " Narrow is the way which leadeth unto life."   Thus, not living according to their own judgment nor obeying their own desires and pleasures, but walking under another's judgment and command, passing their time in monasteries, let them desire an abbot to rule over them.   Without doubt all such live up to that precept of the Lord in which he says : " I am not come to do my own will but the will of him that sent me." . . . .

6. *Concerning silence.*   Let us do as the prophet says: "I said, I will take heed to my ways that I sin not with my tongue, I have kept my mouth with a bridle : I was dumb with silence, I held my peace even from good ; and my sorrow was stirred."   Here the prophet shows that if one

---

[1] Here follow seventy-two quotations from the Bible.

ought at times, for the sake of silence, to refrain from good sayings; how much more, as a punishment for sin, ought one to cease from evil words. . . . . And therefore, if anything is to be asked of the prior, let it be asked with all humility and subjection of reverence; lest one seem to speak more than is fitting. Scurrilities, however, or idle words and those exciting laughter, we condemn in all places with a lasting prohibition: nor do we permit a disciple to open his mouth for such sayings.

7. *Concerning humility.* . . . . The sixth grade of humility is, that a monk be contented with all lowliness or extremity, and consider himself, with regard to everything which is enjoined on him, as a poor and unworthy workman; saying to himself with the prophet: "I was reduced to nothing and was ignorant; I was made as the cattle before thee, and I am always with thee." The seventh grade of humility is, not only that he, with his tongue, pronounce himself viler and more worthless than all; but that he also believe it in the innermost workings of his heart; humbling himself and saying with the prophet, etc. . . . . The eighth degree of humility is that a monk do nothing except what the common rule of the monastery, or the example of his elders, urges him to do. The ninth degree of humility is that a monk restrain his tongue from speaking; and, keeping silence, do not speak until he is spoken to. The tenth grade of humility is that he be not ready, and easily inclined, to laugh. . . . . The eleventh grade of humility is that a monk, when he speaks, speak slowly and without laughter, humbly with gravity, using few and reasonable words; and that he be not loud of voice. . . . . The twelfth grade of humility is that a monk, shall not only with his heart but also with his body, always show humility to all who see him: that is, when at work, in the oratory, in the monastery, in the garden, on the road, in the fields. And everywhere, sitting or walking or standing, let him always be with head inclined, his looks fixed upon the ground; remembering every hour that he is guilty of his sins. Let him think that he is already being presented before the tremendous judgment of God, saying always to himself in his heart what that publican of the gospel, fixing his eyes on

the earth, said: "Lord I am not worthy, I a sinner, so much as to lift up mine eyes unto Heaven."

8. *Concerning the divine offices at night.* In the winter time, that is from the Calends of November until Easter, according to what is reasonable, they must rise at the eighth hour of the night, so that they rest a little more than half the night, and rise when they have already digested. But let the time that remains after vigils be kept for meditation by those brothers who are in any way behind hand with the psalter or lessons. From Easter, moreover, until the aforesaid Calends of November, let the hour of keeping vigils be so arranged that, a short interval being observed in which the brethren may go out for the necessities of nature, the matins, which are always to take place with the dawning light, may straightway follow.

9. *How many psalms are to be said at night.* In the winter first of all the verse shall be said: "Make haste oh God to deliver me; make haste to help me oh God." Then, secondly, there shall be said three times: "Oh Lord open Thou my lips and my mouth shall show forth Thy praise." To which is to be subjoined the third psalm and the Gloria. After this the ninety fourth psalm is to be sung antiphonally or in unison. The Ambrosian chant shall then follow: then six psalms antiphonally. These having been said, the abbot shall, with the verse mentioned, give the blessing. And all being seated upon the benches, there shall be read in turn from the Scriptures—following out the analogy—three lessons; between which also three responses shall be sung. Two responses shall be said without the *Gloria;* but, after the third lesson, he who chants shall say the *Gloria.* And, when the cantor begins to say this, all shall straightway rise from their seats out of honour and reverence for the holy Trinity. Books, moreover, of the old as well as the New Testament of Divine authority shall be read at the Vigils; but also expositions of them which have been made by the most celebrated orthodox teachers and catholic Fathers. Moreover, after these three lessons with their responses, shall follow other six psalms to be sung with the Alleluia. After this a lesson of the Apostle shall follow, to be recited by heart; and verses and the supplication of the Litany,

that is the Kyrie eleison : and thus shall end the nocturnal vigils.

10. *How in summer the nocturnal praise shall be carried on.*   From Easter moreover until the Calends of November, the whole quantity of psalmody, as has been said above, shall be observed : except that the lessons from the Scripture, on account of the shortness of the nights, shall not be read at all.   But in place of those three lessons, one from the old Testament shall be said by memory, and a short response shall follow it.   And everything else shall be carried out as has been said ; that is, so that never less than the number of twelve psalms shall be said at nocturnal vigils ; excepting the third and ninety fourth psalm.

11. *How vigils shall be conducted on Sundays.*   On Sundays they shall rise earlier for vigils.   In which vigils let the following measure be observed ; that is, after six psalms and a verse having been sung—as we arranged above,—all sitting down in their places and in order upon the benches, there shall be read from Scripture, as we said above, four lessons with their responses.   Only in the fourth response, however, shall the Gloria be said by the Cantor.   When he begins this, straightway all shall rise with reverence.   After which lessons shall follow other six psalms in order, antiphonally, like the former ones ; and verses.   After which, there shall again be read other four lessons with their responses, in the same order as above. After which there shall be said three canticles, which the abbot shall have chosen from the prophets : which canticles shall be sung with the Alleluia.   Then after the verse has been said and the abbot has given his benediction, there shall be read other four lessons from the New Testament, in the same order as above.   After the fourth response, moreover, the abbot shall begin the hymn : " We praise Thee O Lord."   This being finished the abbot shall read a lesson from the Gospel with honour and trembling, all standing.   This being read through, all shall answer "Amen."   And the abbot shall straightway cause the hymn : " It is a good thing to praise the Lord " to follow ; and, the benediction being given, they shall begin matins. This order of vigils at all times of summer as well as winter shall be similarly observed on Sunday : unless by

chance (may it not happen) they rise too late, and something from the lessons or responses must be shortened : as to which they must take the greatest care lest it occur. But if it happen, he through whose neglect it came about shall give proper satisfaction for it to God in the oratory.[1] . . . .

16. *How Divine Service shall be held through the day.* As the prophet says : " Seven times in the day do I praise Thee." Which sacred number of seven will thus be fulfilled by us if, at matins, at the first, third, sixth, ninth hours, at vesper time and at " completorium " we perform the duties of our service ; for it is of these hours of the day that he said : " Seven times in the day do I praise Thee." For, concerning nocturnal vigils, the same prophet says : " At midnight I arose to confess unto thee." Therefore, at these times, let us give thanks to our Creator concerning the judgments of his righteousness ; that is, at matins, etc. . . . . , and at night we will rise and confess to him.[1] . . . .

18. *In what order the psalms are to be said.* The order of the daily psalmody having been arranged, all the rest of the psalms that remain shall be equally divided among the vigils of the seven nights, separating, indeed, the psalms that are the longest among them ; and twelve shall be appointed for each night. Laying great stress upon this fact, however, that if this distribution of psalms be not pleasing to any one, he shall arrange it otherwise if he think best ; provided he sees to it under all circumstances that every week the entire psalter, to the number of 150 psalms, is said. And on Sunday at Vigils it shall always be begun anew. For those monks show a too scanty proof of their devotion, who, during the course of a week, sing less than the Psalter with its customary canticles : inasmuch as we read that our holy Fathers in one day rigidly fulfilled that, which would that we—lukewarm as we are— might perform in an entire week.

19. *Concerning the art of singing.* Whereas we believe that there is a divine presence, and that the eyes of the Lord look down everywhere upon the good and the evil : chiefly

[1] Long lists of psalms follow.

then, without any doubt, we may believe that this is the case when we are assisting at divine service. Therefore let us always be mindful of what the prophet says : " Serve the Lord in all fear " ; and again, " Sing wisely " ; and, " in the sight of the angels I will sing unto thee." Therefore let us consider how we ought to conduct ourselves before the face of the divinity and his angels ; and let us so stand and sing that our voice may accord with our intention.

20. *Concerning reverence for prayer.*   If when to powerful men we wish to suggest anything, we do not presume to do it unless with reverence and humility : how much more should we supplicate with all humility, and devotion of purity, God who is the Lord of all. And let us know that we are heard, not for much speaking, but for purity of heart and compunction of tears. And, therefore, prayer ought to be brief and pure; unless perchance it be prolonged by the influence of the inspiration of the divine grace.   When assembled together, then, let the prayer be altogether brief ; and, the sign being given by the prior, let all rise together.

21. *Concerning the deans of the monastery.*   If the congregation be a larger one, let there be elected from it brothers of good standing and of holy character ; and let them be made deans.   And they shall be watchful over their decanates in all things, according to the mandates of God and the precepts of their abbot.   And the deans elected shall be such that the abbot may safely share his burdens with them. And they shall not be elected according to order, but according to their merit of life and their advancement in wisdom.   And, if any one of these deans be found perchance to be blameworthy, being puffed up by pride of something ; and if, being warned once and again and a third time, he be unwilling to better himself, —let him be deposed ; and let another, who is worthy, be chosen in his place.   And we decree the like concerning the provost.

22. *How the monks shall sleep.*   They shall sleep separately in separate beds.   They shall receive positions for their beds, after the manner of their characters, according to the dispensation of their abbot.   If it can be done, they

shall all sleep in one place. If, however, their number do not permit it, they shall rest by tens or twenties, with elders who will concern themselves about them. A candle shall always be burning in that same cell until early in the morning. They shall sleep clothed, and girt with belts or with ropes; and they shall not have their knives at their sides while they sleep, lest perchance in a dream they should wound the sleepers. And let the monks be always on the alert; and, when the signal is given, rising without delay, let them hasten to mutually prepare themselves for the service of God—with all gravity and modesty, however. The younger brothers shall not have beds by themselves, but interspersed among those of the elder ones. And when they rise for the service of God, they shall exhort each other mutually with moderation, on account of the excuses that those who are sleepy are inclined to make.

23. *Concerning excommunication for faults.* If any one is found to be a scorner—being contumacious or disobedient, or a murmurer, or one acting in any way contrary to the holy Rule, and to the precepts of his elders: let such a one, according to the teaching of our Lord, be admonished once, and a second time, secretly, by his elders. If he do not amend his ways, he shall be rebuked publicly in the presence of all. But if, even then, he do not better himself— if he understands how great the penalty is—he shall be subject to excommunication. But, if he is a wicked man, he shall be given over to corporal punishment.

24. *What ought to be the measure of the excommunication.* According to the amount of the fault the measure of the excommunication or of the discipline ought to be extended: which amount of the faults shall be determined by the judgment of the abbot. If any brother, however, be taken in lighter faults, he shall be prevented from participating at table. With regard to one deprived of participation at table, moreover, this shall be the regulation: that he shall not start a psalm or a chant in the oratory, or recite a lesson, until he has atoned. The refreshment of food, moreover, he shall take alone, after the refreshment of the brothers. So that if, for example, the brothers eat at the sixth hour, that brother shall do so at the ninth; if

the brothers at the ninth, then he at Vespers; until by suitable satisfaction he gains pardon.

25. *Concerning graver faults.* That brother, moreover, who is held guilty of a graver fault shall be suspended at the same time from table and from the oratory. None of the brothers may in any way consort with him, or have speech with him. He shall be alone at the labour enjoined upon him, persisting in the struggle of penitence; knowing that terrible sentence of the Apostle who said that such a man was given over to the destruction of the flesh in order that his soul might be saved at the day of the Lord. The refection of food moreover he shall take alone, in the measure and at the time that the abbot shall appoint as suitable for him. Nor shall he be blessed by any one who passes by, nor shall any food be given him.

26. *Concerning those who, without being ordered by the abbot, associate with the excommunicated.* If any brother presume, without an order of the abbot, in any way to associate with an excommunicated brother, or to speak with him, or to give an order to him: he shall suffer the same penalty of excommunication.

27. *What care the abbot should exercise with regard to the excommunicated.* With all solicitude the abbot shall exercise care with regard to delinquent brothers: " They that be whole need not a physician, but they that are sick." And therefore he ought to use every means, as a wise physician, to send in as it were secret consolers—that is, wise elder brothers who, as it were secretly, shall console the wavering brother and lead him to the atonement of humility. And they shall comfort him lest he be swallowed up by overmuch sorrow. On the contrary, as the same apostle says, charity shall be confirmed in him, and he shall be prayed for by all. For the abbot should greatly exert his solicitude, and take care with all sagacity and industry, lest he lose any of the sheep entrusted to him. For he should know that he has undertaken the care of weak souls, not the tyranny over sound ones. And he shall fear the threat of the prophet through whom the Lord says: " Ye did take that which ye saw to be strong, and that which was weak ye did cast out." And let him imitate the pious example of the good Shepherd, who, leaving the

ninety and nine sheep upon the mountains, went out to seek the one sheep that had gone astray : and He had such compassion upon its infirmity, that He deigned to place it upon His sacred shoulders, and thus to carry it back to the flock.

28. *Concerning those who, being often rebuked, do not amend.* If any brother, having frequently been rebuked for any fault, do not amend even after he has been excommunicated, a more severe rebuke shall fall upon him ;— that is, the punishment of the lash shall be inflicted upon him. But if he do no even then amend ; or, if perchance —which God forbid,—swelled with pride he try even to defend his works : then the abbot shall act as a wise physician. If he have applied the fomentations, the ointments of exhortation, the medicaments of the Divine Scriptures ; if he have proceeded to the last blasting of excommunication, or to blows with rods, and if he see that his efforts avail nothing : let him also—what is greater—call in the prayer of himself and all the brothers for him : that God who can do all things may work a cure upon an infirm brother. But if he be not healed even in this way, then at last the abbot may use the pruning knife, as the apostle says : " Remove evil from you," etc. : lest one diseased sheep contaminate the whole flock.

29. *Whether brothers who leave the monastery ought again to be received.* A brother who goes out, or is cast out, of the monastery for his own fault, if he wish to return, shall first promise every amends for the fault on account of which he departed ; and thus he shall be received into the lowest degree—so that thereby his humility may be proved. But if he again depart, up to the third time he shall be received. Knowing that after this every opportunity of return is denied to him.

30. *Concerning boys under age, how they shall be corrected.* Every age or intelligence ought to have its proper bounds. Therefore as often as boys or youths, or those who are less able to understand how great is the punishment of excommunication : as often as such persons offend, they shall either be afflicted with excessive fasts, or coerced with severe blows, that they may be healed.

31. *Concerning the cellarer of the monastery, what sort of a person he shall be.* As cellarer of the monastery there

shall be elected from the congregation one who is wise, mature in character, sober, not given to much eating, not proud, not turbulent, not an upbraider, not tardy, not prodigal, but fearing God: a father, as it were, to the whole congregation. He shall take care of every thing, he shall do nothing without the order of the abbot. He shall have charge of what things are ordered: he shall not rebuff the brethren. If any brother by chance demand anything unreasonably from him, he shall not, by spurning, rebuff him; but reasonably, with humility, shall deny to him who wrongly seeks.

Let him guard his soul, mindful always of that saying of the apostle, that he who ministers well purchases to himself a good degree. He shall care with all solicitude for the infirm and youthful, for guests and for the poor; knowing without doubt that he shall render account for all of these at the day of judgment. All the utensils of the monastery, and all its substance, he shall look upon as though they were the sacred vessels of the altar. He shall deem nothing worthy of neglect; nor shall he give way to avarice; nor shall he be prodigal or a squanderer of the substance of the monastery; but he shall do everything with moderation and according to the order of the abbot. He shall have humility above all things: and when there is nothing substantial for him to give, let a good word of reply be offered, as it is written: "a good word is above the best gift." Every thing which the abbot orders him to have, let him have under his care; what he prohibits let him refrain from. To the brethren he shall offer the fixed measure of food without any haughtiness or delay, in order that they be not offended; being mindful of the divine saying as to what he merits "who offends one of these little ones." If the congregation is rather large, assistants shall be given him; by whose aid he himself, with a calm mind, shall fill the office committed to him. At suitable hours those things shall be given which are to be given, and those things shall be asked for which are to be asked for: so that no one may be disturbed or rebuffed in the house of God.

32. *Concerning the utensils or property of the monastery.* For the belongings of the monastery in utensils, or garments, or property of any kind, the abbot shall provide

brothers of whose life and morals he is sure ; and to them as he shall see fit he shall consign the different things to be taken care of and collected. Concerning which the abbot shall keep a list, so that when in turn the brothers succeed each other in the care of the things assigned, he may know what he gives or what he receives. If moreover any one have soiled or treated negligently the property of the monastery, he shall be rebuked ; but if he do not amend, he shall be subjected to the discipline of the Rule.

33. *Whether the monks should have any thing of their own.* More than any thing else is this special vice to be cut off root and branch from the monastery, that one should presume to give or receive anything without the order of the abbot, or should have anything of his own. He should have absolutely not anything : neither a book, nor tablets, nor a pen—nothing at all.—For indeed it is not allowed to the monks to have their own bodies or wills in their own power. But all things necessary they must expect from the Father of the monastery ; nor is it allowable to have anything which the abbot did not give or permit. All things shall be common to all, as it is written : " Let not any man presume or call anything his own." But if any one shall have been discovered delighting in this most evil vice : being warned once and again, if he do not amend, let him be subjected to punishment.

34. *Whether all ought to receive necessaries equally.* As it is written : " It was divided among them singly, according as each had need " : whereby we do not say—far from it—that there should be an excepting of persons, but a consideration for infirmities. Wherefore he who needs less, let him thank God and not be dismayed ; but he who needs more, let him be humiliated on account of his infirmity, and not exalted on account of the mercy that is shown him. And thus all members will be in peace. Above all, let not the evil of murmuring appear, for any cause, through any word or sign whatever. But, if such a murmurer is discovered, he shall be subjected to stricter discipline.

35. *Concerning the weekly officers of the kitchen.* The brothers shall so serve each other in turn that no one shall be excused from the duty of cooking, unless either through

sickness, or because he is occupied in some important work of utility. For, by this means, charity and a greater reward are acquired. Moreover assistants shall be provided for the weak, so that they may not do this as a burden, but may all have helpers according to the size of the congregation or the nature of the place. If the congregation is a large one the cellarer, or any who, as we have said, are occupied with matters of greater utility, shall be excused from cooking. The rest shall serve each other in turn with all charity. At the end of the week he (the weekly cook) shall, on Saturday, do the cleansing. He shall wash the towels with which the brothers wipe their hands or feet. Moreover as well he who enters into as well as he who goes out (of office) shall wash the feet of every body. He shall give back the vessels of his ministry clean and whole to the cellarer. And he, the cellarer, shall consign them thus to the one entering (into office), so that he shall know what he gives or what he receives. The weekly cooks moreover, one hour before the hour of refection, shall receive the measure of food previously fixed upon : the different drinking vessels, namely, and the bread ; so that at the hour of refection, without murmuring and without heavy labour, they may serve their brothers. On solemn days moreover they shall fast until mass. The incoming and the outgoing weekly officers, moreover, shall, in the oratory, as soon as matins are finished on Sunday, prostrate themselves at the feet of all, begging to be prayed for. Furthermore he who has finished his week shall say this verse: " Blessed art Thou oh Lord God, who hast aided and consoled me." This being said for the third time, he who retires shall receive the benediction. He who is entering shall follow and shall say: "O God come to my aid, O Lord hasten to help me." And this shall be repeated three times by all. And, receiving the benediction, he shall enter (upon his office).

36. *Concerning infirm brothers.* Before all, and above all, attention shall be paid to the care of the sick ; so that they shall be served as if it were actually Christ. For He himself said : " I was sick and ye visited me." And : " Inasmuch as ye have done it unto one of the least of these ye have done it unto me." But let the sick also consider that

they are being served to the honour of God, and let them
not offend by their abundance the brothers who serve
them: which (offences) nevertheless are patiently to be
borne, for, from such, a greater reward is acquired. Wherefore let the abbot take the greatest care lest they suffer
neglect. And for these infirm brothers a cell by itself
shall be set apart, and a servitor, God-fearing, and diligent
and careful. The use of baths shall be offered to the sick
as often as it is necessary: to the healthy, and especially
to youths, it shall not be so readily conceded. But also
the eating of flesh shall be allowed to the sick, and altogether to the feeble, for their rehabilitation. But when
they have grown better, they shall all, in the usual manner,
abstain from flesh. The abbot, moreover, shall take the
greatest care lest the sick are neglected by the cellarer or
by the servitors: for whatever fault is committed by the
disciples rebounds upon him.

37.

Although human nature itself is prone to have pity for
these ages—that is, old age and infancy,—nevertheless the
authority of the Rule also has regard for them. Their
weakness shall always be considered, and in the matter of
food, the strict tenor of the Rule shall by no means be observed, as far as they are concerned; but they shall be
treated with pious consideration, and may anticipate the
canonical hours.

38. *Concerning the weekly reader.* At the tables of the
brothers when they eat the reading should not fail; nor
may any one at random dare to take up the book and begin
to read there; but he who is about to read for the whole
week shall begin his duties on Sunday. And, entering
upon his office after mass and communion, he shall ask all
to pray for him, that God may avert from him the spirit of
elation. And this verse shall be said in the oratory three
times by all, he however beginning it: " O Lord open Thou
my lips and my mouth shall show forth Thy praise." And
thus, having received the benediction, he shall enter upon
his duties as reader. And there shall be the greatest
silence at table, so that the muttering or the voice of no one

shall be heard there, except that of the reader alone. But whatever things are necessary to those eating and drinking, the brothers shall so furnish them to each other in turn, that no one shall need to ask for anything. But if, nevertheless, something is wanted, it shall rather be sought by the employment of some sign than by the voice. Nor shall any one presume there to ask questions concerning the reading or anything else; nor shall an opportunity be given: unless perhaps the prior wishes to say something, briefly, for the purpose of edifying. Moreover the brother who reads for the week shall receive bread and wine before he begins to read, on account of the holy communion, and lest, perchance, it might be injurious for him to sustain a fast. Afterwards, moreover, he shall eat with the weekly cooks and the servitors. The brothers, moreover, shall read or sing not in rotation; but the ones shall do so who will edify their hearers.

39.

We believe, moreover, that, for the daily refection of the sixth as well as of the ninth hour, two cooked dishes, on account of the infirmities of the different ones, are enough for all tables: so that whoever, perchance, can not eat of one may partake of the other. Therefore let two cooked dishes suffice for all the brothers: and, if it is possible to obtain apples or growing vegetables, a third may be added. One full pound of bread shall suffice for a day, whether there be one refection, or a breakfast and a supper. But if they are going to have supper, the third part of that same pound shall be reserved by the cellarer, to be given back to those who are about to sup. But if, perchance, some greater labour shall have been performed, it shall be in the will and the power of the abbot, if it is expedient, to increase anything; surfeiting above all things being guarded against, so that indigestion may never seize a monk: for nothing is so contrary to every Christian as surfeiting, as our Lord says: "Take heed to yourselves, lest your hearts be overcharged with surfeiting." But to younger boys the same quantity shall not be served, but less than that to the older ones; moderation being observed in all things. But the eating of the flesh of quadrupeds shall be abstained from altogether by every one, excepting alone the weak and the sick.

40. *Concerning the amount of drink.* Each one has his own gift from God, the one in this way, the other in that. Therefore it is with some hesitation that the amount of daily sustenance for others is fixed by us. Nevertheless, in view of the weakness of the infirm we believe that a hemina [1] of wine a day is enough for each one. Those moreover to whom God gives the ability of bearing abstinence shall know that they will have their own reward. But the prior shall judge if either the needs of the place, or labour or the heat of summer, requires more; considering in all things lest satiety or drunkenness creep in. Indeed we read that wine is not suitable for monks at all. But because, in our day, it is not possible to persuade the monks of this, let us agree at least as to the fact that we should not drink till we are sated, but sparingly. For wine can make even the wise to go astray. Where, moreover, the necessities of the place are such that the amount written above can not be found,—but much less or nothing at all,—those who live there shall bless God and shall not murmur. And we admonish them as to this above all: that they be without murmuring.

41. *At what hours the brothers ought to take their refection.* From the holy Easter time until Pentecost the brothers shall have their refection at the sixth hour; and at evening they shall sup. From Pentecost, moreover, through the whole summer,—if the monks do not have hard labour in the fields, or the extreme heat of the summer does not prevent them,—they shall fast on the fourth and sixth day until the ninth hour: but on the other days they shall have their repast at the sixth hour. Which sixth hour, if they have ordinary work in the fields, or if the heat of summer is not great, shall be kept to for the repast; and it shall be for the abbot to decide. And he shall so temper and arrange all things, that their souls may be saved on the one hand; and that, on the other, what the brothers do they shall do without any justifiable murmuring. Moreover, from the ides of Sep-

---

[1] Not quite half a liter.—ED.

tember until the beginning of Lent, they shall always have their refection at the ninth hour. But in Lent, until Easter, they shall have their refection at Vesper time. And that same Vesper meal shall be so arranged that those who take their repast may not need the light of a lantern; but everything shall be consumed while it is still daylight. But indeed at all times, the hour, whether of supper or of refection, shall be so arranged, that everything may be done while it is still light.

42. *That after "completorium" no one shall speak.* At all times the monks ought to practise silence, but most of all in the nocturnal hours. And thus at all times, whether of fasting or of eating: if it be meal-time, as soon as they have risen from the table, all shall sit together and one shall read selections or lives of the Fathers, or indeed anything which will edify the hearers. But not the Pentateuch or Kings; for, to weak intellects, it will be of no use at that hour to hear this part of Scripture; but they shall be read at other times. But if the days are fast days, when Vespers have been said, after a short interval they shall come to the reading of the selections as we have said; and four or five pages, or as much as the hour permits having been read, they shall all congregate, upon the cessation of the reading. If, by chance, any one is occupied in a task assigned to him, he shall nevertheless approach. All therefore being gathered together, they shall say the completing prayer; and, going out from the "completorium," there shall be no further opportunity for any one to say anything. But if any one be found acting contrary to this rule of silence, he shall be subjected to a very severe punishment. Unless a necessity in the shape of guests should arise, or the abbot, by chance, should give some order. But even this, indeed, he shall do most seriously, with all gravity and moderation.

43. *Concerning those who come late to Divine Service or to table.* As soon as the signal for the hour of Divine Service has been heard, leaving everything that they had in hand they shall run with the greatest haste; with gravity, however, in order that scurrility may find no nourishment. Therefore let nothing be preferred to the service of God. But if any one should come to the noc-

turnal vigils after the Gloria of the ninety fourth psalm—
which on this account we wish to have said quite lin-
geringly and with delay,—he shall not stand in his place
in the choir, but shall stand last of all, or in a place which
the abbot shall have set apart for such dilatory ones; that
he may be seen by him or by all, until, the Divine Service
being ended, he may show his repentance by giving public
satisfaction. Moreover this is the reason why we have
decreed that they ought to stand last or apart: that, being
seen by all, even for very shame they may amend. For if
they remain outside the oratory, there may be one perhaps
who will either go back and go to sleep, or at any rate
will sit down outside, or will give way to idle thoughts,
and a chance will be given to the evil one. He shall
rather enter within, that he lose not the whole, and that
he amend for the time that remains. Moreover in the
day time he who does not come to the Divine Service after
the verse, and the Gloria of the first psalm which is said
after the verse—according to the rule which we mentioned
above,—shall stand last. Nor shall he presume to join
the choir of singers until he render satisfaction; unless,
indeed, the abbot allow him to do so by his permission,
under condition that the guilty one shall afterwards render
satisfaction. Moreover he who does not come to table
before the verse, so that all together may say the verse
and pray, and all as one may go to table: he who, through
his negligence or fault, does not come, shall be rebuked
for this up to the second time. If again he do not amend,
he shall not be allowed to share in the common table; but,
separated from the companionship of all, shall have his
refection alone, his portion of wine being taken away from
him until he render satisfaction and make amends. He,
moreover, who is not present at that verse which is said
after the meal shall suffer in like manner. Nor shall any
one presume, before the hour fixed, or after it, to take any
food or drink for himself. But if anything is offered to
any one by the prior, and he refuse to accept it: at the
hour when he desires that which he first refused, he shall
not receive it or anything else at all, until he makes suitable amends.

44. *Concerning those who are excommunicated, how they*

shall render satisfaction. He who, for graver faults, is excommunicated from the oratory and from table, shall, at the hour when the Divine Service is being celebrated in the oratory, lie prostrate before the gates of the oratory, saying nothing, his head being placed not otherwise than on the ground, lying headlong before the feet of all who go out from the oratory. And he shall continue doing this until the abbot shall judge that he have rendered satisfaction. And when he shall enter at the order of the abbot, he shall grovel at the feet of the abbot, and then of all, that they may pray for him. And then, if the abbot order it, he shall be received into the choir or into the grade which the abbot decrees: in such wise, nevertheless, that he may not presume to start a psalm, or a lesson, or anything else in the oratory, unless the abbot again order him to. And at all hours when the Divine Service reaches its end, he shall throw himself on the ground in the place where he stands: and shall render satisfaction in this way until the abbot orders him to desist at length from doing so. But those who, for light faults, are excommunicated from table alone, shall render satisfaction in the oratory: they shall do this until the abbot gives the order; until he blesses them and says, "it is enough."

45. *Concerning those who make mistakes in the oratory.* If any one, in saying a psalm, response, or antiphone or lesson, make a mistake: unless he humble himself there before all, giving satisfaction, he shall be subjected to greater punishment, as one who was unwilling to correct by humility that in which he had erred by neglect. But children, for such a fault, shall be whipped.

46. *Concerning those who err in any other matters.* If any one commit any fault while at any labour, in the kitchen, in the cellar, in the offices, in the bakery, while labouring at any art, or in any place; or shall break or lose anything, or commit any excess wherever he may be; and do not himself, coming before the abbot or the congregation, of his own accord give satisfaction and declare his error: if it become known through another, he shall be subjected to greater amends. But if the cause of his sin lie hidden in his soul, he may declare it to the abbot alone or to his spiritual elders; who may know how to cure his

wounds, and not to uncover and make public those of another.

47. *Concerning the announcement of the hour of Divine Service.* The announcing of the hour of Divine Service, by night and by day, shall be the work of the abbot: either to announce it himself, or to enjoin this care on a brother so zealous that everything shall be fulfilled at the proper hours. And those who are ordered to, shall, after the abbot, start the psalms or antiphones in their proper order. No one moreover shall presume to sing or to read unless he can fulfill this duty so that those hearing him shall be edified. And he whom the abbot orders to, shall do this with humility and gravity and trembling.

48. *Concerning the daily manual labour.* Idleness is the enemy of the soul. And therefore, at fixed times, the brothers ought to be occupied in manual labour; and again, at fixed times, in sacred reading. Therefore we believe that, according to this disposition, both seasons ought to be arranged; so that, from Easter until the Calends of October, going out early, from the first until the fourth hour they shall do what labour may be necessary. Moreover, from the fourth hour until about the sixth, they shall be free for reading. After the meal of the sixth hour, moreover, rising from table, they shall rest in their beds with all silence; or, perchance, he that wishes to read may so read to himself that he do not disturb another. And the nona (the second meal) shall be gone through with more moderately about the middle of the eighth hour; and again they shall work at what is to be done until Vespers. But, if the exigency or poverty of the place demands that they be occupied by themselves in picking fruits, they shall not be dismayed: for then they are truly monks if they live by the labours of their hands; as did also our fathers and the apostles. Let all things be done with moderation, however, on account of the faint-hearted. From the Calends of October, moreover, until the beginning of Lent they shall be free for reading until the second full hour. At the second hour the tertia (morning service) shall be held, and all shall labour at the task which is enjoined upon them until the ninth. The first signal, moreover, of the ninth hour having been given,

they shall each one leave off his work; and be ready when
the second signal strikes. Moreover after the refection
they shall be free for their readings or for psalms. But in
the days of Lent, from dawn until the third full hour, they
shall be free for their readings; and, until the tenth full
hour, they shall do the labour that is enjoined on them.
In which days of Lent they shall all receive separate books
from the library; which they shall read entirely through in
order. These books are to be given out on the first day of
Lent. Above all there shall certainly be appointed one or
two elders, who shall go round the monastery at the hours
in which the brothers are engaged in reading, and see to it
that no troublesome brother chance to be found who is
open to idleness and trifling, and is not intent on his reading; being not only of no use to himself, but also stirring
up others. If such a one—may it not happen—be found,
he shall be admonished once and a second time. If he do
not amend, he shall be subject under the Rule to such
punishment that the others may have fear. Nor shall
brother join brother at unsuitable hours. Moreover on
Sunday all shall engage in reading: excepting those who
are deputed to various duties. But if anyone be so negligent and lazy that he will not or can not read, some task
shall be imposed upon him which he can do; so that he be
not idle. On feeble or delicate brothers such a labour or
art is to be imposed, that they shall neither be idle, nor
shall they be so oppressed by the violence of labour as to
be driven to take flight. Their weakness is to be taken
into consideration by the abbot.

49. Although at all times the life of the monk should be
such as though Lent were being observed: nevertheless,
since few have that virtue, we urge that, on those said days
of Lent, he shall keep his life in all purity; and likewise
wipe out, in those holy days, the negligencies of other
times. This is then worthily done if we refrain from all
vices, if we devote ourselves to prayer with weeping, to
reading and compunction of heart, and to abstinence.
Therefore, on these days, let us add of ourselves something
to the ordinary amount of our service: special prayers,
abstinence from food and drink;—so that each one, over
and above the amount allotted to him, shall offer of his

own will something to God with rejoicing of the Holy Spirit. That is, he shall restrict his body in food, drink, sleep, talkativeness, and merry-making; and, with the joy of a spiritual desire, shall await the holy Easter. The offering, moreover, that each one makes, he shall announce to his abbot; that it may be done with his prayers and by his will. For what is done without the permission of the spiritual Father, shall be put down to presumption and vain glory, and not to a monk's credit. Therefore all things are to be done according to the will of the abbot.

50. *Concerning brothers who labour far from the oratory, or who are on a journey.* Brothers who are at work very far off, and cannot betake themselves at the proper hour to the oratory, shall, if the abbot deem this to be the case, celebrate the Divine Service there where they are at work; bending their knees in the fear of God. Likewise as to those who are sent on a journey: the established hours shall not escape them; but, according as they can, they shall perform of themselves, and not neglect to render, the rightful amount of service.

51. *Concerning brothers who do not journey very far.* A brother who is sent for any reply, and is expected to return to the monastery on the same day, shall not presume to eat outside, even if he be asked to by any one; unless perchance he be told to by his abbot. But if he do otherwise he shall be excommunicated.

52. *Concerning the oratory of the monastery.* The oratory shall be that which it is called; nor shall any thing else be done there or placed there. When the Divine Service is ended, let all go out with perfect silence and let reverence be paid to God: so that a brother who perchance especially desires to pray for himself, may not be impeded by the wickedness of another. But, if another wishes perchance to pray more secretly for himself, he shall simply enter and pray; not with a clamorous voice, but with tears, and inclining his heart. Therefore he who does not perform a similar act, shall not be permitted, when the Divine Service is ended, to remain in the oratory—as has been said —lest another suffer hindrance.

53. *Concerning the reception of guests.* All guests who come shall be received as though they were Christ: for

He Himself said: "I was a stranger and ye took me in."
And to all, fitting honour shall be shown; but, most of
all, to servants of the faith and to pilgrims. When, therefore, a guest is announced, the prior or the brothers shall
run to meet him, with every office of love. And first they
shall pray together; and thus they shall be joined together in peace. Which kiss of peace shall not first be
offered, unless a prayer have preceded; on account of the
wiles of the devil. In the salutation itself, moreover, all
humility shall be exhibited. In the case of all guests
arriving or departing: with inclined head, or with pros-
trating of the whole body upon the ground, Christ, who is
also received in them, shall be adored. The guests moreover, having been received, shall be conducted to prayer;
and afterwards the prior, or one whom he himself orders,
shall sit with them. The law of God shall be read before
the guest that he may be edified; and, after this, every
kindness shall be exhibited. A fast may be broken by
the prior on account of a guest; unless, perchance, it be
a special day of fast which can not be violated. The
brothers, moreover, shall continue their customary fasts.
The abbot shall give water into the hands of his guests;
and the abbot as well as the whole congregation shall
wash the feet of all guests. This being done, they shall
say this verse: "We have received, oh Lord, Thy loving-
kindness in the midst of Thy temple." Chiefly in the
reception of the poor and of pilgrims shall care be most
anxiously exhibited: for in them Christ is received the
more. For the very fear of the rich exacts honour for
them. The kitchen of the abbot and the guests shall be
by itself; so that guests coming at uncertain hours, as is
always happening in a monastery, may not disturb the
brothers. Into the control of which kitchen, two brothers,
who can well fulfill that duty, shall enter yearly; and to
them, according as they shall need it, help shall be administered; so that they may serve without murmuring.
And again, when they are less occupied, they shall go out
where they are commanded to, and labour. And not only
in their case, but in all the offices of the monastery, such
consideration shall be had, that, when they need it, help
shall be given to them. And, when they are again at

leisure, they shall obey orders. Likewise a brother, whose soul the fear of God possesses, shall have assigned to him the cell of the guests, where there shall be beds sufficiently strewn; and the house of God shall be administered wisely by the wise. Moreover he who has not been ordered to shall by no means join the guests or speak to them. But if he meet them or see them, saluting them humbly, as has been said, and seeking their blessing, he shall pass by, saying that he is not allowed to speak with a guest.

54. *Whether a monk should be allowed to receive letters or anything.* By no means shall it be allowed to a monk—either from his relatives, or from any man, or from one of his fellows—to receive or to give, without order of the abbot, letters, presents or any gift, however small. But even if, by his relatives, anything has been sent to him: he shall not presume to receive it, unless it have first been shown to the abbot. But if he order it to be received, it shall be in the power of the abbot to give it to whomever he may will. And the brother to whom it happened to have been sent shall not be chagrined; that an opportunity be not given to the devil. Whoever, moreover, presumes otherwise, shall be subject to the discipline of the Rule.

55.

Vestments shall be given to the brothers according to the quality of the places where they dwell, or the temperature of the air. For in cold regions more is required; but in warm, less. This, therefore, is a matter for the abbot to decide. We nevertheless consider that for ordinary places there suffices for the monks a cowl and gown apiece—the cowl, in winter hairy, in summer plain or old,—and a working garment, on account of their labours. As clothing for the feet, shoes and boots. Concerning the colour and size of all of which things the monks shall not talk; but they shall be such as can be found in the province where they are or as can be bought the most cheaply. The abbot, moreover, shall provide, as to the measure, that those vestments be not short for those using them; but of suitable length. And, when new ones are received, they shall always straightway return the old ones, to be kept in the vestiary on account of the poor. It is enough, moreover, for a monk to have two gowns and two cowls; on account of the nights, and on account of washing the things themselves. Every thing, then, that is over this is superfluous, and ought to be removed. And the shoes, and whatever is old, they shall return when they receive something new. And those who are sent on a journey shall receive cloths for the loins from the vestiary ; which on their return they shall restore, having washed them. And there shall be cowls and gowns somewhat better than those which they have ordinarily : which, when they start on a journey, they shall receive from the vestiary, and, on returning, shall restore. As trappings for the beds, moreover, shall suffice a mat, a woollen covering, a woollen cloth under the pillow, and the pillow. And these beds are frequently to be searched by the abbot on account of private property ; lest he find some. And, if any thing is found belonging to any one which he did not receive from the abbot, he shall be subjected to the most severe discipline. And, in order that this special vice may be cut off at the roots, there shall be given by the abbot all things which are necessary : that is, a cowl, a gown, shoes, boots, a binder for the loins, a knife, a pen, a needle, a handkerchief, tablets : so that all excuse of necessity shall be removed. By this same abbot, however, that sentence of the Acts of the Apostles shall always be regarded : " For there was given unto each man according unto his need." Thus, therefore, the abbot also shall consider the infirmities of the needy, not the evil will of the envious. In all his judgments, nevertheless, he shall remember the retribution of God.

56. *Concerning the table of the abbot.* The table of the abbot shall always be with the guests and pilgrims. As often, however, as guests are lacking, it shall be in his power to summon those of the brothers whom he wishes. He shall see. nevertheless, that one or two elders are always left with the brothers, for the sake of discipline.

57. *Concerning the artificers of the monastery.* Artificers, if there are any in the monastery, shall practise with all humility their special arts, if the abbot permit it. But if

any one of them becomes inflated with pride on account of knowledge of his art, to the extent that he seems to be conferring something on the monastery : such a one shall be plucked away from that art; and he shall not again return to it unless the abbot perchance again orders him to, he being humiliated. But, if anything from the works of the artificers is to be sold, they themselves shall take care through whose hands they (the works) are to pass, lest they (the intermediaries) presume to commit some fraud upon the monastery. They shall always remember Ananias and Sapphira; lest, perchance, the death that they suffered with regard to the body, these, or all those who have committed any fraud as to the property of the monastery, may suffer with regard to the soul. In the prices themselves, moreover, let not the evil of avarice crop out: but let the object always be given a little cheaper than it is given by other and secular persons; so that, in all things, God shall be glorified.

58. *Concerning the manner of receiving brothers.* When any new comer applies for conversion, an easy entrance shall not be granted him : but, as the apostle says, " Try the spirits if they be of God." Therefore, if he who comes perseveres in knocking, and is seen after four or five days to patiently endure the insults inflicted upon him, and the difficulty of ingress, and to persist in his demand : entrance shall be allowed him, and he shall remain for a few days in the cell of the guests. After this, moreover, he shall be in the cell of the novices, where he shall meditate and eat and sleep. And an elder shall be detailed off for him who shall be capable of saving souls, who shall altogether intently watch over him, and make it a care to see if he reverently seek God, if he be zealous in the service of God, in obedience, in suffering shame. And all the harshness and roughness of the means through which God is approached shall be told him in advance. If he promise perseverance in his steadfastness, after the lapse of two months this Rule shall be read to him in order, and it shall be said to him : Behold the law under which thou dost wish to serve; if thou canst observe it, enter; but if thou canst not, depart freely. If he have stood firm thus far, then he shall be led into the

aforesaid cell of the novices; and again he shall be proven with all patience. And, after the lapse of six months, the Rule shall be read to him; that he may know upon what he is entering. And, if he stand firm thus far, after four months the same Rule shall again be re-read to him. And if, having deliberated with himself, he shall promise to keep everything, and to obey all the commands that are laid upon him : then he shall be received in the congregation; knowing that it is decreed, by the law of the Rule, that from that day he shall not be allowed to depart from the monastery, nor to shake free his neck from the yoke of the Rule, which, after such tardy deliberation, he was at liberty either to refuse or receive. He who is to be received, moreover, shall, in the oratory, in the presence of all, make promise concerning his steadfastness and the change in his manner of life and his obedience to God and to His saints; so that if, at any time, he act contrary, he shall know that he shall be condemned by Him whom he mocks. Concerning which promise he shall make a petition in the name of the saints whose relics are there, and of the abbot who is present. Which petition he shall write with his own hand. Or, if he really be not learned in letters, another, being asked by him, shall write it. And that novice shall make his sign; and with his own hand shall place it (the petition) above the altar. And when he has placed it there, the novice shall straightway commence this verse: "Receive me oh Lord according to thy promise and I shall live, and do not cast me down from my hope." Which verse the whole congregation shall repeat three times, adding: "Glory be to the Father." Then that brother novice shall prostrate himself at the feet of each one, that they may pray for him. And, already, from that day, he shall be considered as in the congregation. If he have any property, he shall either first present it to the poor, or, making a solemn donation, shall confer it on the monastery, keeping nothing at all for himself : as one, forsooth, who from that day, shall know that he shall not have power even over his own body. Straightway, therefore in the oratory, he shall take off his own garments in which he was clad, and shall put on the garments of the monastery. Moreover those garments which he has taken off shall be placed in the vestiary to be preserved; so that if, at any time, the devil persuading him, he shall consent to go forth from the monastery—may it not happen,—then, taking off the garments of the monastery, he may be cast out. That petition of his, nevertheless, which the abbot took from above the altar, he shall not receive again; but it shall be preserved in the monastery.

59. *Concerning the sons of nobles or of poor men who are presented.* If by chance any one of the nobles offers his son to God in the monastery : if the boy himself is a minor in age, his parents shall make the petition which we spoke of above. And, with an oblation, they shall enwrap that petition and the hand of the boy in the linen cloth of the altar ; and thus they shall offer him. Concerning their property, moreover, either they shall promise in the present petition, under an oath, that they will never, either through some chosen person, or in any way whatever, give him any thing at any time, or furnish him with the means of possessing it. Or, indeed, if they be not willing to do this, and wish to offer something as alms to the monastery for their salvation, they shall make a donation of the things which they wish to give to the monastery ; retaining for themselves, if they wish, the usufruct. And let all things be so observed that no suspicion may remain with the boy; by which being deceived he might perish—which God forbid,—as we have learned by experience. The poorer ones shall also do likewise. Those, however, who have nothing at all shall simply make their petition ; and, with an oblation, shall offer their son before witnesses.

60. *Concerning priests who may chance to wish to dwell in the monastery.* If anyone of the order of priests ask to be received in the monastery, assent, indeed, shall not too quickly be given him. Nevertheless, if he altogether persist in this supplication, he shall know that he must observe all the discipline of the Rule ; nor shall anything be relaxed unto him, that it may be as it is written : " Friend, wherefore art thou come ? " Nevertheless it shall be allowed to him to stand after the abbot, and to give the benediction, or to hold mass ; if, however, the abbot order him to. But, otherwise, he shall by no means presume to do anything, knowing that he is subject to the discipline of

the Rule, and that, all the more, he shall give an example
of humility to all. And if he chance to be present in the
monastery for the sake of an ordination or anything,
he shall expect the position that he had when he entered
the monastery ; not that which has been conceded to him
out of reverence for his priesthood. Moreover, if any one
of the clergy desire similarly to be associated with the
monastery, he shall have a medium position given him.
And he, none the less, shall make promise concerning his observance of the Rule, and concerning his own steadfastness.

61. *Concerning pilgrim monks, how they shall be received.*
If any pilgrim monk come from distant parts,—if he wish
as a guest to dwell in the monastery, and will be content with
the customs which he finds in the place, and do not perchance by his lavishness disturb the monastery, but is
simply content with what he finds : he shall be received for
as long a time as he desires. If, indeed, he find fault with
anything, or expose it, reasonably, and with the humility
of charity : the abbot shall discuss it prudently, lest perchance God had sent him for this very thing. But if,
afterwards, he wish to establish himself lastingly, such
a wish shall not be refused : and all the more, since, in the
time of his sojourn as guest, his manner of life could have
become known. But, if he have been found lavish or
vicious in the time of his sojourn as guest,—not only ought
he not to be joined to the body of the monastery, but also
it shall be said to him, honestly, that he must depart ; lest,
by sympathy with him, others also become contaminated.
But, if he be not such a one as to merit being cast out :
not only if he ask it, shall he be received and associated
with the congregation, but he shall also be urged to
remain ; that by his example others may be instructed.
For in every place one God is served, and one King
is warred for. And if the abbot perceive him to be such a
one, he may be allowed to place him in a somewhat higher
position. For the abbot can place not only a monk, but
also one from the above grades of priests or clergy, in a
greater place than that in which he enters ; if he perceive
their life to be such a one as to demand it. Moreover the
abbot must take care lest, at any time, he receive a monk
to dwell (with him) from another known monastery, with-

out the consent of his abbot or letters of commendation. For it is written : " Do not unto another what thou wilt not that one do unto thee."

62.

If any abbot seek to ordain for himself a priest or deacon, he shall elect from among his fold one who is worthy to perform the office of a priest. He who is ordained, more-over, shall beware of elation or pride. Nor shall he pre-sume to do anything at all unless what he is ordered to by the abbot ; knowing that he is all the more subject to the Rule. Nor, by reason of the priesthood, shall he forget obedience and discipline ; but he shall advance more and more towards God. But he shall always expect to hold that position which he had when he entered the monastery : except when performing the service of the altar, and if, perchance, the election of the congregation and the will of the abbot inclines to promote him on account of his merit of life. He shall, nevertheless, know that he is to observe the rule constituted for him by the deans or provosts : and that, if he presume otherwise, he shall be considered not a priest but a rebel. And if, having often been admonished, he do not amend : even the bishop shall be called in in testimony. But if, even then, he do not amend, his faults being glaring, he shall be thrust forth from the monastery. That is, if his contumaciousness shall have been of such a kind, that he was not willing to be subject to or to obey the Rule.

63. *Concerning rank in the congregation.* They shall pre-serve their rank in the monastery according as the time of their conversion and the merit of their life decrees ; and as the abbot ordains. And the abbot shall not perturb the flock committed to him ; nor, using as it were an arbitrary power, shall he unjustly dispose anything. But he shall always reflect that he is to render account to God for all his judgments and works. Therefore, according to the order which he has decreed, or which the brothers them-selves have held : thus they shall go to the absolution, to the communion, to the singing of the psalm, to their place in the choir. And in all places, altogether, age does not

decide the rank or affect it; for Samuel and Daniel, as boys, judged the priests. Therefore excepting those who, as we have said, the abbot has, for a higher reason, preferred, or, for certain causes, degraded: all the rest, as they are converted, so they remain. Thus, for example, he who comes to the monastery at the second hour of the day, may know that he is younger than he who came at the first hour of the day, of whatever age or dignity he be. And, in the case of boys, discipline shall be observed in all things by all. The juniors, therefore, shall honour their seniors; the seniors shall love their juniors. In the very calling of names, it shall be allowed to no one to call another simply by his name: but the seniors shall call their juniors by the name of brothers. The juniors, moreover, shall call their seniors "nonni," which indicates paternal reverence. The abbot, moreover, because he is believed to be Christ's representative, shall be called Master and Abbot; not by his assumption, but through honour and love for Christ. His thoughts moreover shall be such, and he shall show himself such, that he may be worthy of such honour. Moreover, wherever the brothers meet each other, the junior shall seek a blessing from the senior. When the greater one passes, the lesser one shall rise and give him a place to sit down. Nor shall the junior presume to sit unless his senior bid him; so that it shall be done as is written: "Vying with each other in honour." Boys, little ones or youths, shall obtain their places in the oratory or at table with discipline as the end in view. Out of doors, moreover, or wherever they are, they shall be guarded and disciplined; until they come to an intelligent age.

64. *Concerning the ordination of an abbot.* In ordaining an abbot this consideration shall always be observed: that such a one shall be put into office as the whole congregation, according to the fear of God, with one heart—or even a part, however small, of the congregation with more prudent counsel—shall have chosen. He who is to be ordained, moreover, shall be elected for merit of life and learnedness in wisdom; even though he be the lowest in rank in the congregation. But even if the whole congregation with one consent shall have elected a person con-

senting to their vices—which God forbid ;—and those vices shall in any way come clearly to the knowledge of the bishop to whose diocese that place pertains, or to the neighbouring abbots or Christians : the latter shall not allow the consent of the wicked to prevail, but shall set up a dispenser worthy of the house of God ; knowing that they will receive a good reward for this, if they do it chastely and with zeal for God. Just so they shall know, on the contrary, that they have sinned if they neglect it. The abbot who is ordained, moreover, shall reflect always what a burden he is undertaking, and to whom he is to render account of his stewardship. He shall know that he ought rather to be of help than to command. He ought, therefore, to be learned in the divine law, that he may know how to give forth both the new and the old ; chaste, sober, merciful. He shall always exalt mercy over judgment, that he may obtain the same. He shall hate vice, he shall love the brethren. In his blame itself he shall act prudently and do nothing excessive ; lest, while he is too desirous of removing the rust, the vessel be broken. And he shall always suspect his own frailty ; and shall remember that a bruised reed is not to be crushed. By which we do not say that he shall permit vice to be nourished ; but prudently, and with charity, he shall remove it, according as he finds it to be expedient in the case of each one, as we have already said. And he shall strive rather to be loved than feared. He shall not be troubled and anxious ; he also shall not be too obstinate ; he shall not be jealous and too suspicious ; for then he will have no rest. In his commands he shall be provident, and shall consider whether they be of God or of the world. He shall use discernment and moderation with regard to the labours which he enjoins, thinking of the discretion of St. James who said : " if I overdrive my flocks they will die all in one day." Accepting therefore this and other testimony of discretion the mother of the virtues, he shall so temper all things that there may be both what the strong desire, and the weak do not flee. And, especially, he shall keep the present Rule in all things ; so that, when he hath ministered well, he shall hear from the Lord what that good servant did who obtained meat for his fellow servants

in his day : " Verily I say unto you," he said, " That he
shall make him ruler over all his goods."

65. *Concerning the provost of the monastery.* Very often,
indeed, it happens that, through the ordination of a
provost, grave scandals arise in monasteries ; since there
are some who, inflated with the evil spirit of pride, and
thinking themselves to be second abbots, taking upon
themselves to rule, nourish scandals, and make dissensions
in the congregation ; especially in those places where the
provost is ordained by the same priest, or the same abbots,
who ordain the abbot.   How absurd this is, is easily seen ;
for, commencing with the ordination itself, a reason is
given him for being proud, since it is suggested to him by
his thoughts that he is exempt from the authority of his
abbot in as much as he has been ordained by the same
persons as the abbot.   Hence arise envy, quarrels, detrac-
tions, emulations, dissensions, disturbances.   And when
the abbot and the provost differ mutually in their opinions,
their souls, on the one hand, must be endangered by this
dissension ; and those who are under them, while they
pay court to different sides, go to perdition.   The evil of
which danger is to be referred to those who have made
themselves the causes of such things through the ordination.   Wherefore we foresee that it is expedient, for the
sake of maintaining peace and charity, that the ordering
of his monastery shall rest with the will of the abbot.
And, if it can be done, all the necessities of the monastery
shall, as the abbot disposes, be seen to by deans, as we
arranged before ; so that, by committing them to many,
one may not become proud.   But if either the place
demands it, or the congregation seeks it, the abbot shall,
with the counsel of God-fearing brothers, reasonably and
with humility, himself ordain for himself, as provost,
whomever he shall choose.   Which provost, nevertheless,
shall do with reverence that which is enjoined upon him
by his abbot, doing nothing contrary to the will or order
of the abbot ; for in as much as he is raised above the
others, so much the more carefully should he observe the
precepts of the Rule.   Which provost, if he be found
vicious, or deceived by the elation of pride ; or if he be
proved a despiser of the holy Rule ; he shall be warned by

words up to the fourth time. If he do not then amend, the correction of the discipline of the Rule shall be administered to him. But if he do not, even then, amend, he shall be cast down from the rank of a provost, and another who is worthy shall be called in his place. But if, even in the congregation, he be not quiet and obedient, he shall also be expelled from the monastery. Nevertheless the abbot shall reflect that he is to render account to God for all his judgments; lest perchance a flame of envy or jealousy may burn his soul.

66. *Concerning the doorkeepers of the monastery.* At the door of the monastery shall be placed a wise old man who shall know how to receive a reply and to return one; whose ripeness of age will not permit him to trifle. Which doorkeeper ought to have a cell next to the door; so that those arriving may always find one present from whom they may receive a reply. And straightway, when any one has knocked, or a poor man has called out, he shall answer, " Thanks be to God ! " or shall give the blessing; and with all the gentleness of the fear of God he shall hastily give a reply with the fervour of charity. And if this doorkeeper need assistance he may receive a younger brother.

A monastery, moreover, if it can be done, ought so to be arranged that everything necessary,—that is, water, a mill, a garden, a bakery,—may be made use of, and different arts be carried on, within the monastery; so that there shall be no need for the monks to wander about outside. For this is not at all good for their souls. We wish, moreover, that this Rule be read very often in the congregation; lest any of the brothers excuse himself on account of ignorance.

67. *Concerning brothers sent upon a journey.* Brothers who are to be sent upon a journey shall commend themselves to the prayers of all the brethren and of the abbot. And always, at the last prayer of the Divine Service, there shall be a calling to mind of all the absent ones. Having returned, moreover, from the journey—on the very day on which they return,—at all the canonical hours when the Divine Service is being carried on, prostrated on the floor of the oratory, they shall seek the prayers of all, on account

of their excesses: lest perchance the sight of some evil thing, or the hearing of some idle discourse, may have met or happened to them on the journey. Let not any one presume to tell another what he has seen or heard outside of the monastery; for, very often, it means ruin. And if any one presume to, he shall be subject to the punishment of the Rule. Even so he who presumes to go beyond the confines of the monastery, or to go anywhere, or to do anything however trivial without the order of the abbot.

68. *If impossibilities are enjoined on a brother.* If on any brother by chance any burdensome or impossible tasks are enjoined, he shall receive indeed the command of him who orders with all gentleness and obedience. But if he shall see that the weight of the burden altogether exceeds the measure of his strength, he shall patiently and in due season suggest to him who is in authority the causes of the impossibility, but not with pride, or resisting, or contradicting. But if, after his suggestion, the command of the superior continue according to his first opinion, the junior shall know that thus it is expedient for him; and in all love, trusting in the aid of God, he shall obey.

69. *That, in the monastery, one shall not presume to defend another.* It is to be especially guarded against lest, on any occasion, one monk presume to defend another in the monastery, or to protect him as it were: even though they be joined by some nearness of relationship. Nor in any way shall the monks presume to do this; for thence can arise most grave occasion for scandals. But if any one transgress these commands, he shall be most severely punished.

70. *That no one shall presume to strike promiscuously.*— Every ground for presumption shall be forbidden in the monastery. We decree that it shall be allowed to no one to excommunicate or to strike any of his brothers; unless he be one to whom power is given by his abbot. Sinners, moreover, shall be called to account in the presence of all: so that the others may have fear. The care of disciplining, and the custody of children up to fifteen years of age, however, shall belong to all. But this also with all moderation and reason. For he who presumes in any way against one of riper age, without precept of the abbot; or

who, even against children, becomes violent without discretion,—shall be subject to the discipline of the Rule; for it is written: "Do not unto another what thou wilt not that one do unto thee."

71. *That they shall be mutually obedient.*—The virtue of obedience is not only to be exhibited by all to the abbot, but also the brothers shall be thus mutually obedient to each other; knowing that they shall approach God through this way of obedience. The command therefore of the abbot, or of the provosts who are constituted by him, being given the preference—since we do not allow private commands to have more weight than his,—for the rest, all juniors shall obey their superiors with all charity and solicitude. But if any one is found contentious, he shall be punished. If, moreover, any brother, for any slight cause, be in any way rebuked by the abbot or by any one who is his superior; or if he feel, even lightly, that the mind of some superior is angered or moved against him, however little:—straightway, without delay, he shall so long lie prostrate at his feet, atoning, until, with the benediction, that anger shall be appeased. But if any one scorn to do this, he shall either be subjected to corporal punishment; or, if he be contumacious, he shall be expelled from the monastery.

72. *Concerning the good zeal which the monks ought to have.*—As there is an evil zeal of bitterness, which separates from God and leads to Hell; so there is a good zeal, which separates from vice and leads to God and to eternal life. Let the monks therefore exercise this zeal with the most fervent love: that is, let them mutually surpass each other in honour. Let them most patiently tolerate their weaknesses, whether of body or character; let them vie with each other in showing obedience. Let no one pursue what he thinks useful for himself, but rather what he thinks useful for another. Let them love the brotherhood with a chaste love; let them fear God; let them love their abbot with a sincere and humble love; let them prefer nothing whatever to Christ, who leads us alike to eternal life.

73. *Concerning the fact that not every just observance is decreed in this Rule.*—We have written out this Rule, indeed, that we may show those observing it in the monasteries how to have some honesty of character, or

beginning of conversion. But for those who hasten to the
perfection of living, there are the teachings of the holy
Fathers : the observance of which leads a man to the
heights of perfection. For what page, or what discourse,
of Divine authority of the Old or the New Testament is not
a most perfect rule for human life ? Or what book of the
holy Catholic Fathers does not trumpet forth how by the
right path we shall come to our Creator ? Also the reading
aloud of the Fathers, and their decrees, and their lives; also
the Rule of our holy Father Basil—what else are they
except instruments of virtue for well-living and obedient
monks ? We, moreover, blush with confusion for the idle,
and the evilly living and the negligent.   Thou, therefore,
whoever doth hasten to the celestial fatherland, perform
with Christ's aid this Rule written out as the least of
beginnings : and then at length, under God's protection,
thou wilt come to the greater things that we have mentioned ; to the summits of learning and virtue.

II.

"FORMULAE LITURGICAE" IN USE AT ORDEALS.

(Published by Gengler: "Germanische Rechtsdenkmäler,"
pp. 759-765 ; also by de Rozière, Recueil II., 770-884.)

A.   THE JUDGMENT OF THE GLOWING IRON.

After the accusation has been lawfully made, and three
days have been passed in fasting and prayer, the priest,
clad in his sacred vestments with the exception of his outside garment, shall take with a tongs the iron placed before
the altar ; and, singing the hymn of the three youths,
namely, "Bless him all his works," he shall bear it to the
fire, and shall say this prayer over the place where fire is to
carry out the judgment : "Bless, O Lord God, this place,
that there may be for us in it sanctity, chastity, virtue and
victory, and sanctimony, humility, goodness, gentleness and
plenitude of law, and obedience to God the Father and the
Son and the Holy Ghost."—After this, the iron shall be

placed in the fire and shall be sprinkled with holy water; and while it is heating, he shall celebrate mass. But when the priest shall have taken the Eucharist, he shall adjure the man who is to be tried . . . . and shall cause him to take the communion.—Then the priest shall sprinkle holy water above the iron and shall say : "The blessing of God the Father, the Son, and the Holy Ghost descend upon this iron for the discerning of the right judgment of God." And straightway the accused shall carry the iron to a distance of nine feet. Finally his hand shall be covered under seal for three days, and if festering blood be found in the track of the iron, he shall be judged guilty. But if, however, he shall go forth uninjured, praise shall be rendered to God.

B. JUDGMENT OF THE PLOUGHSHARES.

Lord God omnipotent . . . we invoke Thee, and, as suppliants, exhort Thy majesty, that in this judgment and test Thou will'st order to be of no avail all the wiles of diabolical fraud and ingenuity, the incantations either of men or of women, also the properties of herbs; so that to all those standing around it may be apparent, that Thou art just and lovest justice, and that there is none who may resist Thy majesty. And so O Lord, Ruler of the heavens and the earth, creator of the waters, king of thy whole creation, in Thy holy name and strength we bless these ploughshares, that they may render a true judgment; so that if so be that that man is innocent of the charge in this matter which we are discussing and treating of amongst us, who walks over them with naked feet: thou, O omnipotent God, as thou didst deliver the three youths from the fiery furnace, and Susanna from the false charge, and Daniel from the den of lions,—so thou may'st see fit, by Thy potent strength, to preserve the feet of the innocent safe and uninjured. If, moreover, that man be guilty in the aforesaid matter; and, the devil persuading, shall have dared to tempt Thy power, and shall walk over them: do Thou, who art just and a Judge, make a manifest burn to appear on his feet, to Thy honour and praise and glory; to the constancy and confidence in Thy name, moreover, of us thy servants; to the confusion and repentance of their sins of the perfidious and the blind; so that, against their will, they may perceive, what willingly they would not,—that Thou, living and reigning from ages to ages, art the judge of the living and the dead.   Amen.

C.   THE JUDGMENT OF BOILING WATER.

Having performed the mass the priest shall descend to the place appointed, where the trial itself shall be gone through with; he shall carry with him the book of the gospels and a cross, and shall chant a moderate litany; and when he shall have completed that litany, he shall exorcize and bless that water before it boils.—After this he shall divest him (the accused) of his garments, and shall clothe him or them with clean vestments of the church—that is, with the garment of an exorcist or of a deacon—and shall cause him or them to kiss the gospel and the cross of Christ; and he shall sprinkle over them some of the water itself; and to those who are about to go in to the Judgment of God, to all of them, he shall give to drink of that same holy water.   And when he shall have given it, moreover, he shall say to each one: "I have given this water to thee or to you for a sign to-day."   Then pieces of wood shall be placed under the cauldron, and the priest shall say . . . . prayers when the water itself shall have begun to grow warm.—And he who puts his hand in the water for the trial itself, shall say the Lord's prayer, and shall sign himself with the sign of the cross; and that boiling water shall hastily be put down near the fire, and the judge shall suspend that stone, bound to that measure, within that same water in the accustomed way; and thus he who enters to be tried by the judgment shall extract it thence in the name of God himself.   Afterwards, with great diligence, his hand shall thus be wrapped up, signed with the seal of the judge, until the third day; when it shall be viewed and judged of by suitable men.

D.   TEST OF THE COLD WATER.

Consecration to be said over the man.   May omnipotent God, who did order baptism to be made by water, and did grant remission of sins to men through baptism : may He, through His mercy, decree a right judgment through that water.   If, namely, thou art guilty in that matter, may the water which received thee in baptism not receive thee now ; if, however, thou art innocent, may the water which received thee in baptism receive thee now.   Through Christ our Lord.

Afterwards he shall exorcise the water thus : I adjure thee, water, in the name of the Father Almighty, who did create thee in the beginning, who also did order thee to be separated from the waters above, . . . that in no manner thou receive this man, if he be in any way guilty of the charge that is brought against him ; by deed, namely, or by consent, or by knowledge, or in any way : but make him to swim above thee.   And may no process be employed against thee, and no magic which may be able to conceal that (fact of his guilt).

E.   JUDGMENT OF THE MORSEL.

(*Prayer.*) Holy Father, omnipotent, eternal God, maker of all things visible and of all things spiritual ; who dost look into secret places, and dost know all things ; who dost search the hearts of men, and dost rule as God, I pray Thee, hear the words of my prayer : that whoever has committed or carried out or consented to that theft,—that bread and cheese may not be able to pass through his throat.

(*Exorcism.*) " I exorcize thee, most unclean dragon, ancient serpent, dark night, through the word of truth and the sign of light, through our Lord Jesus Christ the immaculate Lamb generated by the Most High, conceived of the Holy Spirit, born of the Virgin Mary—whose coming Gabriel the archangel did announce ; whom seeing, John did call out : this is the living and true Son of God—that in no wise may'st thou permit that man to eat this bread and cheese, who has committed this theft or consented to it or advised it.   Adjured through Him who is to come to judge the quick and the dead, do thou close his throat with a band, not, however, unto death."

And thou shalt repeat those prayers three times.   And,

before thou sayest those prayers, thou should'st write on the bread itself the Lord's prayer. And of that bread thou should'st weigh out ten denars weight, and of the cheese likewise. And thou should'st place the bread and the cheese at the same time in his mouth, and make two crosses of poplar wood, and put one under his right foot; and the other cross the priest shall hold with his hand above his (the accused's) head, and shall throw above his head that theft written on a tablet. And when thou dost place that bread in his mouth, thou should'st say the following conjuration:

(*Conjuration.*) I conjure thee, O man, through the Father and the Son and the Holy Spirit, and through the twenty-four elders who daily sound praises before God, and through the twelve patriarchs, through the twelve prophets, and through the twelve apostles, and the evangelists, through the martyrs, through the confessors, through the virgins, and through all the saints, and through our Redeemer, our Lord Jesus Christ, who for our salvation and for our sins, did suffer His hands to be affixed to the cross: that if thou werst a partner in this theft, or did'st know of it, or have any fault in it, that bread and cheese may not pass thy gullet and throat: but that thou may'st tremble like an aspen-leaf, amen; and not have rest, O man, until thou dost vomit it forth with blood, if thou hast committed aught in the matter of the aforesaid theft. Through Him who liveth, etc.

F. JUDGMENT WITH THE PSALTER.

One piece of wood shall be made with a button on top, and shall be put in a psalter above this verse: "Thou art just O Lord and righteous are Thy judgments," and the psalter being closed shall be strongly pressed, the button projecting. Another piece of wood also shall be made with a hole in it, in which the button of the former piece shall be placed so that the psalter hangs from it and can be turned. Let two persons, moreover, hold the wood, the psalter hanging in the middle; and let him who is suspected be placed before them. And one of those who holds the psalter shall say to the other, thrice, as follows:

" He has this thing " (*i.e.* the thing stolen).   The other shall reply thrice : " He has it not."   Then the priest shall say : " This He will deign to make manifest unto us, by whose judgment are ruled things terrestrial and things celestial.   Thou art just, O Lord, and righteous are Thy judgments.   Turn away the evils of my enemies, and destroy them with Thy truth."

(*Prayer.*) Omnipotent, everlasting God, who did'st create all things from nothing, and did'st form man from the clay of the earth, we pray thee as suppliants through the intercession of Mary the most holy mother of God . . . . that Thou do make trial for us concerning this matter about which we are uncertain : so that if so be that this man is guiltless, that book which we hold in our hands shall (in revolving) follow the ordinary course of the sun; but if he be guilty that book shall move backwards.

III.

THE DONATION OF CONSTANTINE.

(From Zeumer's edition of the text, published in Berlin in 1888, v. Brunner-Zeumer : " Die Constantinische Schenkungsurkunde.")

In the name of the holy and indivisible Trinity, the Father, namely, and the Son and the Holy Spirit.   The emperor Caesar Flavius Constantine in Christ Jesus, the Lord God our Saviour, one of that same holy Trinity,— faithful, merciful, supreme, beneficent, Alamannic, Gothic, Sarmatic, Germanic, Britannic, Hunic, pious, fortunate, victor and triumpher, always august : to the most holy and blessed father of fathers Sylvester, bishop of the city of Rome and pope, and to all his successors the pontiffs who are about to sit upon the chair of St. Peter until the end of time—also to all the most reverend and of God beloved catholic bishops, subjected by this our imperial decree throughout the whole world to this same holy Roman church, who have been established now and in all previous times—grace, peace, charity, rejoicing, long-suffering, mercy, be with you all from God the Father almighty and from Jesus Christ his Son and from the Holy Ghost. Our most gracious serenity desires, in clear discourse, through the page of this our imperial decree, to bring to the knowledge of all the people in the whole world what things our Saviour and Redeemer the Lord Jesus Christ, the Son of the most High Father, has most wonderfully seen fit to bring about by the intervention of our father Sylvester, the highest pontiff and the universal pope. First, indeed, putting forth, with the inmost confession of our heart, for the purpose of instructing the mind of all of you, our creed which we have learned from the aforesaid most blessed father and our confessor, Sylvester the universal pontiff; and then at length announcing the mercy of God which has been poured upon us.

For we wish you to know, as we have signified through our former sacred imperial decree, that we have gone away from the worship of idols, from mute and deaf images made by hand, from devilish contrivances and from all the pomps of Satan; and have arrived at the pure faith of the Christians, which is the true light and everlasting life. Believing, according to what he—that same one, our revered supreme father and teacher, the pontiff Sylvester —has taught us, in God the Father, the almighty maker of Heaven and earth, of all things visible and invisible; and in Jesus Christ, his only Son, our Lord God, through whom all things are created; and in the Holy Spirit, the Lord and vivifier of the whole creature. We confess these, the Father and the Son and the Holy Spirit, in such way that, in the perfect Trinity, there shall also be a fulness of divinity and a unity of power. The Father is God, the Son is God, and the Holy Spirit is God; and these three are one in Jesus Christ.

There are therefore three forms but one power. For God, wise in all previous time, gave forth from himself the word through which all future ages were to be born; and when, by that sole word of His wisdom, He formed the whole creation from nothing, He was with it, arranging all things in His mysterious secret place.

Therefore, the virtues of the Heavens and all the material

part of the earth having been perfected, by the wise nod of His wisdom first creating man of the clay of the earth in His own image and likeness, He places him in a paradise of delight. Him the ancient serpent and envious enemy, the devil, through the most bitter taste of the forbidden tree, made an exile from these joys; and, he being expelled, did not cease in many ways to cast his poisonous darts; in order that, turning the human race from the way of truth to the worship of idols, he might persuade it, namely, to worship the creature and not the creator; so that, through them (the idols), he might cause those whom he might be able to entrap in his snares to be burned with him in eternal punishment. But our Lord, pitying His creature, sending ahead His holy prophets, announcing through them the light of the future life—the coming, that is, of His Son our Lord and Saviour Jesus Christ—sent that same only begotten Son and Word of wisdom: He descending from Heaven on account of our salvation, being born of the Holy Spirit and of the virgin Mary,—the word was made flesh and dwelt among us. He did not cease to be what He had been, but began to be what He had not been, perfect God and perfect man: as God, performing miracles; as man, sustaining human sufferings. We so learned Him to be very man and very God by the preaching of our father Sylvester, the supreme pontiff, that we can in no wise doubt that He was very God and very man. And, having chosen twelve apostles, He shone with miracles before them and an innumerable multitude of people. We confess that this same Lord Jesus Christ fulfilled the law and the prophets; that He suffered, was crucified, on the third day arose from the dead according to the Scriptures; was received into Heaven, and sitteth on the right hand of the Father. Whence He shall come to judge the quick and the dead, whose kingdom shall have no end. For this is our orthodox creed, placed before us by our most blessed father Sylvester the supreme pontiff. We exhort, therefore, all people, and all the different nations, to hold, cherish and preach this faith; and, in the name of the Holy Trinity, to obtain the grace of baptism; and, with devout heart, to adore the Lord Jesus Christ our Saviour, who, with the Father and the Holy Spirit, lives and reigns through infinite ages; whom Sylvester our father, the universal pontiff, preaches. For He himself, our Lord God, having pity on me a sinner, sent His holy apostles to visit us, and caused the light of His splendour to shine upon us. And do ye rejoice that I, having been withdrawn from the shadow, have come to the true light and to the knowledge of truth. For, at a time when a mighty and filthy leprosy had invaded all the flesh of my body, and the care was administered of many physicians who came together, nor by that of any one of them did I achieve health : there came hither the priests of the Capitol, saying to me that a font should be made on the Capitol, and that I should fill this with the blood of innocent infants; and that, if I bathed in it while it was warm, I might be cleansed. And very many innocent infants having been brought together according to their words, when the sacrilegious priests of the pagans wished them to be slaughtered and the font to be filled with their blood: our serenity perceiving the tears of the mothers, I straightway abhorred the deed. And, pitying them, I ordered their own sons to be restored to them ; and, giving them vehicles and gifts, sent them off rejoicing to their own. That day having passed therefore —the silence of night having come upon us—when the time of sleep had arrived, the apostles St. Peter and Paul appear, saying to me : " Since thou hast placed a term to thy vices, and hast abhorred the pouring forth of innocent blood, we are sent by Christ the Lord our God, to give to thee a plan for recovering thy health. Hear, therefore, our warning, and do what we indicate to thee. Sylvester— the bishop of the city of Rome—on Mount Serapte, fleeing thy persecutions, cherishes the darkness with his clergy in the caverns of the rocks. This one, when thou shalt have led him to thyself, will himself show thee a pool of piety; in which, when he shall have dipped thee for the third time, all that strength of the leprosy will desert thee. And, when this shall have been done, make this return to thy Saviour, that by thy order through the whole world the churches may be restored. Purify thyself, moreover, in this way, that, leaving all the superstition of idols, thou do adore and cherish the living and true God—who is alone and true—and that thou attain to the doing of His will."

Rising, therefore, from sleep, straightway I did according to that which I had been advised to do by the holy apostles; and, having summoned that excellent and benignant father and our enlightener—Sylvester the universal pope—I told him all the words that had been taught me by the holy apostles; and asked him who were those gods Peter and Paul. But he said that they were not really called gods, but apostles of our Saviour the Lord God Jesus Christ. And again we began to ask that same most blessed pope whether he had some express image of those apostles; so that, from their likeness, we might learn that they were those whom revelation had shown to us. Then that same venerable father ordered the images of those same apostles to be shown by his deacon. And, when I had looked at them, and recognized, represented in those images, the countenances of those whom I had seen in my dream : with a great noise, before all my satraps, I confessed that they were those whom I had seen in my dream.

Hereupon that same most blessed Sylvester our father, bishop of the city of Rome, imposed upon us a time of penance—within our Lateran palace, in the chapel, in a hair garment,—so that I might obtain pardon from our Lord God Jesus Christ our Saviour by vigils, fasts, and tears and prayers, for all things that had been impiously done and unjustly ordered by me. Then through the imposition of the hands of the clergy, I came to the bishop himself; and there, renouncing the pomps of Satan and his works, and all idols made by hands, of my own will before all the people I confessed : that I believed in God the Father almighty, maker of Heaven and earth, and of all things visible and invisible; and in Jesus Christ, His only Son our Lord, who was born of the Holy Spirit and of the virgin Mary. And, the font having been blessed, the wave of salvation purified me there with a triple immersion. For there I, being placed at the bottom of the font, saw with my own eyes a hand from Heaven touching me; whence rising, clean, know that I was cleansed from all the squalor of leprosy. And, I being raised from the venerable font—putting on white raiment, he administered to me the sign of the seven-fold holy Spirit, the unction of the holy oil; and he traced the sign of the holy cross on my brow, saying: God seals thee with the seal of His faith in the name of the Father and the Son and the Holy Spirit, to signalize thy faith. All the clergy replied: "Amen." The bishop added "peace be with thee."

And so, on the first day after receiving the mystery of the holy baptism, and after the cure of my body from the squalor of the leprosy, I recognized that there was no other God save the Father and the Son and the Holy Spirit; whom the most blessed Sylvester the pope doth preach; a trinity in one, a unity in three. For all the gods of the nations, whom I have worshipped up to this time, are proved to be demons; works made by the hand of men; inasmuch as that same venerable father told to us most clearly how much power in Heaven and on earth He, our Saviour, conferred on his apostle St. Peter, when finding him faithful after questioning him He said: "Thou art Peter, and upon this rock (petram) shall I build My Church, and the gates of hell shall not prevail against it." Give heed ye powerful, and incline the ear of your hearts to that which the good Lord and Master added to His disciple, saying: "and I will give thee the keys of the kingdom of Heaven; and whatever thou shalt bind on earth shall be bound also in Heaven, and whatever thou shalt loose on earth shall be loosed also in Heaven." This is very wonderful and glorious, to bind and loose on earth and to have it bound and loosed in Heaven.

And when, the blessed Sylvester preaching them, I perceived these things, and learned that by the kindness of St. Peter himself I had been entirely restored to health: I—together with all our satraps and the whole senate and the nobles and all the Roman people, who are subject to the glory of our rule—considered it advisable that, as on earth he (Peter) is seen to have been constituted vicar of the Son of God, so the pontiffs, who are the representatives of that same chief of the apostles, should obtain from us and our empire the power of a supremacy greater than the earthly clemency of our imperial serenity is seen to have had conceded to it,—we choosing that same prince of the apostles, or his vicars, to be our constant intercessors with God. And, to the extent of our earthly imperial power, we decree that his holy Roman church shall be honoured with veneration; and that, more than our empire and earthly throne, the most sacred seat of St. Peter shall be gloriously exalted; we giving to it the imperial power, and dignity of glory, and vigour and honour.

And we ordain and decree that he shall have the supremacy as well over the four chief seats Antioch, Alexandria, Constantinople and Jerusalem, as also over all the churches of God in the whole world. And he who for the time being shall be pontiff of that holy Roman church shall be more exalted than, and chief over, all the priests of the whole world; and, according to his judgment, everything which is to be provided for the service of God or the stability of the faith of the Christians is to be administered. It is indeed just, that there the holy law should have the seat of its rule where the founder of holy laws, our Saviour, told St. Peter to take the chair of the apostleship; where also, sustaining the cross, he blissfully took the cup of death and appeared as imitator of his Lord and Master; and that there the people should bend their necks at the confession of Christ's name, where their teacher, St. Paul the apostle, extending his neck for Christ, was crowned with martyrdom. There, until the end, let them seek a teacher, where the holy body of the teacher lies; and there, prone and humiliated, let them perform the service of the heavenly king, God our Saviour Jesus Christ, where the proud were accustomed to serve under the rule of an earthly king.

Meanwhile we wish all the people, of all the races and nations throughout the whole world, to know: that we have constructed within our Lateran palace, to the same Saviour our Lord God Jesus Christ, a church with a baptistry from the foundations. And know that we have carried on our own shoulders, from its foundations, twelve baskets weighted with earth, according to the number of the holy apostles. Which holy church we command to be spoken of, cherished, venerated and preached of, as the head and summit of all the churches in the whole world—as we have commanded through our other imperial decrees. We have also constructed the churches of St. Peter and St. Paul, chiefs of the apostles, which we have enriched with gold and silver; where also, placing their most sacred bodies with great honour, we have constructed their caskets of electrum, against which no force of the elements prevails. And we have placed a cross of purest gold on each of their caskets, and fastened them with golden keys. And on these churches, for the providing of the lights, we have conferred estates, and have enriched them with different objects; and, through our sacred imperial decrees, we have granted them our gift of land in the east as well as in the west; and even on the northern and southern coast;—namely in Judea, Greece, Asia, Thrace, Africa and Italy and the various islands : under this condition indeed, that all shall be administered by the hand of our most blessed father the pontiff Sylvester and his successors.

For let all the people and the nations of the races in the whole world rejoice with us; we exhorting all of you to give unbounded thanks, together with us, to our Lord and Saviour Jesus Christ. For He is God in Heaven above and on earth below, who, visiting us through His holy apostles, made us worthy to receive the holy sacrament of baptism and health of body. In return for which, to those same holy apostles, my masters, St. Peter and St. Paul; and, through them, also to St. Sylvester, our father,—the chief pontiff and universal pope of the city of Rome,—and to all the pontiffs his successors, who until the end of the world shall be about to sit in the seat of St. Peter : we concede and, by this present, do confer, our imperial Lateran palace, which is preferred to, and ranks above, all the palaces in the whole world; then a diadem, that is, the crown of our head, and at the same time the tiara; and, also, the shoulder band,—that is, the collar that usually surrounds our imperial neck; and also the purple mantle, and crimson tunic, and all the imperial raiment; and the same rank as those presiding over the imperial cavalry; conferring also the imperial sceptres, and, at the same time, the spears and standards; also the banners and different imperial ornaments, and all the advantage of our high imperial position, and the glory of our power.

And we decree, as to those most reverend men, the clergy who serve, in different orders, that same holy Roman church, that they shall have the same advantage, distinction, power and excellence by the glory of which our most illustrious senate is adorned ; that is, that they shall be made patricians and consuls,—we commanding that they shall also be decorated with the other imperial dignities. And even as the imperial soldiery, so, we decree, shall the clergy of the holy Roman church be adorned. And even as the imperial power is adorned by different offices—by the distinction, that is, of chamberlains, and door keepers, and all the guards,—so we wish the holy Roman church to be adorned. And, in order that the pontifical glory may shine forth more fully, we decree this also : that the clergy of this same holy Roman church may use saddle cloths of linen of the whitest colour ; namely that their horses may be adorned and so be ridden, and that, as our senate uses shoes with goats' hair, so they may be distinguished by gleaming linen ; [1] in order that, as the celestial beings, so the terrestrial may be adorned to the glory of God. Above all things, moreover, we give permission to that same most holy one our father Sylvester, bishop of the city of Rome and pope, and to all the most blessed pontiffs who shall come after him and succeed him in all future times—for the honour and glory of Jesus Christ our Lord,—to receive into that great catholic and apostolic church of God, even into the number of the monastic clergy, any one from the whole assembly of our nobles, who, in free choice, of his own accord, may wish to become a clerk ; no one at all presuming thereby to act in a haughty manner.

We also decreed this, that this same venerable one our father Sylvester, the supreme pontiff, and all the pontiffs his successors, might use and bear upon their heads—to the praise of God and for the honour of St. Peter—the diadem ; that is, the crown which we have granted him from our own head, of purest gold and precious gems. But he, the most holy pope, did not at all allow that crown of gold to be used over the clerical crown which he wears to the glory of St. Peter ; but we placed upon his most holy head, with our own hands, a tiara of gleaming splendour representing the glorious resurrection of our Lord. And, holding the

---

[1] This whole paragraph is full of difficulties and probable text corruptions.

bridle of his horse, out. of reverence for St. Peter we performed for him the duty of groom; decreeing that all the pontiffs his successors, and they alone, may use that tiara in processions.

In imitation of our own power, in order that for that cause the supreme pontificate may not deteriorate, but may rather be adorned with power and glory even more than is the dignity of an earthly rule: behold we—giving over to the oft-mentioned most blessed pontiff, our father Sylvester the universal pope, as well our palace, as has been said, as also the city of Rome and all the provinces, districts and cities of Italy or of the western regions; and relinquishing them, by our inviolable gift, to the power and sway of himself or the pontiffs his successors—do decree, by this our godlike charter and imperial constitution, that it shall be (so) arranged; and do concede that they (the palaces, provinces, etc.) shall lawfully remain with the holy Roman church.[1]

Wherefore we have perceived it to be fitting that our empire and the power of our kingdom should be transferred and changed to the regions of the East; and that, in the province of Byzantium, in a most fitting place, a city should be built in our name; and that our empire should there be established. For, where the supremacy of priests and the head of the Christian religion has been established by a heavenly Ruler, it is not just that there an earthly ruler should have jurisdiction.

We decree, moreover, that all these things which, through this our imperial charter and through other godlike commands, we have established and confirmed, shall remain uninjured and unshaken until the end of the world. Wherefore, before the living God, who commanded us to reign, and in the face of his terrible judgment, we conjure, through this our imperial decree, all the emperors our successors, and all our nobles, the satraps also and the most glorious senate, and all the people in the whole world now and in all times previously subject to our rule: that no one of them, in any way, allow himself to oppose or disregard, or in any way seize, these things which, by our

Text much corrupted.

imperial sanction, have been conceded to the holy Roman church and to all its pontiffs. If any one, moreover,—which we do not believe—prove a scorner or despiser in this matter, he shall be subject and bound over to eternal damnation; and shall feel that the holy chiefs of the apostles of God, Peter and Paul, will be opposed to him in the present and in the future life. And, being burned in the nethermost hell, he shall perish with the devil and all the impious.

The page, moreover, of this our imperial decree, we, confirming it with our own hands, did place above the venerable body of St. Peter chief of the apostles; and there, promising to that same apostle of God that we would preserve inviolably all its provisions, and would leave in our commands to all the emperors our successors to preserve them, we did hand it over, to be enduringly and happily possessed, to our most blessed father Sylvester the supreme pontiff and universal pope, and, through him, to all the pontiffs his successors—God our Lord and our Saviour Jesus Christ consenting.

And the imperial subscription: May the Divinity preserve you for many years, oh most holy and blessed fathers.

Given at Rome on the third day before the Kalends of April, our master the august Flavius Constantine, for the fourth time, and Galligano, most illustrious men, being consuls.

IV.

THE FOUNDATION CHARTER OF THE ORDER OF CLUNY. SEPT. 11, 910 A.D.

(Edited anew according to the original by A. Bruel: "Recueil des Chartes de l'Abbaye de Cluny." Paris, 1876.)

To all right thinkers it is clear that the providence of God has so provided for certain rich men that, by means of their transitory possessions, if they use them well, they may be able to merit everlasting rewards. As to which thing, indeed, the divine word, showing it to be possible and altogether advising it, says: " The riches of a man are the redemption of his soul." (Prov. xiii.)   I, William, count and duke by the grace of God, diligently pondering this, and desiring to provide for my own safety while I am still able, have considered it advisable—nay, most neces- sary, that from the temporal goods which have been con- ferred upon me I should give some little portion for the gain of my soul.   I do this, indeed, in order that I who have thus increased in wealth may not, perchance, at the last be accused of having spent all in caring for my body, but rather may rejoice, when fate at last shall snatch all things away, in having reserved something for myself. Which end, indeed, seems attainable by no more suitable means than that, following the precept of Christ: " I will make his poor my friends " (Luke xvi. 9), and making the act not a temporary but a lasting one, I should support at my own expense a congregation of monks.   And this is my trust, this my hope, indeed, that although I myself am unable to despise all things, nevertheless, by receiving de- spisers of the world, whom I believe to be righteous, I may receive the reward of the righteous.   Therefore be it known to all who live in the unity of the faith and who await the mercy of Christ, and to those who shall succeed them and who shall continue to exist until the end of the world, that, for the love of God and of our Saviour Jesus Christ, I hand over from my own rule to the holy apostles, Peter, namely, and Paul, the possessions over which I hold sway, the town of Cluny, namely, with the court and demesne manor, and the church in honour of St. Mary the mother of God and of St. Peter the prince of the apostles, together with all the things pertaining to it, the vills, indeed, the chapels, the serfs of both sexes, the vines, the fields, the meadows, the woods, the waters and their outlets, the mills, the incomes and revenues, what is cultivated and what is not, all in their entirety.   Which things are situated in or about the country of Macon, each one surrounded by its own bounds. I give, moreover, all these things to the aforesaid apostles —I, William, and my wife Ingelberga—first for the love of God; then for the soul of my lord king Odo, of my father and my mother; for myself and my wife—for the salvation, namely, of our souls and bodies ;—and not least for that of Ava who left me these things in her will; for the souls also of our brothers and sisters and nephews, and of all our relatives of both sexes ; for our faithful ones who adhere to our service ; for the advancement, also, and integrity of the catholic religion. Finally, since all of us Christians are held together by one bond of love and faith, let this donation be for all,—for the orthodox, namely, of past, present or future times. I give these things, more-over, with this understanding, that in Cluny a regular monastery shall be constructed in honour of the holy apostles Peter and Paul, and that there the monks shall congregate and live according to the rule of St. Benedict, and that they shall possess, hold, have and order these same things unto all time. In such wise, however, that the venerable house of prayer which is there shall be faith-fully frequented with vows and supplications, and that celestial converse shall be sought and striven after with all desire and with the deepest ardour ; and also that there shall be sedulously directed to God prayers, beseechings and exhortations as well for me as for all, according to the order in which mention has been made of them above. And let the monks themselves, together with all the afore-said possessions, be under the power and dominion of the abbot Berno, who, as long as he shall live, shall preside over them regularly according to his knowledge and ability. But after his death, those same monks shall have power and permission to elect any one of their order whom they please as abbot and rector, following the will of God and the rule promulgated by St. Benedict,—in such wise that neither by the intervention of our own or of any other power may they be impeded from making a purely canonical election. Every five years, moreover, the afore-said monks shall pay to the church of the apostles at Rome ten shillings to supply them with lights ; and they shall have the protection of those same apostles and the defence of the Roman pontiff ; and those monks may, with their whole heart and soul, according to their ability and knowledge, build up the aforesaid place. We will, further, that in our times and in those of our successors, according as the opportunities and possibilities of that place shall allow, there shall daily, with the greatest zeal be performed there works of mercy towards the poor, the needy, strangers and pilgrims. It has pleased us also to insert in this document that, from this day, those same monks there congregated shall be subject neither to our yoke, nor to that of our relatives, nor to the sway of the royal might, nor to that of any earthly power. And, through God and all his saints, and by the awful day of judgment, I warn and objure that no one of the secular princes, no count, no bishop whatever, not the pontiff of the aforesaid Roman see, shall invade the property of these servants of God, or alienate it, or diminish it, or exchange it, or give it as a benefice to any one, or constitute any prelate over them against their will. And that such unhallowed act may be more strictly prohibited to all rash and wicked men, I subjoin the following, giving force to the warning. I adjure ye, oh holy apostles and glorious princes of the world, Peter and Paul, and thee, oh supreme pontiff of the apostolic see, that, through the canonical and apostolic authority which ye have received from God, ye do remove from participation in the holy church and in eternal life, the robbers and invaders and alienators of these possessions which I do give to ye with joyful heart and ready will; and be ye protectors and defenders of the aforementioned place of Cluny and of the servants of God abiding there, and of all these possessions—on account of the clemency and mercy of the most holy Redeemer. If any one—which Heaven forbid, and which, through the mercy of God and the protection of the apostles I do not think will happen, —whether he be a neighbour or a stranger, no matter what his condition or power, should, through any kind of wile, attempt to do any act of violence contrary to this deed of gift which we have ordered to be drawn up for love of almighty God and for reverence of the chief apostles Peter and Paul: first, indeed, let him incur the wrath of almighty God, and let God remove him from the land of the living and wipe out his name from the book of life, and let his portion be with those who said to the Lord God: Depart from us; and, with Dathan and Abiron whom the earth, opening its jaws, swallowed up, and hell absorbed while still alive, let him incur everlasting damnation. And being made a companion of Judas let him be kept thrust down there with eternal tortures, and, lest it seem to human eyes that he pass through the present world with impunity, let him experience in his own body, indeed, the torments of future damnation, sharing the double disaster with Heliodorus and Antiochus, of whom one being coerced with sharp blows scarcely escaped alive; and the other, struck down by the divine will, his members putrefying and swarming with vermin, perished most miserably. And let him be a partaker with other sacrilegious persons who presume to plunder the treasure of the house of God; and let him, unless he come to his senses, have as enemy and as the one who will refuse him entrance into the blessed paradise, the key-bearer of the whole hierarchy of the church, and, joined with the latter, St. Paul; both of whom, if he had wished, he might have had as most holy mediators for him. But as far as the worldly law is concerned, he shall be required, the judicial power compelling him, to pay a hundred pounds of gold to those whom he has harmed; and his attempted attack, being frustrated, shall have no effect at all. But the validity of this deed of gift, endowed with all authority, shall always remain inviolate and unshaken, together with the stipulation subjoined. Done publicly in the city of Bourges. I, William, commanded this act to be made and drawn up, and confirmed it with my own hand.

(Signed by Ingelberga and a number of bishops and nobles.)

V.

SUMMONS OF POPE EUGENE III. TO THE CRUSADE, DEC. 1, 1145.

(Doeberl: "Monumenta Germaniae Selecta," vol. 4, p. 40.)

Bishop Eugene, servant of the servants of God, to his most beloved son in Christ Louis, the illustrious and glorious king of the French, and to his beloved sons the

princes, and to all the faithful ones of God who are
established throughout Gaul,—greeting and apostolic
benediction.   How much our predecessors the Roman
pontiffs did labour for the deliverance of the oriental
church, we have learned from the accounts of the ancients
and have found it written in their acts.   For our predecessor of blessed memory, pope Urban, did sound, as
it were, a celestial trump and did take care to arouse for
its deliverance the sons of the holy Roman church from
the different parts of the earth.   At his voice, indeed,
those beyond the mountain and especially the bravest and
strongest warriors of the French kingdom, and also those
of Italy, inflamed by the ardour of love did come together,
and, congregating a very great army, not without much
shedding of their own blood, the divine aid being with
them, did free from the filth of the pagans that city where
our Saviour willed to suffer for us, and where He left
His glorious sepulchre to us as a memorial of His passion,
—and many others which, avoiding prolixity, we refrain
from mentioning.

Which, by the grace of God, and the zeal of your
fathers, who at intervals of time have striven to the extent
of their power to defend them and to spread the name of
Christ in those parts, have been retained by the Christians
up to this day; and other cities of the infidels have by
them been manfully stormed.   But now, our sins and
those of the people themselves requiring it, a thing which
we can not relate without great grief and wailing, the city
of Edessa which in our tongue is called Rohais,—which
also, as is said, once when the whole land in the east was
held by the pagans, alone by herself served God under the
power of the Christians—has been taken and many of the
castles of the Christians occupied by them (the pagans).
The archbishop, moreover, of this same city, together with
his clergy and many other Christians, have there been
slain, and the relics of the saints have been given over to
the trampling under foot of the infidels, and dispersed.
Whereby how great a danger threatens the church of God
and the whole of Christianity, we both know ourselves and
do not believe it to be hid from your prudence.   For it is
known that it will be the greatest proof of nobility and

probity, if those things which the bravery of your fathers acquired be bravely defended by you the sons. But if it should happen otherwise, which God forbid, the valour of the fathers will be found to have diminished in the case of the sons.

We exhort therefore all of you in God, we ask and command, and, for the remission of sins enjoin: that those who are of God, and, above all, the greater men and the nobles, do manfully gird themselves; and that you strive so to oppose the multitude of the infidels, who rejoice at the time in a victory gained over us, and so to defend the oriental church—freed from their tyranny by so great an outpouring of the blood of your fathers, as we have said,—and to snatch many thousands of your captive brothers from their hands,—that the dignity of the Christian name may be increased in your time, and that your valour which is praised throughout the whole world, may remain intact and unshaken. May that good Matthias be an example to you, who, to preserve the laws of his fathers, did not in the least doubt to expose himself with his sons and relations to death, and to leave whatever he possessed in the world; and who at length, by the help of the divine aid, after many labours however, did, as well as his progeny, manfully triumph over his enemies.

We, moreover, providing with paternal solicitude for your tranquillity and for the destitution of that same church, do grant and confirm by the authority conceded to us of God, to those who by the promptings of devotion do decide to undertake and to carry through so holy and so necessary a work and labour, that remission of sins which our aforesaid predecessor pope Urban did institute; and do decree that their wives and sons, their goods also and possessions shall remain under the protection of ourselves and of the archbishops, bishops and other prelates of the church of God. By the apostolic authority, moreover, we forbid that, in the case of any thing which they possessed in peace when they took the cross, any suit be brought hereafter until most certain news has been obtained concerning their return or their death. Moreover since those who war for the Lord should by no means prepare themselves with precious garments, nor with provision for their personal appearance, nor with dogs or hawks or other things which portend licentiousness : we exhort your prudence in the Lord that those who have decided to undertake so holy a work shall not strive after these things, but shall show zeal and diligence with all their strength in the matter of arms, horses and other things with which they may fight the infidels.   But those who are oppressed by debt and begin so holy a journey with a pure heart, shall not pay interest for the time past, and if they or others for them are bound by an oath or pledge in the matter of interest, we absolve them by apostolic authority. It is allowed to them also when their relations, being warned, or the lords to whose fee they belong, are either unwilling or unable to advance them the money, to freely pledge without any reclamation, their lands or other possessions to churches, or ecclesiastical persons, or to any other of the faithful.   According to the institution of our aforesaid predecessor, by the authority of almighty God and by that of St. Peter the chief of the apostles, conceded to us by God, we grant such remission and absolution of sins, that he who shall devoutly begin so sacred a journey and shall accomplish it, or shall die during it, shall obtain absolution for all his sins which with a humble and contrite heart he shall confess, and shall receive the fruit of eternal retribution from the Remunerator of all.   Given at Vetralle on the Calends of December.

VI.

DECREE OF THE LATERAN COUNCIL OF 1179 A.D. CONCERNING PAPAL ELECTIONS.

(Doeberl, iv. p. 253.)

Concerning the election of the supreme pontiff. Although, for the sake of avoiding discord at the election of a supreme pontiff, clear enough decrees have emanated from our predecessors,—nevertheless, since often, after their promulgation, the church has suffered grave disunion through the audacity of wicked ambition : we, also, by the counsel of our brothers and the approbation of the holy council, have decided to add something to avert this evil. We decree, therefore, that if, by chance, some hostile man sowing discord among the cardinals, full concord cannot be attained with regard to constituting a pope; and, with the two thirds whicn agree, the other third be unwilling to agree, or presume of itself to ordain some one else: he shall be considered Roman pontiff who shall be elected and received by two thirds.   But if any one, trusting in the nomination of one third, shall usurp for himself the name—the real authority he can not—of a bishop: he himself, as well as those who shall have received him, shall be subject to ex-communication, and shall be punished by the privation of all their holy orders; so that the holy Eucharist, except on their death-beds, shall be denied them, and, unless they come to their senses, their lot shall be with Dathan and Abiron whom the earth swallowed up alive. Moreover if any one be elected to the office of pope by fewer than two thirds,—unless greater concord is attained, he shall by no means be accepted, and shall be subject to the aforesaid penalty if he be unwilling to humbly abstain.   From this, however, let no prejudice to the canonical and other eccle-siastical decrees arise, with regard to which the opinion of the greater and the sounder part should prevail; for when a doubt arises with regard to them, it can be defined by the judgment of a higher power.   But, in the Roman church, special decrees are made, because recourse cannot be had to a higher power.

VII.

GENERAL SUMMONS OF POPE INNOCENT III. TO A CRUSADE, A.D. 1215.

("Bullarium Romanum, editio Taurinensis," vol. iii. p. 300.)

Aspiring with ardent desire to liberate the Holy Land from the hands of the ungodly, by the counsel of prudent men who fully know the circumstances of times and places, the holy council approving : we decree that the crusaders shall so prepare themselves that, at the Calends of the June following the next one, all who have arranged to cross by sea shall come together in the kingdom of Sicily ; some, as shall be convenient and fitting, at Brindisi, and others at Messina and the places adjoining on both sides ; where we also have arranged then to be present in person if God wills it, in order that by our counsel and aid the Christian army may be healthfully arranged, about to start with the divine and apostolic benediction.

1. Against the same term, also, those who have decided to go by land shall endeavour to make themselves ready ; announcing to us, in the meantime, this determination, so that we may grant them, for counsel and aid, a suitable legate from our side.

2. Priests, moreover, and other clergy who shall be in the Christian army, subordinates as well as prelates, shall diligently insist with prayer and exhortation, teaching the crusaders by word and example alike that they should always have the divine fear and love before their eyes, and that they should not say or do anything which might offend the divine majesty.   Although at times they may lapse into sin, through true penitence they shall soon arise again ; showing humility of heart and body, and observing moderation as well in their living as in their apparel ; altogether avoiding dissensions and emulations ; rancour and spleen being entirely removed from them.   So that, thus armed with spiritual and material weapons, they may fight the more securely against the enemies of the faith ; not presuming in their own power, but hoping in the divine virtue.

3. To the clergy themselves, moreover, we grant that they may retain their benefices intact for three years, as if they were residing in their churches ; and, if it shall be necessary, they may be allowed to place them in pledge for that time.

4. Lest therefore this holy undertaking should happen to be impeded or retarded, we distinctly enjoin on all the prelates of the churches, that, separately, throughout their districts, they diligently move and induce to fulfil their vows to God those who have arranged to resume the sign

of the cross; and besides these, the others who are signed with the cross, and who have hitherto been signed; and that, if it shall be necessary, through sentences of excommunication against their persons and of interdict against their lands, all backsliding being put an end to, they compel them to fulfil their vows: those only being excepted who shall meet with some impediment on account of which, according to the ordinance of the apostolic chair, their vow may rightly be commuted or deferred.

5. Besides this, lest anything which pertains to the work of Jesus Christ be omitted, we will and command that the patriarchs, archbishops, bishops, abbots and others who obtain the care of souls shall studiously propound to those committed to them the word of the cross, exhorting through the Father and the Son and the Holy Spirit—the one sole true eternal God,—the kings, dukes, princes, margraves, counts and barons and other magnates, also the communities of the cities towns and burghs, that those who do not in person go to the aid of the Holy Land, shall donate a suitable number of warriors, with the necessary expenses for three years, according to their own wealth, for the remission of their sins,—as has been expressed in our general letters, and as, for the greater safety, we shall also express below. Of this remission we wish to be partakers not only those who furnish their own ships, but also those who on account of this work have striven to build new ships.

6. To those that refuse, moreover, if any by chance shall be so ungrateful to our Lord God, they (the clergy) shall firmly protest on behalf of the apostolic see, that they shall know that for this they are about to answer to us, at the final day of a strict investigation, before the tremendous Judgment. First considering, however, with what conscience or with what security they will be able to confess in the presence of Jesus Christ the only begotten Son of God, into whose hands the Father gave all things, if they shall refuse in this matter, as if it were properly their own, to serve Him who was crucified for sinners; by whose gift they live, by whose benefit they are sustained, nay, more, by whose blood they are redeemed

7. Lest, however, we seem to impose upon the shoulders

of men heavy and unbearable burdens which we are unwilling to put a finger to, like those who only say, and do not do ; behold we, from what we have been able to spare beyond our necessary and moderate expenses, do grant and give thirty thousand pounds to this work ; and, besides the transport from Rome and the neighbouring places that we have granted, we assign in addition, for this same purpose, three thousand marks of silver which have remained over to us from the alms of some of the faithful ; the rest having been faithfully distributed for the needs and uses of the aforesaid Land, through the hand of the abbot of blessed memory, the patriarch of Jerusalem, and the masters of the Templars and Hospitallers.

8. Desiring, moreover, to have the other prelates of the churches, as well as the whole clergy, as participators and sharers both in the merit and in the reward, we have decreed with the general approbation of the council, that absolutely the entire clergy, subordinates as well as prelates, shall give the twentieth part of their ecclesiastical revenues for three years in aid of the Holy Land, through the hands of those who shall by the care of the pope be appointed for this purpose ; certain monks alone being excepted, who are rightly to be exempted from this taxation ; likewise those who, having assumed or being about to assume the cross, are on the point of making the expedition.

9. We, also, and our brothers the cardinals of the holy Roman Church, shall pay fully one tenth ; and they shall all know that they are all bound to faithfully observe this under penalty of excommunication ; so that those who in this matter shall knowingly commit fraud shall incur sentence of excommunication.

10. Since, indeed, those who with right judgment remain in the service of the divine Commander ought to rejoice in a special privilege : when the time of the expedition exceeds one year in length, the crusaders shall be free from taxes and talliages and other burdens. Upon their assuming the cross we take their persons and goods under the protection of the blessed Peter and of ourselves, so that they shall remain under the care of the archbishops,

bishops and other prelates of the church. Special protectors, nevertheless, being deputed for this purpose, so that, until most certain news shall have been obtained either of their death or of their return, their possessions shall remain intact and unassailed. And if any one presume to the contrary he shall be restrained by ecclesiastical censure.

11. But if any of those proceeding thither are bound by an oath to pay interest, we command, under the same penalty, that their creditors be compelled to remit the oath given them and to desist from claiming interest. But if any one of their creditors shall compel them to pay interest, we command that, by a similar process, they shall be compelled to restore it. But we command that Jews shall be compelled by the secular power to remit their interest; and, until they shall remit it, all intercourse with them on the part of all the followers of Christ shall be denied, under pain of excommunication. For those, moreover, who are unable at present to pay their debts to the Jews, the secular princes shall so provide, with useful delay, that, from the time when they started on their journey until most certain news is obtained of their death or of their return, they shall not incur the inconvenience of interest. The Jews being compelled to count the income which they in the meantime received from the lands pledged to them, towards the principal of the sum loaned, the necessary expenses being deducted; for such a benefice does not suffer much loss, when it so delays the payment that it is not itself absorbed by the debt. The prelates of the churches, indeed, who shall be found negligent in rendering justice to the crusaders and their families, shall know that they shall be severely punished.

12. Furthermore, since corsairs and pirates excessively impede the aiding of the Holy Land, taking and despoiling those who go to and return from it, we bind with the chain of the anathema their especial aiders and favourers. Forbidding, under threat of the anathema, that any one make common cause with them through any contract of buying or selling; and enjoining on the rectors of their cities and districts to recall and restrain them from this iniquity. Otherwise, since to be unwilling to disturb the

wicked is nothing else than to foster them, and since he is not without suspicion of secret collusion who desists from opposing a manifest crime : we will and command that, against their persons and lands, ecclesiastical severity shall be exercised by the prelates of the churches.

13. Moreover we excommunicate and anathematize those false and impious Christians who, against Christ Himself and the Christian people, carry arms, iron, and wood for ships to the Saracens. Those also who sell to them galleys or ships and who, in the pirate ships of the Saracens, keep watch or do the steering, or give them any aid, counsel or favour with regard to their war machines or to any thing else, to the harm of the Holy Land ;—we decree shall be punished with the loss of their own possessions and shall be the slaves of those who capture them. And we command that on Sundays and feast days, throughout all the maritime cities, this sentence shall be renewed ; and to such the lap of the church shall not be opened unless they shall send all that they have received from such damnable gains, and as much more of their own as aid to the aforesaid Land ; so that. they may be punished with a penalty equal to the amount of their original fault. But if by chance they be insolvent, those guilty of such things shall be otherwise punished; that through their punishment others may be prevented from having the audacity to presume to act similarly.

14. We prohibit, moreover, all Christians, and under pain of anathema, interdict them from sending across or taking across their ships to the lands of the Saracens who inhabit the oriental districts, until four years are past ; so that, in this way, greater means of transport may be prepared for those wishing to cross to the aid of the Holy Land, and the aforesaid Saracens may be deprived of the by no means small advantage which has, as a rule, accrued to them from this.

15. Although, indeed, in different councils, tournaments have been generally forbidden under penalty : inasmuch as at this time the matter of the crusade is very much impeded by them, we, under pain of excommunication, do firmly forbid them to be carried on for the next three years.

16. Since, moreover, in order to carry on this matter it is most necessary that the princes and the people of Christ should mutually observe peace, the holy universal synod urging us: we do establish that, at least for four years, throughout the whole Christian world, a general peace shall be observed; so that, through the prelates of the churches, the contending parties may be brought back to inviolably observe a full peace or a firm truce. And those who, by chance, shall scorn to acquiesce, shall be most sternly compelled to do so through excommunication against their persons, and interdict against their land; unless the maliciousness of the injuries shall be so great, that the persons themselves ought not to have the benefit of such peace. But if by chance they despise the ecclesiastical censure, not without reason shall they fear lest, through the authority of the church, the secular power may be brought to bear against them as against disturbers of what pertains to the Crucified One.

17. We therefore, trusting in the mercy of almighty God and in the authority of the blessed apostles Peter and Paul, from that power of binding and loosing which God conferred on us, although unworthy, do grant to all who shall undergo this labour in their own persons and at their own expense, full pardon of their sins of which in their heart they shall have freely repented, and which they shall have confessed; and, at the retribution of the just, we promise them an increase of eternal salvation. To those, moreover, who do not go thither in their own persons, but who only at their own expense, according to their wealth and quality, send suitable men; and to those likewise who, although at another's expense, go, nevertheless, in their own persons: we grant full pardon of their sins. Of this remission, also, we will and grant that, according to the quality of their aid and the depth of their devotion, all shall be partakers who shall suitably minister from their goods towards the aid of that same Land, or who shall give timely counsel and aid. To all, moreover, who piously proceed in this work the general synod imparts in common the aid of all its benefits, that it may worthily help them to salvation.

Given at the Lateran, on the nineteenth day before the

Calends of January (Dec. 14th), in the eighteenth year of our pontificate.

VIII.

THE RULE OF ST. FRANCIS OF ASSISI.

("Bullarium Romanum, editio Taurinensis," vol. iii. p. 394.)

1. This is the rule and way of living of the minorite brothers: namely to observe the holy Gospel of our Lord Jesus Christ, living in obedience, without personal possessions, and in chastity. Brother Francis promises obedience and reverence to our lord pope Honorius, and to his successors who canonically enter upon their office, and to the Roman Church. And the other brothers shall be bound to obey brother Francis and his successors.

2. If any persons shall wish to adopt this form of living, and shall come to our brothers, they shall send them to their provincial ministers; to whom alone, and to no others, permission is given to receive brothers. But the ministers shall diligently examine them in the matter of the catholic faith and the ecclesiastical sacraments. And if they believe all these, and are willing to faithfully confess them and observe them steadfastly to the end; and if they have no wives, or if they have them and the wives have already entered a monastery, or if they shall have given them permission to do so—they themselves having already taken a vow of continence by the authority of the bishop of the diocese, and their wives being of such age that no suspicion can arise in connection with them:—the ministers shall say unto them the word of the holy Gospel, to the effect that they shall go and sell all that they have and strive to give it to the poor. But if they shall not be able to do this, their good will is enough. And the brothers and their ministers shall be on their guard and not concern themselves for their temporal goods; so that they may freely do with those goods exactly as God inspires them. But if advice is required, the ministers shall have permission to send them to some God-fearing men by whose counsel they shall dispense their goods to the poor. After-

wards there shall be granted to them the garments of probation: namely two gowns without cowls and a belt, and hose and a cape down to the belt; unless to these same ministers something else may at some time seem to be preferable in the sight of God. But, when the year of probation is over, they shall be received into obedience; promising always to observe that manner of living, and this Rule. And, according to the mandate of the lord pope, they shall never be allowed to break these bonds. For according to the holy Gospel, no one putting his hand to the plough and looking back is fit for the kingdom of God. And those who have now promised obedience shall have one gown with a cowl, and another, if they wish it. without a cowl. And those who are compelled by necessity, may wear shoes. And all the brothers shall wear humble garments, and may repair them with sack cloth and other remnants, with the benediction of God. And I warn and exhort them lest they despise or judge men whom they shall see clad in soft garments and in colours, using delicate food and drink; but each one shall the rather judge and despise himself.

3. The clerical brothers shall perform the divine service according to the order of the holy Roman Church; excepting the psalter, of which they may have extracts. But the lay brothers shall say twenty four Paternosters at matins, five at the service of praise, seven each at the first, third, sixth and ninth hour, twelve at vespers, seven at the completorium; and they shall pray for the dead. And they shall fast from the feast of All Saints to the Nativity of the Lord; but as to the holy season of Lent, which begins from the Epiphany of the Lord and continues forty days, which the Lord consecrated with his holy fast—those who fast during it shall be blessed of the Lord, and those who do not wish to fast shall not be bound to do so; but otherwise they shall fast until the Resurrection of the Lord. But at other times the brothers shall not be bound to fast save on the sixth day (Friday); but in time of manifest necessity the brothers shall not be bound to fast with their bodies. But I advise, warn and exhort my brothers in the Lord Jesus Christ, that, when they go into the world, they shall not quarrel, nor contend with words, nor judge others.

But they shall be gentle, peaceable and modest, merciful and humble, honestly speaking with all, as is becoming. And they ought not to ride unless they are compelled by manifest necessity or by infirmity. Into whatever house they enter they shall first say: peace be to this house. And according to the holy Gospel it is lawful for them to eat of all the dishes which are placed before them.

4. I firmly command all the brothers by no means to receive coin or money, of themselves or through an intervening person. But for the needs of the sick and for clothing the other brothers, the ministers alone and the guardians shall provide through spiritual friends, as it may seem to them that necessity demands, according to time, place and cold temperature. This one thing being always regarded, that, as has been said, they receive neither coin nor money.

5. Those brothers to whom God has given the ability to labour, shall labour faithfully and devoutly ; in such way that idleness, the enemy of the soul, being excluded, they may not extinguish the spirit of holy prayer and devotion ; to which other temporal things should be subservient. As a reward, moreover, for their labour, they may receive for themselves and their brothers the necessaries of life, but not coin or money ; and this humbly, as becomes the servants of God and the followers of most holy poverty.

6. The brothers shall appropriate nothing to themselves, neither a house, nor a place, nor anything ; but as pilgrims and strangers in this world, in poverty and humility serving God, they shall confidently go seeking for alms. Nor need they be ashamed, for the Lord made Himself poor for us in this world. This is that height of most lofty poverty, which has constituted you my most beloved brothers heirs and kings of the kingdom of Heaven, has made you poor in possessions, has exalted you in virtues. This be your portion, which leads on to the land of the living. Adhering to it absolutely, most beloved brothers, you will wish to have for ever in Heaven nothing else than the name of our Lord Jesus Christ. And wherever the brothers are and shall meet, they shall show themselves as of one household ; and the one shall safely manifest to the other his necessity. For if a mother loves and nourishes her son in

the flesh, how much more zealously should one love and nourish one's spiritual brother? And if any of them fall into sickness, the other brothers ought to serve him, as they would wish themselves to be served.

7. But if any of the brothers at the instigation of the enemy shall mortally sin : for those sins concerning which it has been ordained among the brothers that recourse must be had to the provincial ministers, the aforesaid brothers shall be bound to have recourse to them, as quickly as they can, without delay. But those ministers, if they are priests, shall with mercy enjoin penance upon them. But if they are not priests, they shall cause it to be enjoined upon them through others, priests of the order; according as it seems to them to be most expedient in the sight of God. And they ought to be on their guard lest they grow angry and be disturbed on account of the sin of any one; for wrath and indignation impede love in themselves and in others.

8. All the brothers shall be bound always to have one of the brothers of that order as general minister and servant of the whole fraternity, and shall be firmly bound to obey him. When he dies, the election of a successor shall be made by the provincial ministers and guardians, in the chapter held at Pentecost; in which the provincial ministers are bound always to come together in whatever place shall be designated by the general minister. And this, once in three years; or at another greater or lesser interval, according as shall be ordained by the aforesaid minister. And if, at any time, it shall be apparent to the whole body of the provincial ministers and guardians that the aforesaid minister does not suffice for the service and common utility of the brothers : the aforesaid brothers to whom the right of election has been given shall be bound, in the name of God, to elect another as their guardian. But after the chapter held at Pentecost the ministers and the guardians can, if they wish it and it seems expedient for them, in that same year call together, once, their brothers, in their districts, to a chapter.

9. The brothers may not preach in the bishopric of any bishop if they have been forbidden to by him. And no one of the brothers shall dare to preach at all to the

people, unless he have been examined and approved by the general minister of this fraternity, and the office of preacher have been conceded to him. I also exhort those same brothers that, in the preaching which they do, their expressions shall be chaste and chosen, to the utility and edification of the people; announcing to them vices and virtues, punishment and glory, with briefness of discourse; for the words were brief which the Lord spoke upon earth.

10. The brothers who are the ministers and servants of the other brothers shall visit and admonish their brothers and humbly and lovingly correct them; not teaching them anything which is against their soul and against our Rule. But the brothers who are subjected to them shall remember that, before God, they have discarded their own wills. Wherefore I firmly command them that they obey their ministers in all things which they have promised God to observe, and which are not contrary to their souls and to our Rule. And wherever there are brothers who know and recognize that they can not spiritually observe the Rule, they may and should have recourse to their ministers. But the ministers shall receive them lovingly and kindly, and shall exercise such familiarity towards them, that they may speak and act towards them as masters to their servants; for so it ought to be, that the ministers should be the servants of all the brothers. I warn and exhort, moreover, in Christ Jesus the Lord, that the brothers be on their guard against all pride, vainglory, envy, avarice, care and anxiety for this world, detraction and murmuring. And they shall not take trouble to teach those ignorant of letters, but shall pay heed to this that they desire to have the spirit of God and its holy workings; that they pray always to God with a pure heart; that they have humility, patience, in persecution and infirmity; and that they love those who persecute, revile and attack us. For the Lord saith: "Love your enemies, and pray for those that persecute you and speak evil against you; Blessed are they that suffer persecution for righteousness' sake, for of such is the kingdom of Heaven; He that is steadfast unto the end shall be saved."

11. I firmly command all the brothers not to have suspicious intercourse or to take counsel with women. And, with the exception of those to whom special permission has been given by the Apostolic Chair, let them not enter nunneries. Neither may they become fellow god-parents with men or women, lest from this cause a scandal may arise among the brothers or concerning brothers.

12. Whoever of the brothers by divine inspiration may wish to go among the Saracens and other infidels, shall seek permission to do so from their provincial ministers. But to none shall the ministers give permission to go, save to those whom they shall see to be fit for the mission.

Furthermore, through their obedience I enjoin on the ministers that they demand from the lord pope one of the cardinals of the holy Roman Church, who shall be the governor, corrector and protector of that fraternity, so that, always subjected and lying at the feet of that same holy Church, steadfast in the catholic faith, we may observe poverty and humility, and the holy Gospel of our Lord Jesus Christ; as we have firmly promised.

IX.

THE INSTITUTION OF THE JUBILEE, 1300.

("Bullarium Romanum.   Ed. Taurinensis."
Vol. iv. p. 156.)

Bishop Boniface, servant of the servants of God, in perpetual memory of this matter.

The relation of the ancients is trustworthy, to the effect that, to those going to the famous church of the Prince of the Apostles in the City, great remissions and indulgences of their sins have been granted.

1. We therefore who, as is the duty of our office, do seek and most willingly procure the salvation of individuals, considering each and all such remissions and indulgences as valid and helpful, do confirm and approve them by apostolic authority; and do also renew them and furnish them with the sanction of the present writing.

2. In order, therefore, that the most blessed apostles Peter and Paul may be the more honoured the more their churches in the City shall be devoutly frequented by the faithful, and that the faithful themselves, by the bestowal of spiritual gifts, may feel themselves the more regenerated through such frequenting: we, by the mercy of almighty God, and trusting in the merits and authority of those same ones his apostles, by the counsel of our brethren and from the plentitude of the apostolic power, do concede, in this present year and in every hundreth year to come, not only full and free, but the very fullest, pardon of all their sins to all who in this present year 1300, counting from the feast just past of the nativity of our Lord Jesus Christ, and in every hundredth year to come, shall reverently go to those churches, having truly repented and confessed, or being about to truly repent and confess.

3. Decreeing that those who wish to become partakers of such indulgence conceded by us, if they are Romans shall go to those churches on at least thirty days, consecutively or at intervals, and at least once in the day; but, if they be pilgrims or foreigners, they shall in like manner go on fifteen days. Each one, however, shall be the more deserving and shall more efficaciously obtain the indulgence, the more often and the more devoutly he shall frequent those churches. Let no man whatever infringe this page of our decree, or oppose it with rash daring. But if any one shall presume to attempt this he shall know that he is about to incur the indignation of almighty God and of His blessed apostles Peter and Paul.

Given at Rome, in St. Peters, on the 23rd day of February 1300, in the sixth year of our pontificate

BOOK IV. CHURCH AND STATE.

INTRODUCTION.

THE whole life of Pope Gregory VII. (1073-1085) was one long effort to raise the papacy and the priesthood into a higher sphere. It was by his influence—for although not yet pope he was at that time the power behind the throne —that in 1059 a document (see No. I.) was drawn up placing the initiative in the matter of electing the pope exclusively in the hands of the cardinal-bishops. The document, indeed, was tampered with at an early date, for two versions of it have come down to us, one of which gives to the king of the Romans a much larger share in the election than the other.

The questions at issue in the war of the investitures will be more or less clear from the documents themselves, which are given under No. II. ; but a slight sketch of the course of this most important struggle is, nevertheless, necessary.

At Gregory's own election in 1073 the forms of the decree of 1059 were not regarded ; but Henry IV. did not lay much stress upon this fact until some years later, when open enmity had been declared between himself and the pope. The "Dictate of the Pope" (No. II. 3) shows most clearly the attitude that Gregory was prepared to take. Exactly what the "Dictate" was intended to be is still a mystery. It may have been either a succession of head-ings for future elaboration, or a summary of utterances already delivered. At any rate it is found in the register of Gregory's letters which was made in his own day, and its authenticity is undeniable.

A Roman synod in 1075 proclaimed sacerdotal celibacy, made war on simony,—excommunicating five of Henry IV.'s councillors for having attained ecclesiastical office by means of it,—and declared lay investiture to be uncanonical. The wording of the last decree has not come down to us, but was probably similar to II. 1 and 2, which were issued respectively in 1078 and 1080.

The forbiddal of lay investiture was especially directed against Henry IV., who had recently, disregarding the papal candidate, taken into his own hands the election of an archbishop of Milan. It was one of the boldest moves imaginable, this measure of Gregory's. A renunciation on the part of the king to the right of choosing the men on whom to bestow the rich bishoprics and abbeys of Germany and Italy meant practical abdication. A bishop at that time was not only a dignitary of the church, but also a prince of the realm, whose duty it was to send his contingents to the king's army, and to act as councillor at his court. The fiefs and jurisdictions of the bishoprics were given therefore to faithful followers, not only as a reward for their past services, but also in consideration of their future ones. And now the king was to desist from exercising any further influence on episcopal elections!

No. 4 of the documents under II. explains itself. Henry had continued to consort with the five councillors who were under the bann for simony, although, in a moment of discouragement, he had promised unqualified submission to the pope. He furthermore disdained to treat concerning the matter of lay investiture, although Gregory seems to have invited and courted discussion. The pope's letter reached him at a time when he was flushed with the pride of his victory over the obdurate Saxons. Gregory's envoys, too, used even stronger terms than were contained in the writing they bore. The result was that the king, in a fury of rage, summoned a council to meet at Worms. Two of the archbishops and two-thirds of all the bishops of Germany were present. After listening to a long series of accusations against the pope, the council decreed that Gregory, having wrongfully ascended the throne of Peter, must straightway descend from it. Two letters were despatched to Rome on the same day, one from the king (see No. 5), and one from the bishops (see No. 6). When the German envoys presented them to the pope, who was sitting in council in the Lateran, a scene of wild excitement ensued, and the bearers of such haughty messages were with difficulty saved from instant death. The pope and his synod retaliated (see No. 7) by banning all the dissentient bishops, as well as the king, and by declaring the latter's royal power forfeit, and all of his subjects loosed from their allegiance. Both parties then proceeded to make public their grievances. Henry issued a summons to the princes for a new council to be held at Worms, in which document (see No. 8) he clearly defined his position, while Gregory sent a long letter of justification, couched in the most tolerant terms, to the German bishops (see No. 9).

It was most disastrous for Henry that there happened to be a strong opposition party among the princes of his own land, to whom even an ally like Gregory, the accomplishment of whose aims would have been the greatest possible national misfortune, was not unwelcome. Nor were the princes long alone in their enmity to the king. Gregory succeeded in winning over a number even of the very bishops who had signed the document of his own deposition. Henry's proposed council at Worms was so scantily attended that it was removed to Mainz. Here

too the German princes were conspicuous by their absence. Of their own accord the latter held a diet at
Tribur, and forced Henry to agree to the convention of
Oppenheim (see No. 10). Among themselves they agreed
that, should Henry fail to obtain absolution from the
bann within a year from the date of the assembly, he
should be deposed from the throne. They furthermore
invited Gregory to be present at an Augsburg diet, where
he was to sit in judgment on their king.

The latter, meanwhile, was relegated to a species of
banishment in Spires, where he was to abstain from all
interference in public affairs until the pope's decision
should have been rendered. It was not long, however,
before Henry found this state of things unbearable, and
made up his mind to the step that was to make him the
most famous suppliant in history. It was absolutely
necessary to break the strong league existing between the
pope and the German princes. The latter demanded that
the king should gain absolution from the bann. He determined to do so at any price. It must be remembered
that the prime teaching of the church was that no repentant sinner who sought God's mercy in the proper way
could possibly fail to obtain it. Gregory's influence as the
spiritual head of Christendom would have been irrevocably
shaken had he refused to pardon one who expressed himself as ready to undergo any depth of penance that might
be enjoined upon him.

What happened at Canossa is described by Gregory
himself in his letter to the German princes (see No. 11).
Henry rode away from the Tuscan castle, bound, indeed,
by promises for the future, but, in reality, a free man—
free to labour and to consult for his own interests. At
the price of a deep personal humiliation he had gained an
undoubted diplomatic victory.

For a time, indeed, this was not apparent. Little more

than a month after the scene at Canossa an assembly of princes at Forscheim elected Rudolf of Swabia as anti-king. But it soon became evident that Henry's following was far more considerable than that of his rival. It was of the greatest advantage to him that, for a time at least, Pope Gregory remained neutral, taking upon himself the rôle of mediator. But in 1080, under pretence that Henry had hindered the calling of such a council as would have put an end to the civil war, the pope renewed the bann against him, and acknowledged Rudolf as the rightful king (see No. 12).

There is a famous manœuvre in the Spanish bull-fights, which may prove successful once, but which means death to the torreador should he attempt to repeat it. The result of Gregory's second bann was not unlike it. A storm of indignation rose against the pope, and the Lombard and German bishops rallied to Henry. First in Bamberg, then in Mainz, and finally in Brixen (see No. 13), Gregory was declared deposed. Wibert of Ravenna was made pope in his stead. Gregory's letter of justification, written to Bishop Herrmann of Metz (see No. 14), shows a power of reasoning worthy of the Jesuits. Gregory's pontificate, as is well known, marks an era in the history of the papacy. He was the first to formulate many dogmas which later formed the bases of the most extravagant claims. Boniface VIII.'s "God has constituted us over kings and kingdoms" is but another form of a doctrine of Gregory's.

It is interesting to note that many of the quotations in the present letter are from the forged Isidorian decretals, which claim for the popes the sanction of antiquity for a jurisdiction far beyond that which they had actually enjoyed.

On Easter day 1084 the anti-pope Wibert crowned Henry in St. Peter's as emperor of the Romans, and in the follow-

ing year Pope Gregory died in exile in Salerno. Henry
followed him to the grave in 1106, still in the bann which
Gregory and his successors had hurled against him.

But the war of the investitures was not yet fought out.
Henry V. was as unwilling and as unable to give up the
royal prerogative as his father had been. Various attempts
were made at a settlement. In 1111 Henry compelled
Pope Paschal II. to draw up an agreement (see 15 a) by
which the crown was to receive back all the temporal
grants that had been made by it in the course of centuries
to the clergy. On these terms, and on no others, was the
king ready to renounce the right of investiture. The
document, when read in St. Peter's before the clergy assembled to celebrate the imperial coronation, aroused the
most violent opposition. The ceremony could not be performed, the day ended in a general uproar, and the pope
and the cardinals were taken prisoners by the king. After
a few weeks of captivity Paschal was ready to make any
concessions, and finally consented to an unqualified resignation of the right of investiture (see 15 b). In the
following year, however, a Lateran council repudiated this
compact, and a synod held at Vienne declared lay investiture to be heresy, at the same time placing Henry under
the bann. In 1118 the question of the investitures led to
the election of a new anti-pope and the beginning of a new
schism. But four years later, under Calixtus II., the long
struggle was at last ended. The famous Concordat of
Worms (see No. 16), issued on September 23, 1122, was a
compromise in which both parties made almost equal concessions. The emperor renounced the investiture with
ring and staff, thus giving to the church the right of
nominating and electing her servants. But the elections
were to be held in the emperor's presence, and he alone, by
a special investiture with the sceptre, might bestow the
temporal fiefs and privileges. By refusing to do this he

could readily nullify an election, and the possibility was
avoided of having men in the bishoprics who might be
hostile to the German or to the imperial interests.

No. III. consists of the documents relating to an interesting episode, which shows how ready the papacy was to put
forth every real or theoretical claim to superiority over
the empire, and how ably, as yet, the latter was able to maintain its dignity.   The date of the correspondence is 1157-8.

Eskil, bishop of Lund, had been captured by German
highwaymen while on his way to Rome, and the pope
had demanded the emperor's interference in the matter.
Frederick had done nothing, for Eskil happened to stand
in disfavour with him at the time.   The pope accordingly
sent two cardinals to Vesançon to press the matter.   In
the letters that they bore Adrian spoke of the imperial
crown as a benefice that he had conferred upon Frederick.
There is scarcely a doubt but that the pope knew the full
force of the words he was using.   Since the time of
Gregory VII., who was the first to receive princes as
vassals of the Roman see, the feudal relation had been
entered into with the papacy more than once, and its
terminology could not have been unfamiliar to Adrian.
In the present case one of the legates had made matters
worse by bursting out with the remark: "from whom
then has the emperor the empire except from the pope?"

Frederick's manifesto (III. c) is a spirited defence of
the imperial independence.   It is to be compared with the
similar utterances of the electors in 1338 (see No. VIII.).
Almost the entire clergy approved of the emperor's attitude in this matter, and the pope, finding the opposition
altogether too strong for him, was fain to explain away
the objectionable clauses.

The documents under No. IV. concern the contest between
Frederick Barbarossa and Alexander III., which lasted from
1160 to 1177, being the longest war that was ever waged

between one and the same emperor and one and the same pope. Alexander was that very chancellor Roland who, as Pope Adrian's envoy, had so angered the emperor at Vesançon ; he was known, too, to favour Frederick's enemy, William of Sicily.

Alexander was chosen pope by a majority of the cardinals, but his rival, Victor, besides a strong minority, had the people of Rome—whose vote, as they claimed, was still necessary to the election—upon his side; Victor also enjoyed the priority of consecration.

The synod of Pavia (see IV. *a*) declared for Victor, and Frederick openly ranged himself upon his side. England and France, however, after much vacillation, took the part of Alexander—who, indeed, for years was forced to fight an uphill fight. On Victor's death (1164) his party elected Paschal, and, as the latter's successor, Calixtus. In 1165 Frederick and a number of his nobles and bishops took a solemn oath at Wurzburg never to acknowledge Roland, or a pope elected by his party.

Alexander found at last, in the Lombard cities and in the king of Sicily, the allies he most needed. After years of stern fighting with the Lombard League fortune turned against the emperor, and he was obliged to flee from Italy to save his life. It was six years before he was able to raise an army and return. He was preparing to strike a final blow for his prestige in Italy when he was deserted by his powerful vassal, Henry the Lion. The battle of Legnano, fought in 1176, proved a great defeat, and paved the way for the peace of Venice (see IV. *c*). With the Lombards and with the King of Sicily a truce was arranged, and a term fixed within which a lasting peace was to be established. The oath of Wurzburg was broken, and the reconciliation between the heads of Christendom was solemnized at Venice with the greatest possible pomp and display. Three red marble slabs in the church of St.

Mark's still show the spot where the emperor knelt before the pope.

The terms of the peace were not so unfavourable to Frederick as might have been expected. A number of the bishops even, who had been consecrated by his anti-popes, were allowed to remain in their own sees, or were otherwise provided for.   But, nevertheless, the papacy had come forth victorious from the long struggle.

No. V. is the act by which King John, in 1213, laid England at the feet of a papal legate, to receive it back, by paying tribute, as a fief from the see of Rome. The course of the struggle between John and Pope Innocent is too familiar to need recapitulation.   The papal candidate, Stephen Langton, was finally received as archbishop of Canterbury, and, after removing the interdict, the pope accepted John's submission in the form here given. Innocent was now at the height of his power. England, Aragon, and Hungary, were fiefs of Rome, and the Latin rulers in the East were completely subject to him.   Never at any time has the papacy so nearly approached its ideal of world rule.

No. VI. is the bull " clericis laicos," which was issued in 1296, in answer to complaints of the clergy of France and England over the taxes imposed upon them by their respective kings.   Edward I. of England obeyed Boniface's menaces, and declared in 1297 that no taxes should be imposed upon his clergy without the papal consent. But Philip of France answered by measures of retaliation, and the conflict began which was to end in the dramatic capture at Anagni, and to lead indirectly to the Babylonian captivity.

No. VII., the bull " unam sanctam," was issued towards the close of the struggle between Boniface and Philip. The last sentence of the bull declares that every human power must be subject to the pope of Rome in order to gain salvation. There have been many attempts to explain away this sentence or to attribute a milder meaning to it, but if one remembers that the bull "ausculta filii" of the same year had contained expressions not dissimilar, and that Boniface had been forced then to claim a milder interpretation, it is not likely but that he knew the effect that his words would produce.

It was in answer to "unam sanctam" that Philip, supported by all classes of the population, by the university and by the monasteries, appealed from the pope to a future general council.

No. VIII., the law "licet juris" of 1338, was issued by the electors during the conflict between Louis the Bavarian and Pope Benedict XII. This was the last of the great mediæval struggles between the papacy and the empire. Louis had been on the point of a reconciliation with his old enemy when the war between France and England broke out. Louis held to Edward of England, the pope to Philip of France. Benedict declared the emperor not really repentant, and demanded a renunciation of his royal and imperial rights. It was clear to the electors that, if the pope could claim the right of deposing an emperor, their own position as the persons who had chosen that emperor would be equivocal to say the least. Hence this energetic protest.

It seemed for a moment—strange spectacle—as if all elements in Germany were to go hand in hand in supporting the dignity of the empire. But the internal dissensions, which were to be the curse of the land for centuries, soon regained the upper hand. "The good odour of the emperor began to stink in the nostrils of the princes," as we are told by a contemporary, and in 1346 Charles of Bohemia was chosen as rival king.

I.

DECREE OF 1059 CONCERNING PAPAL ELECTIONS.

(Doeberl: "Monumenta Germaniae selecta," 3rd vol.)

(a.) PAPAL VERSION.

In the name of the Lord God our Saviour Jesus Christ, in the year of his incarnation 1059, in the month of April, in the 12th indiction—the holy Gospel being placed before us and the most reverend and blessed apostolic pope Nicholas presiding, while the most reverend archbishops, bishops, abbots and venerable priests and deacons assisted —in the church of the Lateran patriarch, which is called the church of Constantine, this same venerable pontiff, decreeing by apostolic authority, spoke thus concerning the election of the supreme pontiff: Ye know, most blessed and beloved fellow bishops and brothers—nor has it been hidden from the lower members also—how much adversity this apostolic chair, in which by God's will I serve, did endure at the death of our master and predecessor, Stephen of blessed memory: to how many blows, indeed, and frequent wounds it was subjected by the traffickers in simoniacal heresy; so that the columns of the living God seemed almost to totter already, and the net of the chief fisher to be submerged, amid the swelling blasts, in the depths of shipwreck. Wherefore, if it please ye brethren, we ought prudently to take measures for future cases, and to provide for the state of the church hereafter, lest—which God forbid—the same evils may revive and prevail. Therefore, strengthened by the authority of our predecessors and of the other holy fathers, we decree and establish:

1. That, when the pontiff of this Roman universal church dies, the cardinal bishops, after first conferring together with most diligent consideration, shall afterwards call in to themselves the cardinal clergy; and then the remaining clergy and the people shall approach and consent to the new election.

2. That—lest the disease of venality creep in through any excuse whatever—the men of the church shall be the leaders in carrying on the election of a pope, the others merely followers. And surely this order of electing will be considered right and lawful by those who, having looked through the rules or decrees of the various fathers, also take into consideration that sentence of our blessed predecessor Leo. "No reasoning permits," he says, "that those should be considered as among the bishops who have neither been elected by the clergy, nor desired by the people, nor consecrated by the bishops of their province with the approval of the metropolitan." But since the apostolic chair is elevated above all the churches of the earth, and thus can have no metropolitan over it, the cardinal bishops perform beyond a doubt the functions of that metropolitan, when, namely, they raise their chosen pope to the apex of apostolic glory.

3. They shall make their choice, moreover, from the lap of this (Roman) church itself, if a suitable man is to be found there. But if not, one shall be chosen from another church.

4. Saving the honour and reverence due to our beloved son Henry who is at present called king, and will be in the future, as it is hoped, emperor by God's grace; according as we now have granted to him and to his successors who shall obtain this right personally from this apostolic see.

5. But, if the perversity of depraved and wicked men shall so prevail that a pure, sincere and free election can not be held in Rome, the cardinal bishops, with the clergy of the church and the catholic laity, may have the right and power, even though few in numbers, of electing a pontiff for the apostolic see wherever it may seem to them most suitable.

6. It is to be clearly understood that if, after an election has been held, a time of war, or the endeavours of any man who is prompted by the spirit of malignity, shall prevent him who has been elected from being enthroned according to custom in the apostolic chair: nevertheless he who has been elected shall, as pope, have authority to rule the holy Roman church and to have the disposal of all its re-

sources; as we know the blessed Gregory to have done before his consecration.

But if any one, contrary to this our decree promulgated by a synodal vote, shall, through sedition or presumption or any wile, be elected or even ordained and enthroned: by the authority of God and of the holy apostles Peter and Paul he shall be subjected, as Antichrist and invader and destroyer of all Christianity, to a perpetual anathema, being cast out from the threshold of the holy church of God, together with his instigators, favourers and followers. Nor at any time shall he be allowed a hearing in this matter, but he shall irrevocably be deposed from every ecclesiastical grade, no matter what one he had previously held. Whoever shall adhere to him or show any reverence to him, or shall presume in any way to defend him, shall be bound by a like sentence. Whoever, moreover, shall scorn the import of this our decree, and shall attempt, contrary to this statute, presumptuously to confound and perturb the Roman church, shall be condemned with a perpetual anathema and excommunication and shall be considered as among the impious who do not rise at the Judgment. He shall feel against him, namely, the wrath of Almighty God, the Father, the Son and the Holy Ghost, and shall experience in this life and in the next the fury of the holy apostles Peter and Paul whose church he presumes to confound. His habitation shall be made a desert, and there shall be none to dwell in his tents. His sons shall be made orphans and his wife a widow. He shall be removed in wrath, and his sons shall go begging and shall be cast out of their habitations. The usurer shall go through all his substance and strangers shall destroy the results of his labours. The whole earth shall fight against him and all the elements oppose him; and the merits of all the saints at rest shall confound him, and in this life shall take open vengeance against him. But the grace of Almighty God will protect those who observe this our decree, and the authority of the blessed apostles Peter and Paul will absolve them from the bonds of all their sins.

I, Nicholas, bishop of the holy catholic and apostolic Roman church, have signed this decree promulgated by us as it stands above. I, Boniface, by the grace of God bishop

of Albano, have signed.   I, Humbert, bishop of the holy
church of Sylva Candida, have signed.   I, Peter, bishop of
the church of Ostia, have signed.   And other bishops to
the number of 76, with priests and deacons have signed.

(b.) IMPERIAL VERSION.

(The beginning and the ending of the imperial version
are, with the exception of a word or two, identical with
those of the papal.   The differences are to be found in the
numbered paragraphs.   The cardinals in general and not
only the cardinal-bishops are to be the prime movers in the
election, and the emperor's share in their proceedings is
largely increased.)

1. That, when the pontiff of this Roman church universal
dies, the cardinals, after first conferring together with most
diligent consideration—saving the honour and reverence
due to our beloved son Henry, who is at present called
king, and will be in the future, as it is hoped, emperor by
God's grace, according as we now, by the mediation of his
envoy W. the chancellor of Lombardy, have granted to
him and to those of his successors who shall obtain this
right personally from this apostolic see,—shall approach
and consent to the new election.

2. That—lest the disease of venality creep in through
any excuse whatever—the men of the church, together with
our most serene son king Henry, shall be the leaders in
carrying on the election of a pope, the others merely
followers.

3. They shall make their choice, moreover, from the lap
of this (Roman) church itself, if a suitable man is to be
found there.   But if not, one shall be chosen from another
church.

4. But, if the perversity of depraved and wicked men
shall so prevail that a pure, sincere and free election can
not be held in Rome, they may have the right and power,
even though few in numbers, of electing a pontiff for the
apostolic see wherever it may seem to them, together with
the most unconquerable king, Henry, to be most suitable.

5. It is to be clearly understood that if, after an election
has been held, a time of war, or the endeavour of any man

who is prompted by the spirit of malignity, shall prevent him who has been elected from being enthroned according to custom in the apostolic chair : nevertheless he who has been elected shall, as pope, have authority to rule the holy Roman church, and to have the disposal of all its resources; as we know the blessed Gregory to have done before his consecration.

But if, etc.

II.

DOCUMENTS RELATING TO THE WAR OF THE INVESTITURES.

(Doeberl: "Monumenta Germaniae selecta," pp. 16-48.)

1. *Decree of Nov.* 19*th*, 1078, *forbidding lay Investiture.*

Inasmuch as we have learned that, contrary to the establishments of the holy fathers, the investiture with churches is, in many places, performed by lay persons; and that from this cause many disturbances arise in the church by which the Christian religion is trodden under foot : we decree that no one of the clergy shall receive the investiture with a bishopric or abbey or church from the hand of an emperor or king or of any lay person, male or female. But if he shall presume to do so he shall clearly know that such investiture is bereft of apostolic authority, and that he himself shall lie under excommunication until fitting satisfaction shall have been rendered.

2. *Decree of March* 7*th*, 1080, *forbidding the same.*

Following the statutes of the holy fathers, as, in the former councils which by the mercy of God we have held, we decreed concerning the ordering of ecclesiastical dignities, so also now we decree and confirm : that, if any one henceforth shall receive a bishopric or abbey from the hand of any lay person, he shall by no means be considered as among the number of the bishops or abbots ; nor shall any hearing be granted him as bishop or abbot. Moreover we further deny to him the favour of St. Peter and the entry of the church, until, coming to his senses, he shall

desert the place that he has taken by the crime of ambition as well as by that of disobedience—which is the sin of
idolatry. In like manner also we decree concerning the
inferior ecclesiastical dignities.

Likewise if any emperor, king, duke, margrave, count,
or any one at all of the secular powers or persons, shall
presume to perform the investiture with bishoprics or with
any ecclesiastical dignity,—he shall know that he is bound
by the bonds of the same condemnation. And, moreover,
unless he come to his senses and relinquish to the church
her own prerogative, he shall feel, in this present life, the
divine displeasure as well with regard to his body as to his
other belongings: in order that, at the coming of the Lord,
his soul may be saved.

3. *The Dictate of the Pope.*

That the Roman church was founded by God alone,

That the Roman pontiff alone can with right be called
universal.

That he alone can depose or reinstate bishops.

That, in a council, his legate, even if a lower grade, is
above all bishops, and can pass sentence of deposition
against them.

That the pope may depose the absent.

That, among other things, we ought not to remain in
the same house with those excommunicated by him.

That for him alone is it lawful, according to the needs
of the time, to make new laws, to assemble together new
congregations, to make an abbey of a canonry ; and, on
the other hand, to divide a rich bishopric and unite the
poor ones.

That he alone may use the imperial insignia.

That of the pope alone all princes shall kiss the feet.

That his name alone shall be spoken in the churches.

That this is the only name in the world.

That it may be permitted to him to depose emperors.

That he may be permitted to transfer bishops if need be.

That he has power to ordain a clerk of any church he
may wish.

That he who is ordained by him many *preside* over

another church, but may not hold a subordinate position; and that such a one may not receive a higher grade from any bishop.

That no synod shall be called a general one without his order.

That no chapter and no book shall be considered canonical without his authority.

That a sentence passed by him may be retracted by no one; and that he himself, alone of all, may retract it.

That he himself may be judged by no one.

That no one shall dare to condemn one who appeals to the apostolic chair.

That to the latter should be referred the more important cases of every church.

That the Roman church has never erred; nor will it err to all eternity, the Scripture bearing witness.

That the Roman pontiff, if he have been canonically ordained, is undoubtedly made a saint by the merits of St. Peter; St. Ennodius, bishop of Pavia, bearing witness, and many holy fathers agreeing with him. As is contained in the decrees of St. Symmachus the pope.

That, by his command and consent, it may be lawful for subordinates to bring accusations.

That he may depose and reinstate bishops without assembling a synod.

That he who is not at peace with the Roman church shall not be considered catholic.

That he may absolve subjects from their fealty to wicked men.

4. *Letter of Gregory VII. to Henry IV., Dec.* 1075.

Bishop Gregory, servant of the servants of God, to King Henry, greeting and apostolic benediction:—that is, if he be obedient to the apostolic chair as beseems a Christian king. Considering and carefully weighing with what strict judgment we shall have to render account for the ministry entrusted to us by St. Peter, chief of the apostles, it is with hesitation that we have sent unto thee the apostolic benediction. For thou art said knowingly to exercise fellowship with those excommunicated by a judgment of the apostolic chair, and by sentence of a synod. If this be true, thou dost know thyself that thou may'st receive the favour neither of the divine nor of the apostolic benediction unless—those who have been excommunicated being separated from thee, and compelled to do penance— thou do first, with condign repentance and satisfaction, seek absolution and indulgence for thy transgression. Therefore we counsel thy Highness that, if thou dost feel thyself guilty in this matter, thou do seek the advice of some canonical bishop with speedy confession. Who, with our permission enjoining on thee a proper penance for this fault, shall absolve thee and shall endeavour by letter to intimate to us truly, with thy consent, the measure of thy penitence.

For the rest it seems strange enough to us that, although thou dost transmit to us so many and such devoted letters; and although thy Highness dost show such humility through the words of thy legates—calling thyself the son of holy mother church and of ourselves, subject in the faith, one in love, foremost in devotion;—although, finally, thou dost commend thyself with all the devotion of sweetness and reverence: thou dost, however, at heart and in deeds most stubborn, show thyself contrary to the canonical and apostolic decrees in those things which the religion of the church enjoins as the chief ones. For, not to mention other things, in the affair of Milan the actual outcome of the matter shows plainly how thou didst carry out—and with what intent thou didst make them—the promises made to us through thy mother and through our confrères the bishops whom we sent to thee. And now, indeed, inflicting wound upon wound, contrary to the establishments of the apostolic chair, thou hast given the churches of Fermo and Spoleto—if indeed a church could be given or granted by a man—to certain persons not even known to us. On whom, unless they are previously well known and proven, it is not lawful even regularly to perform the laying on of hands.

Since thou dost confess thyself a son of the church it would have beseemed thy royal dignity to look more respectfully upon the master of the church,—that is, St. Peter, the chief of the apostles. To whom, if thou art of

the Lord's sheep, thou wast given over by the Lord's voice
and authority to be fed ; Christ Himself saying: " Peter,
feed my sheep." And again : " To thee are given over the
keys of the kingdom of Heaven, and whatsoever thou shalt
bind upon earth shall be bound also in Heaven ; and whatsoever thou shalt loose upon earth shall be loosed also in
Heaven." Inasmuch as in his seat and apostolic ministra-
tion we, however sinful and unworthy, do act as the representative of his power : surely he himself has received whatever, through writing or in bare words, thou hast sent to
us. And at the very time when we are either perusing the
letters or listening to the voices of those who speak, he
himself is discerning, with subtile inspection, in what
spirit the instructions were issued. Wherefore thy Highness should have seen to it that no discrepancy of good
will should have been found towards the apostolic chair in
thy words and messages. And, in those things through
which the Christian faith and the state of the church
chiefly progress towards eternal salvation, thou should'st
not have denied the reverence due, not to us, but to God
Almighty—disregarding the fact that the Lord saw fit to
say to the apostles and their successors : " Who hears you,
hears me ; and who scorns you, scorns me." For we know
that he who does not refuse to show faithful obedience to
God, does not scorn to observe our commands—even as if
he had heard them from the lips of the apostle himself—
and the things which, following the decrees of the holy
fathers, we may have said. For if, out of reverence for
the chair of Moses, the Lord ordered the apostles to observe whatever the scribes and Pharisees sitting above
them should say : it is not to be doubted but that the
apostolic and evangelic teaching, the seat and foundation
of which is Christ, should be received—and observed—by
the faithful with all veneration from the lips of those who
have been chosen for the service of preaching.

In this year, indeed,—a synod being assembled around
the apostolic chair, over which the heavenly dispensation
willed that we should preside ; at which, moreover, some
of thy faithful subjects were present : seeing that the good
order of the Christian religion has now for some time been
falling away, and that the chief and proper methods of

gaining souls had long fallen into abeyance and, the devil
persuading, been trampled under foot, we, struck by the
danger and the clearly approaching ruin of the Lord's
flock, reverted to the decrees and to the teachings of the
holy fathers—decreeing nothing new, nothing of our own
invention. We did decree, however, that, error being
abandoned, the first and only rule of ecclesiastical discipline was again to be followed, and the well-worn way of the
saints to be re-sought. Nor indeed do we know of any
other entrance to salvation and eternal life which lies open
to the sheep of Christ and their shepherds, save the one
which, as we have learned in the gospel and in every page
of the divine Scriptures, was shown by Him who said:
"I am the door, he who entereth through me shall be
saved and shall find pasture," was preached by the
apostles and followed by the holy fathers. This decree,
moreover, which some, preferring human to divine honours,
do call an unbearable weight and immense burden—we,
however, by a more suitable name, as a necessary truth
and light for regaining salvation—we did judge should be
devoutly received and observed, not only by thee and by
those of thy kingdom, but by all the princes and peoples
of the world who confess and cherish Christ. Although
we much desired, and it would have most beseemed thee,
that, as thou dost surpass others in glory, honour and
valour, so thou should'st be superior in thy devotion to
Christ. Nevertheless, lest these things should seem beyond
measure burdensome or wrong to thee, we did send word
to thee through thy faithful servants that the changing of
an evil custom should not alarm thee ; that thou should'st
send to us wise and religious men from thy land, who, if
they could, by any reasoning, demonstrate or prove in what,
saving the honour of the Eternal King and without danger
to our souls, we might moderate the decree as passed by the
holy fathers, we would yield to their counsels. In which
matter, indeed, even though thou had'st not been so
amicably admonished by us, it would nevertheless have
been but right that, before thou did'st violate apostolic decrees, thou should'st, by negotiation, make demands from
us in cases where we oppressed thee or stood in the way of
thy prerogatives. But of how much worth thou did'st

consider either our commands or the observance of justice, is shown by those things which were afterwards done and brought about by thee.

But since, inasmuch as the still long-suffering patience of God invites thee to amend thy ways, we have hopes that, thy perception being increased, thy heart and mind can be bent to the obedience of the mandates of God: we warn thee with paternal love, that, recognizing over thee the dominion of Christ, thou do reflect how dangerous it is to prefer thine own honour to His; and that thou do not impede, by thy present detraction from it, the liberty of the church which He considered worthy to join to Himself as His spouse in celestial union; but that thou do begin, with faithful devotion, to lend it the aid of thy valour, in order that it may best increase to the honour of God Almighty and of St. Peter; by whom also thy glory may deserve to be increased. All of which, in return for the victory recently conferred upon thee over thy enemies, thou should'st recognize to be now most clearly due from thee to them; so that, when they reward thee with noteworthy prosperity, they may see thee the more devout for the benefits granted. And, in order that the fear of God, in whose hand and power is every kingdom and empire, may remain fixed in thy heart more deeply than our admonition, bear in mind what happened to Saul after the victory which, by the prophet's order, he enjoyed; and how he was chidden by God when he boasted of his victory, not carrying out the commands of that same prophet; but what favour followed David for the merit of humility amid the distinctions of valour.

Finally, as to the things which we have seen and noted in thy letter we keep silent; nor will we give thee a sure reply until thy legates, Rapoto, Aldepreth and Udescalc, and those whom we sent with them shall return to us and more fully reveal thy will to us in those matters which we entrusted to them to treat of with thee.

Given at Rome on the 6th day before the Ides of January, in the 14th indiction.

5. *Henry IV.'s Answer to Gregory VII., Jan. 24, 1076.*

Henry, king not through usurpation but through the holy ordination of God, to Hildebrand, at present not pope but false monk. Such greeting as this hast thou merited through thy disturbances, inasmuch as there is no grade in the church which thou hast omitted to make a partaker not of honour but of confusion, not of benediction but of malediction. For, to mention few and especial cases out of many, not only hast thou not feared to lay hands upon the rulers of the holy church, the anointed of the Lord—the archbishops, namely, bishops and priests—but thou hast trodden them under foot like slaves ignorant of what their master is doing. Thou hast won favour from the common herd by crushing them; thou hast looked upon all of them as knowing nothing, upon thy sole self, moreover, as knowing all things. This knowledge, however, thou hast used not for edification but for destruction; so that with reason we believe that St. Gregory, whose name thou hast usurped for thyself, was prophesying concerning thee when he said: "The pride of him who is in power increases the more, the greater the number of those subject to him; and he thinks that he himself can do more than all." And we, indeed, have endured all this, being eager to guard the honour of the apostolic see; thou, however, hast understood our humility to be fear, and hast not, accordingly, shunned to rise up against the royal power conferred upon us by God, daring to threaten to divest us of it. As if we had received our kingdom from thee! As if the kingdom and the empire were in thine and not in God's hand! And this although our Lord Jesus Christ did call us to the kingdom, did not, however, call thee to the priesthood. For thou hast ascended by the following steps. By wiles, namely, which the profession of monk abhors, thou hast achieved money; by money, favour; by the sword, the throne of peace. And from the throne of peace thou hast disturbed peace, inasmuch as thou hast armed subjects against those in authority over them; inasmuch as thou, who wert not called, hast taught that our bishops called of God are to be despised; inasmuch as thou hast usurped for laymen the ministry over their priests, allowing them to depose or condemn those whom they themselves had received as teachers from the hand of God through the laying on of hands of the bishops. On me also who, although unworthy to be among the anointed, have nevertheless been anointed to the kingdom, thou hast lain thy hand; me who—as the tradition of the holy Fathers teaches, declaring that I am not to be deposed for any crime unless, which God forbid, I should have strayed from the faith—am subject to the judgment of God alone. For the wisdom of the holy fathers committed even Julian the apostate not to themselves, but to God alone, to be judged and to be deposed. For himself the true pope, Peter, also exclaims: "Fear God, honour the king." But thou who dost not fear God, dost dishonour in me his appointed one. Wherefore St. Paul, when he has not spared an angel of Heaven if he shall have preached otherwise, has not excepted thee also who dost teach otherwise upon earth. For he says: "If any one, either I or an angel from Heaven, should preach a gospel other than that which has been preached to you, he shall be damned. Thou, therefore, damned by this curse and by the judgment of all our bishops and by our own, descend and relinquish the apostolic chair which thou hast usurped. Let another ascend the throne of St. Peter, who shall not practise violence under the cloak of religion, but shall teach the sound doctrine of St. Peter. I Henry, king by the grace of God, do say unto thee, together with all our bishops: Descend, descend, to be damned throughout the ages.

6. *Letter of the Bishops to Gregory VII., Jan.* 24, 1076.

Siegfried archbishop of Mainz, Udo of Treves, William of Utrecht, Herrman of Metz, Henry of Laudun, Ricbert of Verdun, Bibo of Touls, Hozemann of Spires, Burkhard of Halberstadt, Werner of Strasburg, Burkhard of Basel, Otto of Constance, Adalbero of Wurzburg, Rodbert of Bamberg, Otto of Ratisbon, Ellinard of Frising, Odalric of Eichstädt, Frederick of Münster, Eilbert of Minden, Hezil of Hildesheim, Benno of Osnabrück, Eppo of Naples,

Imadus of Paderborn, Tiedo of Brandenburg, Burkhard of Lausanne, Bruno of Verona : to brother Hildebrand.

Although it was well known to us, when thou didst first invade the helm of the church, what an unlawful and nefarious thing thou, contrary to right and justice, wast presuming with thy well-known arrogance to do : we nevertheless thought best to veil the so vicious beginnings of thy elevation by a certain excusatory silence ; hoping, namely, that such wicked commencements would be recti- fied, and to some degree obliterated by the probity and zeal of the rest of thy reign.   But now, as the lamentable state of the church universal proclaims and bemoans, thou dost, with pertinacious continuance, fulfill the promises of thy evil beginnings through the still worse progress of thy actions and decrees.   For although our Lord and Saviour impressed upon his faithful followers the special advan- tages of peace and charity—in testimony of which too many proofs exist to be comprised in the extent of a letter —thou, on the contrary, striving after profane novelties, delighting more in a widely known than in a good name, being swelled with unheard of pride, hast, like a standard- bearer of schism, torn with proud cruelty and cruel pride all the members of the church, which, following the apostle, were enjoying a quiet and tranquil life before thy times.   Thou hast, with raging madness, scattered through all the churches of Italy, Germany, Gaul and Spain the flame of discord which, through thy ruinous factions, thou didst start in the Roman church.   For by taking away from the bishops, as well as thou wast able, all the power which is known to have been divinely conferred upon them through the grace of the holy Spirit, which chiefly mani- fests itself in ordinations ; and by giving over to the fury of the people all the administration of ecclesiastical affairs —seeing that now no one is bishop or priest over any one unless he has bought this by most unworthy assent from thy magnificence—thou hast disturbed, with wretched con- fusion, all the vigour of the apostolic institution and that most beautiful distribution of the members of Christ which the Teacher of the nations so often commends and inculcates.   And thus, through these thy boasted decrees, —we can not speak of it without tears—the name of Christ has almost perished. Who, moreover, for the very indignity of the thing, is not astounded that thou should'st usurp and arrogate to thyself a certain new and unlawful power in order to destroy rights which are the due of the whole brotherhood? For thou dost assert that no one of us shall have any further power of binding or loosing any one of our parishioners whose crime, or even the mere rumour of it, shall reach thee—save thou alone, or him whom thou dost especially delegate for this purpose. What man that is learned in the sacred Scriptures does not see the more than madness of this decree? Since, therefore, we have decided that it is worse than any evil longer to tolerate that the church of God should be so seriously endangered—nay, almost ruined—through these and other workings of thy presumptions,—we have agreed, by common consent of all of us, to make known to thee that about which we have hitherto kept silent: why it is that thou neither now may'st, nor at any time could'st preside over the apostolic see. Thou thyself, in the time of the emperor Henry (III.) of blessed memory, did'st bind thyself by an oath in person, never while that emperor lived, or his son our master the most glorious king who is now at the head of affairs, thyself to accept the papacy, or, so far as thou could'st prevent it, to permit any one else to receive it without the assent and approbation either of the father during his life, or of the son so long as he too should live. And there are very many bishops who can to-day bear witness to this oath, having seen it at that time with their eyes and heard it with their ears. Remember this also, how, when the ambition of securing the papacy tickled some of the cardinals, thou thyself, in order to remove rivalry, did'st bind thyself by an oath, on the condition and with the understanding that they should do the same, never to accept the papacy. See how faithfully thou hast observed both these oaths! Moreover, when, in the time of pope Nicholas, a synod was held with 125 bishops in session, this was established and decreed: that no one should ever become pope except by election of the cardinals, with the approbation of the people and through the consent and authority of the king. And thou thyself wast the author, the sponsor and the signer of this decree.

Furthermore thou hast filled the whole church, as it were, with the ill odour of a most grave charge concerning the too familiar living together and cohabitation with a strange woman.   By which thing our sense of shame suffers more than our cause, although this general complaint has resounded every where: that all the decrees of the apostolic see have been set in motion by women—in a word, that through this new senate of women the whole circle of the church is administered.   For no amount of complaining suffices concerning the injuries and insults against bishops whom thou most unworthily dost call sons of harlots and the like.   Since, therefore, thy accession has been inaugurated by such perjuries; since, through the abuse of thy innovations, the church of God is in danger through so severe a storm; and since thou has defiled thy life and conversation with such manifold infamy : we renounce the obedience which we never promised to thee, nor shall we in future at all observe it.   And since, as thou did'st publicly proclaim, not one of us has been to thee thus far a bishop, so also shalt thou henceforth be pope for none of us.

7. *First Deposition and Banning of Henry IV. by Gregory VII., February 22, 1076.*

O St. Peter, chief of the apostles, incline to us, I beg, thy holy ears, and hear me thy servant whom thou hast nourished from infancy, and whom, until this day, thou hast freed from the hand of the wicked, who have hated and do hate me for my faithfulness to thee.   Thou, and my mistress the mother of God, and thy brother St. Paul are witnesses for me among all the saints that thy holy Roman church drew me to its helm against my will; that I had no thought of ascending thy chair through force, and that I would rather have ended my life as a pilgrim than, by secular means, to have seized thy throne for the sake of earthly glory.   And therefore I believe it to be through thy grace and not through my own deeds that it has pleased and does please thee that the Christian people, who have been especially committed to thee, should obey me.   And especially to me, as thy representative and by

thy favour, has the power been granted by God of binding
and loosing in Heaven and on earth. On the strength of this
belief therefore, for the honour and security of thy church,
in the name of Almighty God, Father, Son and Holy
Ghost, I withdraw, through thy power and authority, from
Henry the king, son of Henry the emperor, who has risen
against thy church with unheard of insolence, the rule
over the whole kingdom of the Germans and over Italy.
And I absolve all Christians from the bonds of the oath
which they have made or shall make to him; and I forbid
any one to serve him as king. For it is fitting that he
who strives to lessen the honour of thy church should
himself lose the honour which belongs to him. And since
he has scorned to obey as a Christian, and has not returned
to God whom he had deserted—holding intercourse with
the excommunicated; practising manifold iniquities;
spurning my commands which, as thou dost bear witness,
I issued to him for his own salvation; separating himself
from thy church and striving to rend it—I bind him in
thy stead with the chain of the anathema. And, leaning
on thee, I so bind him that the people may know and
have proof that thou art Peter, and above thy rock the
Son of the living God hath built His church, and the
gates of Hell shall not prevail against it.

8. Summons of Henry IV. to the Council of Worms. Royal Justification (1076).

Henry, king by the grace of God, sends favour, greeting,
love—not to all, but to a few.

In very important matters the wisest counsels of the
greates' men are needed—men who shall both outwardly
have the ability and inwardly shall not be without the
will to give their best advice in a matter in which they
are interested. For there is nothing whatever in the
carrying out of which either ability without will or will
without ability avails. Both of which thou, most faithful
one, dost possess, as we think, in equal measure; or to
speak more truly, although thou who art very great art
not lacking in very great ability,—nevertheless, if we
know thee rightly and have noted thy fidelity with proper

care, thou dost abound with a good will greater even than
this very great ability; to our own and to the country's
advantage. For from the faithful services of the past we
are led to hope for still more faithful services in the future.
We rely moreover on thy love not to let thy faithfulness
disappoint our expectations; for from the loyalty of none
of the princes or bishops of the land do we hope for greater
things than from thine, rejoicing, as we have done, not only
in the showing of the past but also in what thou hast led
us to expect from thee in the future. Let, therefore, thy
timely good will be present now with thy ability; for it is
called for not only by our own straits but also by those of
all thy fellow-bishops and brothers—nay, of the whole
oppressed church. Thou art not ignorant, indeed, of this
oppression; only see to it that thou do not withdraw thy
aid from the oppressed church, but that thou do give thy
sympathy to the kingdom and the priesthood. For in
both of these, even as the church has hitherto been exalted,
so now, alas, in both it is humiliated and bereaved. Inasmuch as one man has claimed for himself both; nor has
he helped the one, seeing that he neither would nor could
help either. But, lest we keep from thee any longer the
name of one who is known to thee, learn of whom we are
speaking—Hildebrand, namely, outwardly, indeed, a monk;
called pope, but presiding over the apostolic see rather
with the violence of an invader than with the care of a
pastor, and, from the seat of universal peace, sundering
the chains of peace and unity—as thou thyself dost clearly
know. For, to mention a few cases out of many, he usurped
for himself the kingdom and the priesthood without God's
sanction, despising God's holy ordination which willed
essentially that they—namely the kingdom and the priesthood—should remain not in the hands of one, but, as two,
in the hands of two. For the Saviour Himself, during
His Passion, intimated that this was the meaning of the
typical sufficiency of the two swords. For when it was
said to Him: "Behold, Lord, here are two swords"—He
answered: "It is enough," signifying by this sufficing
duality that a spiritual and a carnal sword were to be
wielded in the church, and that by them every thing evil
was about to be cut off—by the sacerdotal sword, namely,

to the end that the king, for God's sake, should be obeyed; but by the royal one to the end that the enemies of Christ without should be expelled, and that the priesthood within should be obeyed. And He taught that every man should be constrained so to extend his love from one to the other that the kingdom should neither lack the honour due to the priesthood, nor the priesthood the honour due to the kingdom. In what way the madness of Hildebrand confounded this ordinance of God thou thyself dost know, if thou hast been ready or willing to know. For in his judgment no one is rightfully priest save him who has bought permission from his own capricious self. Me also whom God called to the kingdom—not, however, having called him to the priesthood—he strove to deprive of my royal power, threatening to take away my kingdom and my soul, neither of which he had granted, because he saw me wishing to hold my rule from God and not from him— because he himself had not constituted me king. Although he had often, as thou dost know, thrown out these and similar things to shame us, he was not as yet satisfied with that but needs must inflict upon us from day to day new and ingenious kinds of confusion—as he recently proved in the case of our envoys. For a page will not suffice to tell how he treated those same envoys of ours, how cruelly he imprisoned them and afflicted them, when captive, with nakedness, cold, hunger and thirst and blows; and how at length he ordered them to be led like martyrs through the midst of the city, furnishing a spectacle for all; so that one would call him and believe him as mad as Decius the tyrant, and a burner of saints. Wherefore, beloved, be not tardy—may all in common not be tardy— to give ear to my request, and to that of thy fellow-bishops, that thou do come to Worms at Pentecost; and that thou there, with the other princes, do listen to many things a few of which are mentioned in this letter; and that thou do show what is to be done. Thou art asked to do this for love of thy fellow-bishops, warned to for the good of the church, bound to for the honour of our life and of the whole land.

9. *Gregory VII.'s Justification of himself to the Germans.* 1076 A.D. (*April or May*).

Bishop Gregory, servant of the servants of God, to all the bishops, dukes, counts and other loyal defenders of the Christian faith in the land of the Germans, greeting and apostolic benediction.

We have heard that certain among you utter complaints and are doubtful, concerning the excommunication which we have passed against the king, whether he has justly been excommunicated and whether our sentence has proceeded from the authority of a censure that is permissible, and with due deliberation. Therefore, as best we could, our conscience bearing witness, we have taken care to lay before the eyes and intellects of all how we were led to excommunicate him ; not so much in order to throw before the public, with our clamour as it were, the separate causes —which, alas, are too well known—as to satisfy the doubts of those who think that we have seized the spiritual sword rashly, and through a sudden impulse of our mind, rather than through fear of God and zeal of justice.

Previously, when we were exercising the office of deacon, a dark and very disgraceful report of the king's actions having reached us, we, for the sake of the imperial dignity and out of reverence for his father and mother—also with the hope and desire of correcting him—often admonished him, through letters and envoys, to desist from his wickedness and, mindful of his most distinguished race and dignity, to order his life according to rules of conduct suitable for a king and, if God should grant it, a future emperor.

Moreover, his age and his depravity keeping pace with each other,—after we, though unworthy, came to be supreme pontiff, the more diligently did we urge him in every way, by arguing, exhorting, rebuking, to amend his life ; knowing that God Almighty would the more strictly demand his soul at our hands the more we, above all others, had been given permission and authority to rebuke him. He, while often sending to us devoted letters and greetings, excusing himself both with his age, which was pliable and frail, and because evil was often recommended to him by those who had the court in their hands, promised, indeed, in words, from day to day, that he would most readily receive our warnings ; but in fact, and by increasing his faults, he entirely trod them under foot.

In the mean while we called to repentance some of his associates by whose counsels and machinations he had, with simoniacal heresy, defiled bishoprics and many monasteries, introducing, for money, wolves instead of shepherds. For we wished both that, while there was yet time to make amends, they should restore to the venerable places where they belonged the goods of the church which they, through so shameful a traffic, had with sacrilegious hand received— and that they themselves, through the lamentations of penitence, should render satisfaction to God for the iniquity perpetrated. But when we learned that they had scorned the terms appointed for carrying out these things and were obstinately continuing in their accustomed iniquity, we justly separated them, as sacrilegious persons and ministers and members of the devil, from the communion and body of the whole church. And we warned the king to expel them, as excommunicate, from his palace and his counsels and from all intercourse with himself.

But meanwhile the cause of the Saxons gained the upper hand against the king. And when he saw that the forces and the protectors of the land were ready, for the most part, to abandon him, he once more directed to us a letter, supplicatory and full of all humility. In it he acknowledged his guilt towards God Almighty, St. Peter and ourselves ; praying that, whatever faults he might have committed in ecclesiastical matters against the institutions of the canons and the decrees of the holy fathers, we, with our apostolic foresight and authority, should strive to correct. And in this matter he promised us, in every way, obedience, consent and faithful aid. Afterwards, being admitted to penance by our brothers and legates Humbert bishop of Praeneste and Gerald bishop of Ostia whom we sent to him, he renewed to them and confirmed this promise, swearing by the sacred stoles which they bore about their necks.

But when, after a time, a battle was fought with the

Saxons, these are the thanks and the sacrifices which he
offered to God in return for the victory which he gained :
he straightway broke the vows that he had made concerning
his improvement, and, carrying out none of his promises,
received those who had been excommunicated into companionship and intercourse with himself, dragging down
the churches into the same confusion as formerly.

At this we, much afflicted—although, after his scorning
the kindness of the Heavenly King, we had lost almost all
hope of correcting him—decided that an attempt must
still be made to reach his conscience, desiring rather that
he should give ear to the apostolic clemency than experience
its severity.   Accordingly we sent to him admonitory
letters : he was to remember what he had promised and to
whom ; he was not to believe that he could deceive God,
whose wrath, when He commences to judge, is so much the
more severe the more long suffering His patience has been ;
he was not to dishonour God by honouring himself, nor
was he to try and extend his own power to the contempt
of God and to the shame of the papacy—knowing that
while God resists the proud He also gives grace to the
humble.   Moreover we sent to him three men of the
clergy, his own faithful followers, warning him through
them in secret that he should do penance for his crimes
—which are indeed horrible to speak of, known moreover
unto many and divulged in many places ; and, on account
of them, the authority of divine and human laws sanctions
and orders that he should not only be excommunicated
until he renders suitable satisfaction, but that he should
be deprived of all honour in his kingdom without hope of
regaining it.   Finally we warned him that, unless he
should cease to hold intercourse with those who had been
banned, we could judge or decree nothing else of him than
that, being cut off from the church, he should share the
fate of the excommunicate, with whom he preferred to
have his portion rather than with Christ.   But if he should
be willing to receive our warnings and to correct his life,
we called and do call God to witness how greatly we should
rejoice concerning his safety and honour, and with what
love we would fold him in the lap of the holy church as
one who, having been made prince of a people and holding

the reins of a most extended kingdom, ought to be a defender of catholic peace and justice.

But his deeds declare how much he thought either of our writings or of the messages sent through our legates. For, offended at being taken to task or rebuked by any one, he not only could not be induced to make amends for the deeds perpetrated, but, carried away by a still greater fury of spirit, did not cease until he had caused the bishops—nearly all of those in Italy; in German lands as many as he could—to shipwreck the faith of Christ, compelling them to deny the obedience and honour due to St. Peter and the apostolic see and granted to them by our Lord Jesus Christ. We, therefore, seeing his iniquity advance to a climax, for these causes :—first, namely, that he was unwilling to abstain from intercourse with those who had been excommunicated for sacrilege and for the sin of simoniacal heresy; then because, for the criminal acts of his life, he was not willing—I will not say to undergo—but even to promise penance, that repentance which he had promised before our legates having been feigned; finally because he has not flinched at rending the unity of the holy church, which is the body of Christ:—for these faults, I say, we have excommunicated him by sentence of a synod to the end that, since we could not recall him by gentleness, we might either lead him back to the way of salvation by severity, God helping us, or that, should he not even fear the censure of the bann—which God forbid —our soul might not at length succumb to the charge of negligence or fear.

If any one, therefore, thinks that this sentence has been unjustly or unreasonably imposed—if he be such a one as is able to apply his intellect to the sacred canons—let him treat with us in the matter and let him acquiesce after hearing patiently, not what we, but what the divine authority teaches, what it decrees, what the unanimous voice of the holy fathers declares. We, indeed, do not think that there is one of the faithful who, knowing the ecclesiastical statutes, is so bound by this error as not to say in his heart, even though he do not dare to publicly affirm it, that we have acted rightly. But even if we—which God forbid—had bound him with such bann for no sufficiently

grave reason or in a too irregular manner : even then, as
the holy fathers assert, it would not have been right to
scorn the sentence, but absolution should have been sought
with all humility.

But do ye, beloved, who have not been willing because of
the royal indignation or of any danger to desert the justice
of God, paying little heed to those who at the last shall be
announced as cursers and liars, stand boldly and be com-
forted in the Lord ; knowing that ye defend the part of
Him who, as an unconquerable King and glorious Victor, is
about to judge the quick and the dead, rendering unto
each man according to his works. Concerning His manifold retribution ye also can be assured if ye shall to the
end have remained faithful and unshaken in His truth.
Wherefore we also incessantly pray to God for ye that He
may cause ye to be strengthened in His name through the
Holy Spirit, and that He may so turn the heart of the
king to repentance that he also at some time may know
that we and ye more truly love him than those who now
pander to and favour his iniquities. But if by God's
inspiration he be willing to come to his senses, no matter
what he shall attempt against us, he shall always, notwithstanding, find us ready to receive him into the holy communion as ye, beloved, have counselled us to do.

10. *Convention of Oppenheim.*

(*a.*) Promise of the King to offer Obedience to the Pope.

Being admonished to do so by the counsel of our faithful
ones, I promise to observe in all things the obedience due
to the apostolic see and to thee, pope Gregory, and will
take care devoutly to correct and to render satisfaction for
anything whereby a derogation to the honour of that same
see, or to thine, has arisen through us. Since, moreover,
certain very grave charges are brought against us concerning attempts which I am supposed to have made against that
same see and against thy reverence : these, at a suitable
time, I will either refute by the help of innocence and by
the favour of God, or, failing this, I will at length willingly
undergo a suitable penance for them. It behoves thy

holiness also, moreover, not to veil those things which, spread abroad concerning thee, cause scandal to the church —but rather, by removing this scruple too from the public conscience, to establish through thy wisdom the universal tranquillity of the church as well as of the kingdom.

(b.) Edict cancelling the Sentence against Gregory VII., October, 1076.

Henry, king by the grace of God, sends to the archbishops, bishops, margraves, counts and dignitaries of every rank the honourable distinction of his goodwill. Inasmuch as we have been brought to recognize, through the representations of our faithful ones, that we have been wanting in clemency, in some regards, towards the apostolic see and its venerable bishop, pope Gregory : it has pleased us, in accordance with healthful counsel, to change our former sentence and to observe, after the manner of our predecessors and progenitors, due obedience in all things to the holy see and to him who is known to preside over it, our master Gregory the pope. And if we have presumed to act too severely against him we will atone for it by rendering fitting satisfaction. We will, moreover, that ye also, warned by our Highness's example, do not hesitate to render solemn satisfaction to St. Peter and to his vicar ; and that those of you who understand themselves to be bound by his bann do strive to be solemnly absolved by him—by our master, namely, Gregory the pope.

11. *Gregory VII.'s Letter to the German Princes concerning the Penance of Henry IV. at Canossa.* (1077.)

Bishop Gregory, servant of the servants of God, to all the archbishops, bishops, dukes, counts and other princes of the realm of the Germans who defend the Christian faith, greeting and apostolic benediction.

Inasmuch as for love of justice ye assumed common cause and danger with us in the struggle of Christian warfare, we have taken care to indicate to you, beloved, with sincere affection, how the king, humbled to penance,

obtained the pardon of absolution and how the whole
affair has progressed since his entry into Italy up to the
present time.

As had been agreed with the legates who had been sent
to us on your part, we came into Lombardy about twenty
days before the date on which one of the commanders was
to come over the pass to meet us, awaiting his advent that
we might cross over to the other side. But when the term
fixed upon had already passed, and we were told that at
this time on account of many difficulties—as we can readily
believe—an escort could not be sent to meet us, we were
involved in no little care as to what would be best for us
to do, having no other means of crossing to you.

Meanwhile, however, we learned for certain that the
king was approaching. He also, before entering Italy,
sent on to us suppliant legates, offering in all things to
render satisfaction to God, to St. Peter and to us. And
he renewed his promise that, besides amending his life, he
would observe all obedience if only he might merit to obtain from us the favour of absolution and the apostolic
benediction. When, after long deferring this and holding
frequent consultations, we had, through all the envoys who
passed, severely taken him to task for his excesses: he
came at length of his own accord, with a few followers,
showing nothing of hostility or boldness, to the town of
Canossa where we were tarrying. And there, having laid
aside all the belongings of royalty, wretchedly, with bare
feet and clad in wool, he continued for three days to stand
before the gate of the castle. Nor did he desist from im-
ploring with many tears the aid and consolation of the
apostolic mercy until he had moved all of those who were
present there, and whom the report of it reached, to such
pity and depth of compassion that, interceding for him
with many prayers and tears, all wondered indeed at the
unaccustomed hardness of our heart, while some actually
cried out that we were exercising, not the gravity of apostolic severity, but the cruelty, as it were, of a tyrannical
ferocity.

Finally, conquered by the persistency of his compunction
and by the constant supplications of all those who were
present, we loosed the chain of the anathema and at

length received him into the favour of communion and
into the lap of the holy mother church, those being
accepted as sponsors for him whose names are written
below. And of this transaction we also received a confirmation at the hands of the abbot of Cluny, of our daughters
Matilda and the countess Adelaide, and of such princes,
episcopal and lay, as seemed to us useful for this
purpose.

Having thus accomplished these matters, we desire
at the first opportunity to cross over to your parts in order
that, by God's aid, we may more fully arrange all things
for the peace of the church and the concord of the kingdom, as has long been our wish. For we desire, beloved,
that ye should know beyond a doubt that the whole question at issue is as yet so little cleared up—as ye can learn
from the sponsors mentioned—that both our coming and
the unanimity of your counsels are extremely necessary.
Wherefore strive ye all to continue in the faith in which ye
have begun and in the love of justice; and know that we
are not otherwise bound to the king save that, by word
alone as is our custom, we have said that he might have
hopes from us in those matters in which, without danger
to his soul or to our own, we might be able to help him
to his salvation and honour either through justice or
through mercy.

Oath of Henry King of the Germans.

I, king Henry, on account of the murmuring and enmity
which the archbishops and bishops, dukes, counts and
other princes of the realm of the Germans, and others who
follow them in the same matter of dissension, bring to bear
against me, will, within the term which our master pope
Gregory has constituted, either do justice according to his
judgment or conclude peace according to his counsels—unless an absolute impediment should stand in his way or
in mine. And on the removal of this I shall be ready to
continue in the same course. Likewise, if that same lord
pope Gregory shall wish to go beyond the mountains or to
any other part of the world, he himself, as well as those
who shall be in his escort or following or who are sent by

him or come to him from any parts of the world whatever, shall be secure, while going, remaining or returning, on my part and on the part of those whom I can constrain, from every injury to life or limb, or from capture. Nor shall he by my consent have any other hindrance which is contrary to his dignity; and if any such be placed in his way I will aid him according to my ability. So help me God and this holy gospel.

Given at Canossa on the 5th day before the Calends of February (Jan. 28), in the 15th indiction, in the year of our Lord Jesus Christ 1077—there being present the bishops Humbert of Praeneste and Gerald of Ostia; the Roman cardinals Peter of the title of St. Chrisogonus and Cono of the title of St. Anastasius; the Roman deacons Gregory and Bernard, and the sub-deacon Humbert. Likewise, on the part of the king, there were present the archbishop of Bremen, the bishops of Vercelli and Osnabruck, the abbot of Cluny and many noble men.

12. *Second Banning and Dethronement of Henry IV. through Gregory VII., March 7th*, 1080.

St. Peter, chief of the apostles, and thou St. Paul, teacher of the nations, deign, I beg, to incline your ears to me and mercifully to hear me. Do ye who are the disciples and lovers of truth aid me to tell the truth to ye without any of the falsehood which we altogether detest: to the end that my brothers may better acquiesce with me and may know and learn that, after God and his mother the ever-virgin Mary, it is in ye I trust when I resist the wicked and unholy but lend aid to your faithful followers. For ye know that I did not willingly take holy orders. And unwillingly I went with my master Gregory beyond the mountains; but more unwillingly I returned with my master pope Leo to your especial church, in which I served ye as always. Then, greatly against my will, with much grieving and groaning and wailing I was placed upon your throne, although thoroughly unworthy. I say these things thus because I did not choose ye but ye chose me and did place upon me the very heavy burden of your church. And because ye did order me to go up into a high mountain and call out and proclaim to the people of God their crimes and to the sons of the earth their sins, the members of the devil have commenced to rise up against me and have presumed, even unto blood, to lay their hands upon me. For the kings of the earth stood by, and the secular and ecclesiastical princes ; the men of the palace, also, and the common herd came together against the Lord and against ye His anointed, saying : " Let us break their chains and cast off their yoke from us." And they have in many ways attempted to rise up against me in order to utterly confound me with death or with exile.

Among them, especially, Henry whom they call king, son of Henry the emperor, did raise his heel against your church and strive, by casting me down, to subjugate it, having made a conspiracy with many ultramontane bishops. But your authority resisted and your power destroyed their pride. He, confounded and humbled, came to me in Lombardy and sought absolution from the bann. I seeing him humiliated, having received many promises from him concerning the bettering of his way of living, restored to him the communion. But only that ; I did not reinstate him in his kingdom from which I had deposed him in a Roman synod, nor did I order that the fealty from which, in that synod, I had absolved all those who had sworn it to him, or were about to swear it, should be observed towards him. And my reason for not doing so was that I might do justice in the matter or arrange peace—as Henry himself, by an oath before two bishops, had promised me should be done—between him and the ultramontane bishops or princes who, being commanded to do so by your church, had resisted him. But the said ultramontane bishops and princes, hearing that he had not kept his promise to me, and, as it were, despairing of him, elected for themselves without my advice—ye are my witnesses—duke Rudolf as king. This king Rudolf hastily sent an envoy to intimate to me that he had been compelled to accept the helm of state but that he was ready to obey me in every way. And to make this the more credible he has continued from that time to send me words to the same effect, adding also that he was ready to confirm what he had promised by giving his own son and the son of his faithful follower duke Bertald as hostages. Meanwhile Henry commenced to implore my aid against the said Rudolf. I answered that I would willingly grant it if I could hear the arguments on both sides so as to know whom justice most favoured. But he, thinking to conquer by his own strength, scorned my reply. But when he found that he could not do as he had hoped he sent to Rome two of his partizans, the bishops, namely, of Verdun and of Osnabruck, who asked me in a synod to do justice to him. This also the envoys of Rudolf pressed me to do. At length, by God's inspiration as I believe, I decreed in that synod that an assembly should take place beyond the mountains, where either peace should be established or it should be made known which side justice the most favoured. For I—as ye, my fathers and masters, can testify—have taken care up to this time to aid no party save the one on whose side justice should be found to be. And, thinking that the weaker side would wish the assembly not to take place, whereas justice would hold its own, I excommunicated and bound with the anathema the person of any one —whether king, duke, bishop or ordinary man—who should by any means contrive to prevent the assembly from taking place. But the said Henry with his partizans, not fearing the danger from disobedience, which is the crime of idolatry, incurred the excommunication by impeding the assembly. And he bound himself with the chain of the anathema, causing a great multitude of Christians to be given over to death and of churches to be ruined, and rendering desolate almost the whole realm of the Germans. Wherefore, trusting in the judgment and mercy of God and of his most holy mother the ever-virgin Mary, armed with your authority, I lay under excommunication and bind with the chains of the anathema the oft-mentioned Henry—the so-called king—and all his followers. And again, on the part of God Almighty and of yourselves, I deny to him the kingdom of the Germans and of Italy and I take away from him all royal power and dignity. And I forbid any Christian to obey him as king, and absolve from their oath all who have sworn or shall swear to him as ruler of the land. May this same Henry, moreover,—as well as his partizans, —be powerless in any warlike encounter and obtain no victory during his life   Whereas I grant and concede in your name that Rudolf, whom, as a mark of fidelity to ye, the Germans have chosen to be their king, may rule and defend the land of the Germans. To all of those who faithfully adhere to him I, trusting in your support, grant absolution of all their sins and your benediction in this life and the life to come. For as Henry, on account of his pride, disobedience and falseness, is justly cast down from his royal dignity, so to Rudolf, for his humility, obedience and truthfulness, the power and dignity of kingship are granted.

Proceed now, I beg, O fathers and most holy princes, in such way that all the world may learn and know that, if ye can bind and loose in Heaven, so ye can on earth take away empires, kingdoms, principalities, duchies, margravates, counties and all possessions of men, and grant them to any man ye please according to his merits. For often have ye taken away patriarchates, primateships, archbishoprics and bishoprics from the wicked and unworthy and given them to devout men. And if ye judge spiritual offices what are we to believe of your power in secular ones? And if ye shall judge angels, who rule over all proud princes, how will it be with those subject to them? Let kings and all secular princes now learn how great ye are and what your power is; and let them dread to disregard the command of your church. And, in the case of the said Henry, exercise such swift judgment that all may know him to fall not by chance but by your power. Let him be confounded;— would it were to repentance, that his soul may be safe at the day of the Lord!

Given at Rome, on the Nones of March, in the third indiction.

13. *Decision of the Synod of Brixen, June 25th,* 1080.

In the year of our Lord's incarnation 1080, when, in the presence of the most serene king Henry IV. and by his order, in the 26th year of his reign, on Friday the 7th day before the Calends of July and in the 3rd indiction, there was assembled at Brixen in Noricum a convention of thirty bishops and an army of nobles not only from Italy but also from Germany: there was heard from the mouth of all one voice, as it were, terribly complaining over the truculent madness of a certain false monk called pope Gregory VII., and asking why the invincible king allowed the same to rage so long unhindered when Paul, the vase of election, testifies that a prince does not wield the sword without cause ; and when Peter, the chief of the apostles, proclaims that not only is the king pre-eminent but that it is his place to send out commanders to punish, indeed, the evil, but to reward the good. In answer to these representations, therefore, it seemed just to the most illustrious king and to his princes that the judgment of the bishops and the sentence of the divine wrath against this same Hildebrand should precede the material sword ; so that him the royal power might afterwards, with more right, declare an object of pursuit whom the bishops of the churches should first have deposed from his proud eminence. What one of the faithful, indeed, who knows him would fear to hurl against him the javelin of damnation ? For from his earliest years he has striven through vain glory to commend himself in the world as more than man —no merits calling for it—and to prefer his own divinations and those of others to the divine orderings ; to be a monk in dress and not by profession ; to consider himself beyond ecclesiastical discipline, subject to no master ; to assist, more than laymen, at obscene theatrical amusements; for the sake of sordid gain publicly to watch the tables of the money-changers in the path of the passers by. Having accumulated money, then, by such pursuits, he invaded the abbey of St. Paul's, supplanting the abbot. Then, inducing by deception a certain man named Mancius to sell him the office, he seized the archdeaconship; and, against the will of pope Nicholas, in the midst of a popular tumult he had himself raised to the office of administrator. Moreover, by the outrageous death, through poison, of four Roman pontiffs at the hand of a certain intimate of his—John Brachintus—he is convicted of being a murderer ; as the minister of death himself, although repenting late, did testify with dire clamourings when in the very grasp of death—all others having kept silence. Finally this oft-mentioned pest-bearer, on the very night when the body of pope Alexander was being honoured with the funeral ceremony in the church of St. Salvatore, guarded the gates and bridges, towers and triumphal arches of the city of Rome with bands of armed men, occupied the Lateran palace with an armed force that he had brought together with hostile intent, frightened the clergy—lest they, none of whom wished to elect him, should dare to resist—by threatening death through the drawn swords of his satellites, and carried by assault the long-besieged chair before the body of the dead man had obtained burial. But when some persons tried to call to his mind that decree of pope Nicholas promulgated by those 125 bishops under pain of anathema, Hildebrand himself approving,—the tenor of which was that if any one, without the consent of the Roman sovereign, should presume to become pope he should be considered no pope but an apostate : he denied all knowledge of a king and asserted his own right to declare void a decree of his predecessors. What more is there to say ? Not only Rome, indeed, but the whole Roman world bears witness that he was not chosen by God but that he forced his way most impudently by violence, fraud and bribery. For his fruits betray their root and his works manifest his intent, inasmuch as he subverts the order of the church ; has perturbed the rule of a Christian empire ; tries to kill the body and soul of a catholic and pacific king ; defends as king a perjurer and traitor ; has sown discord among the united, strife among the peaceful, scandals among brothers, divorce among husbands and wives ; and has shattered whatever of rest he found being enjoyed by those leading a holy life. Therefore we, congregated together, as has been said, by God's authority, trusting in the legates and letters of the 19 bishops who were assembled at Mainz on the holy day of last Pentecost, do decree against this same most brazen Hildebrand, —who preaches sacrilege and arson, who defends perjury and homicide, who questions the catholic and apostolic faith concerning the body and blood of our Lord, who is an ancient disciple of the heretic Berengar, a manifest believer in dreams and divinations, a necromancer, dealing in the spirit of prophecy and therefore a wanderer from the true faith—that, he shall be canonically deposed and expelled and, unless on hearing this he descend from that seat, forever damned. (Here follow the signatures of the bishops, etc., first the cardinal Hugo Candidus, then the king, etc.)

14. *Letter of Gregory VII. to Bishop Hermann of Metz,* *March 15th,* 1081.

Bishop Gregory, servant of the servants of God, to his beloved brother in Christ, Hermann bishop of Metz, greeting and apostolic benediction. It is doubtless owing to a dispensation of God that, as we learn, thou art ready to bear labours and dangers in defence of the truth. For such is His ineffable grace and wonderful mercy that He never allows His chosen ones completely to go astray— never permits them utterly to fall or to be cast down. For, after they have been afflicted by a time of persecution—a useful term of probation as it were,—He makes them, even if they have passed through some trepidation, stronger than before. Since, moreover, manly courage impels one strong man to act more bravely than another and to press forward more boldly—even as among cowards fear induces one to flee more disgracefully than another,—we wish, beloved, with the voice of exhortation, to impress this upon thee: thou should'st the more delight to stand in the army of the Christian faith among the first, the more thou art convinced that they are the most worthy and the nearest to God the victors. Thy demand, indeed, to be aided, as it were, by our writings and fortified against the madness of those who babble forth with unhallowed mouth that the authority of the holy and apostolic see had no right to excommunicate Henry—a man who despises the Christian law; a destroyer, namely, of the churches and of the empire; a favourer of heretics and a partaker with them—or to absolve any one from the oath of fealty to him, does not seem to us to be altogether necessary when so many and such absolutely certain proofs are to be found in the pages of Holy Scripture. Nor do we believe, indeed, that those who, heaping up for themselves damnation, impudently detract from the truth and run counter to it have joined these charges to the audacity of their defence so much from ignorance as from a certain madness of wretched desperation. And no wonder. For it is the custom of the wicked to strive after protection from their iniquity and to defend those like to themselves; considering it of no importance that they incur perdition for lying.

For, to cite a few passages from among many, who does not know the words of our Lord and Saviour Jesus Christ who says in the gospel: " Thou art Peter and upon this rock will I build my church, and the gates of hell shall not prevail against it; and I will give unto thee the keys of the kingdom of Heaven; and whatsoever thou shalt bind upon earth shall be bound also in Heaven, and whatsoever thou shalt loose upon earth shall be loosed also in Heaven "? Are kings excepted here, or do they not belong to the sheep which the Son of God committed to St. Peter? Who, I ask, in this universal concession of the power of binding and loosing, can think that he is withdrawn from the authority of St. Peter, unless, perhaps, that unfortunate man who is unwilling to bear the yoke of the Lord and subjects himself to the burden of the devil, refusing to be among the number of Christ's sheep? It will help him little to his wretched liberty, indeed, that he shake from his proud neck the divinely granted power of Peter. For the more any one, through pride, refuses to bear it, the more heavily shall it press upon him unto damnation at the judgment.

The holy fathers, indeed, as well in general councils as otherwise in their writings and doings, have called the holy Roman church the universal mother, accepting and serving with great veneration this institution founded by the divine will, this pledge of a dispensation to the church, this privilege handed over in the beginning and confirmed to St. Peter the chief of the apostles. And even as they accepted its proofs in confirmation of their faith and of the doctrines of holy religion, so also they received its judgments—consenting in this, and agreeing as it were with one spirit and one voice: that all greater matters and exceptional cases, and judgments over all churches, ought to be referred to it as to a mother and a head; that from it there was no appeal; that no one should or could retract or refute its decisions. Wherefore the blessed pope Gela-

sius, armed with the divine authority, when writing to the
emperor Anastasius how and what he should think concerning the primacy of the holy and apostolic see, instructed him as follows: "Although," he said, "before
all priests in common who duly exercise divine functions
it is right that the necks of the faithful should be bowed,
by how much more should the bishop of the Roman see
be obeyed, whom both the supreme deity has willed to
predominate over all priests and the subsequent piety of
the whole church in common has honoured?   From which
thy prudence clearly sees that, with him whom the voice
of Christ placed over all, and whom a venerable church
has always professed and devoutly holds as its primate, no
one can, by any human device whatever, gain an equal
privilege and be equally acknowledged."   Likewise pope
Julius, when writing to the oriental bishops concerning
the power of that same holy and apostolic see, said: "It
would have become ye, brethren, to choose your words and
not to speak ironically against the holy Roman and apostolic church, since our Lord Jesus Christ, addressing it as
was fitting, said: 'Thou art Peter, and upon this rock
will I build my church, and the gates of hell shall not prevail against it; and I will give unto thee the keys of the
kingdom of Heaven.'   For it has the power, granted to it
by a special privilege, of opening and closing for whom it
will the gates of the kingdom of Heaven."   Is it not
lawful, then, for him to whom the power of opening and
closing Heaven is granted to exercise judgment upon
earth?   God forbid that it should not be!   Remember
what the most blessed apostle Paul says: "Know ye not
that we shall judge angels?   How much more the things
of earth!"   The blessed pope Gregory also decreed that
those kings should fall from their dignity who should
dare to violate the statutes of the apostolic see, writing to
a certain abbot, Senator, as follows: "But if any king,
priest, judge or secular person, disregarding this the page
of our decree, shall attempt to act counter to it he shall
lose the dignity of his power and honour and shall know
that he, in the sight of God, is guilty of committing a
crime.   And unless he restore the things which have been
wrongfully removed by him, or unless he atone by fitting

penance for his unlawful acts, he shall be kept away from the most sacred body and blood of our Lord and Saviour Jesus Christ and shall undergo a stern vengeance at the eternal judgment."

But if the blessed Gregory, the most gentle of teachers, decreed that kings who should violate his decrees in the matter of a single hospice should not only be deposed but also excommunicated and, at the last judgment, condemned: who, save one like to them, will blame us for having deposed and excommunicated Henry, who is not alone a scorner of the apostolic judgments but also, as far as in him lies, a treader under foot of holy mother church herself and a most shameless robber and atrocious destroyer of the whole realm and of the churches. As we have learned, through St. Peter's teaching, from a letter concerning the ordination of Clement in which it says: "If any one shall be a friend to those with whom he (Clement) does not speak, he also is one of those who wish to exterminate the church of God; and while, with his body, he seems to be with us, he is with heart and soul against us. And such an enemy is far more dangerous than those who are without and who are open enemies. For he, under the guise of friendship, does hostile acts, and rends and lays waste the church." Mark well, beloved, if this pope so severely judges the friend or companion of those with whom, on account of their actions he is angry, with what condemnation he will visit the man himself with whose actions he is displeased.

But to return to the matter in hand. Is not a dignity like this, founded by laymen—even by those who do not know God,—subject to that dignity which the providence of God Almighty has, in His own honour, founded and given to the world? For His Son, even as He is undoubtingly believed to be God and man, so is He considered the highest priest, the head of all priests, sitting on the right hand of the Father and always interceding for us. And He despised a secular kingdom, which makes the sons of this world swell with pride, and came of His own will to the priesthood of the cross. Who does not know that kings and leaders are sprung from those who—ignorant of God—by pride, plunder, perfidy, murders—in a word by

almost every crime, the devil, who is the prince of this
world, urging them on as it were—have striven with blind
cupidity and intolerable presumption to dominate over
their equals; namely, over men? To whom, indeed, can
we better compare them, when they seek to make the
priests of God bend to their footprints, than to him who
is head over all the sons of pride and who, tempting the
Highest Pontiff Himself, the Head of priests, the Son of
the Most High, and promising to Him all the kingdoms
of the world, said: "All these I will give unto Thee if
Thou wilt fall down and worship me?" who can doubt
but that the priests of Christ are to be considered the
fathers and masters of kings and princes and of all the
faithful? Is it not considered miserable madness for a
son to attempt to subject to himself his father, a pupil
his master; and for one to bring into his power and bind
with iniquitous bonds him by whom he believes that he
himself can be bound and loosed not only on earth but
also in Heaven? This the emperor Constantine the Great,
lord of all the kings and princes of nearly the whole world,
evidently understood—as the blessed Gregory reminds us
in a letter to the emperor Mauritius—when, sitting last
after all the bishops in the holy council of Nicæa, he
presumed to give no sentence of judgment over them, but,
even calling them gods, decreed that they should not be
subject to his judgment but that he should be dependent
upon their will. Also the afore-mentioned pope Gelasius,
persuading the said emperor Anastasius not to take offence
at the truth which had been made clear to his senses,
added this remark: "For, indeed, O august emperor, there
are two things by which this world is chiefly ruled—the
sacred authority of the pontiffs and the royal power;
whereby the burden of the priests is by so much the
heavier according as they, at the divine judgment of men,
are about to render account for the kings themselves."
And a little further on he says: "Thou dost know, therefore, that in these matters thou art dependent on their
judgment and that thou art not to wish to reduce them to
do thy will."

Very many of the pontiffs, accordingly, armed with such
decrees and with such authorities, have excommunicated—

some of them kings; some, emperors. For, if any special example of the persons of such princes is needed,—the blessed pope Innocent excommunicated the emperor Arcadius for consenting that St. John Chrysostom should be expelled from his see. Likewise another Roman pontiff —Zacchary, namely—deposed a king of the Franks, not so much for his iniquities as for the reason that he was not fitted to exercise so great power. And he substituted Pipin, father of the emperor Charles the Great, in his place—loosing all the Franks from the oath of fealty which they had sworn him. As, indeed, the holy church frequently does by its authority when it absolves servitors from the fetters of an oath sworn to such bishops as, by apostolic sentence, are deposed from their pontifical rank. And the blessed Ambrose—who, although a saint, was not, indeed, bishop over the whole church—excommunicated and excluded from the church the emperor Theodosius the Great for a fault which, by other priests, was not regarded as very grave. He shows, too, in his writings that, not by so much is gold more precious than lead, as the priestly dignity is more lofty than the royal power; speaking thus towards the beginning of his pastoral letter: "The honour and sublimity of bishops, brethren, is beyond all comparison. If one should compare them to resplendent kings and diademed princes it would be far less worthy than if one compared the base metal lead to gleaming gold. For, indeed, one can see how the necks of kings and princes are bowed before the knees of priests; and how, having kissed their right hands, they believe themselves to be fortified by their prayers." And, after a little: "Ye should know, brethren, that we have thus mentioned all these things in order to show that nothing in this life can be found more lofty than priests or more sublime than bishops."

Thou, brother, should'st also remember that more power is granted to an exorcist, when he is made a spiritual emperor for the casting out of demons, than can be granted to any layman in the matter of secular dominion. Over all kings and princes of the earth who do not live religiously and do not, in their actions, fear God as they should, demons—alas, alas—hold sway, confounding them with a wretched servitude. For such men desire to rule, not, induced by divine love, to the honour of God and for the saving of souls—like the priests of the church; but they strive to have dominion over others in order to show forth their intolerable pride and to fulfil the lusts of their heart. Concerning whom the blessed Augustine says in the first book on the Christian teaching: "For, indeed, whoever strives to gain dominion even over those who are by nature his equals—that is, over men: his pride is altogether intolerable." Exorcists, then, have, as we have said, dominion from God over demons: how much more, therefore, over those who are subject to demons and members of demons? If, moreover, exorcists are so preeminent over these, how much the more so are priests!

Furthermore every Christian king, when he comes to die, seeks as a miserable suppliant the aid of a priest to the end that he may evade hell's prison, that he may pass from the shadows to the light, that, at the last judgment, he may appear absolved from the bonds of his sins. But what man—a layman even, not to speak of priests—has ever implored the aid of an earthly king for the salvation of his soul when his last hour was near? And what king or emperor is able, by reason of the office imposed upon him, to snatch any Christian from the power of the devil through holy baptism, to number him among the sons of God and to fortify him with the divine unction? And who of them —which is the greatest thing in the Christian religion—can with his own lips make the body and blood of our Lord? Or who of them possesses the power of binding and loosing in Heaven and on earth? From which things it is clearly seen how greatly priests excel in power and dignity. Or who of them can ordain any one as clerk in the holy church —much less depose him for any fault? For in the matter of ecclesiastical grades a greater power is needed to depose than to ordain. For bishops may ordain other bishops, but by no means depose them without the authority of the apostolic see. Who, therefore, that is even moderately intelligent can doubt that priests are to be preferred to kings? But if kings are to be judged by priests for their sins, by whom should they be judged with more right than by the Roman pontiff? Finally, any good Christians whatever have much more right to be considered kings than have bad princes. For the former, seeking the glory of God, strenuously rule themselves; but the latter, enemies unto themselves, seeking the things which are their own and not the things which are God's, are tyrannical oppressors of others. The former are the body of the true king, Christ; the latter, of the devil. The former restrain themselves to the end that they may eternally reign with the supreme emperor; but the sway of the latter brings about this—that they shall perish in eternal damnation with the prince of darkness who is king over all the sons of pride.

Nor, indeed, is it much to be wondered at that wicked bishops are of one mind with a bad king whom—having wrongfully obtained honours from him—they love and fear. For they, simoniacally ordaining whom they please, sell God even for a paltry price. And as the good are indivisibly united with their head, so also the bad are pertinaciously banded together—chiefly against the good—with him who is the head of evil. But against them we ought surely not so much to hold discourse as to weep for them with tears and lamentations: to the end that God Almighty may snatch them from the nooses of Satan in which they are held captive and, after their great danger, bring them at length at some time to a knowledge of the truth.

We refer to kings and emperors who, too much swollen by worldly glory, rule not for God but for themselves. But, since it belongs to our office to distribute exhortation to each person according to the rank or dignity which he adorns, we take care, God impelling us, to provide weapons of humility just for emperors and kings and other princes, that they may be able to subdue the risings of the sea and the waves of pride. For we know that mundane glory and worldly cares usually do induce to pride, especially those who are in authority. They, in consequence, neglecting humility and seeking their own glory, always desire to dominate over their brothers. Wherefore to kings and emperors especially it is of advantage, when their mind tends to exalt itself and to delight in its own particular glory, to find out a means of humbling themselves and to be brought to realize that what they have been rejoicing in is the thing most to be feared. Let them, therefore, diligently consider how dangerous and how much to be feared the royal or imperial dignity is. For in it the fewest are saved; and those who, through the mercy of God, do come to salvation are not glorified in the holy church and in the judgment of the Holy Spirit to the same extent as many poor people. For, from the beginning of the world until these our own times, in the whole of authentic history we do not find seven emperors or kings whose lives were as distinguished for religion and as beautified by significant portents as those of an innumerable multitude who despised the world—although we believe many of them to have found mercy in the presence of God Almighty. For what emperor or king was ever honoured by miracles as were St. Martin, St Antony and St Benedict—not to mention the apostles and martyrs? And what emperor or king raised the dead, cleansed lepers, or healed the blind? See how the holy church praises and venerates the emperor Constantine of blessed memory, Theodosius and Honorius, Charles and Louis as lovers of justice, promoters of the Christian religion, defenders of the churches: it does not, however, declare them to have been resplendent with so great a glory of miracles. Moreover, for how many kings or emperors has the holy church ordered chapels or altars to be dedicated to their names, or masses to be celebrated in their honour? Let kings and other princes fear lest the more they rejoice at being placed over other men in this life, the more they will be subjected to eternal fires. For of them it is written: "The powerful shall powerfully suffer torments." And they are about to render account to God for as many men as they have had subjects under their dominion. But if it be no little task for any private religious man to guard his own soul: how much labour will there be for those who are rulers over many thousands of souls? Moreover, if the judgment of the holy church severely punishes a sinner for the slaying of one man, what will become of those who, for the sake of worldly glory, hand over many thousands to death? And such persons, although after having slain many they often say with their lips "I have sinned," nevertheless rejoice in their hearts at

having extended their fame as it were. And they are unwilling not to have done what they have done, nor do they
grieve at having driven their brothers into Tartarus. And,
so long as they do not repent with their whole heart and
are unwilling to let go what has been acquired or retained
through shedding of blood, their penitence before God will
remain without the worthy fruit of penitence. Surely,
therefore, they ought greatly to fear. And it should frequently be recalled to their memory that, as we have said,
in the different kingdoms of the earth, from the beginning
of the world, very few of the innumerable multitude of
kings are found to have been holy: whereas in one see
alone—the Roman one, namely—almost a hundred of the
successive pontiffs since the time of St. Peter the apostle are
counted among the most holy. Why, then, is this—except
that the kings and princes of the earth, enticed by vain
glory, prefer, as has been said, the things that are their own
to the things that are spiritual; but the pontiffs of the
church, despising vain glory, prefer to carnal things the
things that are of God? The former readily punish those
who sin against themselves and are indifferent to those who
sin against God; the latter quickly pardon those who sin
against themselves and do not lightly spare those who sin
against God. The former, too much bent on earthly deeds,
think slightingly of spiritual ones; the latter, sedulously
meditating on heavenly things, despise the things which
are of earth.

Therefore all Christians who desire to reign with Christ
should be warned not to strive to rule through ambition of
worldly power, but rather to keep in view what the blessed
Gregory, most holy pope, tells them to in his pastoral book
when he says: "Among these things, therefore, what is to
be striven for and what to be feared except that he who
surpasses in virtue shall be urged and shall come to rule,
and that he who is without virtues shall not be urged and
shall not come?" But if those who fear God come, when
urged, with great fear to the apostolic chair, in which those
who are duly ordained are made better by the merits of
the apostle St. Peter,—with how much fear and trembling
is the throne of the kingdom to be approached, where even
the good and humble—as is shown in the case of Saul and

David—become worse? For what we have said of the apostolic chair—we know it, too, by experience—is thus contained in the decrees of the blessed pope Symmachus: "He—St. Peter, namely—has sent down to posterity a perennial gift of merits together with a heritage of innocence." And a little further on: "For who can doubt that he is holy who is raised by the apex of so great a dignity? And, if the goods acquired by merit are lacking, those which are furnished by his predecessor suffice. For either he (St. Peter) exalts distinguished men to this summit, or he illumines those who are exalted."

Therefore let those whom holy church, of its own will and after proper counsel, not for transitory glory but for the salvation of many, calls to have rule or dominion, humbly obey. And let them always beware in that point as to which St. Gregory, in that same pastoral book bears witness: "Indeed, when a man disdains to be like to men, he is made like to an apostate angel. Thus Saul, after having possessed the merit of humility, came to be swelled with pride when at the summit of power. Through humility, indeed, he was advanced; through pride, reproved—God being witness who said: ' When thou wast small in thine own eyes, did I not make thee head over the tribes of Israel?' " And a little further on: " Moreover, strange to say, when he was small in his own eyes he was great in the eyes of God; but when he seemed great in his own eyes he was small in the eyes of God." Let them also carefully retain what God says in the gospel: " I do not seek my glory "; and, "He who wishes to be the first among you shall be the servant of all." Let them always prefer the honour of God to their own; let them cherish and guard justice by observing the rights of every man; let them not walk in the counsel of the ungodly but, with an assenting heart, always consort with good men. Let them not seek to subject to themselves or to subjugate the holy church as a handmaid; but chiefly let them strive, by recognizing the teachers and fathers, to honour in due form her eyes—namely the priests of God. For if we are ordered to honour our carnal fathers and mothers—how much more our spiritual ones! And if he who has cursed his carnal father or mother is to be punished with death—what does he merit who curses his spiritual father or mother? Let them not, enticed by carnal love, strive to place one of their own sons over the flock for which Christ poured forth His blood, if they can find some one who is better and more useful than he : lest, loving their son more than God, they inflict the greatest detriment on the holy church. For he who neglects to provide to the best of his ability for such a want—and, as it were, necessity—of holy mother church is openly convicted of not loving God and his neighbour as a Christian should.

For if this virtue—namely, love—has been neglected, no matter what good any one does he shall be without every fruit of salvation. And so by humbly doing these things, and by observing the love of God and of their neighbour as they ought, they may hope for the mercy of Him who said : " Learn of Me, for I am meek and lowly of heart." If they shall have humbly imitated Him they shall pass from this servile and transitory kingdom to a true kingdom of liberty and eternity.

15. *Negotiations between Paschal II. and Henry V.*, 1111.

(*a.*) Paschal's Privilege of the first Convention, Feb. 12th, 1111.

Bishop Paschal, servant of the servants of God. To his beloved son Henry and his successors, forever. It is both decreed against by the institutions of the divine law, and interdicted by the sacred canons, that priests should busy themselves with secular cases, or should go to the public court except to rescue the condemned, or for the sake of others who suffer injury. Wherefore also the apostle Paul says : " If ye have secular judgments constitute as judges those who are of low degree in the church." Moreover in portions of your kingdom bishops and abbots are so occupied by secular cares that they are compelled assiduously to frequent the court, and to perform military service. Which things, indeed, are scarcely if at all carried on without plunder, sacrilege, arson. For ministers of the altar are made ministers of the king's court ; inasmuch as they receive cities, duchies, margravates, monies and other

things which belong to the service of the king. Whence
also the custom has grown up—intolerably for the church
—that elected bishops should by no means receive consecration unless they had first been invested through the
hand of the king. From which cause both the wickedness
of simoniacal heresy and, at times, so great an ambition
has prevailed that the episcopal sees were invaded without
any previous election. At times, even, they have been invested while the bishops were alive. Aroused by these
and very many other evils which had happened for the
most part through investitures, our predecessors the pontiffs Gregory VII. and Urban II. of blessed memory,
frequently calling together episcopal councils did condemn
those investitures of the lay hand, and did decree that
those who should have obtained churches through them
should be deposed, and the donors also be deprived of
communion—according to that chapter of the apostolic
canons which runs thus : " If any bishop, employing the
powers of the world, do through them obtain a church : he
shall be deposed and isolated, as well as all who communi-
cate with him." Following in the traces of which (canons),
we also, in an episcopal council, have confirmed their sentence. And so, most beloved son, king Henry,—now
through our office, by the grace of God, emperor of the
Romans,—we decree that those royal appurtenances are to
be given back to thee and to thy kingdom which manifestly
belonged to that kingdom in the time of Charles, Louis,
and of thy other predecessors. We forbid, and under sentence of anathema prohibit, that any bishop or abbot, present or future, invade these same royal appurtenances. In
which are included the cities, duchies, margravates, counties, monies, toll, market, advowsons of the kingdom, rights
of the judges of the hundred courts, and the courts which
manifestly belonged to the king together with what pertained to them, the military posts and camps of the kingdom. Nor shall they henceforth, unless by favour of the king,
concern themselves with those royal appurtenances. But
neither shall it be allowed our successors, who shall follow
us in the apostolic chair, to disturb thee or thy kingdom
in this matter. Furthermore, we decree that the churches,
with the offerings and hereditary possessions which mani-

festly did not belong to the kingdom, shall remain free; as, on the day of thy coronation, in the sight of the whole church, thou didst promise that they should be. For it is fitting that the bishops, freed from secular cares, should take care of their people, and not any longer be absent from their churches. For, according to the apostle Paul, let them watch, being about to render account, as it were, for the souls of these (their people).

(b.) Paschal's Privilege of the second Convention, April 12th, 1111.

Bishop Paschal, servant of the servants of God, to his most beloved son in Christ, Henry, glorious king of the Germans, and, through the grace of Almighty God, august emperor of the Romans, greeting and apostolic benediction. The divine disposition has appointed that your kingdom should be singularly united with the holy Roman church. Your predecessors by reason of uprightness and greater virtue have obtained the crown of the city of Rome and the empire. To which dignity, viz.: that of the crown and the empire, the divine majesty has, most beloved son Henry, through the ministry of our priestship, brought thy person also. That prerogative, therefore, of dignity which our predecessors did grant to thy predecessors the catholic emperors, and did confirm by their charters, we also do concede to thee, beloved, and do confirm by the page of this present privilege: that, namely, thou may'st confer the investiture of staff and ring, freely, except through simony and with violence to the elected, on the bishops and abbots of thy kingdom. But after the investiture they shall receive the canonical consecration from the bishop to whom they belong. If any one, moreover, without thy consent, shall have been elected by the clergy and people, he shall be consecrated by no one unless he be invested by thee. Bishops and archbishops, indeed, shall have the right of canonically consecrating bishops or abbots invested by thee. For your predecessors have enriched the churches of their kingdom with such benefits from their royal appurtenances, that the kingdom itself should seek its chief safety in protecting the bishops and abbots; and popular dissensions, which often happen at elections, should be restrained by the royal majesty. Wherefore the attention of thy prudence and power ought the more carefully to be applied to this end: that the greatness of the Roman, and the safety of the other churches, should be preserved through still greater benefits—God granting them. Therefore if any person, secular or ecclesiastical, knowing this page of our concession, shall with bold daring strive to act against it: he shall, unless he come to his senses, be entwined in the chain of the anathema, and shall suffer the risk of losing his honour and dignity. The divine mercy, moreover, shall guard those observing it, and shall permit thy person and power happily to reign to His honour and glory. Amen.

16. *Concordat of Worms, Sept. 23rd,* 1122.

(*a.*) Privilege of Pope Calixtus II.

I, bishop Calixtus, servant of the servants of God, do grant to thee beloved son, Henry—by the grace of God august emperor of the Romans—that the elections of the bishops and abbots of the German kingdom, who belong to the kingdom, shall take place in thy presence, without simony and without any violence; so that if any discord shall arise between the parties concerned, thou, by the counsel or judgment of the metropolitan and the co-provincials, may'st give consent and aid to the party which has the more right. The one elected, moreover, without any exaction may receive the regalia from thee through the lance, and shall do unto thee for these what he rightfully should. But he who is consecrated in the other parts of thy empire (*i.e.* Burgundy and Italy) shall, within six months, and without any exaction, receive the regalia from thee through the lance, and shall do unto thee for these what he rightfully should. Excepting all things which are known to belong to the Roman church. Concerning matters, however, in which thou dost make complaint to me, and dost demand aid,—I, according to the duty of my office, will furnish aid to thee. I give unto thee true peace, and to all who are or have been on thy side in the time of this discord.

(b.) Edict of the Emperor Henry IV.

In the name of the holy and indivisible Trinity, I, Henry, by the grace of God august emperor of the Romans, for the love of God and of the holy Roman church and of our master pope Calixtus, and for the healing of my soul, do remit to God, and to the holy apostles of God, Peter and Paul, and to the holy catholic church, all investiture through ring and staff; and do grant that in all the churches that are in my kingdom or empire there may be canonical election and free consecration. All the possessions and regalia of St. Peter which, from the beginning of this discord unto this day, whether in the time of my father or also in mine, have been abstracted, and which I hold : I restore to that same holy Roman church. As to those things, moreover, which I do not hold, I will faithfully aid in their restoration. As to the possessions also of all other churches and princes, and of all others lay and clerical persons which have been lost in that war: according to the counsel of the princes, or according to justice, I will restore the things that I hold ; and of those things which I do not hold I will faithfully aid in the restoration. And I grant true peace to our master pope Calixtus, and to the holy Roman church, and to all those who are or have been on its side. And in matters where the holy Roman church shall demand aid I will grant it; and in matters concerning which it shall make complaint to me I will duly grant to it justice. All these things have been done by the consent and counsel of the princes. Whose names are here adjoined : Adalbert archbishop of Mainz; F. archbishop of Cologne; H. bishop of Ratisbon; O. bishop of Bamberg; B. bishop of Spires ; H. of Augsburg; G. of Utrecht ; Ou. of Constance ; E. abbot of Fulda ; Henry, duke ; Frederick, duke; S. duke ; Pertolf, duke ; Margrave Teipold ; Margrave Engelbert ; Godfrey, count Palatine; Otto, count Palatine ; Berengar, count.

I, Frederick, archbishop of Cologne and archchancellor, have given my recognizances.

III.

THE VESANCON EPISODE.

(Doeberl: "Monumenta Germaniae Selecta," vol. iv.
pp. 107-115.)

(a.) Letter of Adrian IV. to Barbarossa, Sept. 20th, 1157.

Bishop Adrian, servant of the servants of God, to his
beloved son Frederick, illustrious emperor of the Romans,
—greeting and apostolic benediction.   A few days ago we
remember to have written to thy imperial Majesty recal-
ling to thy Highness's memory that, as we believe, that
horrid and execrable crime and impious deed of evil committed in our time in Germany had remained for some
time uninvestigated,—and observing, not without great
wonder, that thou had'st allowed the barbarity of so pernicious a crime to pass until now without taking the severe
vengeance that was fitting.   For in what manner our
venerable brother Eskill, archbishop of Lyon, while returning from the apostolic see, was captured in that land
by certain impious and godless men—we cannot speak of
it without great grief of mind,—and is at present kept in
custody ; how, moreover, in the aforesaid capture the impious men, the seeds of evil, the sons of crime did violently
and with drawn swords rise against him and his followers ;
and how vilely and disgracefully they treated them, taking
away all that they had :—thy serene Highness knows on
the one hand, and, on the other, the fame of so great an
outrage has already reached the most distant and most
unapproachable regions.   In vengeance of which most
violent crime, as one to whom, as we believe, good things
are pleasing and evil ones displeasing, thou should'st have
arisen with more steadfastness ; and the sword, which was
given thee by divine concession to punish evil-doers but to
exalt the good, ought to have raged above the neck of the
impious and most sternly to have destroyed the presump-
tuous.   But thou art said so to have hushed this up—or
rather to have neglected it—that they have no reason to
repent of having committed the deed, inasmuch as they

already feel that they have gained immunity for the sacrilege which they committed. As to the cause of this dissimulation or negligence we are entirely ignorant, since no scruple of conscience accuses our mind of having offended thy serene Highness in any respect; but we have always loved thy person as that of our most dear and special son, and the most Christian prince, whose power we do not doubt to have been founded by the grace of God on the rock of the apostolic confession. And we have treated thee always with the partiality of due benignity. For thou should'st, oh most glorious son, bring before the eyes of thy mind how graciously and how joyfully thy mother the holy Roman church received thee in a former year; with what affection of heart she treated thee; what plenitude of dignity and honour she granted thee; and how, *most willingly conferring upon thee the distinction of the imperial crown*, she strove to cherish in her most bountiful lap thee at the summit of thy sublimity—doing nothing at all which she knew would even in the least be contrary to the royal will. Nor, indeed, do we repent having fulfilled in all things the desires of thy heart, but would, not without right, rejoice if thy excellency had received from our hand even greater *benefices* (beneficia), if that were possible; knowing, as we do, what great increase and advantage can come through thee to the church of God and to us. But now, since thou dost seem to neglect and gloss over so monstrous a crime—which is known, indeed, to have been committed to the shame of the universal church and of thy empire—we suspect and likewise fear lest perhaps thy mind has been led to this dissimulation and neglect for the reason that, at the suggestion of a perverse man sowing discord, thou hast conceived against thy most lenient mother the most holy Roman church, and against our own person, some indignation or rancour—which God forbid! On account of this, therefore, and of other matters which we know to be pressing upon us, we have seen fit at present to despatch to thy serenity from our side two of the best and most beloved men whom we have about us, our dear sons, namely, Bernard, cardinal presbyter of St. Clement, and Roland, cardinal presbyter of the title of St. Mark and our own chancellor—as being men who are conspicuous for their religion and prudence and honesty. And we most urgently request thy Highness to receive them honourably as well as kindly, to treat them fairly and to receive without hesitation, as though proceeding from our lips, whatever they say on our part to thy imperial Majesty concerning this matter and concerning other things which pertain to the honour of God and of the holy Roman church, and also to the glory and exaltation of the empire. And do not doubt to lend faith to their words as though we ourselves had happened to utter them.

(b.) *Manifesto of the Emperor, Oct.* 1157.

Inasmuch as the divine power, from which is every power in Heaven and on earth, has committed to us, his anointed, the kingdom and the empire to be ruled over, and has ordained that the peace of the church shall be preserved by the arms of the empire,—not without extreme grief of heart are we compelled to complain to you, beloved, that, from the head of the holy church on which Christ impressed the character of his peace and love, causes of dissension, seeds of evil, the poison of a pestiferous disease seem to emanate. Through these, unless God avert it, we fear that the whole body of the church will be tainted, the unity riven, a schism be brought about between the kingdom and the priesthood. For recently, while we were holding court at Vesançon and with due watchfulness were treating of the honour of the empire and of the safety of the church, there came apostolic legates asserting that they brought such message to our majesty that from it the honour of our empire should receive no little increase. When, on the first day of their coming, we had honourably received them, and, on the second, as is the custom, we sat together with our princes to listen to their report,—they, as if inflated with the mammon of unrighteousness, out of the height of their pride, from the summit of their arrogance, in the execrable elation of their swelling hearts, did present to us a message in the form of an apostolic letter, the tenor of which was that we should always keep it before our mind's eye how

the lord pope had *conferred* upon us the distinction of the
imperial crown and that he would not regret it if our
Highness were to receive from him even greater *benefices.*
This was that message of paternal sweetness which was to
foster the unity of church and empire, which strove to
bind together both with a bond of peace, which enticed
the minds of the hearers to the concord and obedience of
both. Of a truth at that word, blasphemous and devoid
of all truth, not only did the imperial majesty conceive a
righteous indignation, but also all the princes who were
present were filled with such fury and wrath that, without
doubt, they would have condemned those two unhallowed
presbyters to the punishment of death had not our presence
prevented them. Whereupon, since many similar letters
were found upon them, and sealed forms to be filled out
afterwards at their discretion—by means of which, as has
hitherto been their custom, they intended to strive throughout all the churches of the kingdom of Germany, to scatter
the virus conceived by their iniquity, to denude the altars,
to carry away the vessels of the house of God, to strip the
crosses : lest an opportunity should be given them of
proceeding further, we caused them to return to Rome by
the way on which they had come. And, inasmuch as the
kingdom, together with the empire, is ours by the election
of the princes from God alone, who, by the passion of His
Son Christ subjected the world to the rule of the two
necessary swords ; and since the apostle Peter informed
the world with this teaching, "Fear God, honour the
king" : whoever shall say that we received the imperial
crown as a benefice from the lord pope, contradicts the
divine institutions and the teaching of Peter, and shall be
guilty of a lie. Since, moreover, we have hitherto striven
to rescue from the hands of the Egyptians the honour and
liberty of the church which has long been oppressed by
the yoke of an undue servitude, and are striving to preserve to it all the prerogatives of its dignity : we ask you
as one to condole with us over such ignominy inflicted on
us and on the empire, trusting that the undivided sincerity
of your faith will not permit the honour of the empire,
which, from the foundation of Rome and the establishment
of the Christian religion up to your own times has remained

glorious and undiminished,[1] to be lessened by so unheard of an innovation. And be it known beyond the shadow of a doubt, that we would rather incur danger of death than in our day to sustain the shame of so great a disaster.

(c.) *Letter of Adrian IV. to the German Bishops.*

As often as any thing is attempted in the church against the honour of God and the salvation of the faithful, it ought to be the care of our brothers and fellow bishops— and especially of those who are impelled by the spirit of God—to discover a means of correction pleasing to God for the evil things that have been done. In the present time, indeed,—a thing which we can not mention without extreme grief,—our most beloved son, Frederick emperor of the Romans, has done a thing such as we do not read to have ever been perpetrated in the times of our predecessors. For when we had sent to his presence two of our best brothers, Bernard, namely, of the title of St. Clement, and Roland our chancellor, of the title of St. Mark, cardinal presbyters,—he, when they first came into his presence, received them with open arms. But, on the following day, when they returned to him and our letter was read before him, exception being taken at a certain word which was contained in the course of that letter, viz. : " we conferred upon thee the ' beneficium ' of a crown," he burst forth into a fit of such anger that it is shameful to hear and grievous to mention the insults which he is said to have heaped upon us and our legates, and to relate how disgracefully he compelled them to retire from his presence and swiftly to depart from his land. And when, moreover, they had left his presence, passing an edict that no one from your land should go to the apostolic see, he is said to have placed guards at all the boundaries of that kingdom who should turn back with violence those who wished to approach the apostolic see. Although we were somewhat disturbed by this measure, nevertheless we personally

---

[1] This passage is an excellent illustration of the fact, so often insisted upon by Mr. Freeman, that there is no break in the continuity of history, and that the mediæval emperors considered themselves the direct successors of the Cæsars.

received the greater consolation from the fact that it did not proceed from the counsel of yourselves and the princes. Wherefore we trust that he can easily be recalled from his anger of mind by your counsel and persuasion. And so, beloved brothers, since in this matter not only our interest but yours and that of all the churches is known to be at stake, we urge and exhort ye in the Lord, that ye oppose yourselves as a wall of protection before the house of God and that ye strive to bring back, as quickly as possible, our aforesaid son to the right path—paying most particular heed to this, that he cause so great and such evident satisfaction to be rendered by Rainald his chancellor and by the count Palatine who presumed to vomit forth great blasphemies against our aforesaid legates and your mother also, the holy Roman church, that, according as the bitterness of their words offended the ears of many, so also their atonement may recall many to the right path. Let not this same son of ours acquiesce in the counsels of the wicked; let him consider the newest laws and the old, and let him tread the path along which Justinian and the other catholic emperors are known to have passed. By their example, indeed, and by imitating them, he will be able to heap up for himself honour upon earth and felicity in Heaven. But ye also, if ye bring him back to the right path, shall both perform a service pleasing to St. Peter the prince of the apostles and will preserve your own and your churches' liberty. Otherwise let our aforesaid son know from your admonitions, let him know from the truth of the promise of the gospel—that the holy Roman church is founded on a most firm rock, God placing it there; and that, no matter by how great a whirlwind of words it may be shaken, it will remain firm, God protecting it, throughout all the ages. He ought not, as ye know, to have entered upon so arduous a path without your advice; whence we believe that, hearing your warnings, like a discreet man and catholic emperor, he may most easily be recalled to the enjoyment of a more healthful pursuit.

(d.) *Letter of the German Bishops to the Pope.*

Although we know and are sure that neither the winds nor the waves of tempests can cast down the church of God which is founded on a firm rock: we, nevertheless, being very weak and timid, are shaken and tremble whenever such attacks occur. Wherefore we are very gravely disturbed and frightened concerning those things which seem about to furnish, unless God avert it, a fruitful source of great evil between your Holiness and your most devoted son our lord emperor. Indeed, by those words which were contained in the letter which you sent through your most prudent and honest envoys, master Bernard and master Roland the chancellor, venerable cardinal presbyters, the whole public of our empire has been set in commotion. The ears of the imperial power were not able to hear them patiently nor the ears of the princes to bear them. All present were so deaf to them, that we, saving thy grace, most holy father, on account of the sinister interpretation which their ambiguity permits, do neither dare, nor are we able, to defend or to approve them by any form of consent,—for the reason that they are unusual and have not been heard of up to the present time. Receiving with due reverence, however, and putting into effect the letter which you did send to us, we did admonish your son, our lord emperor, as you did order; and, thanks be to God, we received from him such reply as became a catholic prince. It was to this effect: "There are two things by which our empire ought to be ruled, the holy laws of the emperors and the good customs of our predecessors and fathers. We will not and can not go beyond those limits placed for the church; whatever is counter to them we do not receive. We willingly exhibit due reverence to our father; we look upon the free crown of our empire as a divine benefice alone; we acknowledge that the first vote in the election belongs to the archbishop of Mainz, the remaining ones to the other princes in order; that the royal anointing pertains to the archbishop of Cologne, but the highest, which is the imperial, to the supreme pontiff. Whatever there is besides these is super-

fluous, is evil. It was not in contempt of our most beloved and most reverent father and consecrator that we
compelled the cardinals to depart from the confines of our
land. But with those things and on account of those
things which they bore in writing, or about to be filled in
to the disgrace and scandal of our empire, we could not
permit them to proceed further. The exits and entrances
of Italy we neither closed by an edict nor do we wish in
any way to close them to pilgrims or to those approaching
the Roman see for their reasonable necessities with testimonials from their bishops and prelates. But we do
intend to oppose those abuses through which all the
churches of our land are oppressed and worn out, and
almost all monastic discipline is dead and buried. God,
through the emperor, has exalted the church to be at the
head of the world; at the head of the world the church,
not through God, as we believe, now tries to demolish the
empire. It began with a picture;[1] from a picture it went
on to a letter; from a letter it tries to go on to authority.
We shall not suffer it, we shall not permit it. We will
rather lay aside the crown than to consent that the crown,
together with ourselves, be so abased. Let the pictures
be obliterated, the writings retracted, so that they may
not remain eternal sources of discord between the kingdom
and the priesthood." These and other things, concerning
the peace with Roger and William of Sicily and the other
conventions which have been drawn up in Italy, which we
do not dare to give in full, we heard from the lips of our
lord emperor. The count Palatine, moreover, being absent,
having been already sent ahead to prepare for an expedition into Italy,—we heard nothing from the chancellor,
who was still present there, that did not savour of humility
and peace except that he stood by those men in the danger
to their lives that threatened them from the people. And

[1] The picture referred to is described in the Cologne Annals
(Mon. Ger. xvii. 766). Innocent II. sits upon a throne, while
King Lothar, Frederick's predecessor, bends before him with folded
hands to receive the crown of the empire. Underneath was written,
as we learn from Ragewin, iii. 10: "The king comes before the
gates, first swearing to preserve the rights of the city. He is
afterwards made the pope's vassal, and takes the crown which he
gives."

all who were present testify as to this same fact. For the rest we humbly beg and beseech your holiness to spare our weakness, to soothe like a good pastor your high-souled son by writings which shall sweeten your former writings with honeyed suavity; so that both the church of God may rejoice in tranquil devotion, and that the empire may be raised still higher in its lofty position, He himself mediating and helping—Jesus Christ, who, as mediator between God and men, was made man.

(e.) *Letter of Adrian IV. to the Emperor, Feb.,* 1158.

From the time when, God disposing as it pleased himself, we received the charge of the universal church, we have so taken care to honour thy Highness that, from day to day, thy mind ought to have been inflamed more and more with love for us and with veneration for the apostolic see. Wherefore we can not hear without great astonishment that when—having heard from the suggestions of certain men that thy anger was somewhat aroused against us—in order to learn thy will we sent to thy presence two of our best and greatest brothers, the chancellor Roland, namely, of the title of St Mark, and Bernard of the title of St Clement, cardinal presbyters, who had always been most concerned for the honour of thy Majesty in the Roman church: they were treated otherwise than was becoming to the imperial magnificence. On account of a certain word, indeed,—" beneficium," namely—thy mind is said to have been moved to anger; which word ought not by any means to have aroused the ire of so great a man, nor even of any lesser man. For although this word—namely, " beneficium "—is used by some in a sense different from that which it has by derivation, it should, nevertheless, have been accepted in that sense which we ourselves attri-buted to it and which it is known to retain from its origin. For this word is derived from " bonus " and " factum," and a " beneficium " is called by us not " a fief " but a " bonum factum." It is found in this signification in the whole body of Holy Scripture, where it speaks of the " beneficium " of God not as of a fief but as a benediction and good deed of His by which we are said to be governed and nourished. And thy Magnificence, indeed, clearly recognizes that we did so well and so honourably place the mark of the imperial dignity upon thy head that it may be considered by all a "bonum factum." Wherefore when some have tried to distort from its own to another significa-tion this word and that other one, namely: "we have conferred (contulimus) upon thee the distinction of the imperial crown," they have done this not upon the merits of the case, but of their own will and at the suggestion of those who by no means cherish the peace of the kingdom and the church. For by this word "contulimus" we mean nothing else than what we said above, "imposuimus." But that thou didst afterwards, as it is said, order ecclesi-astics to be restrained from visiting, as they ought, the holy Roman church,—if this is so, thy discretion, as we hope, O dearest Son in Christ, recognizes how wrongly this was done. For if thou didst have against us anything of bitterness, thou should'st have intimated it to us through thy envoys and letters and we would have taken care to provide for thy honour, as for that of our dearest son. Now, indeed, at the instigation of our beloved son, Henry duke of Bavaria and Saxony, we send into thy presence two of our brothers, Henry of the title of Sts. Nereus and Achilles, presbyter, and Jacinctus deacon of St. Mary in Cosmide—both cardinals, prudent and honest men, indeed. And we urge and exhort thy Highness in the Lord to re-ceive them honestly and kindly. And thy Excellency may know that what shall be intimated by them on our part to thy Magnificence has proceeded from the sincerity of our heart; and, on the ground of this, through the mediation of the aforesaid duke, our son, may thy Highness strive to come to an agreement with them, so that between thee and thy mother the holy Roman church no soil for the seeds of discord may henceforth remain.

IV.

THE STRUGGLE BETWEEN FREDERICK BAR-BAROSSA AND ALEXANDER III.

(Doeberl iv. pp. 165-247.)

(a.) *Epistola Minor of the Council of Pavia, Feb. 5-11,*
1160 A.D.   (Encyclic.)

Inasmuch as the turmoil in which the apostolic see has been involved has exceedingly wounded the hearts of Christians, we, who have congregated at Pavia to heal the schisms and to restore the peace of the church, have thought best fully to intimate to all of you the nature of the case and the manner of procedure and the ruling of the holy council. We do this in order that the facts shown forth simply and truly in the present writing may forcibly expel any false impressions which the hearers may have conceived, and that henceforth they may not be deceived by schismatic writings.

When, therefore, all of the orthodox congregated at Pavia in the name of the Lord had taken their seats, the case was lawfully and canonically tried and diligently investigated during 7 successive days. And it was sufficiently and canonically proved in the eyes of the council through capable witnesses, that, in the church of St Peter, our lord pope Victor and no other had been elected and solemnly enmantled by the sounder part of the cardinals—at the request of the people and with the consent and at the desire of the clergy; and that, Roland the former chancellor being present and not objecting, he was placed in the chair of St Peter; and that there, by the clergy of Rome and the cardinals, a grand Te Deum was sung to him; and that thence, wearing the stoles and other papal insignia, he was led to the palace.

And the clergy and people being asked according to custom by the notary if they agreed, replied thrice with a loud voice: " We agree."

It was proved also that Roland, on the twelfth day after the promotion of pope Victor, going forth from Rome was first enmantled at Cisterna where once the emperor Nero, an exile from the city, remained in hiding. It was proved that Roland, being interrogated by the rectors of the Roman clergy and the clergy of his cardinalate as to whether they were to obey pope Victor,—expressly confessed that he himself had never been enmantled, and expressly said: Go and obey him whom you shall see to be enmantled. . . . .

Then the venerable bishops Hermann of Verden, Daniel of Prague and Otto count Palatine, and master Herbert, provost, whom the lord emperor, by the advice of 22 bishops and the Cistercian and Clairvaux abbots and other monks there present, had sent to Rome to summon the parties before the council at Pavia, gave testimony in the sight of the council that they had summoned before the presence of the church congregated at Pavia, through three edicts at intervals, peremptorily and solemnly, all secular influence being removed, Roland the chancellor and his party; and that Roland the chancellor and his party with loud voice and with their own lips manifestly declared that they were unwilling to accept any judgment or investigation from the church. . . . .

Being sufficiently instructed, therefore, from all these things, and the truth being fully declared on both sides, it pleased the reverend council that the election of pope Victor, who, like a gentle and innocent lamb had come to humbly receive the judgment of the church, should be approved and confirmed, and the election of Roland should be altogether cancelled. And this was done.

The election of pope Victor, then, after all secular influence had been removed and the grace of the Holy Spirit invoked, being confirmed and accepted,—the most Christian emperor, last, after all the bishops and after all the clergy, by the advice and petition of the council, accepted and approved the election of pope Victor. And, after him, all the princes and an innumerable multitude of men who were present, being asked three times if they agreed, replied, rejoicing with loud voice: "We agree."

On the following day—that is, on the first Saturday in Lent—pope Victor was led with honour in procession from the church of St. Salvatore without the city, where he had

been harboured, to the universal church. There the most
holy emperor received him before the gates of the church,
and, as he descended from his horse, humbly held his
stirrup, and, taking his hand, led him to the altar and
kissed his feet. And all of us—the patriarch, the archbishops, bishops and abbots and all the princes as well as
the whole multitude that was present—kissed the feet of
the pope. And on the next day—the Sabbath, namely—a
general council being held, the lord pope and we with him,
with blazing candles anathematized Roland the chancellor
as schismatic, and likewise his chief supporters ; and we
handed him over to Satan unto the death of the flesh, that
his spirit might be safe at the day of the Lord.

We wish, moreover, that it be not hidden from your
prudent discernment that Roland the chancellor and certain cardinals of his following had formed a conspiracy
while pope Adrian was still alive. The tenor of this conspiracy was, moreover, that if pope Adrian should happen
to die while they were still living, they should elect one
cardinal from those who were banded together in that
conspiracy.

For the rest, on the part of Almighty God, and of the
blessed apostles Peter and Paul, and of all the saints, and
of the orthodox men who have come together by the divine
will to heal the schism, we humbly implore and admonish
all of you in Christ, that, all doubt and ambiguity being
removed, you will irrefragably confirm and hold fast those
things which the church of God congregated at Pavia has
faithfully ordained for the honour of the Creator and for
the tranquillity of your mother the holy Roman church and
for the salvation of all Christians. And we pray that our
Redeemer Christ Jesus may long preserve the universal
pontiff, our pope Victor, in whose sanctity and religion we
altogether trust ; and that He will grant to him all tranquillity and peace, so that, through him, Almighty God
shall be honoured and the Roman church and the whole
Christian religion may receive an increase pleasing to God.
In order, moreover, that our action may have more weight
with those who read this we have thought best to subscribe
the consent and the names of all of us. I, Peregrin,
patriarch of Aquileija, etc. etc.

*(b.) Letter of John of Salisbury concerning the Council of
Pavia. June, 1160.*

To his master and dearest friend Randolf de Serres,
John of Salisbury sends greeting and whatever there is
better than that. I do not doubt thee to be a sharer, my
beloved, in our difficulties; for the cause which troubles us
is not different or dissimilar, although it affects us diffe-
rently and dissimilarly. For we, from near by, receive in
our hands the arrows of raging fortune, and always before
our eyes there is matter for continual labour and grief and
sorrow. Our bitter lot gives us no time or place for happiness or rest, hardly is even a faint hope of solace left to
us. And that is from God; for now, indeed, we despair of
human help. Want of means, indeed, oppresses me on
account of weight of debt and of the importunity of my
creditors; but grief obliterates this care, and the inroad of
a stronger and a public fear swallows up all that is private.
Thou thyself dost feel also what I feel; what I say, thou
dost, I think, say to thyself in continual meditation; and,
with circumspect mind thou dost anticipate the sad word
which I am about to speak. For thou also, unless thou
dost put off thyself, art with viligant and continual care
occupied with our labours and griefs, inasmuch as thou art
troubled with the misfortune of our common master. For
whilst thou dost look upon the disasters of the universal
church from whose breasts we are nourished, dost weigh
the matter, dost measure the dangers,—the meditation
adds grief to grief, grief such as thou canst not bear.
Nevertheless in all this thou hast been more gently treated
than I. for thou having obtained the lot of a more inde-
pendent condition, art not compelled to be present and to
weep at every breath and at every hour, and at every complaint of a desolate family; nor dost thou by any means
fear that there is hanging over thee either exile or the
necessity of committing some infamous crime. For thou
dost live under a prince who is thought of with joy and
benediction.[1] We, however, fear beyond measure lest the

---

[1] Louis VII. of France.

German emperor circumvent and subvert with his wiles
the serenity of our prince.[1] It seems to me to make
very little difference whom the presumption of the little
Pavian convention supports, unless that the election of
Alexander, if any one doubted of it, is confirmed by the
very testimony of the opposing party.

To pass over the rashness of one who has presumed to
judge the Roman church which is reserved for the judgment of God alone, and who, when he ought to have been
excommunicated—as the disgraceful treatment of the
cardinals at Vesançon shows—cited through a peremptory
edict before his judgment seat two men, and, having
already made up his mind as to the sentence, greeted one
with the name of his old office and dignity, the other with
the appellation of Roman pontiff, revealing to the senators
and people his secret inclination : whatever has been done
at Pavia is found to be contrary, as well to common fair-
ness, as to the lawful constitutions and sanctions of the
fathers. Of course the absent were condemned, and in a
case which was not investigated, nay, which had no right
to be investigated there, or in that way, or by such men,—
impudently and imprudently and iniquitously, a sentence
was hurriedly given.

But perhaps one ought to say "those who absented
themselves," rather than "the absent." Surely so, for
those men ignore or pretend to ignore the privilege of the
holy Roman church. Who has subjected the universal
church to the judgment of a single church ? Who has
constituted the Germans judges of the nations ? Who has
conferred authority on these brutal and impetuous men of
electing at their will a prince over the sons of men ? And,
indeed, their fury has often attempted this, but, God
bringing it about, it has often had to blush, prostrate and
confused, over its iniquity. But I know what this German
is attempting. For I was at Rome, under the rule of the
blessed Eugenius, when, in the first embassy sent at the
beginning of his reign, his intolerable pride and incautious
tongue displayed such daring impudence. For he promised
that he would reform the rule of the whole world, and

[1] Henry II. of England.

subject the world to Rome, and, sure of success, would conquer all things,—if only the favour of the Roman pontiff would aid him in this.   And this he did in order that against whomever he, the emperor, declaring war, should draw the material sword,—against the same the Roman pontiff should draw the spiritual sword.   He did not find any one hitherto who would consent to such iniquity, and, Moses himself opposing—*i.e.* the law of God contradicting—he raised up for himself a Balaamitic pontiff, through whom he might curse the people of God ; the son of malediction (Antichrist), therefore, for the designation and reception of whom, through many generations, from the first father of the family down to him for whom it was reserved, the name and cognomen of " accursed " has been invented.   And perhaps, for the purging and probation of the Roman church, the attack of the Germans, like that of the Canaanite, has been left to hang over it forever, —in order that for her own improvement he should make her uneasy, himself being conquered and giving way ; and that she herself, after her triumph, should be restored more pleasing and more glorious to the embraces of her Spouse.   And so to the renown of the fathers,—witness the Lateran palace where even lay men read this in visible pictures—to the renown of the fathers, the schismatics whom the secular power thrusts in are given to the pontiffs as a foot stool, and posterity looks back with triumph to their memory. . . . .

(c.) *The Peace of Venice,* 1177.

1. The lord emperor Frederick, according as he has received the lord pope Alexander as catholic and universal pope, so he will exhibit to him due reverence, just as his, Frederick's, catholic predecessors have exhibited it to his, Alexander's, catholic predecessors.   He will also exhibit the same reverence to the pope's successors who shall be catholically enthroned.

2. And the lord emperor will truly restore peace as well to the lord pope Alexander, as to all his successors and to the whole Roman church.

3. Every possession and holding, moreover, whether of

a prefecture or of any other thing, which the Roman church enjoyed and which he took away of himself or through others, he will restore in good faith ; saving all the rights of the empire. The Roman church also will restore in good faith, every possession and holding which it took away from him through itself or through others ; saving all the rights of the Roman church.

4. The possessions also which the lord emperor shall restore, he will also aid in retaining.

5. Likewise also all the vassals of the church whom, by reason of the schism, the lord emperor took away or received, the lord emperor will release and will restore to the lord pope Alexander and to the Roman church.

6. Moreover the lord emperor and the lord pope will mutually aid each other in preserving the honour and rights of the church and the empire ; the lord pope as a benignant father will aid his devoted and most beloved son, the most Christian emperor,—and the lord emperor, on the other hand, as a devoted son and most Christian emperor, will aid his beloved and reverend father, the vicar of St. Peter.

7. Whatever things, moreover, at the time of the schism and by reason of it, or without judicial proceedings, have been taken away from the church by the lord emperor or his followers, shall be restored to it.

8. The empress also will receive the lord pope Alexander as catholic and universal pope. The lord king Henry, their son, will likewise receive him and will show due reverence to him and his catholic successors, and the oath which the lord emperor shall take, he also will take.

9. The lord emperor and the lord king Henry, his son, closes a true peace with the illustrious king of Sicily for 15 years, as has been ordained and put in writing by the mediators of the peace.

10. He closes also a true peace with the emperor of Constantinople and all the aiders of the Roman church, and he will make no evil return to them, either through himself or through his followers, for the service conferred on the Roman church.

11. Concerning the complaints and controversies, moreover, which, before the time of pope Adrian were at issue

between the church and the empire, mediators shall be
constituted on the part of the lord pope and the lord emperor, to whom it shall be given over to terminate the
same through a judgment or through an agreement.   But
if the aforesaid mediators can not agree the matters shall
be terminated by the judgment of the lord pope and the
lord emperor, or of him or of them whom they shall choose
for this purpose.

12. To Christian, moreover, the said chancellor, the
archbishopric of Mainz, but to Philip the archbishopric of
Cologne shall be granted ; and they shall be confirmed to
them with all the plenitude of the archiepiscopal dignity
and office.   And the first archbishopric which shall be
vacant in the German realm shall be assigned to master
Conrad by the authority of the lord pope and the aid of
the lord emperor, if, however, it seem suitable for him.

13. To him also who is called Calixtus one abbey shall
be given.   Those, moreover, who were called his cardinals
shall return to the places which they held before, unless
they had renounced them by their own will or judgment ;
and they shall be left in the grades which they had before
the schism.

14. Gero, moreover, now called bishop of Halberstadt,
shall be unconditionally deposed, and Ulrich, the true
bishop of Halberstadt, shall be restored.   Alienations
made and benefices given by Gero, and likewise by all in-
truders, shall be cancelled by the authority of the lord
pope and the lord emperor and shall be restored to their
churches.

15. Concerning the election of the Brandenburg bishop
who had been elected to the Bremen archbishopric an investigation shall be made, and, if it shall be found canonical, he shall be transferred to that church.   And whatever
things have been alienated or given as benefices by Baldwin
who now rules over the Bremen church, shall be restored
to that church as shall be canonical and just.

16. Likewise what was taken from the Salzburg church
at the time of the schism, shall be restored to it in full.

17. All the clergy who belong to Italy or to other
regions outside of the German realm, shall be left to the
disposition and judgment of the lord pope Alexander and

his successors. But if it please the lord emperor to ask for a continuance in their grades of some who canonically received them, he shall be heard to the extent of 10 or 12, if he wish to insist.

18. Garsidonius, moreover, of Mantua, shall be restored to his former bishopric, in such way, however, that he who now is bishop of Mantua shall, by the authority of the lord pope and the aid of the lord emperor, be transferred to the bishopric of Trent; unless, perchance, it shall be agreed between the lord pope and the lord emperor, that provision shall be made for him in another bishopric.

19. The archpresbyter of Sacco, moreover, shall be restored in all plenitude to his former archpresbytery and to the other benefices which he had before the schism.

20. All those ordained by any former primates, or by their delegates, in the realm of Germany, shall be restored to the grades thus received; nor shall they be oppressed by reason of this schism.

21. Concerning, moreover, the said bishops of Strassburg and Basel, who were ordained by Guido of Crema, the matter shall, in that same realm, be committed by the aforesaid mediators to 10 or 8 men whom they themselves shall choose; and these shall swear on oath that they will give such counsel of their own accord to the Roman pontiff and the lord emperor, as they find that they can give according to the canons; without danger, namely, to the souls of the lord emperor and the lord pope and their own; and the lord pope will acquiesce in their counsel.

22. The lord pope, moreover, and all the cardinals, just as they have received the lord emperor Frederick as Roman and catholic emperor, so they will receive Beatrix his serene wife as catholic and Roman empress, Provided, however, that she shall be crowned by the lord pope Alexander or by his legate. They will receive, moreover, the lord Henry their son as catholic king.

23. The lord pope and the cardinals will close a true peace with the lord emperor Frederick and the empress Beatrix, and king Henry their son, and all their supporters, save as to the spiritual matters which by the present writing are left to the disposition and judgment of the

lord pope Alexander, and saving all the rights of the
Roman church against the detainers of the possessions of
St. Peter, and saving those things which are prescribed
above as well on the part of the church as on the part of
the lord emperor and of the empire.

24. Moreover the lord pope promises that he will observe the above peace to the letter, and so will all the
cardinals ; and he shall cause a document to be drawn up
to this effect, signed by all the cardinals.   The cardinals
themselves, also, shall draw up a writing in confirmation
of the above peace, and will place their seals to it.

25. And the lord pope, calling together a council as
quickly as it can be done, shall, together with the cardinal
bishops and the monks and ecclesiastics who shall be present, declare the excommunication against all who shall
attempt to infringe this peace.   Then in a general council
he shall do the same.

26. Many also of the Roman nobles and the chief lords
of the Campagna shall confirm this peace with an oath.

27. The emperor, moreover, shall confirm with his own
oath and that of the princes, the aforesaid peace with the
church, and the aforesaid peace of 15 years with the illustrious king of Sicily, and the truce with the Lombards,—
for six years, namely, from the Calends of next August ;
and he shall cause the Lombards who are of his party to
confirm this same truce, as has been arranged and put
down in the general wording of the truce.   But if there
shall be any one in the party of the emperor who shall refuse to swear to the aforesaid truce, the emperor shall command all who are of his party, by the fealty due him and for
the sake of his favour, to lend no aid to such person, and
not to stand in the way of or oppose those who wish to do
him harm ; and if any one shall do him harm, he shall not
be accountable for it.   The emperor, moreover, will not recall that mandate so long as the truce shall last.   And the
lord king Henry, his son, shall confirm the aforesaid, as
has been stated in the writing.   The lord emperor, also,
shall corroborate the aforesaid peace with the church, and
with the illustrious king of Sicily for 15 years, and the
truce with the Lombards, in a writing of his own, and with
his own signature and that of the princes.

28. But if, which God forbid, the lord pope should die
first, the lord emperor and the lord king Henry, his son,
and the princes shall firmly observe this form of peace and
agreement as regards his successors, and all the cardinals
and the whole Roman church, and the illustrious king of
Sicily and the Lombards, and the others who feel with
them.   Likewise if, which God forbid, the lord emperor
should die first, the lord pope and the cardinals and the
Roman church shall firmly observe the aforesaid peace as
regards his successor, and Beatrix his serene wife, and king
Henry, his son, and all who belong to the German realm,
and all his supporters, as has been said before.

(Signed by Wicmann, archbishop of Magdeburg ; Philip,
archbishop of Cologne ; Christian, archbishop of Mainz ;
Arnold, archbishop of Treves ; Arduin, the imperial proto-
notary.)

V.

JOHN'S CONCESSION OF ENGLAND TO THE POPE. A.D. 1213.

("Stubbs' Charters," p. 284.)

John, by the grace of God, king of England, lord of
Ireland, duke of Normandy and Aquitaine, count of Anjou,
to all the faithful of Christ who shall look upon this present charter, greeting.   We wish it to be known to all of
you, through this our charter, furnished with our seal, that
inasmuch as we had offended in many ways God and our
mother the holy church, and in consequence are known to
have very much needed the divine mercy, and can not
offer anything worthy for making due satisfaction to God
and to the church unless we humiliate ourselves and our
kingdoms :—we, wishing to humiliate ourselves for Him
who humiliated Himself for us unto death, the grace of
the Holy Spirit inspiring, not induced by force or compelled by fear, but of our own good and spontaneous will
and by the common counsel of our barons, do offer and
freely concede to God and His holy apostles Peter and
Paul and to our mother the holy Roman church, and to

our lord pope Innocent and to his catholic successors, the whole kingdom of England and the whole kingdom of Ireland, with all their rights and appurtenances, for the remission of our own sins and of those of our whole race, as well for the living as for the dead; and now receiving and holding them, as it were a vassal, from God and the Roman church, in the presence of that prudent man Pandulph, subdeacon and of the household of the lord pope, we perform and swear fealty for them to him our aforesaid lord pope Innocent, and his catholic successors and the Roman church, according to the form appended; and in the presence of the lord pope, if we shall be able to come before him, we shall do liege homage to him; binding our successors and our heirs by our wife forever, in similar manner to perform fealty and show homage to him who shall be chief pontiff at that time, and to the Roman church without demur. As a sign, moreover, of this our perpetual obligation and concession we will and establish that from the proper and especial revenues of our aforesaid kingdoms, for all the service and customs which we ought to render for them, saving in all things the penny of St. Peter, the Roman church shall receive yearly a thousand marks sterling, namely at the feast of St. Michael five hundred marks, and at Easter five hundred marks—seven hundred, namely, for the kingdom of England, and three hundred for the kingdom of Ireland—saving to us and to our heirs our rights, liberties and regalia; all of which things, as they have been described above, we wish to have perpetually valid and firm; and we bind ourselves and our successors not to act counter to them. And if we or any one of our successors shall presume to attempt this,— whoever he be, unless being duly warned he come to his senses, he shall lose his right to the kingdom, and this charter of our obligation and concession shall always remain firm.

Form of the oath of fealty.

I, John, by the grace of God, king of England and lord of Ireland, from this hour forth will be faithful to God and St. Peter and the Roman church and my lord pope

Innocent and his successors who are ordained in a catholic manner: I shall not bring it about by deed, word, consent or counsel, that they lose life or members or be taken captive. I will impede their being harmed, if I know of it, and will cause harm to be removed from them if I shall be able: otherwise, as quickly as I can I will intimate it or tell of it to such person as I believe for certain will inform them. Any counsel which they entrust to me through themselves or through their envoys or through their letters, I will keep secret, nor will I knowingly disclose it to anyone to their harm. I will aid to the best of my ability in holding and defending against all men the patrimony of St. Peter, and especially the kingdom of England and the kingdom of Ireland. So may God and these holy Gospels aid me.

I myself bearing witness in the house of the Knights Templars near Dover, in the presence of master H., archbishop of Dublin; master J., bishop of Norwich; G., the son of Peter count of Essex, our justice; W., count of Salisbury, our brother; W. Marshall, count of Pembroke; R., count of Boulogne; W., count of Warren; S., count of Winchester; W., count of Arundel; W., count of Ferrières; W. Briwer; Peter, son of Herbert; Warin, son of Gerold; on the 15th day of May, in the 14th year of our reign.

VI.

THE BULL "CLERICIS LAICOS," 1296 A.D..

(Rymer's "Foedera," ed. 1816, vol. i. pt. ii. p. 836.)

Bishop Boniface, servant of the servants of God, in perpetual memory of this matter. Antiquity teaches us that laymen are in a high degree hostile to the clergy, a fact which also the experiences of the present times declare and make manifest; inasmuch as, not content within their own bounds, they strive after what is forbidden, and loose the reins in pursuit of what is unlawful. Nor have they the prudence to consider that all jurisdiction is denied them over the clergy—over both the persons and the goods of ecclesiastics. On the prelates of the churches and on ecclesiastical persons, monastic and secular, they impose heavy burdens, tax them and declare levies upon them. They exact and extort from them the half, the tenth or twentieth or some other portion or quota of their revenues or of their goods; and they attempt in many ways to subject them to slavery and reduce them to their sway. And, with grief do we mention it, some prelates of the churches and ecclesiastical persons, fearing where they ought not to fear, seeking a transitory peace, dreading more to offend the temporal than the eternal majesty, without obtaining the authority or permission of the apostolic chair, do acquiesce, not so much rashly, as improvidently, in the abuses of such persons. We, therefore, wishing to put a stop to such iniquitous acts, by the counsel of our brothers, of the apostolic authority, have decreed: that whatever prelates, or ecclesiastical persons, monastic or secular, of whatever grade, condition or standing, shall pay, or promise, or agree to pay as levies or talliages to laymen the tenth, twentieth or hundredth part of their own and their churches' revenues or goods— or any other quantity, portion or quota of those same revenues or goods, of their estimated or of their real value—under the name of an aid, loan, subvention, subsidy or gift, or under any other name, manner or clever pretence, without the authority of that same chair: likewise emperors, kings, or princes, dukes, counts or barons, podestas, captains or officials or rectors—by whatever name they are called, whether of cities, castles, or any places whatever, wherever situated; and any other persons, of whatever pre-eminence, condition or standing who shall impose, exact or receive such payments, or shall any where arrest, seize or presume to take possession of the belongings of churches or ecclesiastical persons which are deposited in the sacred buildings, or shall order them to be arrested, seized or taken possession of, or shall receive them when taken possession of, seized or arrested—also all who shall knowingly give aid, counsel or favour in the aforesaid things, whether publicly or secretly:—shall incur, by the act itself, the sentence of excommunication. Corporations, moreover, which shall be guilty in these matters, we place under the ecclesiastical interdict. The prelates and above-mentioned ecclesiastical persons we strictly command, by virtue of their obedience and under penalty of deposition, that they by no means acquiesce in such demands, without express permission of the aforesaid chair; and that they pay nothing under pretext of any obligation, promise and confession made hitherto, or to be made hereafter before such constitution, notice or decree shall come to their notice; nor shall the aforesaid secular persons in any way receive anything. And if they shall pay, or if the aforesaid persons shall receive, they shall fall by the act itself under sentence of excommunication. From the aforesaid sentences of excommunication and interdict, moreover, no one shall be able to be absolved, except in the throes of death, without the authority and special permission of the apostolic chair; since it is our intention by no means to pass over with dissimulation so horrid an abuse of the secular powers. Notwithstanding any privileges whatever—under whatever tenor, form, or manner or conception of words—that have been granted to emperors, kings, and other persons mentioned above; as to which privileges we will that, against what we have here laid down, they in no wise avail any person or persons. Let no man at all, then, infringe this page of our constitution, prohibition or decree, or, with rash daring, act counter to it; but if any one shall presume to attempt this, he shall know that he is about to incur the indignation of Almighty God and of His blessed apostles Peter and Paul.

Given at Rome at St. Peter's on the sixth day before the Calends of March (Feb. 25), in the second year of our pontificate.

VII.

THE BULL "UNAM SANCTAM."

(From the latest revision of the text in "Revue des
Questions historiques," July, 1889, p. 255.)

We are compelled, our faith urging us, to believe and
to hold—and we do firmly believe and simply confess—
that there is one holy catholic and apostolic church, outside of which there is neither salvation nor remission of
sins; her Spouse proclaiming it in the canticles: "My
dove, my undefiled is but one, she is the choice one of her
that bare her;" which represents one mystic body, of
which body the head is Christ; but of Christ, God. In
this church there is one Lord, one faith and one baptism.
There was one ark of Noah, indeed, at the time of the
flood, symbolizing one church; and this being finished in
one cubit had, namely, one Noah as helmsman and commander. And, with the exception of this ark, all things
existing upon the earth were, as we read, destroyed. This
church, moreover, we venerate as the only one, the Lord
saying through His prophet: "Deliver my soul from the
sword, my darling from the power of the dog." He prayed
at the same time for His soul—that is, for Himself the
Head—and for His body,—which body, namely, he called
the one and only church on account of the unity of the
faith promised, of the sacraments, and of the love of the
church. She is that seamless garment of the Lord which
was not cut but which fell by lot. Therefore of this one
and only church there is one body and one head—not two
heads as if it were a monster:—Christ, namely, and the
vicar of Christ, St. Peter, and the successor of Peter. For
the Lord Himself said to Peter, Feed my sheep. My sheep,
He said, using a general term, and not designating these
or those particular sheep; from which it is plain that He
committed to Him *all* His sheep. If, then, the Greeks or
others say that they were not committed to the care of
Peter and his successors, they necessarily confess that they
are not of the sheep of Christ; for the Lord says, in John,

that there is one fold, one shepherd and one only. We are told by the word of the gospel that in this His fold there are two swords,—a spiritual, namely, and a temporal. For when the apostles said "Behold here are two swords"— when, namely, the apostles were speaking in the church— the Lord did not reply that this was too much, but enough. Surely he who denies that the temporal sword is in the power of Peter wrongly interprets the word of the Lord when He says : " Put up thy sword in its scabbard." Both swords, the spiritual and the material, therefore, are in the power of the church; the one, indeed, to be wielded for the church, the other by the church; the one by the hand of the priest, the other by the hand of kings and knights, but at the will and sufferance of the priest. One sword, moreover, ought to be under the other, and the temporal authority to be subjected to the spiritual. For when the apostle says " there is no power but of God, and the powers that are of God are ordained," they would not be ordained unless sword were under sword and the lesser one, as it were, were led by the other to great deeds. For according to St. Dionysius the law of divinity is to lead the lowest through the intermediate to the highest things. Not therefore, according to the law of the universe, are all things reduced to order equally and immediately ; but the lowest through the intermediate, the intermediate through the higher. But that the spiritual exceeds any earthly power in dignity and nobility we ought the more openly to confess the more spiritual things excel temporal ones. This also is made plain to our eyes from the giving of tithes, and the benediction and the sanctification ; from the acceptation of this same power, from the control over those same things. For, the truth bearing witness, the spiritual power has to establish the earthly power, and to judge it if it be not good. Thus concerning the church and the ecclesiastical power is verified the prophecy of Jeremiah : "See, I have this day set thee over the nations and over the kingdoms," and the other things which follow. Therefore if the earthly power err it shall be judged by the spiritual power ; but if the lesser spiritual power err, by the greater. But if the greatest, it can be judged by God alone, not by man, the apostle bearing

witness. A spiritual man judges all things, but he himself is judged by no one. This authority, moreover, even
though it is given to man and exercised through man, is
not human but rather divine, being given by divine lips
to Peter and founded on a rock for him and his successors
through Christ himself whom he has confessed; the Lord
himself saying to Peter: "Whatsoever thou shalt bind,"
etc. Whoever, therefore, resists this power thus ordained
by God, resists the ordination of God, unless he makes
believe, like the Manichean, that there are two beginnings.
This we consider false and heretical, since by the testimony
of Moses, not "in the beginnings," but "in the beginning" God created the Heavens and the earth. **Indeed we declare, announce and define, that it is
altogether necessary to salvation for every human
creature to be subject to the Roman pontiff.** The
Lateran, Nov. 14, in our 8th year. As a perpetual memorial of this matter.

VIII.

THE LAW "LICET JURIS" OF THE FRANKFORT
DIET OF 1338 A.D.

(Altmann u. Bernheim, p. 38.)

Although the proofs of both kinds of law (civil and
canon) manifestly declare that the imperial dignity and
power proceeded from of old directly through the Son of
God, and that God openly gave laws to the human race
through the emperor and the kings of the world; and
since the emperor is made true emperor by the election
alone of those to whom it pertains, and needs not the confirmation or approbation of any one else, since on earth he
has no superior as to temporal things, but to him peoples
and nations are subject, and our Lord Jesus Christ Himself ordered to be rendered unto God the things that are
God's, and unto Cæsar the things that are Cæsar's; because, nevertheless, some, led by the blindness of avarice

and ambition, and having no understanding of Scripture, but turning away from the path of right feeling into certain iniquitous and wicked deceptions, and, breaking forth into detestable assertions, do wage war against the imperial power and authority and against the prerogatives of the emperors, electors, and other princes, and of the faithful subjects of the empire, falsely asserting that the imperial dignity and power come from the pope and that he who is elected emperor is not true emperor or king unless he be first confirmed and crowned through the pope or the apostolic see; and since, through such wicked assertions and pestiferous dogmas the ancient enemy moves discord, excites quarrels, prepares dissensions and brings about seditions:—therefore, for the purpose of averting such evil, by the counsel and consent of the electors and of the other princes of the empire we declare that the imperial dignity and power comes directly from God alone ; and that, by the old and approved right and custom of the empire, after any one is chosen as emperor or king by the electors of the empire concordantly, or by the greater part of them, he is, in consequence of the election alone, to be considered and called true king and emperor of the Romans, and he ought to be obeyed by all the subjects of the empire.   And he shall have full power of administering the laws of the empire and of doing the other things that pertain to a true emperor ; nor does he need the approbation, confirmation, authority or consent of the apostolic see or of any one else.

And therefore we decree by this law, to be forever valid, that he who is elected emperor concordantly or by the majority of the electors, shall, in consequence of the election alone, be considered and regarded by all as the true and lawful emperor ; and that he ought to be obeyed by all the subjects of the empire, and that he shall have, and shall be considered and firmly asserted by all to have and to hold, the imperial administration and jurisdiction and the plenitude of the imperial power.

Moreover, whatever persons shall presume to assert or say any thing contrary to these declarations, decrees or definitions, or any one of them ; or to countenance those who assert or say anything ; or to obey their mandates or letters or precepts : we deprive them from now on, and decree them to be deprived by the law and by the act itself, of all the fiefs which they hold from the empire, and of all the favours, jurisdictions, privileges and immunities granted to them by us or our predecessors.   Moreover, we decree that they have committed the crime of high treason and are subject to all the penalties inflicted on those committing the crime of high treason.   Given in our town of Frankfort on the 8th day of the month of August A.D. 1338.

APPENDIX.

LIUTPRAND'S REPORT OF HIS MISSION TO CONSTANTINOPLE.

THIS remarkable and exceedingly original piece of writing has been relegated to the appendix not because it is less important than the other documents in this collection, but because, being more of a narrative, it differs from them in character.

We first hear of Liutprand at the court of Berengar and Willa, who, in the middle of the tenth century, ruled over northern Italy. Becoming estranged from his royal patrons he wrote against them the "Antapodosis," or book of retribution, which is one of our most valued historical sources for those times. In 963 Liutprand was envoy of Otto the Great to the shameless Pope John XII., and wrote the only connected account which we have of the latter's condemnation and deposition.

The journey to Constantinople took place in 968. Otto had, in his efforts to bring Italy into his power, come into collision with the Greeks, who regarded Benevento and Capua as belonging to the provinces of the Eastern Empire. Otto went so far as to occupy Apulia and to besiege the Greek town of Bari, but soon came to the conclusion that more was to be gained by negotiations than by war. Liutprand, now Bishop of Cremona, advised peace, and suggested that a Greek princess should be sought in marriage for the

young emperor Otto II., who had commenced to reign
conjointly with his father. It was upon the princess
Theophano that the hopes of the emperor were fixed, and it
was thought that Nicephorus would give Apulia and
Calabria as her dowry. It was to arrange this matter that
Liutprand, accompanied by a large suite, went to Constantinople. The reception that he met with will be
explained in his own words.

Liutprand bishop of the holy church of Cremona desires,
wishes and prays that the Ottos, the unconquerable august
emperors of the Romans,—and the most glorious Adelaide
the august empress—may always flourish, prosper and be
triumphant.

Why it was that ye did not receive my former letters or
my envoy, the following explanation will make clear. On
the day before the Nones of June (June 4) we came to
Constantinople, and there, as a mark of disrespect to yourselves, being shamefully received, we were harshly and
shamefully treated. We were shut up in a palace large
enough, indeed, but uncovered, neither keeping out the
cold nor warding off the heat. Armed soldiers were made
to stand guard who were to prevent all of my companions
from going out and all others from coming in. This
dwelling, into which we alone who were shut up could
pass, was so far removed from the palace that our breath
was taken away when we walked there—we did not ride.
To add to our calamity the Greek wine, on account of
being mixed with pitch, resin and plaster was to us
undrinkable. The house itself was without water, nor
could we even for money buy water to still our thirst. To
this great torment was added another torment—our warden,
namely, who cared for our daily support. If one were to
look for his like, not earth, but perhaps hell, would furnish
it ; for he, like an inundating torrent, poured forth on us
whatever calamity, whatever plunder, whatever expense,
whatever torment, whatever misery he could invent. Nor
among a hundred and twenty days did a single one pass
without bringing us groaning and grief.

On the day before the Nones of June (June 4), as

stated above, we arrived at Constantinople before the
Carian gate and waited with our horses, in no slight rain,
until the eleventh hour. But at the eleventh hour, Nicephorus, not regarding us, who had been so distinguished
by your mercy, as worthy to ride, ordered us to approach;
and we were led to the aforesaid hated, waterless, open
marble house. But on the eighth day before the Ides
(June 6), on the Saturday before Pentecost, I was led into
the presence of his brother Leo, the marshal of the court,
and chancellor; and there we wearied ourselves out in a
great discussion concerning your imperial title. For he
called ye not emperor, which is Basileus in his tongue,
but, to insult ye, Rex, which is king in ours. And when
I told him that the thing signified was the same although
the terms used to signify it were different, he said that I
had come not to make peace but to excite discord; and
thus angrily rising he received your letters, truly insultingly,
not in his own hand, but through an interpreter. He was
a man commanding enough in person but feigning humility;
whereon if a man lean, it will go into his hand and pierce it.

On the seventh day before the Ides (June 7), moreover,
on the sacred day of Pentecost itself, in the palace which
is called the crown hall, I was led before Nicephorus—a
monstrosity of a man, a pygmy, fat-headed and like a mole
as to the smallness of his eyes; disgusting with his short,
broad, thick, and half hoary beard; disgraced by a neck an
inch long; very bristly through the length and thickness
of his hair; in colour an Ethiopian; one whom it would
not be pleasant to meet in the middle of the night; with
extensive belly, lean of loin, very long of hip considering
his short stature, small of shank, proportionate as to his
heels and feet; clad in a garment costly but too old, and
foul-smelling and faded through age; shod with Sicyonian
shoes; bold of tongue, a fox by nature, in perjury and
lying a Ulysses. Always my lords and august emperors
ye seemed to me shapely, how much more shapely after
this! Always magnificent, how much more magnificent
after this! Always powerful, how much more powerful
after this! Always gentle, how much more gentle henceforth! Always full of virtues, how much fuller henceforth. At his left, not in a line but far below, sat two

petty emperors, once his masters, now his subjects. His
discourse began as follows :

" It would have been right for us, nay, we had wished to
receive thee kindly and with honour ; but the impiety of
thy master does not permit it since, invading it as an
enemy, he has claimed for himself Rome ; has taken away
from Berengar and Adalbert their kingdom, contrary to
law and right; has slain some of the Romans by the sword,
others by hanging, depriving some of their eyes, sending
others into exile ; and has tried, moreover, to subject to
himself by slaughter or by flame cities of our empire. And,
because his wicked endeavour could not take effect, he now
has sent thee, the instigator and furtherer of this wickedness, to act as a spy upon us while simulating peace."

I answered him: " My master did not by force or
tyrannically invade the city of Rome ; but he freed it from
a tyrant, nay, from the yoke of tyrants. Did not the
slaves of women rule over it ; or, which is worse and more
disgraceful, harlots themselves ? Thy power, I fancy, or
that of thy predecessors, who in name alone are called
emperors of the Romans and are it not in reality, was
sleeping at that time. If they were powerful, if emperors
of the Romans, why did they permit Rome to be in the
hands of harlots ? Were not some of the most holy popes
banished, others so oppressed that they were not able to have
their daily supplies or the means of giving alms ? Did not
Adalbert send scornful letters to the emperors Romanus
and Constantine thy predecessors ? Did he not plunder
the churches of the most holy apostles ? What one of you
emperors, led by zeal for God, took care to avenge so unworthy a crime and to bring back the holy church to its
proper condition ? You neglected it, my master did not
neglect it. For, rising from the ends of the earth and
coming to Rome, he removed the impious and gave back to
the vicars of the holy apostles their power and all their
honour. But afterwards those who had risen against him
and the lord pope, according to the decrees of the Roman
emperors Justinian, Valentinian, Theodosius and the others
he slew, strangled, hung, and sent into exile as violators of
their oath, as sacrilegious men, as torturers and plunderers
of their lords the popes. Had he not done so he would

have been impious, unjust, cruel, a tyrant. It is well known that Berengar and Adalbert, becoming his vassals, had received the kingdom of Italy with a golden sceptre from his hand, and that they, taking an oath, promised fealty in the presence of servants of thine who still live and are at present in this city. And because, at the devil's instigation they perfidiously violated this promise, he justly deprived them as deserters and rebels against himself, of their kingdom. Thou thyself would'st do the same to those who had been thy subjects, and who afterwards rebelled."

"But Adalbert's vassal," he said, "does not acknowledge this." I answered him: "If he denies it one of my suite shall, at thy command, show by a duel to-morrow that it is so." "Well," he said, "he may, as thou sayest, have done this justly. Explain now why with war and flame he attacked the boundaries of our empire. We were friends, and were expecting by means of a marriage to enter into an indissoluble union."

"The land," I answered, "which thou sayest belongs to thy empire belongs, as the nationality and language of the people proves, to the kingdom of Italy. The Lombards held it in their power, and Louis, the emperor of the Lombards, or Franks, freed it from the hand of the Saracens, many of them being cut down. But also Landulph, prince of Benevento and Capua, subjugated and held it in his power for seven years. Nor would it until now have passed from the yoke of his servitude or that of his successors, had not the emperor Romanus, giving an immense sum of money, bought the friendship of our king Hugo. And it was for this reason that he joined in marriage to his nephew and namesake the bastard daughter of this same king of ours, Hugo. And, as I see, thou dost ascribe it not to kindness but to weakness that, after acquiring Italy and Rome, he left it to thee for so many years. The bond of friendship, however, which thou didst wish, as thou sayest, to form through a marriage, we look upon as a wile and a snare: thou dost demand a truce, which the condition of affairs neither compels thee to demand nor us to grant. But, in order that now all deceit may be laid bare and the truth not be hidden, my master (Otto) hast sent me to thee, so that if thou art willing to give the daughter of the emperor Romanus and of the empress Theophano to my master his son, Otto the august emperor, thou may'st affirm this to me with an oath; whereupon I will affirm by an oath that, in return for such favours, he will observe and do to thee this and this. But already my master has given to thee, as to his brother, the best pledge of his friendship in restoring to thee, by my intervention, at whose suggestion thou declarest this evil to have been done, all Apulia which was subject to his sway. Of which thing there are as many witnesses as there are inhabitants in all Apulia."

"The second hour," said Nicephorus, "is already past. The solemn procession to the church is about to take place. Let us now do what the hour demands. At a convenient time we will reply to what thou hast said."

May nothing keep me from describing this procession, and my masters from hearing about it! A numerous multitude of tradesmen and low-born persons, collected at this festival to receive and to do honour to Nicephorus, occupied both sides of the road from the palace to St. Sophia like walls, being disfigured by quite thin little shields and wretched spears. And it served to increase this disfigurement that the greater part of this same crowd in his (Nicephorus') honour, had marched with bare feet. I believe that they thought in this way better to adorn that holy procession. But also his nobles who passed with him through the plebeian and barefoot multitude were clad in tunics which were too large, and which were torn through too great age. It would have been much more suitable had they marched in their everyday clothes. There was no one whose grandfather had owned one of these garments when it was new. No one there was adorned with gold, no one with gems, save Nicephorus alone, whom the imperial adornments, bought and prepared for the persons of his ancestors, rendered still more disgusting. By thy salvation, which is dearer to me than my own, one precious garment of thy nobles is worth a hundred of these, and more too. I was led to this church procession and was placed on a raised place next to the singers.

And as, like a creeping monster, he proceeded thither, the singers cried out in adulation: "Behold the morning star approaches ; Eos rises ; he reflects in his glances the rays of the sun—he the pale death of the Saracens, Nicephorus the ruler." And accordingly they sang : " Long life to the ruler Nicephorus ! Adore him, ye people, cherish him, bend the neck to him alone ! " How much more truly might they have sung : "Come, thou burnt-out coal, thou fool ; old woman in thy walk, wood-devil in thy look ; thou peasant, thou frequenter of foul places, thou goatfoot, thou horn-head, thou double-limbed one ; bristly, unruly, countrified, barbarian, harsh, hairy, a rebel, a Cappadocian ! " And so, inflated by those lying fools, he enters St. Sophia, his masters the emperors following him from afar, and, with the kiss of peace, adoring him to the ground. His armour-bearer, with an arrow for a pen, places in the church the era which is in progress from the time when he began to reign, and thus those who did not then exist learn what the era is.

On this same day he ordered me to be his guest. Not thinking me worthy, however, to be placed above any of his nobles, I sat in the fifteenth place from him, and without a tablecloth. Not only did no one of my suite sit at table, but not one of them saw even the house in which I was a guest. During which disgusting and foul meal, which was washed down with oil after the manner of drunkards, and moistened also with a certain other exceedingly bad fish liquor, he asked me many questions concerning your power, many concerning your dominions and your army. And when I had replied to him consequently and truly, " Thou liest," he said, " the soldiers of thy master do not know how to ride, nor do they know how to fight on foot ; the size of their shields, the weight of their breast-plates, the length of their swords, and the burden of their helms permits them to fight in neither one way nor the other." Then he added, smiling : " their gluttony also impedes them, for their God is their belly, their courage but wind, their bravery drunkenness. Their fasting means dissolution, their sobriety panic. Nor has thy master a number of fleets on the sea. I alone have a force of navigators ; I will attack him with my ships, I will overrun his maritime cities with war, and those which are near the rivers I will reduce to ashes. And how, I ask, can he even on land resist me with his scanty forces? His son was there, his wife was there, the Saxons, Swabians, Bavarians, were all with him: and if they did not know enough and were unable to take one little city that resisted them, how will they resist me when I come, I who am followed by as many troops as

'Gargara corn-ears hath, or grape-shoots the island of Lesbos,
Stars in the sky are found, or waves in the billowy ocean'?"

When I wished to reply to him and to give forth an answer worthy of his boasting, he did not permit me; but added as if to scoff at me: "You are not Romans but Lombards." When he wished to speak further and was waving his hand to impose silence upon me, I said in anger: "History teaches that the fratricide Romulus, from whom also the Romans are named, was born in adultery; and that he made an asylum for himself in which he received insolvent debtors, fugitive slaves, homicides, and those who were worthy of death for their deeds. And he called to himself a certain number of such and called them Romans. From such nobility those are descended whom you call world-rulers, that is, emperors; whom we, namely the Lombards, Saxons, Franks, Lotharingians, Bavarians, Swabians, Burgundians, so despise, that when angry we can call our enemies nothing more scornful than Roman—comprehending in this one thing, that is in the name of the Romans, whatever there is of contemptibility, of timidity, of avarice, of luxury, of lying: in a word, of viciousness. But because thou dost maintain that we are unwarlike and ignorant of horsemanship, if the sins of the Christians shall merit that thou shalt remain in this hard-heartedness: the next battle will show what you are, and how warlike we."

Nicephorus, exasperated by these words, commanded silence with his hand, and bade that the long narrow table should be taken away, and that I should return to my hated habitation—or, to speak more truly, my prison. There after two days, as a result of vexation as well as of heat and thirst, I was taken with a severe illness. And, indeed, there was not one of my companions who, having drunk from the same cup of sorrow, did not fear that his last day was approaching. Why should they not sicken, I ask, whose drink instead of the best wine was brine; whose resting place was not hay, not straw, not even earth, but hard marble; whose pillow was a stone, whose open house kept off neither heat, nor showers, nor cold? Salvation itself, to use a common expression, if it had poured itself out upon them could not have saved them. Weakened therefore by my own tribulations and those of my companions, calling my warden, or rather my persecutor, I brought it about, not by prayers alone but through money, that he should carry my letter containing what follows, to the brother of Nicephorus:

"To the coropalate and logothete of the palace, Leo,— Bishop Liutprand. If the most illustrious emperor thinks of granting the request on account of which I have come, the suffering which I here endure shall not exhaust my patience; only his lordship must be instructed by my letters and by an envoy that I will not remain here without reason. But if the contrary be the case, there is a transport ship of the Venetians here which is just about to start. Let him permit me who am ill to embark, so that, if the time of my dissolution be at hand, my native land may at least receive my corpse."

When he had read these lines he ordered me to come to him after four days. There sat with him, according to their tradition, to discuss your affair the wisest men, strong in Attic eloquence: Basilius the chief chamberlain, the chief state secretary, the chief master of the wardrobe and two other officials. They began their discourse as follows: "Tell us, brother, why thou hast taken the trouble to come hither." When I had told them that it was on account of the marriage which was to be the ground for a lasting peace, they said: "It is an unheard of thing that a daughter born in the purple of an emperor born in the purple should be joined in marriage with strange nations. But although ye seek so high a favour, ye shall receive what ye wish, if ye give what is right: Ravenna, namely, and Rome with all the adjoining places which extend from thence to our possessions. But if ye desire friendship without the marriage, let thy master permit Rome to be free; but the princes, of Capua, namely, and Benevento, who were formerly slaves of our empire and now are rebels, let him give over to their former subjection."

I answered them: "You yourselves can not but know that my master rules over Slavonian princes who are mightier than Peter king of the Bulgarians who has wedded the daughter of the emperor Christophorus." "But Christophorus," they said, "was not born in the purple."

"But Rome," I said, "which, as you exclaim, you wish to have free, who does it serve, to whom does it pay tribute? Did it not formerly serve harlots? And, while you were sleeping, nay, powerless, did not my master the august emperor free it from so disgraceful a servitude? Constantine, the august emperor who founded this city and called it after his name, as world-ruler gave many gifts to the holy apostolic Roman church, not only in Italy but in almost all the western kingdoms; also in the eastern and southern—in Greece, namely, Judea, Persia, Mesopotamia, Babylonia, Egypt, Libya: as his own privileges witness, which are preserved in our land. Now whatever there is, in Italy and also in Saxony and Bavaria or in any of the dominions of my master, that belongs to the church of the blessed apostles: he has conferred it on the vicar of those same most holy apostles. And may I deny God if my master has retained from all of these a city, an estate, a vassal or a serf. But why does your emperor not do the same? Why does he not restore to the church of the apostles what lies in his kingdom; so that he may make it, rich and free as it is by the labour and munificence of my master, still richer and more free?"

"But this," said the first chamberlain Basilius, "he will do as soon as Rome and the Roman church shall be subordinated to his will." "A certain man," I said, "having suffered much injury from another, approached God with these words: 'Lord, avenge me upon my adversary!' To whom the Lord said: 'I will do it at the day when I shall render unto each man according to his works!' 'Alas,' said he, 'how late that will be!'"

At which all except the emperor's brother shook with laughter. They then ended the interview and ordered me to be led back to my hated abode, and to be guarded with great care until the day, honoured by all religious persons, of the holy apostles. On this festal occasion the emperor commanded me—I was very ill at the time—and also the Bulgarian envoys who had arrived the day before, to meet him at the church of the holy apostles. And when, after the garrulous songs of praise (to Nicephorus) and the celebration of the mass we were invited to table, he placed above me on our side of the table, which was long and narrow, the envoy of the Bulgarians who was shorn in Hungarian fashion, girt with a brazen chain, and as it seemed to me, a catechumen; plainly in scorn of yourselves my august masters. On your behalf I was despised, rejected and scorned. But I thank the Lord Jesus Christ whom ye serve with your whole soul that I have been considered worthy to suffer contumely for your sakes. However, my masters, not considering myself but yourselves to be insulted, I left the table. And as I was about indignantly to go away, Leo the marshal of the court and brother of the emperor, and Simeon the chief state secretary came up to me from behind, barking out at me this: "When Peter the king of the Bulgarians married the daughter of Christophorus articles were mutually drawn up and confirmed with an oath to the effect that with us the envoys of the Bulgarians should be preferred, honoured and cherished above the envoys of all other nations. That envoy of the Bulgarians although, as thou sayest and as is true, he is shorn, unwashed and girt with a brazen chain, is nevertheless a patrician; and we decree and judge that it would not be right to give a bishop, especially a Frankish one, the preference over him. And since we know that thou dost consider this unseemly, we will not now, as thou dost expect, allow thee to return to thy quarters, but shall oblige thee to take food in a separate apartment with the servants of the emperor.

On account of the incomparable grief in my heart I made no reply to them, but did what they had ordered; judging that table not a suitable place where—I will not say to me, that is, the bishop Liutprand, but to your envoy—an envoy of the Bulgarians is preferred. But the sacred emperor soothed my grief through a great gift, sending to me from among his most delicate dishes a fat goat, of which he himself had partaken, deliciously (?) stuffed with garlic, onions and leeks; steeped in fish sauce: a dish which I could have wished just then to be upon your table, so that ye who do not believe the delicacies of the sacred emperor to be desirable, should at length become believers at this sight!

When eight days had passed and the Bulgarians had already departed, thinking that I thought very highly of his table he compelled me, ill as I was, to dine with him in the same place. There was present also, with many bishops, the patriarch; in whose presence he asked me many questions concerning the Holy Scriptures; which, the divine Spirit inspiring me, I expounded with elegance. And at last, in order to make merry over ye, he asked me what synods we recognized. When I had mentioned to him Nicea, Chalcedon, Ephesus, Carthage, Ancyra, Constantinople,—"Ha, Ha, Ha," said he, "you have forgotten to mention Saxony, and, if you ask us why our books do not contain it, I answer that your beliefs are too young and have not yet been able to reach us."

I answered: "That member of the body where the infirmity has its seat must be burned with the burning iron. All heresies have emanated from you, have flourished among you; by us, that is by the western nations they have been here strangled, here put an end to.—A Roman or a Pavian synod, although they often took place, I do not count here. A Roman clerk, indeed, afterwards the universal pope Gregory who is called by you Dialogus, freed Eutychius the heretical patriarch of Constantinople from his heresy. This same Eutychius said, nor did he only say but taught, proclaimed and kept writing, that we would assume at the Resurrection not the true flesh which we have here, but a certain fantastic flesh. The book containing this error was, in an orthodox manner, burned by Gregory. Ennodius, moreover, bishop of Pavia, was, on account of a certain other heresy, sent here, that is to Constantinople, by the Roman patriarch. He repressed it, and restored the orthodox catholic teaching.—The race of the Saxons, from the time when it received the holy baptism and the knowledge of God, has been spotted by no heresy which would have rendered a synod necessary for the correction of an error which did not exist. Since thou declarest the faith of the Saxons to be young, I am willing also to affirm the same; for always the faith of Christ is young and not old with those whose works second their faith. Faith is there not young but old where works do not accompany it; but faith is scorned, as it were, for its age, like a worn-out garment. But I know for certain of one synod that was held in Saxony in which it was decreed and confirmed that it was more fitting to fight with the sword than with the pen, and better to submit to death than to turn one's back to the enemy. Thy own army has experienced the truth of this." In my heart I said: "And may they (the Saxons) soon have occasion to show how warlike they are!"

On this same day, after midday, he ordered me to meet him on his return from the palace, although I was so weak and changed that the women who, before when they met me, called out in astonishment "Mana,[1] mana," now, pitying my misery, beat their breasts with their hands and said: "Poor sick man." What then, raising my hands to Heaven, I wished him,—Nicephorus, namely, as he approached—and ye who were absent: oh that it might be fulfilled! But ye may well believe me, he made me laugh not a little, for he sat on an impatient and unbridled horse—a very little man on a very big beast. My mind pictured to itself one of those dolls which your Slavonians tie on to a foal, allowing it then to follow its mother without a rein.

After this I was led back to my fellow citizens and fellow inmates five lions, into the aforesaid hated abode; where, during a space of three weeks I was treated to the conversation of no one save my companions. On account of which my mind pictured to itself that Nicephorus wished never to let me go, and my unbounded sadness brought on one illness after another, so that I should have died had not the Mother of God, by her prayers, obtained my life from the Creator and His Son; as was shown to me not through a fancied but through a true vision.

Untranslatable.

During these three weeks, then, Nicephorus had his camp outside of Constantinople, in a place that is called "At the Fountains"; and thither he ordered me to come. And, although I was so weak that not only standing but even sitting seemed a heavy burden to me, he compelled me to stand before him with uncovered head; a thing which was entirely wrong in my state of ill health. And he said to me: "The envoys of thy king Otto who were here before thee in the preceding year promised me under oath —and the wording of the oath can be produced—that he would never in any way bring scandal upon our empire. Dost thou wish for a worse scandal than that he calls himself emperor, that he usurps for himself the provinces of our empire? Both of these things are unbearable; and if both are insupportable, that especially is not to be borne, nay, not to be heard of, that he calls himself emperor. But if thou will'st confirm what they promised our majesty will straightway dismiss thee happy and rich." This, moreover, he said not in order that I might expect ye to observe the engagement, even if in my foolishness I had made it; but he wished to have in hand something that he might show in time to come to his praise and to our shame.

I answered him: "My most holy master, most wise as he is and full of the spirit of God, foreseeing this which thou dost desire, wrote me instructions which he also signed with his seal lest I should act counter to them: to the effect that I should not transcend the bounds which he set for me."—Thou knowest, my august master, what I relied upon when I said this.—"Let these instructions be produced, and whatever he shall order, will be confirmed by an oath from me to thee. But as to what the former envoys, without the order of my master, promised, swore or wrote,—in the words of Plato: 'the guilt is with the wisher, the god is without fault.'"

After this we came to the matter of the most noble princes of Capua and Benevento, whom he calls his slaves, and on account of whom an inward grief is troubling him. "Thy master," he said, "has taken my slaves under his protection; if he will not let them go and restore them to their former servitude, he must do without our friendship.

They themselves demand to be taken back under our rule; but our imperial dignity refuses them, that they may know and experience how dangerous it is for slaves to fall away from their masters and to flee slavery. And it is more becoming for thy master to give them over to me as a friend, than to renounce them to me against his will. Indeed they shall learn, if my life holds out, what it is to deceive their lord; what it is to desert their servitude. And even now, as I think, they feel what I say,—our soldiers who are beyond the sea having brought it to pass!"

To this he did not permit me to reply; but, although I desired to go away, he ordered me to return to his table. His father sat with him, a man, it seemed to me, a hundred and fifty years old. Before him, as before his son, the Greeks call out with hymns of praise—nay, with blatancies—that God may multiply his years. From this we can gather how foolish the Greeks are; how fond of such glory; how adulatory; how greedy. For, not only to an old man but to an utterly worn-out graybeard, they wish what they know for certain that nature itself will not grant. And the worn-out graybeard rejoices that that is wished to him which, as he knows, God will not grant him; and which, if He did, would be to his disadvantage and not to his advantage. And Nicephorus, if you please, could rejoice at being called the prince of peace, and the morning star! To call a weakling strong, a fool wise, a short man tall, a black man white, a sinner holy,—is, believe me, not praise but contumely. And he who rejoices in having strange attributes called after him, rather than those that are rightly due to him, is altogether like those birds whose eyes the night illumines, the day blinds.

But let us return to the matter in hand. At this meal, —a thing that he had not done before—he ordered to be read with a loud voice a homily of St. John Chrysostom on the Acts of the apostles. At the end of this reading, when I sought permission to return to you, nodding affirmatively with his head, he ordered my persecutor to take me back to my fellow citizens and co-denizens, the lions. When this had been done I was not received by him until the thirteenth day before the Calends of August (July 20), but was diligently guarded lest I might enjoy the discourse of any one who might indicate to me his actions. Meanwhile he ordered Grimizo, Adalbert's messenger, to come to him and bade him return with the imperial fleet. This consisted of twenty four Chelandian, two Russian, and two Gallic ships; —I do not know if he sent others which I did not see. The bravery of your soldiers, my masters and august emperors, does not require to be encouraged by the weakness of their adversaries, although this has often been the case with other nations; the hindmost of which, and the weakest in comparison, have struck down the Greek bravery and made it tributary. For just as it would not intimidate ye if I announced that they were very strong and comparable to the Macedonian Alexander, so also I do not put courage into ye when I narrate their weakness, true as it is. I wish ye might believe me, and I know ye will believe me, that ye with four hundred of your warriors can slay that whole army, if ditches or walls do not prevent. And over this army, in scorn of ye, as I think, he has placed in command a sort of man—a sort of, I say, because he has ceased to be a male and was not able to become a female. Adalbert has sent word to Nicephorus that he has eight thousand knights in armour, and says that, if the Greek army helps him, he can, with them, put ye to flight or annihilate ye. And he asks your rival to send him money, that he may the more readily induce his troops to fight.

Now, however, my masters,

Hark to the wiles of the Greeks, and from one single example Learn all.

Nicephorus gave that slave, to whom he had entrusted the army which he had brought together and hired, a considerable sum of money to be disposed of as follows: if Adalbert, as he had promised, should join him with seven thousand and more knights in armour, then he was to distribute among them that sum; and Cono, Adalbert's brother, with his and the Greek army was to attack ye; but Adalbert was to be diligently guarded in Bari, until his brother should come back having gained the victory. But if Adalbert when he came should not bring with him so many thousands of men, he ordered that he was to be taken, bound, and given over to ye when ye came; moreover that

the money which was destined for him, Adalbert, should
be paid over into your hands! Oh what a warrior, oh
what fidelity. He wishes to betray him for whom he prepares a defender; he prepares a defender for him whom
he wishes to destroy. Towards neither is he faithful,
towards both untrue. He does what he did not need to
do, he needed to do what he has not done. But so be it,
he acted as one might expect from Greeks! But let us
return to the matter in hand.

On the fourteenth day before the Calends of August
(July 19) he dismissed that motley fleet, I looking on from
my hated abode. On the thirteenth day, moreover
(July 20), on which day the flippant Greeks celebrate with
theatrical plays the ascension of the prophet Elias, he
ordered me to go to him and said : " Our imperial majesty
thinks to lead an army against the Assyrians, not as thy
master does, against followers of Christ. Already last year
I wished to do this, but hearing that thy master intended
to invade the territory of our empire, letting the Assyrians
go, we turned our reins against him. His envoy, the
Venetian Dominicus met us in Macedonia, and, with much
labour and exertion, induced us to return, affirming to us
with an oath that thy master would never think of such a
thing, much less do it. Return therefore,"—when I heard
this I said to myself, " Thank God!"—"and announce
this and this to thy master; if he give me satisfaction,
return hither again."

I answered : " If thy most holy majesty shall command
me quickly to fly to Italy, I know for certain that my
master will fulfil what thy majesty wishes, and I will joyfully return to thee." In what spirit I said this did not,
alas, remain hid from him. For, smiling, he nodded his
head and ordered me, as I was adoring him to the ground,
and was going away, to remain outside and come to his
meal, which smelt strongly of garlic and onions and was
filthy with oil and fish-juice. On this day I brought it
about through many prayers that he deigned to accept my
gift, which he had often scorned.

As we were sitting at his long narrow table, which was
covered for some ells—for the most part, however, uncovered—he made merry over the Franks, under which

name he included the Latins as well as the Germans ; and
he asked me to tell him where the city of my bishopric was
situated and in what name it rejoiced. I said, "Cremona,
quite near to the Eridanus (Po), the king of the rivers of
Italy. And since thy imperial majesty hastens to send
Chelandian ships there, may it be of advantage to me to
have seen and known thee! Grant peace to the place, that
at least by thy favour it may continue to exist, since it
cannot resist thee." But the sly fellow saw that I said
this ironically, and with submissive mien promised that he
would do this ; and he swore to me by virtue of his holy
empire, that I should suffer no ill, but should prosperously
and quickly arrive at the port of Ancona with his Chelandian ships. And this he swore to me, striking his
breast with his fingers.

But mark how impiously he had sworn. These things
were said and done on the thirteenth day before the
Calends of August (July 20) on the second day of the
week (Monday) ; from which day, until the ninth day, I
received no supplies from him. And this was at a time
when the famine in Constantinople was so great that for
three gold pieces I was not able to provide a meal for my
twenty five companions and the four Greek guards. On
the fourth day of that week Nicephorus left Constantinople
to march against the Assyrians.

On the fifth day his brother called me before him and
addressed me as follows: "The holy emperor has gone
forth and I have remained at home to-day at his command. Tell me, then, now, if thou dost desire to see the
holy emperor, and if thou hast any thing which thou
hast not yet imparted." I answered him: "I have no
reason for seeing the holy emperor or for narrating any
thing new ; I ask this alone, that, according to the promise
of the holy emperor, he allow me to cross on his Chelandian
ships to the port of Ancona." On hearing this,—the
Greeks are always ready to swear by the head of another
—he began to swear that he would do so by the head of
the emperor, by his own life, by his children whom God,
according as he spoke truly, was to preserve. When I
asked him: "When?" he answered: "As soon as the
emperor is gone; for the 'delongaris' in whose hand all

the power over the ships rests, will see to thee when the holy emperor goes away." Deceived by this hope, I went away from him rejoicing.

But two days after, on Saturday, Nicephorus had me summoned to Umbria, which is a place eighteen miles from Constantinople. And he said to me: "I thought that thou wert come hither, as a distinguished and upright man, in order altogether to accede to my demands and to establish a perpetual friendship between me and thy master. But as, on account of thy hardness of heart, thou art not willing to do this: at least bring about this one thing, which thou may'st with perfect right do;—promise, namely, that thy master will lend no aid to the princes of Capua and Benevento, my slaves whom I am about to attack. Since he gives us nothing of his own, let him at least give up what is ours. It is a well-known thing that their fathers and grandfathers gave tribute to our empire, and that they themselves shall shortly do the same,—for that the army of our empire will labour."

I answered him: "Those princes are nobles of the first rank and vassals of my master; and, if he see that thy army attacks them, he will send to them aid which will enable them to annihilate thy forces and to take away those two provinces which are thine beyond the sea." Then, swelling like a toad and very angry: "Go away," he said; "by myself, by my parents who engendered me such as I am, I will make thy master think of other things than of protecting rebellious slaves."

As I was going away, he ordered the interpreter to invite me to table; and summoning the brother of those two princes, and Bysantius of Bari, he ordered them to give vent to gross insults against yourselves and against the Latin and the Teuton race. But as I was going away from the foul meal, they sent word to me secretly through messengers and swore that what they had growled out had been said not of their own will, but because of the wishes and threats of the emperor. But Nicephorus himself asked me at that meal if ye had parks and if in your parks ye had wild asses and other animals. When I had answered him that ye had parks and animals in the parks, but no wild asses, he said: "I will take thee into our park

and thou wilt be surprised to see its size and to look at
the wild asses." I was led therefore into a park which
was rather large, hilly and fruitful, but not at all pleasing
to the view; and as I was riding along with my hat on
and the marshal of the court saw me from afar, he quickly
dispatched his son to me to say that it was wrong for any
one to be with his hat on where the emperor was and that
I must wear the Teristra. I answered: "With us the
women wear hoods and veils; the men ride with their
hats on. And you have no right to compel me here to
change the custom of my country, considering that we
permit your envoys who come to us to keep to the custom
of theirs. For with long sleeves, swathed, spangled, with
long hair, clad in tunics down to their ankles, they ride,
walk and sit at table with us; and, what to all of us seems
too disgraceful, they alone kiss our emperors with covered
heads."—"May God not allow it to be done any longer"
I said to myself.—"Thou must turn back, then," he said.

As I did this there met us, herded together with goats,
the so-called wild asses. But why, I ask, wild asses? Our
tame ones at Cremona are the same. Their colour, shape
and ears are the same; they are equally melodious when
they begin to bray; they resemble each other in size, have
the same swiftness, and are equally pleasant food for
wolves. When I saw them I said to the Greek who was
riding with me: "I never saw the like in Saxony." "If,"
he said, "thy master shall be friendly to the holy emperor,
he will give him many such; and it will be no little glory
to him himself to possess what no one of his distinguished
predecessors has ever seen." But believe me, my august
masters, my brother and fellow bishop, master Antony (of
Brixen) can furnish ones that are not inferior, as is witnessed by the markets which are held at Cremona; and
there they walk about not as wild asses but as tame ones.
But when my escort had announced the above words to
Nicephorus, he sent me two goats, and gave me permission
to go away. On the following day he himself started
towards Syria.

But mark now why he led his army against the Assyrians. The Greeks and Saracens have books which they
call the Visions of Daniel; I would call them Sibylline

Books. In them is found written how many years each emperor shall live; what things, whether peace or war, are to happen during his reign; whether fortune is to be favourable to the Saracens, or the reverse. And so it reads, that, in the time of this Nicephorus, the Assyrians will not be able to resist the Greeks, and that he, Nicephorus, will only live seven years; and that after his death an emperor shall arise worse than he—only I fear that none such can be found—and more unwarlike; in whose time the Assyrians shall so prevail, that they shall bring all the regions as far as Chalcedon, which is not far from Constantinople, under their sway. For both peoples have regard for their favourable seasons; and from one and the same cause the Greeks press on encouraged, and the Saracens, in despair, make no resistance; awaiting the time when they themselves may press on, and the Greeks, in turn, may not resist.

Hippolytus, indeed, a certain Sicilian bishop, wrote similarly concerning your empire and our people—I call " our people," namely, all those who are under your rule;—and would that it were true what he prophesied concerning the present times. The other things have hitherto come to pass as he foretold, as I have heard from those who know these books. And of his many sayings I will mention one. For he says that now the saying is to be fulfilled : " The lion and his whelp shall together exterminate the wild ass." The interpretation of which is, according to the Greeks: Leo —that is, the emperor of the Romans or Greeks—and his whelp,—the king, namely, of the Franks—shall together in these days drive out the wild ass—that is, the African king of the Saracens. Which interpretation does not seem to me true, for this reason, that the lion and the whelp, although differing in size, are nevertheless of one nature and species or kind ; and, as my knowledge suggests to me, if the lion be the emperor of the Greeks, it is not fitting that the whelp should be the king of the Franks. For although both are men, as the lion and the whelp are both animals, yet they differ in habits as much—I will not say alone as one species from another—but as rational beings from those who have no reason. The whelp differs from the lion only in age ; the form is the same, the ferocity the same, the roar the same. The king of the Greeks wears long hair, a tunic, long sleeves, a hood; is lying, crafty, without pity, sly as a fox, proud, falsely humble, miserly, and greedy; lives on garlic, onions, and leeks, and drinks bath-water. The king of the Franks, on the contrary, is beautifully shorn; wears a garment not at all like a woman's garment, and a hat; is truthful, without guile, merciful enough when it is right, severe when it is necessary, always truly humble, never miserly; does not live on garlic, onions and leeks so as to spare animals and, by not eating them, but selling them, to heap money together. Ye have heard the difference; do not be willing to accept their interpretation, for either it refers to the future, or it is not true. For it is impossible that Nicephorus, as they falsely say, can be the lion and Otto the whelp, and that they together shall exterminate any one. For "sooner mutually changing their bounds shall the Parthian exile drink the Araris, or the German the Tigris," than that Nicephorus and Otto shall become friends and close a treaty with each other.

Ye have heard the interpretation of the Greeks; hear now that of Liutprand, bishop of Cremona. For I say— and not alone do I say, but I affirm—that if the prophecy is to be fulfilled in the present time, the lion and the whelp are the father and the son, Otto and Otto, unlike in nothing only differing in age,—and that they together shall, in this present time, exterminate the wild ass Nicephorus; who not incongruously is compared to the wild ass on account of his vain and empty glory, and on account of his incestuous marriage with his fellow god-parent and mistress. If now that wild ass shall not be exterminated by our lion and his whelp—by Otto and Otto, the father, namely, and the son, the august emperors of the Romans—then that which Hippolytus wrote will not have been true; for that former interpretation of the Greeks is entirely to be discarded. But oh blessed Jesus, eternal God, the Word of the Father—who dost speak to us, unworthy as we are, not by voice but by inspiration—may'st Thou be willing to see in this sentence no other interpretation than mine. Command that that lion and that whelp may exterminate and bodily humble this wild ass; to the end that, retiring into himself, subjecting himself to his masters the emperors

Basilius and Constantine, his soul may be saved at the Day of the Lord!

But the astronomers prophesy alike concerning yourselves and Nicephorus. Truly wonderful, I say. I have spoken with a certain astronomer who truly described thy form and habits, most illustrious master, and that of thy august namesake; and who related all my past experiences as if they were present. Nor were the names mentioned of any of my friends or enemies concerning whom I thought of asking him, but that he could tell me their appearance, form and character. He foretold all calamity that has happened to me on this journey. But may all that he said to me be false, I only ask that one thing alone be true— that which he foretold ye would do to Nicephorus. Oh may it come to pass! Oh may it come to pass! And then I shall feel that the wrongs I have suffered are as nothing at all.

The aforesaid Hippolytus writes also that not the Greeks but the Franks shall put an end to the Saracens. Encouraged by which prophecy the Saracens, three years ago, engaged in battle near Scylla and Charybdis in the Sicilian waters, with the patrician Manuel, the nephew of Nicephorus. And when they had laid low his immense forces they took his own self and beheaded him and hung up his corpse. And when they had captured his companion and colleague, who was of neither gender, they scorned to kill him; but having bound him and kept him to pine in long imprisonment, they sold him for a price at which no mortals who were sound in their heads would have bought him. And with no less spirit, encouraged by this same prophecy, they shortly after met the general Exachontes. And when they had put him to flight, they destroyed his army in every way.

Another reason also compelled Nicephorus at this time to lead his army against the Assyrians. For at this time, by the will of God, a famine had so laid waste all the land of the Greeks, that not even two Pavian sextares could be bought for a piece of gold: and this in the very realm of plenty, as it were. This misfortune, the field mice aiding him, Nicephorus increased by collecting for himself, at the time of harvest, whatever corn there was anywhere; giving a minimum price to the despairing owners. And when he had done this on the side towards Mesopotamia, where the supply of grain on account of the absence of the mice was greater: the amount of corn that he had equalled the amount of the sands of the sea. When, therefore, on account of this vile transaction, famine was everywhere shamefully raging, he brought together eighty thousand men under pretext of a military expedition; and he sold to them, during one whole month, for two gold pieces what he had bought for one. These, my master, are the reasons which compelled Nicephorus now to lead his forces against the Assyrians. But what sort of forces? I ask. Truly, I answer, not men, but only images of men; whose tongue only is bold, but whose right hand is frigid in war. Nicephorus did not look for quality in them, but only for quantity. How perilous this is for him he will learn to his sorrow, when the multitude of unwarlike ones, brave only on account of numbers, shall be put to rout by a handful of our men who are skilled in war—nay, thirsting for it.

When ye were besieging Bari only three hundred Hungarians seized five hundred Greeks near Thessalonica and led them into Hungary. Which attempt, inasmuch as it succeeded, induced two hundred Hungarians in Macedonia, not far from Constantinople, to do the like; of whom forty, when they were retreating incautiously through a narrow pass, were captured. These Nicephorus, freeing them from custody and adorning them with most costly garments, has made his body guard and defenders—taking them with him against the Assyrians. But what kind of an army he has ye can conjecture from this,—that those who are in command over the others are Venetians and Amalfians!

But no more of this! Learn now what happened to me. On the sixth day before the Calends of August (July 27), I received at Umbria, outside of Constantinople, permission from Nicephorus to return to ye. And when I came to Constantinople, the patrician Christophorus, the eunuch who was the representative of Nicephorus there, sent word to me that I could not then start to return because the Saracens at that time were holding the sea and the Hungarians the land—I should have to wait until they retired. Both of which facts, oh woe is me, were false! Then wardens were placed over us to prevent myself and my companions from going out of our habitation. They seized and slew or put in prison the poor of Latin race who came to me to beg alms. They did not permit my Greek interpreter to go out even to buy supplies—but only my cook, who was ignorant of the Greek tongue and who could speak to the vendor, when he bought of him, not with words but by signs of his fingers or nods of his head. He bought for four pieces of money only as much as the interpreter for one. And when some of my friends sent spices, bread, wine and apples,—pouring them all on the ground, they sent the bearers away overwhelmed with blows of the fist. And had not the divine pity prepared before me a table against my adversaries, I should have had to accept the death they arranged for me. But He who permitted that I should be tempted, mercifully granted then that I should endure. And these perils tried my soul at Constantinople from the second day before the Nones of June (June 4), until the sixth day before the Nones of October (Oct. 2)—one hundred and twenty days.

But, to increase my calamities, on the day of the Assumption of the Virgin Mary the holy mother of God, there came—an evil augury for me—envoys of the apostolic and universal pope John, through whom he asked Nicephorus "the emperor of the Greeks" to close an alliance and firm friendship with his beloved and spiritual son Otto "august emperor of the Romans." Before the question as to why this word, this manner of address, sinful and bold in the eyes of the Greeks, did not cost its bearer his life—why he was not annihilated before it was read, I, who, in other respects, have often shown myself enough of a preacher and with words enough at my command, seem dumb as a fish! The Greeks inveighed against the sea, cursed the waves, and wondered exceedingly how they had been able to transport such an iniquity and why the yawning deep had not swallowed up the ship. "Was it not unpardonable," they said, "to have called the universal emperor of the Romans, the august, great, only Nicephorus: 'of the Greeks';—a barbarian, a pauper: 'of the Romans'? Oh sky! Oh earth! Oh sea!" "But what," they said, " shall we do to those scoundrels, those criminals? They are paupers, and if we kill them we pollute our hands with vile blood; they are ragged, they are slaves, they are peasants; if we beat them we disgrace not them, but ourselves; for they are not worthy of the gilded Roman flail and of such punishments. Oh would that one were a bishop, another a margrave! For sewing them in sacks, after stinging blows with whips, after plucking out their beards or their hair, they would be thrown into the sea. But these," they said, " may continue to live; and, until the holy emperor of the Romans, Nicephorus, learns of this atrocity, they may languish in narrow confinement."

When I learned this I considered them happy because poor, myself unhappy because rich. When I was at home, my desire was to excuse my poverty; but placed in Constantinople, fear itself taught me that I had the wealth of a Crœsus. Poverty had always seemed burdensome to me —then it seemed welcome, acceptable, desirable; yes, desirable, since it keeps its votaries from perishing, its followers from being flayed. And since at Constantinople alone this poverty thus defends its votaries, may it there alone be considered worth striving after!

The papal messengers, therefore, being thrown into prison, that offending epistle was sent to Nicephorus in Mesopotamia; whence no one returned to bring an answer until the second day before the Ides of September (Sept. 12). On that day it came, but its import was concealed from me. And after two days—on the eighteenth day, namely, before the Calends of October (Sept. 14)—I brought it about by prayers and gifts that I might adore the life-giving and salvation-bringing cross. And there in the great crowd, unnoticed by the guards, certain persons approached me, and rendered my saddened heart joyful through stolen words.

But on the fifteenth day before the Calends of October (Sept. 17), as much dead as alive, I was summoned to the palace. And when I came into the presence of the patrician Christophorus—the eunuch, receiving me kindly, rose to meet me with three others. Their discourse began as follows: " The pallor in thy face, the emaciation of thy whole body, thy long hair, and thy beard—flowing, contrary to thy custom—show that there is immense grief in thy heart because the date of thy return to thy master has been delayed. But, we pray thee, be not angry with the holy emperor nor with us. For we will tell thee the cause of the delay. The Roman pope—if indeed he is to be called pope who has held communion and worked together with the son of Alberic the apostate, with an adulterer and unhallowed person—has sent letters to our most holy emperor, worthy of himself, unworthy of Nicephorus, calling him the emperor ' of the Greeks,' and not ' of the Romans.' Which thing beyond a doubt has been done by the advice of thy master."

" What do I hear ? " I said to myself. " I am lost; there is no doubt but what I shall go by the shortest way to the judgment-seat."

" Now listen," they continued, " we know thou wilt say that the pope is the simplest of men ; thou wilt say it, and we acknowledge it." " But," I answered, " I do not say it."

" Hear then ! The stupid silly pope does not know that the holy Constantine transferred hither the imperial sceptre, the senate, and all the Roman knighthood, and left in Rome nothing but vile minions—fishers, namely, pedlars, bird catchers, bastards, plebeians, slaves. He would never have written this unless at the suggestion of thy king ; how dangerous this will be to both—the immediate future, unless they come to their senses, will show." " But the pope," I said, " whose simplicity is his title to renown, thought he was writing this to the honour of the emperor, not to his shame. We know, of course, that Constantine, the Roman emperor, came hither with the Roman knighthood, and founded this city in his name ; but because you changed your language, your customs, and your dress, the most holy pope thought that the name of the Romans as well as their dress would displease you. He will show this, if he lives, in his future letters ; for they shall be addressed as follows: 'John, the Roman pope, to Nicephorus, Constantine, Basilius, the great and august emperors of the Romans ! " And now mark, I beg, why I said this.

Nicephorus came to the throne through perjury and adultery. And since the salvation of all Christians per-

tains to the care of the Roman pope, let the lord pope send
to Nicephorus an epistle altogether like to those sepulchres
which without are whited, within are full of dead men's
bones; within let him show to him how through perjury
and adultery he has obtained the rule over his masters;
let him invite Nicephorus to a synod, and, if he do not
come, let him hurl the anathema at him. But if the address be not as I have said, it will never reach him.

But to return to the matter in hand. When the princes
I have mentioned heard from me the aforesaid promise
concerning the address, not suspecting any guile: "We
thank thee," they said, "oh bishop. It is worthy of thy
wisdom to act as mediator in so great a matter. Thou art
the only one of the Franks whom we now love; but when
at thy behest they shall have corrected what is evil, they
also shall be loved. And when thou shalt come to us
again thou shalt not go away unrewarded."

I said to myself: "If I ever come back here again, may
Nicephorus present me with a crown and a golden sceptre!"

"But tell us," they continued, "does thy most holy
master wish to close with the emperor a treaty of friendship through marriage?"

"When I came hither he wished it," I said, "but since,
during my long delay, he has received no news; he thinks
that you have committed a crime, and that I have been
taken and bound; and his whole soul, like that of a lioness
bereft of her whelps, is inflamed with a desire through just
wrath to take vengeance, and to renounce the marriage and
to pour out his anger upon you."

"If he attempts it," they said, "we will not say Italy,
but not even the poor Saxony where he was born—where
the inhabitants wear the skins of wild beasts—will protect
him. With our money, which gives us our power, we will
arouse all the nations against him; and we will break him
in pieces like a potter's vessel, which, when broken can not
be brought into shape again. And as we imagine that
thou, in his honour, hast bought some costly garments, we
order thee to bring them before us. What are fit for thee
shall be marked with a leaden seal and left to thee; but
those which are prohibited to all nations except to us
Romans, shall be taken away and the price returned."

When this had been done they took away from me five most costly purple stuffs; considering yourselves and all the Italians, Saxons, Franks, Bavarians, Swabians—nay, all nations—as unworthy to be adorned with such vestments. How unworthy, how shameful it is, that these soft, effeminate, long-sleeved, hooded, veiled, lying, neutral-gendered, idle creatures should go clad in purple, while you heroes—strong men, namely, skilled in war, full of faith and love, reverencing God, full of virtues—may not! What is this, if it be not contumely? "But where," I said, "is the word of your emperor, where the imperial promise? For when I said farewell to him, I asked him up to what price he would permit me to buy vestments in honour of my church. And he said: 'Buy whatever ones and as many as thou dost wish;' and in thus designating the quantity and the quality, he clearly did not make a distinction as if he had said 'excepting this and this.' Leo, the marshal of the court, his brother, is witness; Enodisius, the interpreter, John, Romanus, are witnesses. I myself am witness, since even without the interpreter, I understood what the emperor said."

"But," they said, "these things are prohibited; and when the emperor spoke as thou sayest he did, he could not imagine that thou would'st even dream of such things as these. For, as we surpass other nations in wealth and wisdom, so also we ought to surpass them in dress; so that those who are singularly endowed with virtue, should have garments unique in beauty."

"Such a garment can hardly be called unique," I answered, "when with us the street-walkers and conjurers wear them."

"Where do they get them?" they asked.

"From Venetian and Amalfian traders," I said, "who, by bringing them to us, support themselves from the food we give them."

"Well, they shall not do so any longer," they said. "They shall be closely examined, and if any thing of this kind shall be found on them they shall be punished with blows and shorn of their hair."

"In the time of the emperor Constantine, of blessed memory," I said, "I came here not as bishop but as deacon; not sent by an emperor or king but by the margrave Berengar; and I bought many more and more precious vestments, which were neither looked at nor viewed by the Greeks nor stamped with lead. Now, having become a bishop by the mercy of God, and being sent by the magnificent emperors Otto and Otto, father and son, I am so insulted that my vestments are marked after the manner of the Venetians; and, as they are being transported for the use of the church entrusted to me, whatever seems of any worth is taken away. Are you not weary of insulting me, or rather my masters, for whose sake I am derided? Is it not enough that I am given into custody, that I am tortured by hunger and thirst, that I could not return to them, being detained until now,—without, to fill the measure of their disrespect to them, my being robbed of my own things? Take away from me at least only what I have bought; leave me those things that have been given me as a gift by my friends!"

"The emperor Constantine," they said, "was a mild man, who always stayed in his palace, and by such means as this made the natives friendly to him; but the emperor Nicephorus, a man given to war, abhors the palace as if it were the plague. And he is called by us warlike and almost a lover of strife; nor does he make the nations friendly to him by paying them, but subjects them to his rule by terror and the sword. And in order that thou may'st see what is our opinion of thy royal masters, all that has been given to thee of this colour, and all that has been bought shall revert to us by the same process."

Having done and said these things they gave to me a letter written and sealed with gold to bring to ye; but it was not worthy of ye, as I thought. They brought also other letters sealed with silver and said: "We judge it unseemly that your pope should receive letters from the emperor; but the marshal of the court, the emperor's brother, sends him an epistle which is good enough for him—not through his own poor envoys but through thee—to the effect that, unless he come to his senses, he shall know that he shall be utterly confounded."

When I had received this, they let me go, giving me kisses which were very sweet, very loving. But as I went away they sent me a message right worthy of themselves but not of me—to the effect, namely, that they would give me horses for myself personally and for my companions, but none for my luggage. And thus, being very much annoyed, as was natural, I had to give to my guide as pay, objects of the worth of fifty pieces of gold. And as I had no means of retaliating upon Nicephorus for his ill deeds, I wrote these verses on the wall of my hated habitation, and upon a wooden table :

False is Argolian faith, be warned and mistrust it O Latin ;
Heed thee and let not thine ear be lent to the words that they utter.
When it will help him the Argive will swear by all that is holy !
Lofty, with windows tall, ornate with varying marble,
This dwelling, deficient in water, admits the sun in its confines,
Fosters the bitterest cold, nor repels the heat when it rages.
Liutprand a bishop I, from Cremona a town of Ausonia,
Hither for love of peace to Constantinople did journey ;
Here I was kept confined throughout the four months of the summer.
For before Bari's gates had appeared the emperor Otto,
Striving to take the place by flame alike and by slaughter.
Thence, by my prayers induced, he hastens to Rome, his own city,
Greece meanwhile having promised a bride for the son of the victor.
O had she ne'er been born, and I had been spared this grim journey ;
Safely avoiding the wrath that Nicephorus since has poured on me—
He who prohibits his stepchild from wedding the son of my master !
Lo, the day is at hand, when war, impelled by fierce furies,
Wildly shall rage o'er earth's limits, should God not see fit to avert it.
Peace which is longed for by all, because of his guilt will be silent !

After writing these verses, on the sixth day before the Nones of October (Oct. 2), at the tenth hour, I entered my boat with my guide, and left that once most rich and flourishing, now half-starved, perjured, lying, wily, greedy, rapacious, avaricious, vain-glorious city ; and after forty-nine days of ass-riding, walking, horse-riding, fasting, thirsting, sighing, weeping, groaning, I came to Nau-pactus, which is a city of Nikopolis. And here my guide deserted me after placing us on two small ships, and committing us to two imperial messengers who were to bring me by sea to Hydronto. But since their orders did not include the right of levying from the Greek princes, they were everywhere repulsed ; so that we were not supported by them, but they by us. How often did I revolve within me that verse of Terence : "They themselves need help whom thou dost choose to defend thee."

On the ninth day before the Calends of December, then (Nov. 23), we left Naupactus and I arrived at the river Offidaris in two days—my companions not remaining in the ships, which could not hold them, but advancing along the shore. From our position on the river Offidaris we looked over to Patras, eighteen miles distant, on the other shore of the sea. This place of apostolic suffering, which we had visited and adored on our way to Constantinople, we now omitted—I confess my fault—to visit and adore. My unspeakable desire, my august lords and masters, of returning to ye and seeing ye was the cause of this; and if it had not been for this alone, I would, I believe, have forever perished.

A storm from the south rose against me—madman that I was,—disturbing the sea to its lowest depths with its ragings. And when it had continued to do this for several days and nights: on the day before the Calends of December (Nov. 30)—on the very day, namely, of His passion—I recognized that this had happened to me of my own fault. Trouble alone taught me to give ear to its meaning. Famine, indeed, had begun to violently oppress us. The inhabitants of the land thought to kill us, in order to take our goods from us. The sea, to hinder our flight, was raging high. Then, betaking myself to the church which I saw, weeping and wailing, I said : "Oh holy apostle Andrew, I am the servant of thy fellow fisherman, brother and fellow apostle, Simon Peter ; I have not avoided the place of thy suffering or kept away from it through pride ; the command of my emperors, the love of them, urges me to return home. If my sin has moved thee to indignation, may the merit of my august masters lead thee to mercy. Thou hast nothing to bestow on thy brother ; bestow something on the emperors who love thy brother by putting their trust in Him who knows all things. Thou knowest with what labour and exertion, with what vigils and at what expense—snatching it from the hands of the godless—they have enriched, honoured, exalted, and brought back to its proper condition, the Roman church of thy brother the apostle Peter. But if my works cast me into peril, let their merits at least free me ; and let not those whom thy aforesaid brother in the faith and in the flesh, Peter the chief apostle of the apostles, wishes to have rejoice and prosper, be saddened by this—that is, through me whom they themselves had sent ! "

This is not, oh my masters and august emperors, this is not flattery. I tell ye truly, and I do not sew pillows under my arms—the thing, I say, is true : after two days, through your merits the sea became calm and so tranquil, that when our sailors deserted us, we ourselves sailed the boat to Leucate—a hundred and forty miles, namely—suffering no danger or discomfort, except a little at the mouth of the river Acheloi, where its current running down rapidly is beaten back against the waves of the sea.

How then, most mighty emperors, will ye repay the Lord for all that which for your sakes He did to me. I will tell ye how God wishes this and demands this to be done. And although He can do it without ye, He wishes nevertheless that ye shall be His instruments in this matter. For He himself furnishes what shall be offered unto Him—keeps what He demands from us, in order to crown His own work. Pay attention then, I beg. Nicephorus, being a man who scorns all churches, on account of the wrath in which he abounds towards ye, has ordered the patriarch of Constantinople to raise the church of Hydronto to the rank of a bishopric, and not to permit any longer, throughout all Apulia and Calabria, that the divine mysteries be celebrated in Latin, but to have them celebrated in Greek. He says that the former popes were traders and that they sold the Holy Spirit—that Spirit by which all things are vivified and ruled ; which fills the universe ; which knows the Word ; which is co-eternal, and of one substance with God the Father and His Son Jesus Christ, without beginning, without end, for ever true ; who (Christ) is not valued at a fixed price, but is bought by the clean-hearted for as much as they hold Him to be worth. And so Poly-

euctus, the patriarch of Constantinople, wrote a privilege
for the bishop of Hydronto to this effect : that he should
by his authority have permission to consecrate bishops in
Acerenza, Tursi, Gravina, Matera and Tricarico : which,
however, evidently belong to the diocese of the lord pope.
But why need I say this when, indeed, the church of Constantinople itself is rightly subject to our holy catholic
and apostolic church of Rome.   We know—nay, we have
seen—that the bishop of Constantinople did not use the
pallium except with the permission of our holy father.
But when that most godless Alberic,—whom cupidity, not
by drops, but, as it were, by torrents, had filled—usurped
for himself the Roman city, and held the lord pope like his
own slave in his dwelling, the emperor Romanus made his
own son, the eunuch Theophylactus, patriarch.   And since
the cupidity of Alberic was not hidden from him, he sent
to him very great gifts, bringing it about that, in the
name of the pope, letters were sent to the patriarch Theophylactus, by the authority of which he and his successors
alike might use the pallium without permission from the
popes.   From which vile transaction the shameful custom
arose that not only the patriarchs but also the bishops of
all Greece should use the pallium.   How absurd this is, I
do not need to make clear.   It is therefore my plan that a
sacred synod be held, and Polyeuctus be summoned to it.
But if he be unwilling to come and to amend the faults
that have been mentioned above, then let that be done
which the holy canons shall decree.   Do ye in the meantime, most potent emperors, continue to labour as ye have
done ; bring it about that, if Nicephorus be unwilling to
obey us when we arrange to proceed against him canonically, he will hear ye, whose forces this half-corpse will not
dare to meet.   This, I say, is what the apostles, our
masters and fellow fighters, wish us to do.   Rome is not to
be despised by the Greeks because Constantine went away
from it ; but rather to be the more cherished, venerated
and adored for the reason that the apostles, the holy
teachers Peter and Paul, came thither.   But may what I
have written concerning this suffice until, being snatched
from the hands of the Greeks, through the grace of God
and the prayers of the most holy apostles I may come to

ye. And then it may not weary me to say what it burdens me now here to write. Now let us return to the matter in hand.

On the eighth day before the Ides of December (Dec. 6) we came to Leucate, where, by the bishop of that place—a eunuch, as by other bishops everywhere, we were most unkindly received and treated. In all Greece—I speak truly and do not lie—I found no hospitable bishops. They are at the same time poor and rich; rich in gold, with which they play from full coffers; poor in servants and implements. Alone they seat themselves at their bare little tables, placing before themselves their ship-biscuit; and then not drinking, but sipping their bath-water from a very small glass. They themselves sell and buy; they themselves close and open their doors; they are their own stewards, their own ass-drivers, their own " capones "—but ha! I was going to write " caupones," but the thing itself is so true that I was compelled to write the truth even when I did not wish to—for really, I say, they are " caupones "—that is, eunuchs—which is against the ecclesiastical law; and they are also " capones," that is, tavern keepers; which is also against the canons. One can say of them:

Lettuce doth end the meal that with lettuce hath had its
     beginning,
Lettuce, which too was wont to close the meals of their fathers.[1]

I would consider them happy in their poverty if this were an imitation of the poverty of Christ. But nothing impels them to this save sordid gain and the cursed thirst for gold. But may God spare them! I think they do this because their churches are tributary. For the bishop of Leucate swore to me that every year his church had to pay to Nicephorus a hundred pieces of gold; and in like manner the other churches, more or less, according to their means. How wicked this is is demonstrated by the acts of our most holy father Joseph; for when he, in the time of famine, made all Egypt tributary to Pharaoh, he permitted the land of the priests to be free from tribute.

[1] V. Martial, Ep. xiii.

Leaving Leucate, then, on the nineteenth day before the Calends of January (Dec. 14), and navigating ourselves— since, as we said above, our sailors had fled—on the fifteenth (Dec. 18) we came to Corfu; where, before we had left the ship, a certain war-commander met us— Michael by name, a Chersionite, born in the place called Cherson. He was a hoary-headed man, jovial faced, good-natured in his discourse, always pleasantly laughing; but, as it afterwards turned out, a devil at heart—as God showed to me even then by clear enough proofs, if only my mind could then have understood them. For at the very time when, with a kiss, he was wishing me the peace that he did not bear in his heart, all Corfu—a great island, namely—trembled; and not only once but three times on the same day did it tremble. Four days later, moreover, —namely on the eleventh day before the Calends of January (Dec. 22)—while, sitting at table, I was eating bread with him who was treading me under foot, the sun, ashamed at such an unworthy deed, hid the rays of his light, and, suffering an eclipse, terrified that Michael, but did not change him.

I will explain, then, what I had done to him for the sake of friendship, and what I received from him by way of reward. On my way to Constantinople I gave to his son that most costly shield, gilded and worked with marvellous art, which ye, my august masters, gave to me with the other gifts to give to my Greek friends. Now, returning from Constantinople, I gave the father a most precious vestment; for all of which he gave me the following thanks: Nicephorus had written that, at whatever hour I should come to him, without delay he should place me or a Greek ship and send me to the chamberlain Leo. He did not do this; but detained me twenty days and nourished me not at his own but at my expense; until an envoy came from the aforesaid chamberlain Leo, who rated him for delaying me. But because he could not bear my reproaches, laments, and sighs, he went away and handed me over to a man so sinful and utterly bad that he did not even permit me to buy supplies until he had received from me a carpet worth a pound of silver. And when, after twenty days, I did go away from there, that man to whom I had given the carpet ordered the ship's master, after passing a certain promontory, to put me ashore and let me die of hunger. This he did because he had searched my baggage to see if I had any purple vestments concealed, and, when he had wanted to take one, I had prevented him. Oh ye Michaels, ye Michaels, where have I ever found so many of you and such ones! For my keeper in Constantinople gave me over to his rival Michael —a bad man to a worse, the worse one to a rascal. My guide was also called Michael—a simple man, indeed, but one whose saintly simplicity harmed me almost as much as the wickedness of the others. But from the hands of these little Michaels I came into thine, O great Michael— half hermit, half monk! I tell thee and I tell thee truly; the bath will not avail thee, in which thou dost assiduously get drunk for love of St. John the Baptist! For those who seek God falsely, shall never merit to find Him!

*   *   *   *   *

(*The manuscript containing Liutprand's report breaks off here suddenly.*)